Anna
Amalia

Anna Amalia

GRAND-DUCHESS

PATRON OF GOETHE AND SCHILLER

FRANCES A. GERARD

FONTHILL

Fonthill Media Limited
www.fonthillmedia.com
office@fonthillmedia.com

This edition first published in the United Kingdom 2012

British Library Cataloguing in Publication Data.
A catalogue record for this book is available from
the British Library.

ISBN 978-1-78155-016-8 (print)
ISBN 978-1-78155-137-0 (e-book)

Typeset in 11pt on 13pt Bembo.
Printed and bound in England.

Connect with us
❶ facebook.com/fonthillmedia ❷ twitter.com/fonthillmedia

CONTENTS

LIST OF ILLUSTRATIONS
(Between pages 128 and 129)

28. Anna Amalia portrait by Johann Friedrich August Tischbein
29. Angelica Kaufmann, a self-portrait
30. Anna Amalia, portrait by Angelica Kaufmann, 1788
31. Tiefurt
32. Charles Gore, 17 July 1793, by Georg Melchior Kraus
33. Eliza Gore
34. Emily Gore
35. Goethe and Corona Schröter in "Orestes" and "Iphigenia"
36. Corona Schröter with Goethe and Karl August
37. The Newest Thing from *Plundersweilern*, by Goethe, with Goethe on stilts
38. Corona Schröter
39. Silhouette of Goethe
40. Prince Constantine, the second son of Ernestine Constantine and Anna Amilia
41. A scene from *The Fisher Maiden* drawn by Georg Melchior Kraus
42. The old theatre at Weimar, built 1779 and destroyed by fire in 1825
43. The 1830 theatre, replaced in 1908.
44. Portrait of Goethe's mother, Frau Aja
45. View of Goethe's house on the Frauen Platz as it was in 1781
46. View of Goethe's house, 1901
47. Portrait of Goethe by Angelica Kaufmann, 1787
48. Portrait of Wolfgang Heribert Dalberg
49. Karl August Böttiger
50. A group of Weimar's celebrities: 1 Goethe; 2 Schiller; 3 Weiland; 4 Klopstock; 5 Lessing; 6 Herder.
51. Portrait of Duchess Louise of Saxe-Weimar-Eisenach, created Grand Duchess in 1814
52. Karl August in the park with his dogs, 1828
53. Karl Friedrich, 1783-1853, the son of Karl August and Louise
54. The legitimate children of Karl August and Duchess Louise of Saxe-Weimar-Eisenach; Karl Friedrich, the future Grand Duke, Karoline Louise and Karl Bernhard
55. Portrait of Goethe, 1802
56. The grand ducal library
57. Theobald von Oer 1807-1885: The Weimar Court of the Muses

INTRODUCTION
TO THE 2012 EDITION

Francis A. Gerard was the pen-name of Geraldine Fitzgerald. This latter name is not uncommon and as a consequence, information about her has been difficult to find. Searches in the census records and birth, marriage and death records have been equally inconclusive, therefore little has been discovered about her. She wrote numerous works including: *Some Celebrated Irish Beauties of the Last Century*, 1895; *Some Fair Hibernians, being a supplementary volume to "Some Celebrated Irish Beauties of the Last Century"*; *Angelica Kauffmann: a biography*, 1893; *The Romance of King Ludwig II of Bavaria*, 1901 and *Wagner Bayreuth And The Festival Plays*, 1901. These, in addition to *Anna Amalia*, which was published in 1902 and which appears to have been her last work. She also translated *Black Diamonds* by Hungarian novelist Mór Jókai, (1825-1904), which was published in English in 1896.

With her name and with the title of her first work it may be surmised that she was born in Dublin, or at least somewhere in Ireland. She obviously received an excellent education and was presumably fluent in German, French and Hungarian as well as her native language. She is mildly sarcastic about 'Girton girls', and there is a clear inference thrown out that she considers her own education to have been far superior.

How and why she came to be interested in German subjects and how she learnt to speak Hungarian are unknown, but she was clearly cultivated and mixed in good circles.

Francis Gerard's work is of a distinct 'belles-lettres nineteenth-century style'. She begins ominously with the words: *I am not going to enter upon so deep a subject as the early history of Thuringia. Those who wish to know more of the warriors, whose names and brave deeds fill the pages of the ancient histories, should read the early annals of Thuringia. It will be enough for our present purpose to mention a few facts which may, or may not, be familiar to my readers.* The first few pages are therefore somewhat dated in style, but when Frances gets into her subject proper, the pace picks up and the sickly melodramatic history falls away. The resulting book is a pleasure to read and one has to bear in mind that it was written one-hundred-and-ten years ago — half of the way back to the period on which she is narrating.

I have not done much to amend the text, and any alteration has been of the slightest touch. The reader therefore has to bear in mind that this was written well before the epoch-shattering events of the First World War when Saxe-Weimar-Eisenach still had a ducal family. Even though dated in style, this work is a welcome addition to the understanding of Anna Amelia, Goethe, and their world.

Frances made some dating errors which have been corrected when spotted. Her spelling is also idiosyncratic, especially of the German names, but these have largely been left as she wrote them. She relied very heavily on the ducal archives and I am not qualified to comment on her translation, but I have no reason to believe it is not of a good standard. What she did miss out of the work was a better explanation of Weimar society at large and this was unfortunate. It is also surprising that she could not find any information on Charles Gore and his two daughters Eliza and Emily, for the family was very influential in Weimar.

Charles Gore, (1729-1807), was born in Horkstow Hall, Lincolnshire and educated at Westminster School. He was trained in a London trading house with his uncle John Gore, and married, 1751, Mary Cockerill, who inherited Yorkshire estates from Thomas Cockerill of Scarborough. With this wealth, Charles gave up trade to follow his own interests including painting. The coupled settled first at York and in 1759, following the death of his father, the family moved to Southampton, seemingly for another interest, the sea, sailing and maritime science. He designed his own vessel, the cutter *Snail*, and from her decks executed many of his watercolour paintings.

In 1773 the family went to Lisbon for the benefit of Mary who was ailing and then from there they sailed on a frigate to Gibraltar and onwards to Livorno. In Florence, in 1775, their youngest daughter, Hannah Anne, (1759-1826) married George Nassau Clavering-Cowper, (1738-1789), who succeeded as 3rd Earl Cowper in 1789.

While in Italy, Charles Gore fell into the company Richard Payne Knight, (1750-1824) and fellow-artist Jakob Philipp Hackert, (1737-1807). In 1777 the three men made a trip to Sicily. In the following years, Gore travelled with Hackert in Switzerland and to Venice, then only with his family to France, Austria and northern Netherlands, back to England.

In 1785 he took Mary to a spa where she died, and then travelled onwards with his daughters Emily and Elizabeth to Weimar where they arrived in 1787. After visits to Berlin and Dresden the family finally settled in Weimar in 1791. Charles quickly became on good terms with the Duke, who gave him the Lodge, previously inhabited by Goethe. Charles, Elizabeth, (1754-1802), and Emily, (1756-1826), were favourites of the Ducal family. Together with Georg Melchior Kraus, (1737-1806) Charles Gore recorded the siege of Mainz and he also made an extensive trip with him to Austria and Italy.

Both Elizabeth and Emily were noted artists in their own right and made an impact on Weimar society; Schiller named one of his daughters 'Emilie'.

Charles Gore was an interesting man with divergent talents. In 1799 he published *Result of two series of experiments towards ascertaining the respective velocity of floating bodies varying in shape, and towards Determining form best adapted to stability, or possessing most power of resisting the force of the wind in carrying sail: intended to cobvey useful hints to the constructors of ships, with observations: in a letter to the Society for Improvement of Naval Architecture.*

There is another interesting coincidence which may be relevant to the Gore family deciding upon Weimar, and this is the connection with Joseph Mellish.

Joseph Charles Mellish, (1769-1823), was the son of Charles Mellish, (1737-1797), of Blyth, Nottinghamshire, a barrister at Lincoln's Inn; and his wife Judith, née Stapleton, (d. 1806). He was educated at Eton and Trinity College, Cambridge; and was then disinherited by his father on account of his extravagance and gambling. In Charles Mellish's will, made in 1794, he was bequeathed £1,000, compared to £9,000 for each of his two sisters, and the Blyth estate was entailed upon his younger brother Henry Francis Mellish and his heirs, with remainder to the two sisters. He followed his father at Lincoln's Inn, in 1787, but does not appear to have continued with a legal career. He married a German Baroness, Karolina Ernestina Friederike Sophia von Stein, (1777-1824), of Nord-und Ostheim, and had a house in Weimar itself, as well as the schloss at Dornburg. He appears to have been on very friendly terms with the ducal family. Karolina was a relation of Charlotte von Stein, Goethe's close friend. To enable the marriage, the Duke gave Mellish the title of a Prussian *Kammerherr* (chamberlain). Quite why he needed to 'enable' it is unclear, but it shows that Mellish was well regarded in Weimar.

Joseph Charles was the grandson of Joseph Mellish and Dorothy née Gore; she being the sister of the director of the Hamburg Company. Both the Mellish and Gore families were London merchants. Therefore, although probably not closely related, it seems that Charles Gore and Joseph Charles Mellish were cousins of one degree or another, and this may have been a factor in Gore's decision to settle in the locality. Although disinherited, it appears that the Mellish family looked after Joseph Charles well enough, for in 1802 Friedrich Schiller bought the Weimar house from Mellish and the messuage to the Esplanade for 4,200 Thaler.

Relatively little is known about Joseph Charles Mellish, but he appears to have led an interesting life and he was an accomplished linguist. He wrote and translated poetry and plays in German, English, and Latin. He translated Friedrich Schiller's *Mary Stuart* into English and he was on very friendly terms with his co-residents at Weimar, Schiller and Goethe, in fact this may have been one of the reasons why he was attracted there. It may have been that his wife's family relationship to Charlotte von Stein brought him further into the Goethe circle and Goethe became godfather to Mellish's son, Richard. Schiller said that Mellish combined 'alle Liebenswürdigkeiten eines Deutschen und eines Engländers' (all the most agreeable features of a German and an Englishman). Goethe, some twenty years later was to write a poem in his honour, *An Freund Mellish*.

The Gore and Mellish families were therefore very close to the ducal family and to Goethe and Schiller; in fact there was a noted 'English' community at Weimar, a point on which Frances Gerard is surprisingly silent upon, leading to the conclusion that supplementary research apart from the archives was not as thorough as it might have been. Part of the 'magnet' for this community was the academy maintained by Jean Joseph Mounier, a French emigré, who maintained (at the Duke's behest) an academy at the Belvedere, the baroque Schloss Belvedere. This Schloss was a pleasure-house designed for house-parties, built in 1724-1732 to designs of Johann August Richter and Gottfried Heinrich Krohne for Ernst August, Duke of Saxe-Weimar. The corps de logis is flanked by symmetrical pavilions. Today it houses part of the art collections of Weimar, with porcelains and faience, furniture and paintings of the eighteenth century. As the summer residence, its gardens, laid out in the French style in 1728-1748, were an essential amenity. After 1811, much of the outer gardens was altered to conform to the English landscape garden style, as an Englischer Garten, for Grand Duke Carl Friedrich, who died at Belvedere in 1853.

In the late 1790s, Duke Carl Friedrich invited Mounier to use the building for an academy, where his own son received some of his education. The academy was designed primarily for young Englishmen of good family, and among the tutors were Böttiger, Melos and Eckermann. The academy closed in 1801, but a stream of British youngsters continued to pour into the Weimar 'colony' which was considered a cheaper (and more entertaining) alternative to Oxford and Cambridge. Apart from young men, Weimar, due to Anna Amalia and Goethe became a highly fashionable stopping-off point.

Due to the large English community there was a an annual 'Englishman's ball held at Weimar. Francis Witts, (1783-1854), living in Weimar with his parents Edward and Agnes Witts recorded many of the events in Weimar at the time (*The Complete Diary of a Cotswold Parson*, volume 1). His mother Agnes Witts also maintained a diary, (*The Complete Diary of a Cotswold Lady*, volume 2); and both are full of fascinating snippets. Agnes records the first four days in Weimar; they arrived on 3 September 1798 and within 48 hours they were taken under the wing of Dr Böttiger and one of the Miss Gores:

Monday Sep^t 3rd.
A fine Morning, but raind hard at noon for two or three hours ceased in the evening, but was still damp & gloomy, our Young Gentlemen came to us early, & took us all with them to their Lodgings where we were introduced to Mr Boettiger, to whom we had brought a Letter of introduction from Mr Dalziel, he is Rector of the College & high in reputation for learning, spoke English well & was very civil.

Tuesday Sep.^t 4th.

An uncommon fine hot day quite sultry in the evening, Messrs. Hunter, Martin, & Boettiger here in the Morning, the two former walk'd with us a little in the gardens before Dinner, they dined with us instead of the Table d'hote, we drank Tea with them at their Lodgings & afterwards walk'd in the Gardens till it was dark.

Wensday Sep.^t 5th.

A fine but very hot Day staid within all Morning, our two young Gentlemen friends dined in our room & soon after Mr Boettiger call'd to go with us hunting Lodgings wch was not successful, on our return rec'd a visit from Miss Gore a pleasant well bred Woman, when she went walk'd in the Gardens till it was dark.

Thursday Sep.^t 6th.

Quite as hot weather if not more so sat for an hour on the most shady benches we could pick out to read & work, we dined alone & in the evening again went Lodging hunting with Mr Boettiger, hoping with something better success finish'd our walk in the Gardens our young friends also.

By 11 October 1798 the family was beginning to get settled, and to mix in Weimar society:

Thursday Octr 11th.

Rather a cloudy stormy day & in the afternoon a little rain, walk'd no more than to the new house for a little while to see how matters went on went to Tea to Messrs. Hunter & Martins to meet a party of 22, among whom were the Prince & Princess several French people, Miss Gores, Sir Thos. Tancred, Mr Oakely & Mr Benyon from the Belvedere 2 Card Tables much mirth & abundance of Confectionary & good entertainment of various kinds. a perfect new scene.

Friday Octr 12th.

After a night of very severe rain it was a shewey Morning, but at noon became both stormy & showery, but by active exertion, we had mov'd all our baggage from our old, to our new Lodgings before 11 o'clock & by night got tolerably settled & realy very comfortable; & much delighted by our change of situation.

Saturday Octr 13th.

Something of a Frost in the night, but it proved a stormy disagreable Day, & extremely cold hard at work all Morn: with unpacking, receiving Tickets for the Play from Miss Gores to sit in their Box, were tempted to accept of them & were more entertain'd than we expected the Theatre tho not large is handsome being newly fitted up in an elegant taste, & the Dukes Box large & Princely, the Dutchess was there with a small suit, the House not full, the entertainment consisted of two small pieces one entitled the elopement, the other the

Camp of Wallanstine, a shewey fine thing, the actors in general good & performd with spirit & the Band of Music excellent.

By 28 October 1798, the Edward and Agnes Witts were presented at Court:

Sunday Octr 28th.

As fine if not more so than any of the former uncommon Days, the young Men went to service at the Belvedere we did not being preparing to go to Court, to be presented, Miss Gores call'd a little before two to carry us in their Coach, the Ceremony took up very little time, & I was less alarm'd than I expected. Dinner very soon follow'd in the great Hall where were about 40 people, much the greater part Gentlemen & the larger number Military, went home with Miss Gores from ½ past four to six, Tea on our return & at 7 a Concert from the Band of the Theatre & Madam^lle. Jagemann sang afterwards till nine 6 or 7 Tables I play'd Whist at the Reigning Dutchess's Table & Mr Witts at that of the Dowager Dutchess, went thro an amazing number of introductions tired with making Curtseys & standing so much, supp'd at nine, not near so many people as at Dinner, & home at 10 o'clock.

On Wednesday 31 October, Edward and Agnes were invited to dine with Anna Amalia:

Wensday Octr 31st.

Dry but rather cloudy in the Morning, but in the afternoon much sun & being fine busy all the forenoon preparing to Dine at the Dutchess Dowagers where we had been invited, went at two, 21 people there, much the same stile as at Court, but pleasanter from being fewer people & much better entertainment, the old Lady very gracious, Coffee as soon as Dinner was over when all seperated, we went home for an hour, when we went to the Opera, where we were well entertain'd, sat pleasantly among all our young English friends.

On 8 November Edward and Agnes went to a concert, where they were invited by the Duke, and also met all of the young Englishmen from the Belvedere:

Thursday Novr 8th.

The same kind of showery lowering weather in the Morning, but after Dinner settled & very severe rain equally confining till evening when we had been invited to a Concert a large party above 40 performers & all among the rest the Duke & the Prince & Princess, somewhat formal but agreable enough all the Gentlemen from the Belvedere.

By 25 November, Edward and Agnew were well integrated with the Ducal family and from this point onwards Agnes became a regular attendee at Anna Amalia's card table:

Sunday Nov.ʳ 25ᵗʰ.
Still very hard frost, with trifling snow showers, but no wind therefore not near so cold till night accompanied Miss Gores in their Coach to dine at Court, a fuller table than usual & better served, some strangers play'd as usual 6 rubbers at Whist 3 with Dutchess Mother before the Concert & 3 with R.ᵍ Dutchess after did not stay supper.

Monday Novr. 26ᵗʰ.
After a night of very intense frost, it was a clear & very fine day, from constant sunshine, lucky for Mʳ Witts who had accepted of the Dukes invitation to go a Hunting in his party in a Sledge, was absent from home from eight in the Morning till near 6 at night, breakfasting & Dining also with the Duke, & well amused by the novelty of the sport, w.ᶜʰ in fact was shooting rather than Hunting & between 4 & 500 Hares brought home.

By 14 December it was the turn of young Francis to be introduced to Weimar society, and two days later Agnes met the Duchess Louise's brother, the Duke of Hesse Darmstadt: :

Friday Decʳ 14ᵗʰ.
Hard frost as usual, & extremely cold being a wind & no sun, never stirr'd out all Morn: went to the Club Ball in the evening, taking Frank with us his first introduction into the great World where he was received very graciously & conducted himself extremely well staid supper & much amused by some new Polish Dances admirably well perform'd lost my money horridly at Dow Dutchess's Table.

Sunday Decʳ 16ᵗʰ.
A mild air & cloudy sky, & before Noon several hard showers but dry in the evening, Mʳ Witts & Frank went up to the Belvedere to Service, we went to Court in the evening, very pleasant & the scene rather varied by the Prince of Hesse Darmstadt being there with whom I play'd at Whist at the Reigning Dutchess's Table

On 6 January 1799, Agnes was introduced to the Mellish family, and this was the beginning of a new friendship, they later visited the Mellishes at their schloss at Dornburg:

Sunday Jan: 6ᵗʰ.
Sharp frost & some showers of snow at various times of the day, & extremely cold at night after our Morning service our young Men walk'd, went to the evening Court & staid supper, made chearful & pleasant by Monʳᵉ & Madame Mellech being there play'd Whist w.ʰ the Dutchess Mother. wrote to Miss MacFarlan.

On 14 February, Agnes took her younger son, fourteen-year-old George to Court for the first time:

Friday Feb: 1st.

Having been a very severe fall of snow in the night, & continuing to snow the greater part of the day, it was as miserable as ever could be however we all ventured to go to the Redoute at night it being a famous one on account of the Dutchess recent birth day, George in the character of an English Sailor, it was a very good one all the Court being there, & admitted every one in their Box to pay their Compliments not at home till between 1 & 2

This introduction is not the place for the complete diary, but by the summer one highlight was the visit of the King and Queen of Prussia:

Monday July 1st.

Very hot but extremely fine, quite propitious for the arrival of the King & Queen of Prussia, who were hourly expected with eager impatience by a large multitude but did not come till past eight at night, too late for the Opera w.ch was therefore postponed, tho ourselves & a large & genteel audience had been seated in the Theatre for more than three hours waiting, we sat in the Balcony, & had much lively converse with our compatriots & many others.

Tuesday July 2nd.

Most oppressively hot, appearance of thunder but too distant to be heard if any kept as quiet all Morning as I could in order to be better enabled to go thro the fatigues of the afternoon. Mr. & Mrs. Tuthill visited here while my hand was decorating, Mr Witts & his Son dined in one of the Court parties which were wholly appointed to Gentlemen to the number of near 200, the Table they were at being in the Saloon in the Garden, soon after 4 Miss Gores sent their Coach for Madame de Danckelmann & myself & having taken up the 2 Ladies themselves we adjourn'd to the Court which was very numerous & brilliant indeed as besides the King & Queen, there was her Brother the Prince of Michlenburgh Melitz her Sister the Princess of Thurn et Taxis, the Hereditary Prince & Princes of Saxe Gotha, Prince Frederick of Saxe Gotha with attendants inumerable, besides a great number of stranger Noblesse the introduction to the Queen rather a formidable bussiness but because of polite manner took off much, her countenance is fine, her person handsome her dress elegant more than fine, she conversed with much affability the Court was over about six, when all the Royals, & a very large number of the company, proceeded to the Theatre, all in their splendid habilements, it was a fine sight to see the Court Box so nobly fill'd, I sat in the Balcony within s of it very agreably between Madame de Wester & Madame de Danckelmann the representation Wallenstein, acted in a very superior manner to what it had been on any prior occasion, miserably hot there, got home about nine well fatigued.

Another example of the large English Weimar community is the entry for 21 June 1800, this was the day when Edward and Agnes said 'good bye' to Anna Amalia:

*Saturday June 21*st
An intire wet Day till two o'clock in the evening bright & pleasant tho damp, extremely busy all Morning, & at 5 o'clock Mr *Witts & myself & the young Men went to the Duchess Mothers at Tiefurth where we found a small circle mostly English, drank Tea & came home very early stupid enough, tho the leave taking was obliging enough.*

Four days later the family left Weimar for good, but not before the reigning Duke and Duchess requested their presence at a private dinner:

*Wensday June 25*th.
A most charming fine Day, more & & more occupied, & some vexatious circumstances arose to give us pain & anxiety, Mad.^{selle} *d'Ortel call'd, & accompanied us to the Theatre, to a concert which proved most pleasant & flattering to us from the civilities of every one & more particularly the Duke & Dutches's who proposed making a private Dinner for us the next Day at the Roman House which we try'd to decline walk'd with M*^r *Walker in the gardens afterwards who return'd home to Tea with us.*

The diaries of young Francis echo the closeness of the family to the Ducal family, to the extent that the duchess was anxious for Francis to befriend her awkward and shy son, Carl Friedrich the Erb Prince, (Carl Friedrich Grossherzog von Saxe-Weimar-Eisenach; 1783-1853), a youth two weeks older than himself. This was somewhat at the duchess's 'insistence' (and to his own chagrin) and he felt 'forced' to play at what he considered to be childish games with the prince — beneath his dignity — for he considered himself adult. The game 'prison bases' was a form of tag. It was played in the Stern, the star-shaped paths complex in the Ducal Park. The diary entries from Francis commence 28 August 1799:

Wen'sday 28.
Wind S. A fine Day. To the Drawing Academy. To Mr *Schmids. To the Park to play at Prison Bases with the Prince. To M*^r *L. Harens. at my usual Occupations.*

Friday 30.
Wind N.W.A fine warm Day, to Mr. Schmid's. took a walk in the Evening, for the Prince Hereditary was gone to Rudolstadt, of course the sports of the meadow did not take place. At my usual Business.

For the purposes of illustrating life at Weimar from the young man's perspective, one typical evening out is given by Francis in his own words:

Wednesday Feb. 19.
A Charming day walked in the Morning after having been at the Academy & Library and after having called on Mr *Lawrence to the Scating Meadow, joining Mad. de Helldorf &*

*her Sister Mademoiselle de Beist — my Father and Mother dined at the Duchess Mothers.
with my Mother at the Play Gleiches mit Gleichem nach dem Italienischen von Federici
von Vogel. The Piece itself tho' one of the best of Federici nothing remarkable, tho all the
Characters chiefly those of Vohs, Graff, Beckin, Casper, Becker, Haide, Malkolmi, Genast,
& Schall were well kept up.*

The diary entries above are a discursive deviation away from the subject of
Frances Gerard's text, but are provided in the hope that they throw additional
light on society at Anna Amalia's Weimar. They are published separately, and in
full in *An English Family's Life at the the Weimar of Anna Amalia.*

   In conclusion, Frances Gerard did good service in trawling through letters and
documents in the Ducal Archives and has provided a pleasing and readable text.
This book forms a useful contribution to the period of Anna Amalia, Goethe and
Schiller.

Alan Sutton
November 2011

APPENDIX TO THE
INTRODUCTION

In the summer of 1800, shortly before the Witts family left Weimar, Francis Witts, then a youth of seventeen, wrote a Journal of the family's residence in the town (from August 1798 to July 1800). This journal was in *addition* to his diary, and his mother's diary, extracts from which have been included above. The extract relating to Weimar has been reproduced below in whole as it throws light from a young contemporary witness on to the condition of the town and of Weimar society in general. The Witts family became favourites of Anna Amalia, and Francis's mother, Agnes became a frequent companion to the Grand Duchess at her card table. I have added some explanatory notes at the end of this journal extract. Please also note, that this is a faithful transcription from Francis Witts's original and the spelling and grammar are his, completely un-edited.

The Journal of Francis Witts

The Chaussée from Weimar to Erfurt is superb. The Country is not remarkable and yet very fine open Corn Country: at a distance we see the Ettersberg the mountains which extend in a Range farther to the Northward behind Naumburg &c. Ettersberg & the other Elevations in the Neighbourhood of Weimar, together with a distant view of the Seeberg a Mountain in the Neighbourhood of Gotha. Behind a Mountain on the Highland as you leave Erfurt is Romeburg a handsome old Castle in a picturesque Situation. Continuing on this Charming Road thro' Cornfields we arrive at an Hospital where the Weimar Territory commences: some wood is seen on the right Hand otherwise the face of the Country is uniform tho' prettily diversified by various Villages. In the years 1770, 71. this road was made: in those dear times which extended very far besides in these Parts. The Execution of this Plan was worthy the Humanity of the Duchess Amalia, then Regent.— As the Want extended chiefly over the Poor People, for the rich could not afford to give them work, she with the Consent of her Council employed them all in the formation of this Road, paying them chiefly in provisions ready prepared, & providing them with wages enough with their Family.

At that time also were made the fine alley leading to Belvedere & the Chaussée to Jena.— This Town so long the Residence of the Dukes of Weimar is situated in the little valley which serves as bed to the Ilm which rising not far from Ilmenau falls into the Saale; surrounded by a picturesque Amphitheatre of mountains the Chief of which is the Ettersberg. Yet Weimar is by no means the most beautiful Situation in the Duchy the Towns, Apolda, Sulza, Dornburg, Jena &c. are as advantageously & much more picturesquely placed.— The population of Weimar amounts at least to 7 or 8000 Souls. It is in general very ill built, & ill paved: the principal houses are the Statehouse. The Original Purpose of this building is for the accomodation of the States of the Duchy of Weimar which are assembled every Year, tho' it is now the temporary dwelling of the Ducal Family, during the rebuilding of the Castle: It is plain & simple with nothing particular to recommend it:— the Salle is a handsome room with galleries all round totally unfurnished. It was built by a man of the name of Hauptmann Hofjäger who besides this Edifice & the Theatre built several other Houses in the Town & Neighbourhood with little Elegance & less durability.— The principal Church the Town Church situated in a Square in the Centre of the Town is a heavy old building: it contains the Tombs of the different Princes and Princesses of the Weimar Family.— the Head Preacher in this Church is the amiable & Eloquent Superintendent & Vice President Herder an amiable, learned, liberal & affable Man; among the many learned who were attracted to this Town During Minority of the present Duke by the Duchess Mother Amalia Princess of Brunswick now above 60 Years of Age, a Woman who without great Part, or extensive Science &c. endowed with some weakness gave a fine Example in her Regency, by extending the splendor of the Character of the Dominions of her Son. — Besides this Church there is one other in the Suburbs: St. Jacobs Church. —The orphan Hospital here under the direction of Consistorialrathforber is very extensive & emits yearly many well educated subjects of both Sexes.— The Theatre is small but handsome & elegantly fitted up; it is in fact the only public place for amusement in Weimar. It belongs to the Duke who supplies out of his own private Purse which amounts to about 10,000 Stlg. Pr. Ann. — & out of which besides the Expences of the Park &c. he must answer all his menus plaisirs,[1] all the necessary Expences for Garderobe, wages, Decorations &c. which are not liquidated by the receipts of the House. According to the new Improvements, the House is fitted up like the Theatre at Cassel.[2] — The Salle, namely, Orchestra Parquet & Parterre,[3] form the Ballrooms, Salle de Redoute &c.[4] — & is surrounded by elegant Arcades which support the Boxes (les Loges)[5] & the Balcon,[6] together with a very handsome Centre Box for the Court elegantly furnished & fitted up. — The Gallery is supported by handsome wooden Pillars & the whole House holds nearly seven hundred spectators. The whole Edifice is light & airy, the Ornaments, Classical, & Elegant, the Colours, good & the Guilding Chaste. — If any thing it were to be wished that the Number of Theatrical Masks some of them most hideous & disgusting were not so great. The Stage itself is small & it were to be wished that under the direction of Göthe the Decorations were more adapted & elegant. — However such little Reproaches are counterpoised by the Company at present on this Theatre which under the administration of the great Göthe who so well understands the management of the Theatre, is become one of the chief Dramatis Personae in Germany, & are capable of leading the path in representing with success for the first time the best pieces of a Kotzebue, a Schiller, a Göthe and an Iffland. During my Residence here they represented Kotzebues, Graf Burgund, several of his Comedies besides, his Gustav Vasa, his Sonnenjungfrau, & his Bayard, Schillers three Pieces Wallenstein, Piccolomini, Wallensteins Lager, his Robbers, his translation of Macbeth his Maria Stuart, Goethes Mahomet from Voltaire &c. Vohs is one of the best Actors of lovers, heros &c. in Germany, his Max Piccolomini is masterly, his Charles Moor excellent, and so in most Characters which he attempts his voice is powerful & his action very fine. Some Scenes by him in the Sonnenjungfrau as Rolla are excellent — His wife is a tolerable actress, naïve with sensibility, she acts with success Margaretha Löwenhaupt, Thekla, &c. Mademoiselle Jagemann the chief singer in the Opera is the greatest ornament of this Stage, with a little figure, but with an enchanting Voice tho' not high enough for several parts, equally adapted for Tragedy or Comedy which she shines as much in as in the opera, she is the admiration of every Stranger, who is astonished to see her paid the greatest Notice to even by the Duke & his Family; but her lively, easy manner enchants everyone, & to see her without wishing to be acquainted with her were impossible. Her best Characters are few in Number (for she acts but just what she likes) Elsbeth, Margaretha Vasa, Blanka, Thekla &c. particularly the two latter are impossible to be better acted.—In the opera she represents with the greatest success the Astasia in Tarare the Chief Character, in Cosa Fan Tutte, la Molinara, Cosa Rara, Titus (Sextus). yet her perfect acquaintance with the Italian Language (for her Father is the Jagemann so well known by his profound acquaintance with & excellent works on that Tongue) enables her in the Concert at Court to sing some of the finest Italian Music to the words originally adapted to it. — Graff, the hoary villain, the old General, in short the storming Character of this Stage is one of the best actors in Germany could he only regulate his Voice he would be inimitable in many Parts. — He represents in a fine stile, Hermit Peter, Christern II. Paola Manfrone, the Priest of the Sun, Wallenstein, Schweizer (in the Robbers which from an Inferior Character he elevates in a great Degree. Zopyz &c. Mad. Feller is at an advanced age with a disgusting face one of the best actresses I know, her Fortis the Gräfin Orsina in Lessings Emilia Galotti, her Gräfin Terzky, & her Lady Macbeth are almost inimitable. — An Englishman of the Name Schall, is a poor actor except in the Character of sneaking Villain, his fort is the Chamberlain in Emilia Galotti &c.[7] For low Comedy Becker is very good besides those I have mentioned, Malkolmi, Spangler, Haide, Cordeman &c. are very tolerable Performers, among the actresses,

Malkolmi, Göbe, &c. hardly deserve mention, a Mad. Beck in Comedy, & a pretty girl by Name Caspers who shared with Mad.Vohs, the Prime Donna, are however very tolerable. — The Opera is not now (Summer 1800) in so flourishing a Condition as when first I came, Stermins as bass, was much superior to Spitzeder, & Weyrauch acted excellently in the Opera buffa, but as for the rest, they have no tolerable Tenor, & besides Madselle Jagemann not one good Actress. The Orchestra is extremely good. Concertmeister Kranz, though not a good Player, leads a Band very well, Destouches, without being a very great Composer, plays extremely well on the Harpsichord, & some fid violins & German Flutes are well executed. The Theatre does not remain at Weimar, during Summer, it then goes to Lauchstädt,[8] Rudolstadt, & Nuremburg. Actors are here tolerably well paid, Vohs & his wife 1500 Dollars, & Madselle Jagemann at 600 Pr. Ann. — Very few Houses in Weimar are tolerable, that of Mr. Bertink with the Garden attached to it, is among the best. — Of Collections & Cabinets the Dukes Library is the most valuable, it contains upwards of 30000 Volumes, with many interesting Manuscripts; some old Editions of Homer, & Thycydides, of the Bible, one Illuminated of the original Aurea Bulla[9] of the German Constitution — The building is airy three stories high, & prettily fitted up in Amphitheatre, crouded with Portraits of the Electors of Saxony, Dukes of Weimar &c. — none good except that of the Duchess Mother; an old greasy Portrait however, on inspection, found to be well painted, is supposed to be Oliver Cromwell. — The library is filled with busts of many famous men, of Herder, Goethe the venerable Wieland, the learned Villeneuve, the Illuminé Amelius Bodo &c. &c. This Collection is better filled with ancient than modern books, but however several new Publications are to be met with always. It is taken Care of by three Librarians, the Head of whom Schmid is a very agreable man, without great Abilities his Talent for learning Languages, has lead him to read so many Books in all Languages, that he has gathered many Anecdotes & Facts which render him an agreable Instructor for he is well enabled to give Lessons in his own, in the ancient, in the Italian & Spanish Tongues. As an Author, his merits lie in translating, his best work is Lord Monboddy translated & a Spanish & German dictionary, He is a would be Poet, but his verses are tedious & often incorrect totally without fire or genius. — On applying to Mr. Goethe who is the Director of the Library any Person may have Books borrowed without any Security but writing a Receipt for them. — You may keep them three Months, & have as many as you chuse.

There is also a Ducal Cabinet of Medals & a Cabinet of Curiosities. The Duchess Dowager has a good Library & a Collection also. — Besides several Private Libraries &c. — That of Oberconsistorialrath Böttiger, Rector of the Gymnasium, is pretty extensive & well collected. — With the invinuation of an Illuminé, this Gentleman does not possess the reserve of secrecy of the members of that diabolical Sect. — He has been stiled the don Quixote of Illuminists,[10] I should have preferred the Epithet, a literary weathercock, for as the wind changes, he changes, & in the space of 12 Hours who he will adopt the opinion, & not only from but really coincide in the Ideas, of the last Person with whom he has conversed. Nevertheless he is a great Scholar, & a Worthy successor of Lessing in his mode of treating the Greek Antiquities: his Lectures on Encyclopædie, are very interesting, and his conjectures on the ancient History of the Heroic Times, throw much light on the general History of Mankind. As an author his Style whenever out of the Sphere of Antiquities, appertains to Bombast & Justials,[11] he is no Poet, except some Latin verses which he has written with correctness. His Politeness to Strangers, who bring Introductions to him, is very extensive, his Library is always at their Command, & I should be very ungrateful not to acknowledge the obligations I lay under to him, not only for the Public Instructions, but for his private Advice in my Course of Reading. — The literary & useful Establishments here, and the College, founded by Duke William. Under the Inspection of Herder. — The Rector Böttiger — The Comcetor Schwabe — Also in the Philosophical & historical line, Mr. Hästner has considerable merit —This College brings the Students into the University, Instructing them in the Hebrew Greek & Latin Languages, Moral & Natural Philosophy, Mathematics, History &c. Most of these Instructions are delivered free of all Cost, the remainder are at very small Expence to the Student, who does not lodge in the School, but are boarded about the Town. — The Drawing Academy here is under the direction of the well known Counsellor Kraus, whose Execution is well known to exceed his taste, Messrs. Femler, Müller, Herdig & Hornÿ, Keinert &c. give also Instructions, in every Branch of Painting and Drawing. There are no famous Drawings nor Paintings in the Academy; the chief are the well known works of Mr. Kraus, these are very interesting to Strangers, particularly his Landscapes, which give a very just Idea of most celebrated views on the Continent: his Costumes are beautiful, & with the rest of his performances are engraved & sold at the Industrie Comton, Messrs. Bertuck & Kraus, at Weimar.

In the Academy are several fine busts, & Statues, some the work of the Hofbildhauer Klaurez of in this Town whose workshop is well worthy the Inspection of the Inquisitor Traveller. His works are very moderate in price, & tho' not first rate, his busts are on account of their great resemblance, much sought after, & even exported to America. — The best Inns at Weimar are the Prince Hereditary, and the Elephant. — The Court at Weimar is extremely hospitable and polite, to Strangers, & very encouraging to artists of every description. besides Dinners, Concerts, & Suppers at Court, every Sunday, and often intermediate Societies at Court, where you come not only into the Intimacy of the Nobility of the Town, but also if of certain consequence, into that of the Ducal Family, who are all in their different ways extremely partial to Strangers. The Reigning Duke, a man of 43 Years old, is a small figure, & rather a forbidding Countenance, fond of Music, & of reading, attached to particular people, & fond of the fair Sex. Ambitions that his Court & Town should be visited by Strangers, yet fond of ease

& social joviality. His genius is martial, & violent, fond of exercise, & passionately attached to the Chase, which he pursues with great ardor. If anything, inclined to expence, and fond of travelling to foreign Courts &c. Without much taste, he is fond of improving his Park, in which however he is chiefly assisted by Privy Counsellor Göethe, & Baron Wohlzogen. He is also Duke of Eisenach, Margrave of Ravensberg, &c. &c. His states occupy a surface of 36 square German Miles, his revenues amount to 600000 Rix dollars a year;[12] the population about 93400, Two thirds of which is furnished by Weimar & Jena. And his troops besides the militia consist of a body of Chasseurs, & one a Corps of Hussars. — These Troops were formerly more numerous, but even now the fixed Contingent must march, as they did with the Austrian and Saxon Troops at the commencement of the war; The Duke of Weimar must also, his dominions being in the Circle of Upper Saxony, contribute his Share in the fournishing the war allowance of 1½ millions for the Empire, this amounts in the Circle of Upper Saxony, to 156,360 florins 15 Kreutzer.[13] — The Reigning Duchess, Louise Princess of Saxe Darmstadt, is aged 45 Years; Her figure is rather majestic, than handsome, her face pleasing, tho' the features are not regular, she is affable, yet not free in her Conversation, she always maintains the Dignity of her rank, without stiffness or Affectation, & suits her conversation admirably to the person with whom she speaks. Adapted much to reading, particularly to History & Politics, an adherent of Lavaters System,[14] & always more ready to obtain Knowledge than to display her own talents, and acquirements. The Hereditary Prince, a youth of 17 Years, is tall & well made, rather of a dark complexion, his Natural Abilities are good, he is good tempered, & inclined to be friendly, his Manners are more constrained than could be wished, arising from the flattery which has been bestowed on him, & the particular partiality of his amiable Mother. His habit of body is at present weak, & he is in general Averse to all bodily Exercise. The Princess, between 14 & 15 years of age, small in stature is a Brunette, lively, & clever, extremely fortunate in her Governess, a Mademoiselle de Knebel. The little Prince Bernard is only 8 Years old, his Character of Course not yet decided, tho' he appears to partake much of that of his father. Several other Children, the fruit of this marriage both older & younger than the Prince Hereditary have died & these three are alone alive. — The Nobility belonging to the Duchy, who reside here are few in number, of strangers there are many. The chief are Count Marschall, the Egloffstein, Seebach, Helldorf, Luc, Lasberg, Wolfskiel, Gormar, Oldorthausen, Families &c. all of whom almost have some Office either in the Civil, Military or Immediate Court Service. Although for the saving of expence many unnecessary Offices at Court have within this four Years been done away. There are about 30 French Nobility here, emigrants chiefly from the Southern Provinces of France, the chief Family of Importance, is that of the Marquis de Fouquet, — that of Marquis de Fumel — & Comte du Masion. Of English, there were here in the Town besides ourselves, Mr. Gore & his two Daughters, formerly of Southampton, a gentleman of very

good fortune, who has for many Years been absent from England. As age &
infirmities are heaped on him, it appears improbable that he will ever leave
Weimar, he has a very handsome house the daily resort of French & English, but
of very few Germans. — Mr. Gore has often Concerts & Musical Parties, is
extremely attached to drawing, fond of Politics, & they are much in favour at
Court. — At the latter place is much Card playing, though at a very low stake, the
chief Games Whist, l'ombre, Teisette, Tarock, Casino & Boston. — One of the
amusements at Court, which however only happens twice or thrice in the Course
of the Year, are the Petits Jeux, in which all the young Nobility of the Town,
Princely &c. take part. They consist in the Elegant Games of Blind mans buff,
Mussli,[15] and so forth; surely a sad employment for a set of rational People, who
are no longer Children. The Confirmation of the Prince of Weimar, while we
were there, was an awful & serious celebration: it happened in the Court, & all
the Nobility here in the Town, and in the neighbourhood were present. The
Ceremony consisted in an Examination, an Exhortation and a Blessing: the
Clergyman was Herder; his forcible Language, his sweet melodious voice, the
silence & attention, together with the seriousness of all surrounders, was a moving
sight: the whole Circumstances have since been published here in a few Copies, a
Manuscript of which I have made. The attendance at Court, besides numerous
Servants, in and out of livery, are 5 or 6 Pages, sons of the surrounding poor
Nobility, who by submitting their Children to a few Years hard & ignominious
Work, put it in their power to obtain a very good Education, in the ancient &
modern Languages, riding, fencing &c; & the assistance of the Duke if necessary,
in their future Pursuits in Life. The Dukes Manege is very good,[16] as indeed
every article relating to his Stables &c: he has many handsome English Horses, &
some are reared in the Neighbourhood: tho' the greatest Number of the Horses
here come from Hesse, Hanover, Holstein, & Mecklenburg: Besides the Court, is
a very pleasant Club of Noblesse here, who subscribe at a very moderate Price to
a certain Number of Balls, where the Nobility whoever they be are all welcome;
they are very pleasant, in the Theatre, begin at 6 o'clock, supper at 9, & end
towards eleven; the chief dances danced there, are the English Country dances,
the dreher, & Walzer, the German & French Quadrilles, the Scottish Reels, & the
Grossvater, a kind of medley which can be continued as long as the dancers like
it. There is also a Club of Savans, the admittance into which is very easy, these
meet every Thursday to dinner & Supper in the Hofjägers at the Saxon Post, & is
a Society by which a young Man can profit much, having there an Opportunity
of becoming acquainted with some of the most famous men in the Town &
Neighbourhood. The Secretary, M. de Seckendorff is a very well informed young
Man, singular in his manners, reserved to the world, & open to particular people.
This Club is visited also by the Prince Hereditary:— attended by his Tutor a
Dutchman, by name de Haren, a man of real worth, but haughty, & sometimes
rather Frivolous. — The evening Parties to tea &c, here, are not very frequent, the

poverty of the Noblesse in general not allowing them to exhibit their Hospitality, & the constant resort of all persons to the reigning Count, & that of the Duchess Mother, who during Winter gives every week a dinner & a Card Society, to the Play, Balls &c. precludes the necessity of those frequent parties which form the agrèment of other Towns. — Still, some few people do receive Society in the Evening, the Helldorffs, Werthern, Fouquet, Fumel, Rictgenstein &c. There are during the whole winter, masked balls every fortnight, or three: weeks these meetings are very poor, tiresome, vulgar, & stupid in the greatest degree, the resort of all those people whose conduct in life, precludes them every other society but that where they do not shew their faces. You seldom see a single Mask, a few Chauve Souris,[17] a few duty Monks, &c, are the more distinguishable as they are the only persons who are without the dismal black Domino,[18] which however the men only wear, as the ladies (rather a perversion of the Name) have no sign of masquerade, but a pair of Evires with Black Silk over them which covers surrounds their Eyes: those People who do not dance, either play at Pharaoh,[19] or drink, & from 12 at night, till 4 or 5 in the Morning, the whole assembly is a scene of gaming, drunkenness, & obscenity — It may easily supposed that this is not a favorite Amusement among the higher Classes, two or three Redoutes at most are tolerable, on the Duchess Mother's Birthday, on the Reigning Duchess's Birthday, & on the Ashwednesday Eve; when the Court, & some ladies of that society, are there. It is at the Redoute only, that a Faro Table is allowed, the permission of holding it, which is rented by respectable Gotha Merchants, costs 500 rix dollars Pr. An. — The Chief Walk here is the Dukes beautiful English Garden, which is always open to every person. — Seldom was any ground better adapted for the purpose to which it is appropriated, as this Garden, & it equals in beauty, Hagley, the Leasowes,[20] & many other Celebrated Gardens in the native Country of the true Taste. — The grand Walk leading from the present Palace over a neat Bridge, over a small stream which flows into a stream the Ilm is of Gravel, wide enough for two Carriages Abreast, & is continued nearly in a serpentine line, of more than half a mile long to the Belvedere road; thro' a beautiful diversified Landscape. In a Plantation of fine fir trees on the left Hand, is the Schmecke, an Edifice of which there is only one more in Europe, namely in Italy: it is built of a strong wooden scaffolding which runs like a Gallery tier over tier on gentle slope between two rows of flourishing Lime Trees, forming two Platforms by which you mount in cross directions to two Turrets, formed by Scaffolding and the Top Branches of the two highest Trees from each of which you have an excellent view of the Town & Country surrounding it. On the right hand as you proceed in the great Walk, is a handsome broad alley of a few very fine lofty lime Trees — Proceeding with an open Lawn on the left Hand, on the right a Shrubbery, we come to the Salon, on the left hand, a building in the Gothic Taste, in which in Summer, the Courts are often held: it is prettily constructed, the windows are down to the Ground, only on one side of the

Edifice, & looks into a Circle of fine foliage: the Apartment is furnished with some very good pictures of hunting: one in particular placed in a bad light, the Rider seized by the Lion, is well worthy of observation. The Walk continues thro' an Alley of Popler Trees, which conceals from immediate view the Greenhouses & Hothouses, & the Kitchen Garden, on the left hand side: all of which are under good Care, & advancing thro' a now open aspect we approach the Roman House: a Summer retreat of the Duke, which he occupies for six Months in the Year & occasionally entertains there the Strangers who visit his Court, en passant. — The building is oblong, in the lower story which is deeper than the front, by some feet, & opens to a walk lower than the great walk, are the Offices built of stone, & well squared stone, the back Part of the Edifice rests on fluted Pillars, forming a Kind of Open Vestibule, in which is a Stone bench for the accomodation of Passengers. — The ornaments and besides a cistern of spring Water with a small Fountain, a dance of the nine Muses of Apollo in Stucco with other antique Ornaments. The upper story level with the grand Walk, is divided into a Vestibule, with a moderate Picture, two handsome Apartments square, & not very large, a Bed Chamber, & dressing Room, together with a Staircase; these Apartments are very handsomely furnished with Embroidered Satin, handsome B_____ Stoves, &c. & decorated by several good Paintings, some by a Miss Gore. — The building is of a fine Plaster made to imitate True Stone, and on the whole the deception is good. The Door is handsome & enters into a Portico supported by four very handsome Stop Pillars, above which is a very well executed Burrelief representing an Antique. Soon after this the great walk terminates in the Belvedere Alley, and the Stranger generally takes the lower walks, these to thro' the wood each equally beautiful, on the side of the Hill which hangs from the top of the Garden down to the Meadows below partly on & partly under some picturesque Rocks, one of which in particular follows by nature, & assisted by art, form a cavern large enough to hold twenty or thirty persons. At every pretty View, a Seat is placed, shewing the Village of Oberweimar, &c. Under the Roman House a small stream of superfluous water is brought by pipes to the Top of a rock from which it falls into a Bason apparently constructed of a heap of rude Stones. These two walks unite again into one, near the Monument of the Prince of Dessau: This Monument consists of an Immense triangular Rock, placed on several other small ones, & is a Stone found in a Quarry, between Weimar & Belvedere, & transported here only with the greatest Difficulty. It is a rough Sandstone, crept round by Ivy, in which a Copper Plate, engraved with the words, in Gold Characters, "Francisco Dessaviæ Princips".[21] This Prince of Dessau, was the first Person who introduced into Germany, the English Stile of Gardens, of which he gave a beautiful Example, in his English Gardens at Woerlitz, which however do not approach the Beauty of the Weimar Gardens. — Continuing onwards, you pass three Seats, each of which gives a beautiful View of the river & meadows, & turning to the walk on the right Hand, you soon come to the Monument inscribed "Genis hujus loci":[22]

it consists of an Altar intwined by a Serpent, who is in the act of devouring one of the sacrifice Cakes. The whole in Sandstone very finely executed by Klaurez, and surrounded by a little Hedge of Thorns. The idea is taken out of Virgils Enid. — Continuing this walk, you come to the Ruins, these are artificial, well made, & represent the wall of an old Castle, the ruined Stones, Statues &c. around add much to the Effect & present to the Stranger a much more agreable sight than it did formerly when it was merely an old Bastion: descen opposite these Ruins is a pretty enough stone inscribed with the words "Remember Leo" in memory of a dog of that name, belonging to Mr. Gore, which was buried there. — Descending from these Ruins, by steps, we pass by Louisa's Kloister, a small dark Defile of wood, to resemble a Hermitage, within, nicely fitted up, and so entitled by the Duke, after his wife; this was the general Summer Retreat of his Highness, till the Roman House was erected. Near this Edifice, is the entrance into the Gravel Pit, which supplies the Gardens: it is a long avenue, in the east, of nearly half a mile in length: and most dreadfully cold, & dangerous for the Inspection of Strangers. — In the Centre, is a side vault, where is kept the English Beer. This is a Sort of Ale, not very wholesome, but agreable to the Taste, which is brewed by the Duke; the Brewer spent some years in England. The general Beer of the Town is however very good, brown Beer, & more wholesome than the other. Two paths here lead you, one thro' the meadows, the other into the stern. The latter former leads thro' very beautiful walks chiefly by the River side, nearly as far as the Village of Oberweimar, thro' meadows whose verdure is delightful & which are beautifully diversified by Trees &c. There are three bridges, one, consisting of two fine oak trees in nature, the others light & elegant, & a small ferry Boat on an easy Construction, which by means of Ropes, can be with the greatest facility used. The fertility of these meadows are much assisted by the water, drawn from the river by the wheels; which in the shape of a mill wheel, with boxes in the Circumference, throws a certain Quantity of Water out of the Stream, into Spouts which conduct it throughout the whole meadow. The bathing House of the Duke is also a pretty little square thatched building: consisting of three Apartments, elegantly furnished, out of which you come into a small portion of the River seperated off by curtains. The Summer Dwellings of privy Counsellors Goethe, & the venerable, & economical Schmid, sister of Klopstocks Fanny, add much to the lively scene: from the field above the latter Gentleman's House, is the best view of the Park altogether; on entering into the Stern, by the Centre Walk you pass the part of the meadow, where the Prince, with the young Nobility of the Court, diverts himself often at the Game of Prison Bases.[23] The Stern is a grove of fine handsome trees, fir, Beech, Birch, Lime, Chesnuts, &c. which are so intersected by walks concentering in a circle, in the Centre, that it exhibits the appearance of a Star, from which Circumstance it has its name; the grand avenue which is very fine, terminates in an open green, shaded by fine Horse Chesnuts, & terminated by a handsome Bridge, coming from the Old Palace, to an Avenue of Lime trees leading to the Jena Chaussée: the decorations of this part of the Garden are, a fine Sphinx, in Sandstone by Klaurez, reclining under a well laid Rock: over which formerly, a Cascade, drawn from the River, fell into a Bason formed by a natural Spring of fine Clear water, which forms a Brook which afterwards runs into the Ilm; another Spring of the same sort, forms a little Brook conveyed under ground, Exhibits, when it bursts out, a little fountain, among a Collection of aquatic plants & shrubs. — Passing thro' the second Arch of the Castlebridge, as it is called, & over the little Brook already mentioned, you pass thro' by a Path, across a little Lawn, near the Dukes Wood, under a venerable ancient Lime Tree, to that Part of the Park which is called Rothaüser Garten, properly a Shrubbery, lying on the hill contiguous to the Jena Road; prettily intersected by walks, it is ornamented chiefly by three Corinthian Pillars, an Imitation of the Portico in the Temple of Jupiter Zator in Rome: there is also a Monument erected to the memory of a famous Actress, Mad. Becker, on an Eminence, which commands very handsome & extensive view, it is a Pedestal & Pillar of Sandstone, crowned with an Urn, on which in Bass Relief, well carved at Gotha the four Seasons, & the twelve Signs of the Zodiac, together with the masks of a Virgin, a Youth, a middle aged man, & a Greybeard to personify, Spring, Summer, Autumn & Winter. Out of this part of the Garden, it is very easy to come to the Wewicht,[24] a small wood adjacent to the Jena Chaussée, intersected by various Alleys, within the Compass of a Walk from Weimar. The most remarkable places among the Environs of Weimar are the Belvedere: a Castle of the Dukes, two English Miles distant from Weimar, with which it is connected by an Alley, & Chaussée of fine Limes & Chestnuts. You pass by the Deposit of floating Wood, chiefly fir, which comes down the Ilm from the further parts of the Dukes Dominions, and at least 24000 Clafters are used yearly here, & in the neighbouring Village of Oberweimar, where is a large Distillery of Brandy. A Clafter is a pile of Wood, six foot high, six foot long & three feet broad. We pass in view of the village of Ehringsdrys & enter into the Grove, which surrounds the Mansions, Gardens &c. of Belvedere. The Edifice was built by the Dukes Great Grandfather, & consists besides the body of the House, of two Wings, with two Pavillons, two Ranges of Stabling & Coachhouses, Guardhouses, a large Garden, Hothouses & Orangery. It was built for a Summer Residence of the Dukel Family, tho' now appropriated by the Dukes Beneficence, to an Academy kept by Mr. Mounier, a Frenchman of the highest & worthiest Character, a Protestant, a liberal & well informed man, bold & steady in his Conduct, & beloved by all the worthy who know him intimately of every age. — No man was ever better adapted to be the Head of an Institute, than Mr. Mounier, & there are few places on the Continent, where young Persons could be placed with more safety: for in Weimar you can enjoy the Privileges, Politeness, & Good manners without the vices, attending Society, in a great Town. The Plan is to admit young Gentlemen of fortune, from the age of fifteen Years onwards, at the sum of 150£ Pr. Ann.

besides which, their private Expences, cost nearly 100£ more. They are instructed in the ancient Languages, the German & French, & if they wish it, the Italian Tongue, Mathematics, Politics, History, Moral & Natural Philosophy. — While Drawing, & the Genteel Accomplishments, can easily be main obtained. — They are received into the best Society in the Town, & are often more paid attention to than most other strangers. From the Price however of the Yearly Board, & Instruction, being so high, few can avail of this most unexceptionable Institute, but English, & I beg leave to remark, that if a young Man comes here, with a steady Character, & firm, religious, & moral Principles the benefits he will receive at the Belvedere, will enhance to him the Respectability & happiness, both in his future, public, & private Life. — Mr. du Vaux as a Mathematician, du Stuat as natural philosopher, and M. Mathir as Linguist, are all able Professors, & from their age are rather the Steady Companions, than the Preceptors of their Pupils. — Mr. Walker, a Clergyman of the Church of England, keeps up the youths of that Country in the Practice of their Religion, & gives to foreigners ample Instruction in the English Language.

The Castle of Ettersburg at the same distance from Weimar, on the other side, is situated on the hill, & in the forest of that name:— pleasant Allies, Avenues, & Paths, traverse the forest, & conduct to its romantic Situations. — The beautiful Garden of Tieffurth, at the same distance from Weimar, is the Summer Retreat of the Duchess Dowager, a Situation totally Different from that of the Park at Weimar, is equally well laid out. — We admire particularly a Small Temple, a monument to the late Prince Constantine, one to a Nightingale with an elegant Inscription by Goethe, & various other ornaments. The Duchess Dowager has Company here in summer, her Tea parties are very agreable. The small Town of Apolda, not far from Weimar is remarkable by its manufacture of stockings: there are sold annually more than 53,000 Pairs.

Notes to the Appendix
1. *Menus Plaisirs.* Simple pleasures, small personal expenses or gratifications.
2. Cassel is presumably Kassel.
3. Orchestra Parquet & Parterre. The parquet is a small marked off area, in this case for the orchestra itself; the parterre is the part of the ground floor of the theatre behind the orchestra.
4. *Salle de Redoute.* Redoubt—a public assembly hall in Germany used for gambling and other entertainments.
5. *Les Loges.* A box in a theatre or opera house.
6. *Balcon.* A railed or balustraded platform. It was usual in early theatres to have a stage box referred to as a '*balcon*'. The theatre programmes refer to the '*Parket und Balkon*' as costing twelve *Groschen*, with the *Parterre* and *Gallerie* being respectively eight and four *Groschen*. A *Groschen* was a small silver coin.
7. The use of *fortis* in relation to Madam Feller and *fort* for Schall is in relation to Francis' opinion of their strongest parts. The *fortis* in particular is Francis playing with his Latin.
8. Lauchstädt is Bad Lauchstädt, some thirty-five miles to the north-west. A Goethe theatre remains there to this day. Rudolstadt is nineteen miles to the south where

the Duke was a frequent visitor to Schloss Heidecksburg. There were no known connections with Nuremberg.

9. *Aurea Bulla.* Golden Bull. A document whose importance was signified by a golden seal; specifically, the term is used to describe the edict of Emperor Charles IV in 1356 defining the seven Electors of the Holy Roman Empire.

10. '… this Gentleman does not possess the reserve of secrecy of the members of that diabolical Sect.—He has been stiled the don Quixote of Illuminists.' Unfortunately, Francis was right at the very right-hand edge of the page when writing the last word and in cramping it in it has become illegible. It looks as is he has written 'illuminipu,' but this makes no sense. The word 'illuminists' has been assumed. The Illuminato were followers of a sect that sprang up in Spain in 1575, later adopted in Germany as a secret society founded by Adam Weishaupt in Bavaria in 1776, holding deistic and republican principles and organized like the Freemasons.

11. Justials. This last word is very difficult to understand. It could be 'fustials', 'tustials', 'frestials', etc. None of these make sense.

12. The rix dollar was the silver state (*Rijk*) *Daler* (also *Thaler*), a silver coin of various European countries at this and earlier times. It was not a real coin or currency in Germany, but was used to denote comparisons. The main currency was the *Gulden* (sixteen *Groschen*) and Double *Gulden* (thirty-two *Groschen*). A rix dollar was usually calculated at twenty-four *Gulden*.

13. The *Kreutzer* is a cross-bearing penny, a silver or copper coin stamped with the shape of a cross.

14. Johann Kaspar Lavater (1741–1801), physiognomist, theologian and writer, born in Zürich. In 1769 he received Protestant orders and made himself known by a volume of poems. He was a close friend of the artist Fuseli. He also invented the science of phrenology, which was based on the reading of significance into the bumps on the heads of a remarkable range of gullible clients. His works on physiognomy were written with the assistance of Goethe. He died of wounds sustained during the capture of Zürich by André Masséna and after tending others amongst the wounded.

15. Mussli. This word is hard to decipher, but nothing else appears to make sense. Muss was a game where small objects are thrown down to be scrambled for—a scramble.

16. *Manège.* A riding school or the movements in which the horse is trained.

17. *Chauve Souris.* A bat—to fly around like a bat.

18. Domino. A garment worn to cover the head and shoulders; a lose cloak with a mask covering the upper part of the face to wear at masquerades.

19. Pharaoh. Faro—a card game.

20. Hagley was the birthplace of Lady Lyttelton's husband, the 'wicked' Lord Lyttelton. The Leasowes is a Lyttelton garden at Halesowen in Worcestershire. The Leasowes was the property bought by his aunt after she returned from India, and before she married Lord Lyttelton. Francis would have been aware of these properties from his parents, but had never visited them.

21. *Francisco Dessaviæ Princips.* To Franz, Prince of Dessau.

22. *Genis hujus loci.* To the genius (spirit) of this place.

23. Prison Bases. Prisoners' Base is a chasing game (a form of tag), played by two sides occupying distinct areas, the object being to catch and make prisoner any player from the other side running from his or her home area.

24. Wewicht. The Webicht.

CHAPTER I

I am not going to enter upon so deep a subject as the early history of Thuringia. Those who wish to know more of the warriors, whose names and brave deeds fill the pages of the ancient histories, should read the early annals of Thuringia. It will be enough for our present purpose to mention a few facts which may, or may not, be familiar to my readers.

In the first place, I would recall to the recollection of readers of history that Thuringia, where the duchies of Weimar and Eisenach are situated, is one of the choicest spots in all Germany. So dear was it to the early German rulers, that, when the rest of that extensive country was parcelled out into dukedoms, the emperors reserved for themselves Thuringia, placing stewards, or supervisors–noblemen of high estate–to exercise the duty of governors, giving them the title of Landgraf, or, later, Markgraf. These deputy governors, who resided at the watch castle or tower of Eisenach, well known nowadays as the Wartburg, were hard fighters, men of courage and cruelty, who flit through the pages of Thuringian history and give it a romantic interest.

Especially interesting is the story of Ludwig IV and his wife, the sainted Elizabeth, who figure in Wagner's setting of the legend of the Knight Tannhäuser, so intimately associated with the Wartburg.[1] The holy Elizabeth, who was a Hungarian Princess; was brought to the Wartburg when three years old, and affianced at that tender age to her future husband, Ludwig IV, surnamed the Pious (AD 1223). The young pair were both holy and God-serving. Ludwig's worldly-minded mother, did everything, we are told, that a wicked woman could do to wean her son's affections from his affianced wife. But Elizabeth's piety and, let us add, her beauty, prevailed, and they were formally wedded and lived happily for many years in the castle. At last the idea seized upon the pious Ludwig that he should make a pilgrimage to Jerusalem. His holy wife would not interfere, but accompanied him on his journey for three days, and then returned to Eisenach "sorrowing." She never saw her beloved husband again; he died at Jerusalem, and was buried there.[2] Her son being only a child, his cousin or uncle, Heinrich der Raspe, undertook the guardianship, and in the usual course drove out the widow and children. Elizabeth had to wander about for years, poor and helpless, but always saintly. At last the wicked Heinrich's heart was touched by the admonitions of a monk, named Rudolph. He sent for Elizabeth, and restored to her and her children the duchies he had usurped. Elizabeth spent the remaining years of her life in prayer and good works. She laid aside all appearance of her rank, wore coarse garments, and gave everything to the poor. Her health speedily gave way, and soon she passed to a better life, an example of a saintly death. Some years later a church was built on the spot where she was buried, and dedicated to her. Pope Gregory IX in the year AD 1324, beatified her.

In course of time, the Thuringian Landgrafs disappear from the pages of the old chronicles, and we find their places taken by the Markgrafs of Meissen. Presently these too go their way, and we come to a new leader, who may be called the founder of the reigning family of Dukes of Weimar and Eisenach. They were a strong race, these Saxons or Ernestines, who dwelt by the shores of the Elbe and the Weser. They grew and multiplied over the land, and, ever on the lookout for new pastures, suddenly swooped down upon beautiful Thuringia, and made it and Meissen their own, the very name being blotted out and that of Saxony taking its place; whilst, in lieu of the ancient lions which were to be seen on the shields and armour of the Markgrafs, there now appeared the *rautenkranz* or rue plant of the Saxons.

It would be writing history, were I to go through the long line of Saxon heroes who distinguished themselves in love and war. Their chronicles teem with romantic episodes, such as the carrying away of Eric and Albert, the two sons of the Elector of Saxony. Then came the blast of the Reformation, which may be said to have had its rise at Eisenach, where Luther lived in the castle that had once been the refuge of the sainted Elizabeth.

One of the first converts was Frederick, called the Wise, son of the Elector Ernst, and his example was followed by John the Steadfast, who fought tooth and nail for Luther and his creed. This storm subsiding, by degrees we come to a certain Duke William, who, with his brothers — by some writers said to be seven, by others eleven in number,— played a great part in the history of the little duchy. One of these, Bernard, acquired great military fame during the Thirty Years' War while another brother earned for himself by his excesses such a reputation, that his name became a by-word. In 1626, an outlaw and an outcast from his own country, he took service with the King of Denmark, who accorded him the rank of colonel; but his conduct was such that he had to be dismissed. He then betook himself to Austria, where he affected a desire to embrace the religion of that country, and was welcomed with joy as an illustrious convert. Soon, however, he showed his true character, and, having killed an Austrian nobleman, he was thrown into prison. Finally, he was claimed by the duke, his brother, and sent back to Weimar, where he was confined in an iron cage, like a wild beast. One day he was found weltering in a pool of blood at the bottom of his cage, and all manner of stories were circulated ascribing his death to supernatural causes. It was believed by the people that he had a compact with the devil, who used to visit him in his cage.

It is more probable that either he died by his own hand, or was removed by the duke's order. It must, however, be said that Duke William's subsequent conduct was not in harmony with the theory of fratricide. He was an honest, open-hearted man; his reign of twenty years was peaceable, and neither in life nor death did he exhibit any symptoms of remorse such as might have been expected in one guilty of so terrible a crime.

His successor, who was theologically inclined, thought more of writing pamphlets than governing his duchy. His grandson, who succeeded him — by name Ernest Augustus — was one of the most powerful princes of the House of Saxony. His appearance, it is true, was mean and unprepossessing. He was diminutive in stature and lean as a skeleton. His eccentricities might have led a stranger to think him at times insane; but when it came to matters of importance, he showed extraordinary shrewdness.

In the memoirs of the Lively Wilhelmina, Margravine of Bayreuth, there is an amusing account of the marriage of this Duke of Weimar with her sister-in-law Charlotte, who was beautiful as an angel, but at times only fit for a lunatic asylum.

The duke, who was looking out for a consort, had seen the portrait of Charlotte, and fell fathoms deep in love with the sweet presentment of girlish loveliness. He at once demanded her hand in marriage, on the condition that his proposal should be kept secret until his arrival at Bayreuth. This was agreed to. Nevertheless, preparations for the wedding were made quietly. The suitor duly arrived, and at first his behaviour was as it should be. He frequently looked at the beautiful princess, whose charms were set off to the best advantage by her toilette, which had been carefully supervised by Wilhelmina. She was evidently most anxious to get the half-crazy princess, who, however, showed no signs of flightiness on this occasion, off her hands. Everything having, so far, gone off well, there was great dismay when, on the following day, the eccentric lover seemed to have forgotten his matrimonial intentions. He did nothing but talk, and "the lies he told were so extravagant that the devil himself could not exceed them." In spite of his disagreeable eccentricities, the match was too advantageous to be allowed to slip, and by dint of diplomacy the wedding of this strangely assorted pair took place. The Margravine Wilhelmina showed no pity for her unfortunate, half-mad sister-in-law, who, when it was made clear to her disordered brain that she was to be the wife of the duke, "fell on her knees weeping like an idiot." Her tears, however, availed her little with the resolute Wilhelmina, who herself dressed the unwilling bride for the sacrifice, put a crown on her head, and brought the poor princess down to the audience chamber, where the chaplain gave the nuptial benediction. The newly married pair remained at Bayreuth for a week, during which time there was a constant dread lest one or other of the eccentric couple should run away. This, however, did not occur.

As may be supposed, the marriage did not turn out happily. We get, however, only fragmentary glimpses of the couple. We know the beautiful Charlotte died after giving birth to a son, Constantine, who became an orphan at eleven years old, the wayward duke dying of fever. We shall hear again of Constantine, but, for the present, must leave him under the care of the two guardians appointed by the Emperor of Austria — Duke Frederick III, of Gotha, and Duke Josias of Coburg, the latter being next heir to the Duchy of Weimar.

We must now turn to another portion of Germany and make acquaintance with another reigning duke, who, in his own person and in the surroundings of his ducal court, presented a great contrast to the eccentric ruler of Weimar.

In 1737 the Duchy of Brunswick was governed by Duke Karl, who has a distinct interest for us, as being father to Anna Amalia, the heroine of our story.

We learn from memoirs and contemporary literature at the beginning of the eighteenth century that Germany was much behind other European nations in refinement and mental cultivation. We read in Doctor Vehse's voluminous histories of the manners and customs which prevailed at the electoral court of Celle, of the immorality, drunkenness, and illiterate state of the reigning dukes all over Germany; whilst the royal court of Prussia afforded anything but a bright example to the smaller states. Readers of biographies and memoirs will recall some very lively incidents described by the Margravine of Bayreuth, who was a princess of the royal house of Prussia, and her testimony is supported by many other writers. The treatment of men of genius, artists, and musicians, was of the shabbiest character. Klopstock, the founder, as we may call him, of German poetry, owed to a foreign prince the small pension which kept him from starvation.[3] England came to the rescue of Schubart; while Lessing, too proud to make known his condition, suffered actual want.

It is pleasant to find a different position of affairs prevailing at the Court of Brunswick, which seems to have served as a pioneer to Attic Weimar. At Wolfenbüttel, the capital of Brunswick, there was every inducement to attract men of letters and artists: a fine picture gallery, a handsome library and academy, and the Collegium Carolinum, founded by Duke Karl, to which a number of learned professors were attached.

Unfortunately the Duchess of Brunswick,[4] who had been brought up in a different school, did not share her husband's scholarly tastes, and if it had been left to her, the duke's children, and especially the daughters, would have fared badly.

On 24 October 1739, the bells of Wolfenbüttel rang out to announce that Her Royal Highness had given birth to a daughter; this was a grievous disappointment which, after the manner of the time, was resented as being the fault of the unwelcome intruder. Having caused her parents this first trial, she was never looked upon with affection; the duchess especially preserved a grudge against her

daughter which lasted her lifetime, and which tinged the childhood of the little
Anna Amalia with bitterness, and clouded her early girlhood.

This conduct on the part of the duchess bears out the character given of her by
her sister, the Margravine of Bayreuth,[5] "Charlotte is very handsome, very satirical,
false, jealous and selfish." She adds: "The Prince her husband is handsome, but stern
and disagreeable, and it is said regarded his children, and especially his daughters,
as mere household appendages." This may have been true, but, like many others,
Duke Karl had different sides to his character, and on many occasions showed a
much warmer heart than is compatible with the description given of him.

With such surroundings Amalia's childhood could not have been happy. In her
Gedanken, or hook of recollections, she says: "When I look back to my childhood,
that spring-time of life, what do I see? An ever-recurring round of sacrifices made
for others. I was not loved by my parents, who on every occasion kept me in the
background, my brothers and sisters being always considered first. I was treated,
in fact, like an outcast, and yet Thou, O my Creator, hadst endowed me with a
sensitive, loving heart, which suffered misery from this want of tenderness and
pined for affection. I was starving for love, and I received the hard crust of mere
duty."

Then she goes on to speak of those who were entrusted with her education,
especially her governess. "She, who was to form my mind and discipline my young
heart, gave way to every ignoble passion, and vented all her ill-humour on me."
The perpetual scolding of this woman broke the spirit of the child, who shrank
away from a harsh word, and could find no answer to give to her tormentor.
Her nature was, however, so generous, that she was always ready to forget the
treatment she had received. An interesting letter from the little princess to her
father, when she was seven years old, contains a covert reproach for the distinction
made between her and her brothers and sisters. It was written in French, the
language then used at royal courts.

"MY VERY DEAR PAPA,

Permit me, my dear Papa, to remind you of your little daughter Amalia, who
loves you as well, if not better, than her brothers and sisters, although she has
not the same opportunity of expressing her affection. When I am older I shall
acquit myself much better in every way, and give you satisfaction in my lessons.
Therefore, my dear Papa, I beg of you to have patience with me, and you will find
que je m'en recule pour mieux sauter. I hope, dearest Papa, you will return soon, and
that you will always honour me with your precious affection. With every assurance of my fond love and with every sentiment of profound respect, I remain, my
very dear Papa,

"Your obedient and devoted daughter,
"ANNA AMALIA."

This letter, if really the composition of a child of such tender years (and it has undoubtedly certain marks of being genuine), is a wonderful production. It does not seem, however, to have altered the position of the poor little princess, who, as she grew older and wiser, ceased to make any complaints, finding them, no doubt, useless. She tells her pitiful tale in her *Gedanken.* "Driven to despair by the unkind treatment I received, I withdrew into myself. I suffered myself to be reproached, insulted, beaten, without uttering a word, and as far as possible persisted in my own course. By degrees I became indifferent to the slights put upon me. I submitted to the indignity of having my place as the eldest taken from me, and withdrew without murmuring into the background."

This simple statement fills the reader with compassion. At the same time there was profit to be derived from this school, hard as it was. Anna Amalia learned how to withdraw into herself, and how to keep her feelings under command, to measure the worth of men and of things, and how to appraise the value of love and applause. She accustomed herself to a proper reserve, which kept all familiarity at a distance, and, guarded by this shield, she filled her mind with mental riches. For this purpose no place was better suited than the court of the duke, her father.

Here the greatest sympathy for art and artists was encouraged, and the galleries were filled with the finest masterpieces. Herr Graun, a musician of note, who had written the fine oratorio, *The Death of Jesus,* was an honoured friend; so, too, was Fleischer, Anna Amalia's music teacher and also professor at the Collegium Carolinum, which had been founded by Duke Karl for the cultivation of German literature and art. The duke's openly expressed opinion was that the greatest gift any one can give to his children is a taste for knowledge. These words show that those who represented Duke Karl as an indifferent father, judged only by the coldness or haughtiness of his manner. But it must be remembered this sort of distance between parent and child was the rule, not the exception, in the eighteenth century.

There is no doubt that, as the young Amalia grew older, she was taken more notice of by the duke, who found her an intelligent and appreciative listener. The praises of her different instructors had, moreover, flattered his parental vanity. All those who had to do with the formation of the young princess's mind prophesied that she would make a mark in the intellectual world. Her studies were pressed forward with great zeal, Amalia finding no labour too much to attain knowledge. There can be no doubt that the atmosphere of learning, and the studious habits inculcated in early youth, together with the constant association with men celebrated in every branch of literature and science, laid a foundation in the young girl's mind of reverence for genius and appreciation of talent, and that this feeling was the incentive, which caused her in after-years to gather round her little court at Weimar a group of the most intellectual and artistic men and women of the time.

But we are looking a long way ahead; the young princess had to pass through many changes and new developments, before, like the chrysalis, she entered on a more brilliant phase, not as a butterfly, but as a *femme savante* of the eighteenth century.

Her studious life at Wolfenbüttel was interrupted by a not unusual event in a woman's, and more especially in a princess's life. The reader will guess without my telling that this event was a proposal of marriage, which came from the young Duke Constantine of Weimar, whose story has a romantic interest. It will be remembered that, by his father's will, Constantine was left a ward of the Emperor of Austria, who appointed two guardians, Duke Frederick III of Gotha, and Duke Josias of Coburg. The last named was to supervise the duchy of Weimar during the minority of the heir, while Duke Frederick was to have the care of his person and education, and likewise to administer the little duchy of Eisenach. Both guardians are said to have played the part of the wicked uncle in the story-book. We are told that "the boy duke was allowed no other companion but the court fool, or jester, who, however, showed himself anything but a fool. It is said that he managed to give his young charge a fair amount of education, and when the opportunity offered, got the young duke out of the hands of his unkind guardians.

This tale, not being supported by any trustworthy evidence, must be looked upon as an exaggeration of the actual facts. The delicacy and constant ill-health of the young duke, together with his shy and nervous nature, made it impossible for him to be often seen by his people. On his rare appearances in public his pallid face, nervous manner, weary, subdued and altogether crushed appearance, gave the idea that he was "terrorised and unhappy." He evinced none of the activity or love of amusement common to his age. Still, there seems no reason to suppose he had been unfairly treated in any way; although it could not be said that either of his guardians had administered their trust, in regard to the two duchies of Weimar and Eisenach, as honourable guardians should.

When, in 1756, the young duke, who had attained his eighteenth year, became of age to manage his own affairs, it was found that a most shameless course of peculation had been permitted. Grievous was the condition of the poorer classes, from the amount of taxation imposed upon them; yet, in spite of these exorbitant imposts and customs duties, the treasury was practically empty. The ducal residences were in a ruinous condition, and everything that was valuable had disappeared. Such had been the shameful conduct of these unjust stewards.

Anna Amalia's father was well acquainted with the condition of Weimar; but he was a farseeing man and he knew that the duchy would, with good management, speedily recover from its present depleted condition. The duke was, therefore, by no means a bad match for his daughter, who, as she was the eldest, was bound to make way for the others coming after her.[6]

In those days there was no such thing as disputing parental authority; so, when Amalia was told that her future husband was coming, and that her new clothes were being got ready, she made no protest. She frankly acknowledges that she was glad to be released from "the bondage in which she was kept," and experienced no regret at leaving a home where she had been shown so little affection, but felt like a caged bird who, at last, receives its freedom — or rather, she says, "like a sick person" who has been long deprived of every healthy enjoyment and, "rising from a sick bed, breathes the fresh air of heaven."

But nevertheless Amalia, like all young girls, must have had her dreams as to what her lover would be like. She could hardly have imagined he would turn out so poor a creature as this pale, depressed and listless boy, only two years older than herself, with little education, but with kind and gentle ways. He was accompanied by his chief minister and adviser, Count von Bünau, who had been placed in this position by the emperor. Bünau was a man of great ability who for many years had held posts of importance at the Austrian Court. After the death of Charles VII he retired to his estates near Dresden, where he occupied himself in the formation of his celebrated library. He was fortunate in possessing the friendship of the learned philosopher, Winckelmann. In 1731 he was called to the Court of Frederick III, of Gotha, where he occupied the post of Governor or Statthalter in Eisenach.

Duke Constantine had known the minister at Gotha and had engaged him to enter his service. Bünau's sharp eyes took note of the girlish princess, and, later, these two came into conflict, as we shall see. In the suite of the young duke there was likewise a man destined to play an important part in the young duchess's life. This was Anton von Fritsch, at this time only twenty-five years old, a clever and a rising man. We shall meet him again later on.

Bünau, assisted by Fritsch, arranged all the preliminaries of the marriage; and, when once the money question was settled, "the wooing was not long a-doing." No one gave much thought to the poor bride wedded to this sickly duke, who needed a nurse more than a wife. It was altogether what may be called a marriage of convenience. Amalia, indeed, honestly acknowledges that love had nothing to do with the affair. "At sixteen," she writes, "I was given in marriage, as most princesses are, without being consulted. But I did not complain. I was glad to break the chains that had held me so long in bondage, and like a young falcon who longs to fly through the air, I was eager to try my wings alone."

Of her feelings in regard to the husband given to her by parental order she says nothing. He was undoubtedly not fashioned so as, to take a young girl's fancy; nevertheless, his portrait represents an amiable and gentle-looking youth. There is neither obstinacy nor vice in his face, and it was not long before his amiable qualities and the good sense which made him respected as well as loved, endeared him to his young wife, who, for the rest, only required a moderate amount of kindness to make her happy.

The marriage took place on 16 March 1756. (The festivity with all its countless ceremonies, which are fully detailed in the different accounts of the wedding, need not be repeated here.) The young pair then set out on their homeward journey, the preparations for which were similar to those for "a journey through the desert." They were accompanied by a suite of thirty-seven persons, amongst whom was the composer, Bach, who held the office of *kapellmeister*.

The newly married pair travelled in a berline or roomy coach, and what with the bad roads and the breakdown of one of the carriages, did not reach their destination until 24 March, when they made a triumphal entry into Weimar. The young duke, aware that his subjects had suffered considerably through the pernicious system of government pursued by the regent, had ordered that no expense was to be incurred in decorating or illuminating the town. The soldiers made a military display, lining the streets through which the youthful couple drove in an open carriage, so that all those who wished could see them.

Duke Constantine, his pale face working with nervous emotion, made a curious contrast to his rosy young bride, who wore a purple dress embroidered in gold, with an underskirt also embroidered. Her hair, which was powdered, was drawn high over a cushion, with a rose at the side. Her youthful face beamed with happiness, and her large and beautiful eyes danced like a child's, as she now and again drew aside the priceless lace veil lent by her mother, and looked at the crowd. The childish face wore such a friendly look, there was such goodness and determination to like her people and her surroundings, and to do her duty, however ungrateful the task might be, that each one felt that a friend and not a stranger had entered Weimar.

And yet the outlook that lay before her was by no means a bright one. Let us listen for a moment to the sharp voice of Henrietta von Eggloffstein.

"Poor Amalia!" she writes, "instead of the luxurious arrangements at Brunswick, she finds at Weimar nothing but the remains of former greatness. During the minority everything of value has disappeared, and even the household has been dismissed. Accustomed to a circle of cultured people, amongst whom she has grown up, nourished from her childhood on a love of the arts, and educated to appreciate all that is best in knowledge, only able to express herself fluently in French; imagine her feelings, poor child, when she finds in Weimar a set of savages, who absolutely don't understand a word of the language of society; these townspeople are, in fact, indifferent to everything, except the small tittle-tattle which goes on amongst the women; and as for the men, they do not understand how to behave in the society of *ladies*, and prefer their own brutal amusements."

Henrietta von Eggloffstein had a sharp tongue, and when she wrote to her correspondents her pen was quite as incisive as her speech, so we must hope this picture was exaggerated. We find, however, the young duchess giving her father a rather depressing account of her surroundings. She describes the town as "insignificant," the castle or residence having small windows sunk in the thickness of the wall; it had all the air of a watch-tower, and stood on the bank of the river Ilm. "Piper," she adds, (the maid given by her mother), "says the doors in the castle are so loosely hung that they can be closed with a carrot, just as in the peasants' cottages at home." In another letter she complains "that no proper respect is paid to either the duke or myself, all the royal prerogatives being set aside." Even the correspondence of the young couple was interfered with.

In August the Margrave Frederick of Brandenburg, writing to the Duke of Brunswick, tells him that it is reported *everywhere* that letters addressed to the duke and duchess were kept from them, and that it was not *convenable* that such a liberty should be allowed.

Later (in August) we find the young duchess complaining to the duke, her father, that her husband wishes her to have some lady of experience in court etiquette about the court: someone who would act as lady-in-waiting and know her duties. "But this is just the sore point," says Anna Amalia, "there is no such treasure to be found, and for my part I am determined not to be made a *cat's-paw*." This expression shows that living in the atmosphere of a court all the days of her youth had early initiated her into court intrigues. Her suspicions, however, were probably unfounded; for her father sided with Duke Constantine. "I have no wish to command, even if I had now the right to do so," he says, in answer; "but I look upon the difficulty of finding a suitable person to fill the post you mention as a misfortune. Every human being, and more especially those of our rank, has need of help from others, both in small as well as in great things, and for a princess the need is of more importance."

He writes a second time, urging her to choose one or two ladies, if possible, to have always about her, — people whom she could trust. "You can only find out," he says (evidently in answer to some objection of hers) "by making the experiment, in whom confidence can be placed. For my part I do not believe that human nature is so black as it is painted; and, as a rule, there are not so many who betray the secrets of those whom they serve — at least, this is not my experience." This letter concludes with the most tender expressions of fatherly, affection. It is somewhat remarkable and bears out what has been said as to the Duke of Brunswick's conduct as a father, that, from the time of the young duchess's marriage, a true affection and confidence seems to have existed between father and daughter. And this leads the reader of the very voluminous correspondence to the conclusion that the duke had not any share in the cruel neglect and unkindness, which had poisoned Anna Amalia's childhood.

We hear nothing more of the lady-in-waiting affair, which naturally fell into the background by reason of so many weightier matters taking up attention. There were rumours and signs in the air of the coming Seven Years' War, which was only held in abeyance by reason of the death of Frederick the Great's grandmother, the Hanoverian princess, wife to George, Elector of Hanover and King of England. She was also grandmother to Anna Amalia who duly went into mourning for her august relative. The period of mourning had not expired when, on the morning of 5 September 1757, the joybells of Weimar rang out a right merry peal to announce that a prince had been born to the youthful duke and duchess. The whole town was in a tumult of delight.

New life seemed to come into the face of the dying duke, whose heart was bound up in his young wife, her influence being now omnipotent. It did not much matter that Minister Bünau, who exercised dictatorial right over the sickly prince, came often to the castle and showed the draft of the will he had begun to prepare; "for," said he to the duke, "now that an heir is born to succeed, the question of the guardianship *must* be settled." And then came the usual platitudes, such as are made to do duty when a sick man is asked to make his last dispositions. Duke Constantine understood, for he knew full well that he was in truth sick unto death. Therefore when Bünau produced from his pocket the draft he had prepared, and, sitting opposite to the sofa where lay the pale-faced duke, proceeded to read out his proposals, the first of which was that the newly born prince should have as guardians the Duchess Amalia and Frederick V, King of Denmark, he knew well and so did Constantine, that this was equivalent, although it was not so stated, to making Bünau co-regent with the duchess. And where would the duchess be with such a coadjutor?

Bünau on this occasion reckoned without his host, or rather he under-estimated alike the love of the duke for his young wife and the capacity the latter possessed in matters of business. He went away quite content with the draft of the will in his pocket. He had it engrossed, duly signed and sealed, locked it up in his safe, and then waited the course of events, the whole business being finished by 21 February 1758.

A few more months went by. The little Prince had been baptized Karl August. He was now five months old, had a little gilt sleigh in which he was driven over the ice and, being a strong, sturdy baby, he clapped his hands with delight. But his sickly father lay on the sofa in his sitting-room, shivering under a weight of furs. No doubt the cold hand of death was already upon him. He lingered on till May came, and then, when the leaves were beginning to sprout and tokens of summer were at hand, the feeble flicker of life suddenly stopped, and poor Constantine looked his last on his young wife and baby boy.

On the day of his decease, in fact, only a few hours later, Count Bünau called together a council (as is necessary on such occasions), and to them read the will, which he had locked up in his bureau, and with the provisions of which we are acquainted. When the reading was concluded the *kammerdiener* (groom of the chambers) of the deceased duke entered the Council Chamber, and presented to Minister von Bünau a sealed packet with the following superscription: —

"We, Ernest Augustus Constantine, Duke of Saxe Weimar and Eisenach, do hereby order by this undertaking that this our last codicil or disposition which has been executed, signed and delivered by us, on this February the 28th, 1758, shall be read publicly on the day of our decease. Given at Wilhelmsburg, March 22nd, 1758."

The codicil was then read aloud, the dispositions therein set forth causing the utmost astonishment. The King of Denmark's office was limited to a mere honorary guardianship over the young duke, Anna Amalia being appointed sole guardian of her son, with the duke of Brunswick as joint guardian until the duchess reached the age of twenty-one.

The Council was still more amazed to find a "conclusion" from the emperor added to the codicil, stating that the duchess had accepted the guardianship of the hereditary prince on the condition that His Majesty the King of Poland, as Elector of Saxony, would accept the office of co-trustee; which office His Majesty had accepted in writing, and was therefore dispensed from being sworn as trustee or guardian.

The consternation caused by this last clause of the codicil was universal. Nothing but mischief could come of such a choice as the Elector of Saxony for guardian. Each one asked the other who could have counselled such an injudicious step. The private secretary of Minister von Bünau, Fritsch, writing to his father, tells him that the report in Weimar was that this codicil had been drawn up by Assistant Counsellor Nonne, who was suspected of having influenced both the duke and duchess, and had acted in this underhand manner in order to advance himself.

The immediate result of the codicil was to throw ministerial and official business into the utmost confusion, as nothing could be done without the signature of the duchess, and that was valueless so long as she was under age (she was just nineteen). It was necessary either that the duke, her father, should act, or that an application should be made to the emperor to extend to her the *veniam aetatis*, or majority. Now came a new surprise. On this motion being made, a conclusion was put in by the court advocate to the effect that the emperor had six months previously, August 1758, granted to the duchess the *veniam aetatis*.

This *coup d'état* completely annihilated Bünau and his party, their only remaining chance being to raise a clamour as to the Elector of Saxony, whose appointment as guardian was unpopular with all classes in Weimar. It might well be said: "*Que diable allait il faire dans cette galère?*" Nothing but mischief could ensue from his inter-meddling, especially at this critical moment, when he was at war with Prussia. "No, we will have nothing to do with the Elector, or we too will be dragged into his quarrels." So said the magnates of Hildburghausen, of Coburg, of Saalfeld, of Meiningen, and of Gotha. The Duke of Brunswick in alarm writes to Bünau. Bünau, sulky at his defeat, says Vienna is resolved that the Elector shall remain guardian. Vienna is bombarded with petitions from all parts of Weimar, Eisenach, Gotha, etc., praying that the Elector may be set aside. But Vienna is obstinate; the Elector must stand. In despair Bünau is approached. Will he not use his powers of persuasion? And Bünau yields. Not to Austria, but to Denmark does he turn for help, and gets it. The personal influence of King Frederick brings about the desired release from the dreaded danger, and the resignation of the Elector restores confidence to Weimar and the surrounding states, But there is still Vienna to be accounted with. She will want *her* price for yielding, and this price will be help against the advance of the Prussian Army — the army of her uncle Frederick, to whom the girl regent looked for powerful help.

No wonder the young heart felt weary of her load of troubles. She must have made a pathetic picture, sitting at her council-table with grave, elderly men around her, her fair head covered with a long crêpe veil reaching to the ground, the sign of her widowed state. Not often has a girl in her teens, such weighty matters laid before her. And as we think of her we recall another picture nearly a century later, when another young princess was roused from her sleep in the early dawn of a summer's morning, to hear that greatness had come to her and that she was Queen of England.

Although Anna Amalia's responsibilities as regent of a little duchy may not compare with the cares of a great empire, still the burden laid upon each of these two was more nearly equal than might at first sight appear. Amalia's lack of money and friends at this juncture should be thrown into the balance, making her charge more heavy. She had plenty of courage and a superabundant energy. It was a strong character, that of this little duchess, and its force and decision are eminently remarkable in her struggle with Minister von Bünau, who, having been disappointed in his ambitious attempt to become ruler of the duchy, now tried to place Weimar altogether under the thumb of Austria. This was not a loyal act, and in the young regent's mind it discounted the service the minister had done in the matter of the Elector of Saxony.

When, later, the doubts she entertained of the minister's sincerity were no longer mere suspicions, but became in her opinion certainties, the duchess resolved to act. On a trifling contradiction taking place between her and the minister, she wrote him a letter, hurriedly put together, conveying the impression that she had lost her confidence in him and that his retirement would be pleasing to her. Bünau at once recognised that he could not, with regard to his own dignity, retain office any longer, and sent in his resignation.

One can easily understand that, although Amalia had brought about this event, she was a little afraid of the consequences of her own act. In her letter announcing the news to her father, she puts forward the plea that Bünau had embittered the last days of her husband by his overbearing and insatiable love of power. Duke Karl passes this by as childish nonsense, and practically tells his daughter he washes his hands of the mess she has got into; if she won't follow his advice and ask the minister to withdraw his resignation, he, the duke, will do nothing. But Amalia has a spirit, and she will not "knuckle under"; she "takes the responsibility of what may happen" and accepts the great man's resignation, who accordingly packs his trunks and retires in high dudgeon.[7]

"There, you see what comes of putting girls out of the nursery into important positions," cried all the wiseacres of Weimar; but they did not know the soul that animated the childish form of the little duchess. She braced herself to the work before her and looked her responsibilities in the face. The first and most necessary duty was to replace Bünau. Fortunately, Geheimerath von Rhediger, who, by right of being the most important member of the Cabinet or Council, now succeeded to the post of minister, was a man of great sense and judgment,[8] no cavil could be made against him; but the sudden elevation and favour bestowed upon the assistant Geheimerath Nonne was something to set the gossips in Weimar talking. It was well known that the secret codicil, which had been sprung upon the ministers, had been the work of Nonne; and here was now his reward-promotion over the heads of his colleagues as second minister and adviser to the duchess-regent.

All this talk and gossip, which was inevitable in so small a place as Weimar, was annoying to the duchess, who, for the rest, had many anxieties on her mind. She must have missed the devotion of her young husband, who had shown his love and confidence in so remarkable a manner. The cares and anxieties of life had come all too early on one so young and inexperienced. As she writes in her *Gedanken*:

"Never did I pray with such devotion as I did in this my hour of need. I believe I might have become a saint. The situation was indeed peculiar. So young to be regent, to command, to rule, I, who all my life had been humiliated, depressed." And then she adds with great frankness: "I am afraid that after a little time I began to look upon my position with a certain amount of vanity. But a secret voice whispered: 'Beware!' I heard it, and my better reason came to my help. Truth and self-love struggled for the mastery, and truth prevailed."

On 8 September 1758, the duchess gave birth to a son, who was named after his father, Constantine. This event seems to have infused new life and spirit into the young mother, who rose up from her trial full of zeal and determination to do her duty towards her children and her subjects to the best of her capacity.

CHAPTER II

The first use Amalia made of her recovery was to commence the work which she had planned on her sick-bed. She was resolved to make herself and her little duchy a feature of the century. We find in a letter to her father this determination distinctly expressed "that every ruler owes to the country which he governs the duty of raising it to a higher position;" and she goes on to instance Prussia and her father's Duchy of Brunswick. That Weimar should win a special reputation for refinement and culture was her ambition.

We generally find that those who have a steady purpose, nearly always reach the goal they have in view, and so it fell out with Amalia, whose dearest wishes were in the end realised. But not for many years did the fruition come. Meantime she tells us how she studied day and night to make herself mistress of her new duties, "I longed for success — for praise. I also felt the absolute need I had of a friend, in whom I could place entire confidence. There were several who sought to be my confidants or my advisers. Some tried flattery, others commended themselves by a show of sincerity, but in none could I detect the ring of true affection which is above all temptations." And then the duchess adds these remarkable words: "If a prince and the individual he selects as an intimate or confidant are *both* noble-minded, the sincerest affection may exist between them; and this is the only way to answer the question, 'Can kings have true friends?'"

Amalia had indeed need of a good friend and counsellor to guide her over a very slippery road, where a false step was easily made. There can hardly be a parallel found in history of so heavy a burden being laid upon such young shoulders.

The condition of the duchy was deplorable: the treasury was empty, agriculture neglected; the upper classes were extravagant, whilst the people were miserably poor and discontented. She had to face the heavy task of bringing order into the general disorder, of replenishing by some means the empty exchequer, of giving her subjects a measure of education, of providing hospitals for the sick and asylums for the aged poor.

What a task for a girl under twenty! Anna Amalia naturally looked to her ministers, and especially to Nonne, for assistance. She had given him many marks of favour. He was now called Herr von Nonne, and enjoyed the position of Geheimerath, or Privy Councillor. But he was not a satisfactory minister. It is difficult, as it generally is in such cases, to grasp what the cause of his falling into disfavour actually was. One account represents his disgrace to have been due to his answer to his royal mistress's demand for an increased vote, for the maintenance of the court and the court ceremonials, which the master of the ceremonies, Von Witzleden, had estimated at 1,253 thalers. "Could not the country afford this yearly sum to keep up its duchess?" asked the young regent. Von Nonne went too far, when in his reply he said: "Your highness's poor subjects are drained of the last halfpenny they earn by the sweat of their brow, to supply luxuries and display, at the court of the best princess in the world." A pretty manner of expressing yourself, Herr von Nonne, but not pleasing to your gracious princess.

Close on this friction came what was called the *Pro Memoria*,[9] issued by Amalia to her ministers, in which she announced her intention to see into all matters of state business herself, and to give her signature to every document, first having read and approved the contents.

At the next sitting of the Council, however, a respectful amendment was made to the *Pro Memoria*, by which Her Serene Highness was limited in the matter of her signature to such papers as had to do with foreign powers, or memorials, etc.; all others were to go through the usual routine. This limitation of her authority was not pleasing to the duchess. It soon became evident that neither Geheimerath von Rhediger nor Geheimerath von Nonne had succeeded in obtaining her confidence or friendship. This privilege was conferred upon a third member of the cabinet, Greiner, to whom the duchess-regent had been first attracted by the fact that he had been tutor to her young husband, who had given him the rank of Assistant Geheimerath. In 1761, during Amalia's guardianship, he was raised to that of Geheimerath, and in 1763 a decree of the emperor elevated him to the peerage.

In her *Gedanken*, Anna Amalia speaks of the character of Greiner with warm admiration. "I found at last in this noble-minded man the treasure which all of us seek but few find — the treasure which is greater than gold or silver, a true friend. A true friend! How happy I was to possess such an one! And now how glad I am to speak of this excellent man and to let the world know what obligations he has conferred upon me. His name is Greiner, his rank Privy Councillor. He was not a great genius, but a thoughtful man, gifted with much intelligence. He had worked his way up from the bottom, so that he was conversant with every department of affairs. Just and delicate feeling animated him, and he was capable of sincere friendship. He was the friend of his friend; and his soul being animated with the loftiest feelings, there was no room for the ignoble vice of flattery. This was the character of the man into whose arms I threw myself. I loved him as if he were my father, and like a child I sat at his feet. From him have I heard the truth, and from him have I learned to love it."

Such expressions as "into whose arms I threw myself," "his soul was animated," etc., belong to the high-flown style of the day, which was all sentiment. Even the healthy, joyous mind of the duchess was tinged with a *soupçon*, or breath, of this mock sentimentality.

It must not be thought, however, that Amalia had devolved the cares of the duchy on Greiner. The energetic princess followed to the letter the programme she had sketched in the *Pro Memoria*.

"The Regent, following the example of her honoured and gracious father, will not spare herself any trouble or pains, but will look into everything with her own eyes, and hear every one's complaints with her own ears. She will be present at the sittings of the council; and, during the time when it is not in session, she will receive reports in writing or by word of mouth, and give to each one attention, consult over them with her advisers and judge accordingly."

And, as the *Memoria*, so was the daily programme of the regent, who went through every detail of state business, foreign or otherwise. The clear, sensible eyes of the youthful regent examined carefully into the workings of every department, and while the intelligent and quick penetration she possessed went to the bottom of every intrigue, her small, energetic hands, with narrow, pointed fingers, were ready to work at all hours for the good of the people. And none the less well did she govern her duchy, because she cared little for the opinion of men, so long as she had the consciousness that she was doing her duty.

She had a difficult part to play; and those who counselled her, deserved infinite credit for the manner in which they directed her policy through the troubled years of the Seven Years' War, — that nightmare "which pursued her even in her sleep." On one side there was Austria, who considered Amalia owed her gratitude for the help she had received in the matter of the Elector of Saxony and King of Poland; on the other hand, the ties of blood and the feeling of veneration Amalia had from childhood entertained for her uncle, Frederick the Great (whom she resembled both in looks and character) drew her irresistibly to his side. Fortunately, by the prudence of her ministers and the pity her youth and widowed condition excited, Weimar came out of the long struggle with small hurt. On more than one occasion Amalia stood up bravely in defence of her little duchy.

It is certain that, in her appreciation of Greiner, she in no way overestimated his services. Without his advice and ever ready co-operation, it would have been impossible for one, so young and inexperienced as Amalia was, to have steered her course through such a sea of difficulty. Unlike the preceding ministers, Greiner gave his full approbation to her plans for improving the duchy. The country was undoubtedly impoverished, and the approaching war was likely still further to drain its resources; but still, with economy (and for so great a purpose, he felt sure the duchess would herself set an example) much might be accomplished. Here was diplomacy on the part of Minister Greiner, and good results followed therefrom. The duchess, delighted at having a friendly collaborator in her schemes, set to work with zeal. Weimar, the capital of the duchy wanting in all necessaries of a capital, should be taken in hand first. In truth it needed supervision. There was the lighting of the streets. Since 1732 Weimar had been lighted by lanterns, which were carried for the higher classes by their servants, who walked before their masters; or, if of lower rank, by the persons themselves. There were few private carriages, and the principal conveyance, for ladies especially, was the sedan chair, or *chaise à porteurs.* This method of getting about had this inconvenience, that, as the chairman also exercised the office of watchman, he often deposited the chair and its occupant on the pavement, while he proceeded to perform the duty of crying out the time of night in a leisurely manner.

There were graver matters that required immediate attention. There was a pressing need for schools for the children, for additions to the public library, and for making some sort of attempt at a museum.

Anna Amalia courageously set to work, beginning with the library. This had already been the object of much interest to the earlier Dukes of Weimar. It had, however, been of late years neglected. Now it was rearranged. The shelves in the library at Wilhelmsburg were denuded of their books, which were carted down to the library for which they had been originally intended, and where they made a goodly show.[10] This was Anna Amalia's work.[11]

Now for the school. In the *Gymnasium Illustre* there were three hundred and twenty pupils who had only seven teachers and two unpaid assistants. In the school for the nobility there was a preceptor who received thirty gulden yearly, the stipend of a mere village schoolmaster in England. Measures were taken to set this matter right, but it nevertheless took considerable time. Herder, who came many years later to Weimar, found that the masters in the Gymnasium, after thirty-one years of study, had not got through the New Testament.

But if Weimar was not altogether satisfactory, Jena filled the heart of the young duchess with pride. There the court had long been patrons of learning and art; it was a bright spot or beacon, which led the duchess forward in her task of bringing Weimar to a similar standard of excellence. The reputation of the learned body of professors in Jena remains to the present day; but it is not too much to say that, well-founded as this reputation was, Jena owed something to the interest taken and the assistance given by Anna Amalia, whose early training in her father's house had imbued her with a deep reverence for knowledge in all its branches. The professors of the Jena University were made welcome at Weimar, where they found in this girlish duchess an intelligent sympathiser in the intellectual developments in progress. Her bright face as she listened to their grave discourse, and eager co-operation so far as her limited means went, acted as an incentive and spur to their zeal for the diffusion of knowledge.

Unfortunately, the means at her disposal, were not in these early days of her regency, equal to her desire to do universal good. Nevertheless, by the prudent management of Geheimerath Greiner, who had cut down all useless expenses, and the careful administration of the ducal household — a task undertaken by the duchess, who looked into the smallest items and *contracted no debts* — economies were effected which left a small sum (small in view of the expenditure of royal courts nowadays) available for the objects this girl of barely twenty years old had at heart.

Four hundred thalers was a small sum (it would now be termed a pittance) wherewith to start collections of statuary, pictures, books, and *objets d'art*. It is a great thing, however, to know precisely what you want, and not to be led astray into wider fields. Amalia possessed this somewhat rare quality; and in reading her correspondence with artists, both in France and Italy, and with friends who travelled in far countries, one is surprised at the clearness and decision with which she makes known exactly what she wants and what she will pay. It must also be said that, in the matter of friends, she was blessed to a degree not very usual in persons of her rank. Those who assisted her did their work in a remarkable manner; and to them was, in a measure, due the success which attended her efforts to, educate the people committed to her care. It was no doubt trying to a young, enthusiastic nature like Amalia's, to find herself curbed and thwarted by the necessary economy she had to practise. In a letter to her father dated 1763 she complains bitterly that she is obliged, in consequence of the strain of the war, to give out of her private purse eight thousand thalers to pay the expenses of the court. She lays the blame on Witzleben, the Comptroller, "who allows the lower class of servants to pillage as much as they like, and when reproved gets on his high horse and is offended." She has made up her mind (stout-hearted little woman!) to get rid of him. But then comes a prudent answer from Duke Karl. "No, my daughter, you must not get rid of Witzleben; it would raise disturbance. Wait awhile, have patience, in time all will go well." And so the young, impetuous heart curbed itself, and we do not hear what happened to the "unjust steward."

The impression made on her own people by Amalia's goodness and extraordinary capacity for governing (which was the more remarkable from her youth and sex) was confirmed by the respect she commanded from foreign nations, to whom the reputation of this young and "wonderful duchess" came, from travellers as well as from other sources. Also, at the Court of Brunswick, where she had been in her youth humiliated and despised, now that it was known that the great king, her Uncle Frederick, had said she was too good for the land over which she was duchess, a complete change took place and she was honoured by all.

"God preserve thee for the happiness of thy country and thy family," writes Anna Amalia's brother, the hereditary Prince Karl II of Brunswick (20 December 1759). "Thou art adored by thy subjects, Heaven has bestowed on thee her choicest blessings, and thou hast only to continue in the same course and no misfortune will come to thee. May Heaven grant that this unhappy war may cease."

According to the portrait of her person given by another of her brothers, Prince Frederick Augustus of Brunswick, Anna Amalia was not handsome, or even decidedly pretty; nevertheless "she gave the impression that she *was* handsome. In her first youth, especially, she charmed by the bright expression of her full round face, which was lit up by remarkably brilliant eyes, like stars, which could soften at will into the sweetest and most loving tenderness. A Roman nose (which others, not blinded by fraternal affection, called a Brunswick nose, inherited from papa, but slightly softened in height and ponderosity), a beautiful profile (some people called it more; a strong-minded, energetic profile, with the aquiline Brunswick nose, again reminiscent of papa), and the sharp pointed little chin, reminiscent of mamma. She is not tall, but looks taller than she is from her elegant proportions."

The affectionate brother then gives a detailed description of the beauties of the duchess's mind, which surpassed those of her person. "Her modesty is one of her greatest charms; and, although she is all gentleness, she has the courage and firmness of a man. She listens to the advice of experience, but is a slave to no one. She gives generously, but never allows herself to be importuned. Her temper is lively and her will is strong, but every emotion of her mind is subject to the dictates of reason. Slow in making friends, she is steadfast and constant. She cares not to listen to gossip; she is a distinguished musician, and her talent has been cultivated in the best school. In her relations to her children she is ideal."

Brothers are not always so alive to their sister's perfections as was Frederick Augustus; but he had a literary turn, which accounts for his exaggerated style. Putting this aside, his testimony is worth having. Another member of the family also bears witness to the feelings entertained by the people of Weimar for their duchess. "They adore her," he writes on one occasion.

Her correspondence with her uncle, Frederick the Great, preserved in the state archives at Weimar, is most interesting, and exhibits both the great king and the little duchess (his niece), in a most favourable light. The feeding of the large army of Frederick, and the recruiting which was carried on extensively, were the two great causes of complaint. The last named especially excited Amalia's indignation. Her first letter to the Prussian king, dated February 1759, deals with this point, and is written in very spirited terms.

"SIRE,

"A requisition has been made to me by Monsieur d'Anhalt to furnish him with 150 recruits for your army. Your Majesty knows too well my feelings of respect and affection to doubt my submission to any order of Your Majesty's, but Your Royal Highness is too merciful to command me to do what would cause the ruin of the country over which I have to govern.

"Your Majesty will call to mind the violence with which the Imperial Court has forced us to supply contingents to the army of the so-called Empire. Nevertheless we have managed to evade this order as much as possible and have only sent as few men as we could spare. If I am obliged to furnish the 150 recruits asked for by d'Anhalt, I must take them from the plough and from the workshops, which will infallibly cause the total ruin of a country as near annihilation as it can be. This terrible situation has induced me to oppose the demands made by Vienna, which, during the last three months, has been pressing me to complete the before-mentioned contingent. I do not deny, Sire, that it was my reliance on your goodness that gave me strength boldly to refuse the demands of Austria; and now I implore you to grant your protection to this my unfortunate and ruined country. I beseech Your Majesty to cancel the order for the levy of the before-named 150 recruits and to believe that I shall return this great favour by the most grateful affection. These sentiments have, in fact, filled my heart since my early childhood when I was first made aware that I had the honour of belonging to you, and these feelings will remain in my heart as long as I continue to live."

To this letter are attached the different appellations and titles of the Duchess Regent: "By God's grace Anna Amalia Duchess of Saxony, Cleves and Berg, also of Engern and Westphalia; by birth Duchess of Brunswick and Lüneburg, Countess of Thuringia, Markgräfin of Meissen, Royal Countess of Henneberg, Countess of Mark and Ravensberg, Frau of Rasenstein, Guardian and Regent of the country,

"Your Majesty's

    "humble and submissive

        "Niece, God-daughter and Servant,

           "AMALIA."

In Eisenach the inhabitants suffered sorely from the exactions of *both* armies, which were constantly passing through this district. Amalia, accompanied by Von Nonne, visited Eisenach and greatly cheered the spirits of the inhabitants by the glad tidings that, by her influence, Frederick had given up the idea of besieging the town. She could not, however, free her duchy from the constant exactions of the recruiting officers. On one occasion the duchess, having got timely notice that one of these, Lieutenant Reim, was coming to Weimar to lay his hands on every man and boy in the place, advised the young men to conceal themselves in the woods; and with true motherly care gave them warm cloaks lest they should catch cold. After this *coup d'état* we find her writing to His Majesty the King of Prussia.

"As I told Your Majesty, we have absolutely no young men, and Reim has taken decrepit old men and aged farmers; and, when he found there were no young or strong men to be got, he said he would proceed to extremities. I have too much confidence in Your Majesty's goodness to believe that you will allow him to act in such a manner. I implore you to be merciful towards me and my unhappy people. March 20th, 1761. *I await with impatience Your Majesty's reply.*"

The answer from the king came ordering that the duchess should be treated with consideration, and her duchy spared as much as possible; but that the necessary recruits must be got. Also the duchess must not believe everything told to her; as, in war-time, many irregularities would naturally take place.

Soon, however, worse things came to pass. In November 1762 a "bureau of Directors" had been established in Saxony, which had for its principal object the levy of troops. From Weimar four hundred men were demanded. Out of all patience at this horrible tyranny, Amalia again has recourse to her pen. She writes an imploring letter begging that this terribly cruel recruiting may be stopped. She calls almost hysterically upon her uncle to save her poor harassed subjects; and this time the king replies in a letter dated Meissen, November 30th, 1762.

"MADAM MY NIECE,

"I have just received the letter you were good enough to write to me on the 28th. However well disposed to comply with your Highness's request, I cannot in this case, when my need for recruits is so urgent, that it is quite impossible for me to cancel the order for recruiting in Weimar.

"I flatter myself that, when you take into consideration that recruits are the only demand I have made on Weimar, you will realise that this demand cannot compare with the burdens which would have been imposed upon your duchy and the inconveniences your subjects would have suffered if, under different circumstances, the Austrians or their allies had occupied winter quarters in your duchy. I also beg Your Highness to remember that it is only out of consideration for *yourself* that I gave orders that, with the exception of the recruits, no other levy should be made on Weimar, and my esteem and friendship for you will always continue, etc., etc."

Poor harassed little duchess! It was well for the great king, her uncle, to talk of what might have happened if Austria had occupied winter quarters. Did not that much offended nation, which considered it had been tricked badly in the matter of the Elector of Saxony, threaten to force her to pay an exorbitant indemnity, for not keeping faith; a threat which the Duke of Brunswick, her, father, characterises as an instance of the hard-heartedness produced by this accursed war? There seemed no refuge on any side except, perhaps, in Uncle Frederick; and so she continues to apply to hint on every occasion, with a childlike confidence that at last seems to have secured his friendship.

From this time the relations between uncle and niece become most cordial. Anna Amalia sends fruit from the gardens of Belvedere, which pleases the king; who in return sends what he calls a trifling present, but is really a royal gift which evidently much delights the duchess, from her rapturous letter of thanks. At different intervals we find her visiting the great king at Potsdam and Berlin, at which court she made a lasting friendship with the Landgräfin of Hesse Darmstadt Caroline Henrietta, called the Great on account of qualities of her mind. There is no doubt that Anna Amalia gained much from her intercourse with the Landgräfin, and, as we shall see later, this friendship led to a closer connection between the duchies of Weimar and Hesse Darmstadt.

We left Amalia fighting the battle for her little duchy, which was in truth nearing total extinction when, at the critical moment, the joyful news came of the cessation of the cruel and never-to-be-forgotten seven years of suffering that Germany had gone through valiantly. To add to Amalia's happiness she had the joy of receiving Uncle Frederick at Weimar, on his homeward journey, and presenting to him her children. With the young Karl August the great king was well pleased, prophesying that he had the makings of a fine soldier and good ruler, if only niece Amalia did not make a milksop of him; and Amalia, overflowing with pride at this praise of her boy, promised she would be guided in all things by Uncle Frederick, and so the visit ended happily. Peace was made and hopes of coming prosperity were in all minds; the duchess, for the first time since her marriage, made a short journey from home and visited Aix-la-Chapelle, then the fashionable watering-place, which was resorted to by crowned heads and princes. The journey there must have been somewhat perilous; for, in a letter home, she expresses astonishment that she arrived at her journey's end without breaking an arm or a leg, and more surprised still that her berline had held out through such a journey. The letter in which these expressions occur is written in gay spirits, and ends with her compliments to the court circle.

On her return Weimar gave its duchess a warm welcome. She was met by a torchlight procession, and serenaded by the school children. The pleasure of feeling that she was understood and loved, by those for whom she had done so much, gratified the youthful duchess. Her return home was, however, saddened by the loss of one whom she prized, not only for his valuable services, but also for his warm friendship for her and her children. That princes do not have many sincere friends is unfortunately too true; but in Greiner the duchess-regent had one who never swerved from his duty towards her. She had, in many ways, shown her appreciation of this friendship. On more than one occasion Greiner, who was advanced in years, had petitioned Anna Amalia to allow him to retire from office. This request she, on the first occasion, absolutely refused to grant.

Greiner, however, after a short interval renewed his demand and this time couched the request in such pressing terms that the duchess, in great distress of mind, took counsel with the minister's colleague, von Fritsch, who, since Herr von Nonne's death in 1762, had been advanced to a place in the Cabinet. In her letter to Fritsch she talks of the services her aged minister had rendered to her, and to the duchy she had been called to govern; of his devotion to her interest and to the country generally; of the order he had brought into the disorder he had found; and of the irreparable loss it would be to her if she were robbed of the help of this able counsellor, especially in times when men from day to day grew more and more hard to fathom.

She then goes on to say that the thought had come to her mind to propose to pay his debts, although she was not instructed as to their amount; but that could be easily ascertained; or at least to return to him the bond for six hundred thalers which he had signed on borrowing that sum a few years previous. At the last sitting of the Council this same proposal had been started by some of the members, but it had been opposed by others, and there the matter had rested.

"I suppose," she adds, "that I, as regent, have the power to give an order on the Treasury for the return of the bond to Minister von Greiner."

Von Fritsch with great astuteness replied: "Greiner has certainly *no debts*, being one who always lived within his income. To retain him in the ministry is all important. It would be well to return him the bond for the six hundred thalers, but not from the Treasury: that would make a disturbance, and it would injure Your Royal Highness, if the people thought you conferred favours at the expense of the State. But the sum could be paid from the Privy Purse, over which fund Your Highness has sole authority."

Anna Amalia acted on this suggestion and had the comfort of keeping her good friend and adviser until his death, which occurred in 1765. It can be well imagined she missed the counsel of one so experienced and so devoted to her interests. And at this juncture the loss of Greiner was all the more felt, as a terrible famine spread all over the land, bringing in its train the usual horrors of pestilence of different kinds, which affected not only human beings, but also the cattle and horses, amongst which a terrible mortality took place. The young duke, writing to Minister von Fritsch in July 1777 says:

"My heart is deeply moved by this terrible misfortune, and I would like of all things to give a little help. You would oblige me much, Herr Geheimerath, if you would help me to get my mother's permission to give 400 thalers out of my own purse, to be divided between the poor in this town, and those in Eisenach. I could not find a better use for my money." And then he adds what one must think was a suggestion of his tutor's: "A Prince's sole happiness should be in doing good."

The plague of famine and sickness lasted a couple of years; for we find the distinguished Italian writer, Micheless, writing in 1773: "Sadness hangs over Weimar, and those who escape from the town do not escape the fatal illness, which pursues them wherever they go." And then he pays a high compliment to Anna Amalia: "A princess whose fine qualities and the wisdom of whose government are acknowledged by the whole world."

Anna Amalia possessed to a wonderful extent the art (one not born with all princes) which is much prized by the German race, that of representation — a word which possesses a wide meaning. On Sundays the regent showed herself to the people in the garden of the old castle of Wilhelmsburg called the Welsche Garten. This garden was extensive; it was laid out in the French fashion — somewhat after the pattern of Versailles — with broad, straight walks, or alleys, extending south, east and west. There were four-cornered beds of flowers, canals with rustic bridges, a Babylonian watch-tower, with a spiral staircase, while the many walks were inviting for lovers' rambles or pleasant picnics.[12] On Sundays the duchess walked in the broad alleys; the court marshal went before her, pages carried her train. After them came the tall halberdiers and a dwarf. She fed the goldfish in the pond, and drank tea in the grotto of the Guard house.

In winter the Sunday programme was different. A procession of court sleighs drove through the streets, each sleigh being driven by a gentleman, who sat behind the ladies. Before each sleigh rode an outrider, and on short winter afternoons the drive was generally to Tiefurt or Ettersburg, where tea would be taken, the company returning by torchlight. Or, again, the duchess, dressed in a long-skirted riding habit, green or black, and mounted on a white horse, rode through the streets. The people gazed at her in admiration; her small feet causing the greatest wonder. It became the fashion for gentlemen to wear on their watch-chains, as a charm, or *breloque*, a tiny gold shoe with a red heel, in imitation of those worn by their beloved duchess. For it was her custom to put on every day a pair of new shoes with red heels which, when once used, were given to the ladies-in-waiting, who wore them, thereby inflicting on their poor feet unspeakable suffering.

At the theatre (where it was the custom for none but the court party to applaud) the duchess appeared in a cloak of different coloured silks, which was thrown over her dress and had long falling sleeves.

In the delightful description of Weimar and its little court, given by Lewes, there is an account of the gaieties of the season.

"This evening there was a *redoute* (entertainment ball) at the Court House, the tickets being one gulden each. The Court party arrived at eight o'clock. The duchess was splendid in a domino, and was set off by some fine jewels. She danced with a light step really beautifully, and with much dignity. The young princes, who wore fancy dresses as Zephyr and Cupid, also danced well. The masquerade was very crowded and animated, and there were a number of masks. There was also a faro table, the smallest stake half a gulden; the duchess never put down less than half a louis d'or, but she liked to dance better than to play, and remained at the table only a short time. She danced with every mask who was presented to her, and remained till nearly three o'clock. Then all was nearly over.

"At another *redoute* the duchess was dressed as a Grecian queen — a very splendid costume which became her well. This was an exceptionally brilliant affair, and the room was crowded. Some students from Jena were present, this being the last *redoute* of the season. The duchess sent me one of her own Savoyard costumes. I was dressed by the Countess von Görtz. Her maid dressed my hair like a lady's, and, together with the young Count von Görtz, who was also dressed in female costume, I presented myself at court, dined, and went with the duchess's party to the *redoute*, where we stayed till six o'clock in the morning.

Let us listen for a moment to Henrietta von Eggloffstein's account of the change effected by the young duchess, whose unfortunate position she at one time deplored so feelingly, for having her lot cast among a set of ignorant creatures, who didn't understand French, the language of good society, which Anna Amalia was accustomed to hear at the "polite" Court of Brunswick.

"Amalia's creative spirit," says Henrietta, "and her pure mind have cast a spell over these people, who did not appear to have a spark of higher aspirations, or a desire to rise above their surroundings, but were quite happy in their intellectual degradation. Like Prometheus Amalia has kindled heavenly fire, and has given a higher life to her subjects. She has drawn round her the youth of both sexes, made them her companions in pleasant and elegant festivities; wherein refined and elegant amusements, such as music, charades and figure dances, have taken the place of the vulgar games and rough horseplay which disgraced the court. Amalia sought out those who were distinguished for any talent or accomplishment, and made these welcome, so that they felt at ease; for she was accomplished in the art of giving every one their right place, and, there being no such thing as restraint or stiffness in her drawing-room, every one was natural and unrestrained. So she learnt to know each person well."

"It must be acknowledged," adds Henrietta, "that she had her favourites, whose faults she excused; and this sometimes gave rise to unkind reports, such as that she overstepped the rigid limits which separate the classes, and that knowledge and talent were a better passport to her favour than old lineage or rank."

CHAPTER III

I have now to introduce two little personages — Duke Ernst Karl August and Prince Constantine. Karl August, the elder by twelve months and the future Duke of Weimar, was possessed of a royal will of his own and a distinct sense of his importance. In Ettersburg there is a portrait of this baby duke in his baby frock, his round little face full of childish obstinacy. "A handful," the nurses called him. "A naughty wicked boy!" cried his *gouvernante*, whose face he scratched, to Amalia's distress. The duchess wrote to tell her usual counsellor, Duke Karl, who, when he read how his grandson had gone to bed without his supper, because he would not apologise to mademoiselle, rapped out an oath which consigned mademoiselle and a much higher person to a hot place. "Those women will spoil as fine a little fellow as ever lived," said the boy's grandfather, who had been all severity to his own children, but could not be severe to the second generation. He writes to his daughter (of whom he now stands a little in awe) that he is sending her a proper person, who has been teaching in the gymnasium at Brunswick, by name J. W. Seidler, and who is a very useful piece of furniture and understands how to manage a boy better than her fool of a mademoiselle. And Amalia, after some "womanish" scruples as to the exact time not having arrived (as mentioned in her husband's will) when Karl August was to be given over to masculine supervision, submits, and Seidler is despatched from Wolfenbüttel.[13]

But Seidler did not give satisfaction: his system of education, excellent in some ways, lacked firmness; and this was the attribute most necessary in dealing with a nature like the young duke's. Punishment had no effect upon him; even if Seidler would have resorted to a system which he condemned. He was a man of theories, and one of his theories was very injurious to his pupil; for he allowed him to grow up with a consciousness of his own elevated rank, a feeling that it gave him privileges not accorded to those beneath him, and that, in fact, it dispensed him from obedience and other lowly virtues. This doctrine was extremely pleasant to the little duke, who became so inflated with the idea of his own greatness as to grow insubordinate and unbearable.

Amalia soon recognised the incapacity of kind, good-natured Seidler. She saw that, with the best will possible, he was incapable of mastering such a proud, obstinate nature as her eldest son possessed. Anxious to do all she could for her child, the duchess first made herself acquainted with every particular of her dead husband's education, and then proceeded to work on the same lines. On 11 May 1761, she addressed a long letter to the council, in which she detailed her maternal anxiety to do her best to train her young son in his father's footsteps, and to prepare him to be a good ruler over his dominions. She said that the first step must be to find a proper governor for him, and that she had for some time devoted her whole attention to this point; the result of her researches being that a certain Count von Görtz appeared to her to have the qualities necessary for so difficult a task. "He is an accomplished gentleman; he has travelled and speaks French well, but he has a turn for sarcasm." "Worse than that," reply the members of the Privy Council, "Count Görtz is malicious and his tongue is pungent with satire. This fault is not of grave magnitude in a private individual, but it is a fatal error in a prince. Europe would be at peace today if Frederick the Great had restrained a satirical observation."

This objection was put aside and Count Görtz, in accepting office, wrote the following letter, which will not impress the reader with a favourable view of his character.

"The wish to be of some use in the world is the sole motive which has decided me to accept an office which brings with it such heavy responsibilities. I sacrifice to the dear prince my best years. I deny myself the pleasures of this world and the affectionate intercourse with my family. All obstacles which may cross my path shall be (so far as human foresight can ensure such a result) resisted to the best of my ability."

He then goes on to speak of his plans for the mental training and education of the young duke. "My first care shall be to foster a tender affection and love for his mother." (This would seem to be a somewhat unnecessary assurance.) "After that the prince shall be taught to regard with affection, friendship, and esteem those who are about him in their separate stations and capacities. He must become master of himself; he must consider his high position as a favour bestowed by the Almighty. Good feelings shall be cultivated and flattery, that most poisonous weed, shall be driven away as if it were the plague itself."

The whole strain of this letter "promises too much," and there is a total lack of sincerity; and, as we shall see later, Count von Görtz's system of training was wanting in the very points on which he insists so emphatically.

At the time Görtz entered on his duties he was twenty-five; his pupil was entering his fifth year, his brother Constantine being still in the nursery. According to the method of education in force in the eighteenth century, Latin was begun by the five-year-old pupil, who learned by heart Ovid's elegies, together with Gellert's fables and the history of the world. How the poor little brain must have been confused! Better training was the fencing lesson, and music lesson to which one hour was given daily. It is a real pleasure to hear that, when Karl was eight years old, he smashed the bow of his violin and the notes of the piano; and had likewise made the walk to Belvedere quite unsafe, by constantly firing off small cannon. Count Görtz uses strong language in detailing these offences; but Amalia, wisely, only laughed. "When the heart is good," she says, "all is right. You tell me my little son loves his mother; let us hope for the best."

This making a fuss over a child's naughtiness does not increase one's belief in Count Görtz's capabilities; and presently the duchess's optimistic view proved correct. At nine years Karl became a very good boy, broke no more violins, fired no more cannon; but concentrated his young mind on learning his lessons and "training himself for his high position." The reader will perhaps exclaim, as I did: "What an odious little prig!" But, no. I am bound to say the boy duke was a manly little fellow. At this early age he did credit to Görtz, or, rather, to the duchess, whose tenderness had subdued the roughness and softened the obstinacy of the childish nature. Karl August at this time adored his mother. Pity it was that this saving influence ever diminished.

Anna Amalia deserved the love of her children; she had sacrificed much for their sakes. Especially had she striven to educate Karl August as a German ruler — although such was not the rule at the German Courts, where the French language and foreign manners prevailed. For the rest, Karl August was a clever youth, and he preferred the company of grown up people to companions of his own age. Contemporary writers speak of the astonishing manner, in which he kept on a level with the elder generation.

The time was now approaching when it would be necessary to send the young princes, especially Karl August, to a foreign college. Anna Amalia, whose anxiety to do her duty towards her sons was most praiseworthy, took counsel with those best able to advise her. Amongst these was an old friend of her youth, the learned Abbot Jerusalem of Brunswick, who was not in favour of university education, either at Geneva, where there was no good system and only a few "uneducated Englishmen," or at Strasbourg, which was a military depôt, where the morals of the princes would be destroyed. The duchess, in great alarm at such a prospect, resolved to keep her sons under her own eye.

But then, what about the university course? Surely there was a university at Erfurt, and, belonging to that university, a distinguished scholar, who, so lately as 1769, had made a name by a philosophical work entitled Der Goldene Spiegel, in which he set forth what the great and the noble should learn in order to make the people happy. Wieland (for that was the name of the author) had expected that the Emperor Joseph II would have extended his patronage to the book and its author; but in this hope he was disappointed, the emperor noticing neither the one nor the other. Amalia, therefore, seized the opportunity to secure the co-operation of so learned a man in the task of educating her sons.

Wieland, who in the year 1769 had been Summoned to Erfurt to take the chair of Primarius Professor of Philosophy, was at the same time given the rank of Crown Counsellor to the Elector of Mayence, or Mainz. There he had written his *Goldene Spiegel*, in which, under the name of "Danischwende,"[14] he instructs kings, rulers and nobles in the history of mankind. This Golden Looking Glass was a remarkable work. Its sentimental tone would not suit the practical taste of today; but sentimentality and romanticism were the fashion in 1769, so the book was much read and talked about.

Anna Amalia was greatly impressed, and anxious to draw the writer into the circle of distinguished men with which she desired to surround her sons. If only she could secure the original of Danischwende, it would be a good beginning. Count Görtz was a friend of the Primarius Professor, but Görtz was not inclined to move in the matter; so Amalia, who, it must be confessed, was at heart somewhat of a "lion-hunter," commissioned Count Dalberg, who had an appointment at Erfurt, to negotiate the matter.

Dalberg, however, was not successful; so brave Anna Amalia takes it in hand herself, and, true to "*ce que femme veut,*" carries it through triumphantly. The duchess goes to a *redoute* at Erfurt and there first approaches the philosopher. She gives him a sunny smile and talks to him of his great book and her admiration for "Danischwende,"[15] her difficulties about her son, and her plans for his education, which she would dearly love to talk over with "Danischwende" (or Wieland). This interview is followed by a lengthy correspondence, which, in its complete form, is to be found in the State archives of Weimar. Each letter from Wieland occupies at least thirteen to fifteen pages. The Primarius Professor, therefore, although he had translated Shakespeare, had evidently not taken to heart the maxim, that Brevity is the soul of wit."[16]

It would seem from these letters that Wieland had paid a visit to the court at Weimar; for otherwise how could he have known that the duchess "was happy in possessing a son of whose understanding the first of living kings (Frederick the Great) had spoken so highly," or that the young Karl August "does not show much sensibility, but that this defect is compatible with the most exalted virtue." He goes on to say that the prince possesses a sound judgment, natural intelligence, and a remarkable abhorrence of flattery; that he is capable of taking a high place amongst the rulers of the age, and repeats his former statement, only now from personal observation, as to the goodness of his heart.

This flattering estimate of her son from the original of "Danischwende" was most pleasing to the duchess's maternal pride, and her answer contains an astounding proposal: Will "Danischwende" come to Weimar for six months to instruct her dear son in philosophy, and thus give the finishing touch to all his other fine qualities? Then we have another lengthy correspondence, in the course of which the duchess grows very philosophical and propounds several important questions; first, whether the great ones of the earth can be happy; second, if a woman must have a strong soul; also her own conviction that, if she could retrace her steps, she would have given her son a different training; and, lastly, she wishes his opinion as to the want of frankness in her eldest son's character.[17]

To all these questions come long-winded replies; only in the matter of the six months' residence there is a good deal of coquetting on the part of the philosopher. There are various objections; first, the separation from wife and family. Then he throws out a hint: it is not instruction in philosophy that the prince requires, but to have a philosopher always with him.

"Then," writes Anna Amalia delightedly, "come yourself as philosopher, friend, and instructor, and bring your wife and family."

The answer is characteristic of the man. "I did not think of offering myself, and I esteem myself and my merits as an instructor sufficiently to be aware that no money could repay my services. But there is my friend and patron the Elector of Mainz; you will have to settle with him; without his permission I make no permanent arrangement." This lands us in another long correspondence, with which I shall not weary my readers. In the end the negotiations were favourable to the duchess's desires, and the professor and all his belongings arrived in Weimar September 1772.

At first everything went smoothly, the education of both princes took a new start, and Wieland in his letters to his friends at Erfurt and elsewhere, speaks in high terms of the talents and disposition of Karl August. There were several assistant-masters. Counsellor Schmid, Major Duvernois, instructor in French, and others. Every month a written report of the progress and general conduct of the princes was sent to the duchess.

One would have supposed that under these circumstances, and in view of the simple and family life at the Court (the two princes spent several hours of each day with their mother), everything would have gone smoothly and without any shoals or quick sands. Unfortunately, the expectations the duchess had formed on the arrival of Wieland were doomed to disappointment. The choice of the incomparable "Danischwende" as a preceptor for the princes was not viewed with approbation by the people of Weimar; and this feeling was strengthened by the uproar that arose in 1774 against the unchristian and immoral tendency of his writings. The crusade against him was led by one of his oldest friends and admirers, Lavater, who called for prayers to be said in all churches for the unhappy sinner. His writings and teaching were openly denounced from various pulpits with exceptional severity.

During this crusade, which commenced in 1774, Anna Amalia stood firmly by her sons' preceptor, and it is doubtful if, without her support, Wieland could have made head against the storm. It therefore comes as a surprise, and is suggestive of the uncertainty of human friendship, to find that the last two years of the duchess's regency were embittered by the relations between her and Karl August, these relations being in her opinion mainly due to Wieland's influence, joined to that of Count Görtz.

In all such cases of domestic friction it is difficult for outsiders to judge correctly as to where, or with whom lies the fault. It should, however, be remembered that in this instance the duchess had acted in regard to her duty as guardian to her son, in a singularly upright and unselfish spirit. She had devoted all the faculties of her mind, all the energy of her nature, she had sacrificed the joys common to her age and the pleasures of her youth, to the duties of a mother and the harassing cares of government. It was but natural that she should be indignant, when she found that so much self-denial and devotion met with what she considered an inadequate return of affection and gratitude. She forgot that youth is seldom grateful, and is apt to look upon the sacrifices made in its interest as only the natural and proper duty of a parent.

It was truly a sad experience, and one that makes the reader indignant, to find that after all her anxiety and toil the two last years of her regency should have been embittered by these unpleasant experiences, which, although perhaps aggravated by her naturally hasty temper, at last drove her to take a resolution which, fortunately, she did not in the end put into execution.

When we recall the pressing invitations given by Amalia to Wieland in March 1772, which induced him to come to Weimar in September of the same year, it is a surprise to read the following letter written but little more than a year after his arrival. The letter is addressed to Minister von Fritsch:

"I have long wished to communicate with you on the subject of my children, and I think it is better to do so in writing than by word of mouth. For the last year my son has altered strangely in his conduct towards me. I have tried to open his eyes as to Görtz and Wieland, but I have met with the most stubborn, opposition. Karl's self-love is his great enemy, vanity and ambition his predominant defects; his judgment is good and he has a noble heart. May God preserve him from a great or absorbing passion of any sort. One consolation is that love for a woman will not be *his* danger; that is not in his temperament, which is most constant; nothing will turn him when once he has chosen his friend. And there is the misfortune. You know Count *Görtz* as well as I do — a restless, intriguing, ambitious man. To attain his own ends he stops at nothing; he is not judicious in his system, which is temporising and cajoling, but has neither method nor firmness. When he is alone with Karl he speaks to him in a most commanding and imperious manner. You can ask old Hermann, and he will let you into a good deal. As for Wieland, he has a feeling, sensitive heart and means well; but he is nothing but a weak enthusiast, full of vanity and self-love. I realise, unfortunately when it is too late, that he is utterly unfit for the situation in which I have placed him; he does not understand youth or how to fit a young prince for his future position, and both Wieland and Görtz (the first I acquit of any bad motive) unite in a system of flattery. They flatter one another and they flatter my son, who, in addition to his other faults, has the weakness to see no fault in those he loves or likes; therefore it is more than useless to think of opening his eyes when he imagines these two men *to be perfect*.

"You see, therefore, how difficult is the position. To make a scene and to go the length of dismissing Wieland and Görtz would only make matters worse and give food to the gossips, and would probably increase the influence of a certain family whom you know as well as I do. In short, I am tired of the life I am compelled to lead. I am not politic enough to conceal my distaste and displeasure from the persons who have merited it by their conduct. At the same time I am quite aware that I gain nothing by this mode of procedure, and therefore I am determined to apply to the court of Vienna for sanction to resign the regency as soon as Karl is seventeen. I don't think a year more or less will make any great difference. I am the more inclined to take this step on account of the deplorable condition of the Privy Purse. It is quite useless to make representations to Herr von Witzleben, either gently or with firmness, it is always the same answer; and I confess it does annoy me that, whereas the treasury can always supply the demands made by my son for his pleasures, towards me there is ever the cry of "Poverty" and "No funds!"

"I confess I am too proud to put up with such treatment without showing my displeasure; and, above all, I see clearly that I possess no longer either the firmness to control, or the patience to endure, such abuses. Everyone now looks to the rising sun. But do not imagine I am therefore jealous. I am content to have given the people an amount of happiness which they never enjoyed before my regency. That is my best reward, and I shall always treasure it in my heart. I hope you will approve of my determination and rejoice with me on my deliverance from a great burden, for I repeat I desire ardently to be set free."

At first we read this letter with astonishment that the duchess, who was now thirty-four, and had held the reins of government for more than fifteen years, should have been surprised into such a childish exhibition of temper as this; but, reading through the lines, one can easily find the clue. It was the mother's heart, not the wisdom of a wise politician, that prompted this outbreak. Amalia felt herself struck in the tenderest point. She best knew all the sacrifices she had made; how she had given up the pleasures of youth to the hard study of learning how to govern, and how she had toiled and striven to keep the little duchy for the son, who now turned to other counsellors. It was no wonder she felt sore at heart; not that she blamed Karl so much; she threw the blame on Count Görtz and Wieland.

Both men had been her own choice, and as Görtz had now been in his office something over ten years, it seems strange that it was only now his evil qualities came to the front in so conspicuous a manner. Wieland had been but one year in the office, which the duchess herself had forced upon him. We have also to consider that here again it was the duchess who was the prime mover in inducing him to undertake the position he now held about her son; also that, once this cloud had passed away, he remained on terms of the greatest friendship with the duchess for the rest of his life. Taking these two points together, it is evident that the whole matter was nothing but a fit of jealousy on the part of Anna Amalia.

Fortunately she had in Minister von Fritsch a wise counsellor and devoted friend. The calm, judicial manner in which he replied to her proposal to resign the office she held as regent must have acted as a sort of "douche" to her feminine and maternal excitement.

"Your Highness cannot resign your office until the prince attains his eighteenth year. He has still to complete his studies; and later he must be introduced to the chamber, where he will learn his duties. In this way he will see for himself how much truth there is in what his flatterers tell him, and he will learn to appreciate what his mother has done for him. From what you say of the Privy Purse and Finance Chamber, it is plain that some stricter organisation is necessary. Some arrangement must also be made for Prince Constantine, whose military education must be taken in hand."

He winds up his exhortations by reminding the duchess that it was the last wish of her late husband, the duke, that his son should not begin to govern the duchy till his majority; and that, therefore, the young prince would have every reason to complain if this express wish of his father were controverted. "And as to the idea of your highness's that one year more or less makes no difference, I must with all respect contradict this sentiment. It is true that a year sometimes passes quickly, but its flight does not prevent much progress in good being made by those who employ the time well; and this without compliment would be the case with your highness. At the same time we all know how much evil can be wrought in the space of a year by inexperienced rulers, with bad counsellors perhaps. I do not say Karl August would be a bad ruler; he certainly would be inexperienced, and his choice of counsellors might be doubtful. Now, for these evils, with their irreparable consequences, you, and you *alone* would be responsible by your sudden action in upsetting the present existing arrangements."

Fritsch then goes on to point out to the duchess how many things still remain to be done before the young heir is fit for his position. "I have always thought it a rash act to send a young, undisciplined youth straight from the schoolroom to the throne. It is at all events a dangerous experiment. I think Your Highness will do well to consider this, and to return to your former idea, that the prince, like other princes, should travel and see a little, at all events, of the world before undertaking the government of the duchy."

This admirable letter, the frankness of which is rare to find amongst the advisers of royalty, ends by drawing the duchess's attention to Prince Constantine, "who has frankly told me that he feels himself neglected." The communication ends with a prophecy that the intimate friendship which at the present time existed between Görtz and Wieland would, as a natural consequence (violent friendships having generally violent endings) terminate in enmity.

Anna Amalia, fortunately, was able to appreciate the frankness which characterised von Fritsch's advice; and not only did she appreciate but she followed the counsel given. There was no more talk of resignation, and all the reforms he had mentioned, beginning with the military education of Prince Constantine, were put into execution.

Curiously enough, his prophecy concerning the friendship between Wieland and Görtz being of short duration was realised. Writing to Zimmermann, January 1773, Wieland, who had then been only a short time in Weimar, says:

"I love my prince and my prince loves me. His mentor, Count von Görtz, is my friend. Don't shake your head at this rash assertion of mine. He is my friend, and I will give you the reason why we are and must be friends to one another: it is because we are as lonely here as if we were on the top of a mountain, or in the desert of Sahara. With the exception of the prince, Görtz has not a single friend but me. I have no friend but him. Do you need any further proof?"

Three years later the story is quite different. In a letter to Merck, dated 5 July 1776, we find the following: —

"Here is news for the gossips. Count Görtz is getting ready to go to your neighbourhood, and from thence to Mainz and Mannheim, to raise a whirlwind against Goethe and me. The wretch! Not another word about such a reptile!"

But in 1773 the friendship was at its height and the coalition was giving the duchess infinite annoyance. Many other causes were added to disquiet her, and to crown all these everyday recurring annoyances, came a calamity.

On 5 May 1774, a storm broke over Weimar; it raged with unexampled fury all that day and the next. On the night of the 5th lightning struck the residence, or castle;[18] a fire burst out which no efforts could subdue, the wind fanning the flames till the building lay in ruins. As soon as the consternation caused by this event was over, the first and most necessary step was to choose a suitable residence for the duchess and her family; and here there arose a renewal of the differences which had been silenced during the excitement of the misfortune; the mother and son were diametrically opposed in their views of a suitable residence. This time the difference of opinion was accentuated by the determination shown by the prince to have his own way. On the other hand, the duchess considered (as mothers, even in our own advanced days, sometimes consider) that she was the one who held the decision in her hands. She had set her mind upon three houses in the town which, with little trouble and small outlay, could be made to suit the purpose. Karl wished to buy the Landschaft, or Assembly House, an official residence, handsome externally but badly built, as the prince was later to find to his cost. His obstinacy in this matter seems to have strangely irritated the duchess, who writes an agitated letter to Minister von Fritsch.

"I have gone through all the suitable houses accompanied by my sons and Herr von Witzleben. As I told you yesterday, Karl has got it into his head that he must have the Landschaft House, because it is a more royal looking residence, and therefore flatters his ridiculous vanity. I told him, in presence of President von Kalb and Herr Berendis, that he can do as he chooses; and he has determined to make this house the Fürstenhaus. I have therefore told the architect to prepare plans for knocking the three houses I showed you into one for my own residence, and also to see what alterations are needed to make the Assembly House suitable for Karl. Berendis has my orders to submit these plans to you, and also to repeat to you verbatim what passed between Karl and myself. You will oblige me by speaking openly of the matter at the council meeting, so that the council may talk it over with my son and explain to him how unfit the Assembly House is for the purpose he requires, and what an endless source of expense and discomfort this fancy of his (which has been put into his head by someone) will prove. When I saw he was so bent on having his own way (or, rather, on following *the advice* he had received) I told Karl to buy the house he fancied — that is, if he had the money. Enough about it. I shall concern myself no further with this utterly wretched, miserable business."

To this agitated epistle an answer comes speedily, signed by the three members of the council, Fritsch, Schmid, and Schnauss. It is couched in the most respectful terms, but entreats the duchess regent to calm herself and try to recover her influence with her son, and to persuade him to give up the idea of buying the Assembly House, "which is eminently unsuited for a dwelling, being merely built for official purposes in a somewhat hasty and inefficient manner." The council entreated the duchess to induce her son to wait until the architect's plans for a royal residence were ready for his inspection. In conclusion they asked her to remember that so long as she filled the position of regent nothing should, or could, be done without her authority.

But after all the correspondence, and the talking and the general fuss, the outcome was what might have been expected; regent and ministry had to give way to "Karl's indomitable will," and the Assembly House became the prince's residence.

It was a poor satisfaction to those who had been against the purchase that, in a few years, Karl August had to acknowledge the truth of their warnings. Writing to Merck in 1781 he tells a lamentable tale of all the repairs he had to make; "the house is only twelve years built, and already the ceiling in the great hall has fallen down and the foundations are sinking. It is altogether a mere shell."

Anna Amalia had a different story to tell as to her habitation. Some years previously Herr von Fritsch had begun to build for himself and his newly married wife a house at the corner of the esplanade. At this time the Schillerstrasse was not built, and Fritsch's house stood in a charming garden, which was surrounded by a quickset hedge, and through which ran a clear and refreshing rivulet. This delightful residence Fritsch offered to his royal mistress, and until her death Anna Amalia made the Witthumshaus (Dower House) as it was called, her winter residence.[19]

The friction between mother and son (which had begun even before the choice of a house had aggravated matters) unfortunately continued all through 1774, the flame being fanned by the mischievous advisers of the young prince. We find Fritsch writing to his father, an experienced courtier and diplomat, to ask his advice as to his own conduct in the strained relations existing between the duchess and her son. The old diplomatist answers in a long-winded epistle, clothing his excellent advice in flowery language. The pith of his discourse was contained in his affected admiration for those wise courtiers who unite the worship of the *rising sun* with due respect for the *setting sun*, both being the one constellation, only now shining in different orbits. "I have little doubt that you, my son, being of a stronger character, would probably look upon such a temporising course as mere cowardice. Do not for this reason utterly reject the course I advise, but consider calmly if you cannot, serve the two constellations for the sake of the general good. Where there are two altars, why should they not contribute to the same end?" This wily Talleyrand concludes with these words: "I believe that if the setting sun could be brought to stifle all feelings of jealousy, and the rising sun could be induced to show the affection which no doubt exists, this course would be the most judicious that a wise and prudent astrologer could adopt."

Following this good advice, which accorded so thoroughly with his own ideas, Fritsch took "the bold course" and urged upon the duchess the necessity of initiating Karl August into affairs of state, the first step to this being his introduction to the council.

This was not very quickly accomplished, the chief obstacle not being so much jealousy on the part of the duchess (as the elder Fritsch supposed), as the fact that the whole system of education for the two princes had to be suddenly broken up and put on a new footing.

Fritsch's remarks as to the neglect shown in regard to Prince Constantine had borne fruit, and the duchess turned her attention first of all to giving her younger son, who had been too long neglected, a military tutor. This was Herr von Knebel, who had been eight years in the Prussian service and was at the same time a cultivated man, enjoying the friendship of several of the *literati* of the day. Knebel was a dilettante poet and author of some praiseworthy, if not very brilliant, literary efforts. At the same time Prince Karl's establishment was increased by the appointment of the master of the horse, Herr von Stein, to be his gentleman-in-waiting.

Fritsch writes to his father of these changes and of the introduction of the prince into the council, and the diplomatist answers, October 1774: "Your news gives me infinite satisfaction. The prince's presence in the cabinet will have a wonderful effect and his royal mother will find her influence materially strengthened by this wise step. He will now forget the vexation that he has felt at being treated always as only the *Crown Prince*, which is not the custom at other courts, where the superior title is invariably *given to a prince under age*."

Here we have the key to the misunderstanding between the duchess and her son. There were those about the young heir who were ready enough to point out that he was not only unfairly kept in subjection by his mother, but was deprived of his right to enjoy a rank superior to his brother and equal to what she possessed. The duchess, rightly or wrongly, considered that it was Görtz and Wieland who had put into her son's mind this idea, which so worked upon him as to make him withdraw his confidence from her and to give it altogether to her enemies. Minister Fritsch shared this opinion of men, whom he considered satellites of the rising sun. But although this judgment no doubt was just in so far as Count Görtz was concerned, it does not seem to have been fair as regarded Wieland, whose letters to his numerous friends point altogether in the opposite direction. Wieland, moreover, was a man of warm affections, and inclined, as such generally are, to endow the object of his regard with every virtue under the sun.

CHAPTER IV

Following the advice of Minister von Fritsch, Anna Amalia had, as we know, appointed a military tutor to prepare Prince Constantine for his future career. Whether Karl Ludwig von Knebel was exactly the right man in the right place is to be doubted. He was nevertheless a gentleman of undoubted honour, while his amiability of character and his accomplishments (he was a poet of a minor order and an agreeable musician) recommended him to the favour of the dilettante duchess.

The assiduous court paid by this young officer to Minister von Fritsch could not but be gratifying to the older man. Knebel, who was twenty-nine, had, during his stay at Berlin and elsewhere, been thrown in company of men of distinction in art and letters. Moses Mendelssohn was his friend, he enjoyed an intimate correspondence with Nicolai, who kept him supplied with all the newest publications, while with both Gleim and Bode he was on friendly terms. Fritsch speedily felt convinced that here was the needful trainer he had been in search of, and became eager to secure him. Nevertheless it seems that Knebel left Weimar without anything definite being concluded. It was after he had been in Nuremberg some little time that he received, through Kapellmeister Wolf, a proposal from Minister Fritsch, originating from the duchess regent, that he should undertake the duties of military tutor to her son, Prince Constantine, as well as the post of Master of the Ceremonies to the little Court — a curious enough jumble of appointments; but we must remember the civil list was not a large one.

Knebel seems to have been somewhat overpowered by the idea of becoming the guide, philosopher and tutor of a real prince.

"What! I am to be the instructor of a prince!" he writes in an ecstasy of self-humiliation. And then he goes on to ask that he may come on a year's probation. "During this period I will ask your gracious highness," he writes, "to be patient with my shortcomings, which are due to a natural timidity of temperament, from which springs a disinclination for all society and especially for a court life. Therefore I would ask you, gracious lady, to take me under your protection and benevolently to support me in my office, and in return I will make use of every effort in my power to merit the great favour which you have conferred upon me."

Shortly after this letter was written the disastrous burning of the castle put a stop to all plans of education; but when things began to settle down again the negotiations were renewed. Everything was settled. But now began the usual intrigues against the new appointment. Unfortunately, Minister von Fritsch left Weimar to take his usual course of baths at Goddula; before his departure the official agreement with Knebel, was ready for his signature. The terms, however, were not in accordance with the verbal agreement; and Knebel, accordingly, refused to sign it, and wrote to his friend and patron to give his reasons, in an epistle of extraordinary length. After sending this letter Knebel returned to Anspach, where his father held an appointment as minister, where also he had a friend in the Margraf, and remained quietly awaiting further developments.

Meantime all manner of reports were flying about. The duchess was plagued with anonymous letters warning her against the new military instructor. When Fritsch returned he found an organised opposition had been set on foot against Knebel. It seemed as if this opposition proceeded from a very high quarter; and soon there was evidence that Count Görtz was adverse to the new appointment. Fritsch, however, calmed the fears of his protégé by giving him satisfactory assurances of his continued support. In the letter which confirms his appointment as tutor to Prince Constantine, the minister says:

"I have been here (at Weimar) for the last fortnight, and I can bear testimony (most unwillingly) to the manner in which certain people, if they cannot compass their designs by any other means, take refuge in calumnies, untruths, and exaggerations of what may contain a mole-hill of truth, which is expanded into a mountain by the mendacity of evil-minded persons, whose testimony presents such a hopeless tangle of falsehood that I find it an impossible task to get any of their statements to hang together, being as they are for the most part utterly improbable or exaggerated. I can, therefore, only repeat to those concerned in the matter that I go bail for my friend. I feel sure that when once his merits have been recognised, the prejudice which has been raised against him by evil reports will change into a warm recognition of his merits, and general acclamation will silence the voice of calumny. And to this end, my worthy and dear friend, you must turn your whole attention. You must be careful and not leave a loophole in your armour of defence. You must remember you have enemies only too anxious to undo you, and you must watch your words and actions — yes, even your very thoughts, lest any ground should be given of which your enemies could take advantage. Only be circumspect and prudent, and I see no reason why you should not in time silence the tongue of the scandal-monger, and, it may be, have full justice done to you by those who are now your enemies."

This letter, which is of great length, seems to have exercised a salutary effect in rousing Knebel from the dejection in which he had been sunk by the machinations of his enemies. He quotes a saying of Caesar's as applicable to his situation.

"We may die," said the Roman emperor, as he put to the sea in a great storm, "but we must set sail."

Acting on this courageous sentiment, Knebel set out for Weimar, where he arrived in the first week of October 1774. Here he found the whole social atmosphere changed in regard to him. Not only did he find himself surrounded by enemies, but his duties were curtailed; so, too, was his salary, whilst his position and his entire official status was lowered.

Under these circumstances Knebel did not hesitate a moment in sending in his resignation (which it seems he had the power to do). It must be owned he was somewhat of a thorn in Fritsch's side, but the minister was a large-hearted man and could make allowances for the easily wounded susceptibilities of a weak nature such as Knebel's. He flatly refused to accept the young man's ill-considered resignation. Anna Amalia, influenced by Fritsch, and attracted by the artistic personality of Knebel, was anxious to retain him in her son's service, and gave orders that a new agreement should be executed allowing the conditions and giving the terms demanded by the officer. On October 12th, the duchess writes to Fritsch as follows:

"The civil war is at an end. Yesterday evening Görtz came to tell me that Knebel has accepted the proposal which I made to him. Görtz repeated the demands made by Knebel. I asked him what Karl had answered in regard to himself. It appears my son said that he was not in a position to promise anything for the future, but that he assured Knebel he had no objection to him; or against my choosing him. I then sent to Knebel and told him that all was settled, and for the future he might take up his residence in the castle, where he is now located. This afternoon I had Görtz, my children, and Knebel with me. I introduced Constantine to his new tutor, and I begged Görtz to assist his new colleague in every way, and asked both men to be good friends. Görtz promised me that it should be so, and added that he had already begun and would go on doing all in his power to carry out my wishes. Previous to these peace ratifications I took Karl into my own room and asked him to select from the gentlemen-in-waiting those whom he would like best to have about him, and I added I would like him to have a little court of his own.

This idea enchanted him. He at once chose Seckendorf. I answered that he had not understood my proposal. I had particularly said I did not wish him to choose from the pages, which would not be suitable; but from the gentlemen-in-waiting.

"He reflected for a few minutes, and then said 'Give me Stein or Klinkowström.' I answered I did not wish to limit or interfere with his choice, but that I thought as Stein was master of the horse, and as he (Karl) esteemed him and had known him a long time, and had confidence in him, and Görtz seemed friendly with him, and that also, as long as I had known Stein, he had impressed me as being a worthy man; therefore on all these grounds I thought he would be a good choice;

but, I added, if he preferred Klinkowström I had nothing against him; it was altogether for him to decide.

"No, no, dear mamma, let me have Stein;[20] since I was a child I have always liked him, and I shall be pleased to have him always with me; and please let me tell him that I *chose him myself.*

"I agreed that it should be as he wished. Later I told Görtz, who seemed very well pleased with the arrangement."

She then goes on to ask directions as to informing the council of the new appointments and other, minor details, of business.

Knebel took the oath, or, as we would say, kissed hands on entering on his duties, and almost immediately the duchess began the preparations for her sons' tour, a matter she had greatly at heart. Both princes were to travel for some months under Knebel's supervision — an astonishing proof of confidence in an almost total stranger, which should have soothed the sensitive character of the new governor. In the eighteenth century it was a matter of necessity that every royal princeling, as well as every nobleman and gentleman of condition, should make what was called "the grand tour," which sometimes occupied a couple of years. Anna Amalia did not contemplate anything so ambitious for her sons, but her clear sense and sound judgment told her that it would be well if they were removed, even for a short time, from the small circle where they (especially Karl) were the cynosure of all eyes. It would take down the young heir's opinion of his own importance, thought the wise duchess, to see how small a space he and his duchy occupied amongst other nations. So the two princes set out with Knebel, "who is, as usual, depressed and nervous at the greatness of the responsibility," Frankfurt was their first stopping-place.

Frankfurt is about eight hours' journey from Weimar by rail. Consequently, we can calculate that it took the prince at least two days to reach this beautiful city. And here occurred an event which was destined to have, in the near future, the most surprising issues. And in this connection we must always remember that it was to Knebel, and his introduction of Karl August to Goethe, that we owe the great literary event which raised Weimar from its insignificance, and gave to it the proud title of the Modern Athens.

In Goethe's autobiography we come on the following passage: —

"I was one day writing in my apartment, which being partly shut up and hung with sketches has the appearance of an artist's study, when a gentleman entered who introduced himself as von Knebel, tutor to Prince Constantine of Weimar."

This visit, accidental though it at first appeared, was a turning-point in the poet's life, as well as in that of Karl August. Knebel told Goethe how desirous was the elder of the princes (who had just read *Götz von Berlichingen*) to make his acquaintance. In accordance with this wish, the poet visited the princes and was received with flattering kindness, especially by Karl August. He dined with his royal hosts in a quiet way and left them, having received and produced an agreeable impression. They were going to Mainz, whither he promised to follow them. His father, a typical sturdy old burgher who held aloof from princes, shook his sceptical head at the idea of this visit to Mainz. The poet nevertheless went a day or two afterwards and spent several days there as the guest of the royal princes. This was his first contact with men of such high rank. Goethe was at this period twenty-five years of age; in the full splendour of his wonderful beauty, and in the full possession of his extraordinary gifts, he had already produced two masterpieces — *Götz* and *Werther*. The first was the product of a somewhat unhealthy senti-mentalism, *Werther* the outcome of a love episode. And yet, although both these early works represent the tendencies of the time, they are both far removed from the ridiculous sentimentalism and extravagant romance of the day, which were all imbued with the most "hysterical enthusiasm."[21]

In the grand-ducal archives in Weimar there is a certain blue portfolio which bears the inscription: "Letters from my sons Karl August and Constantine, from 1774-1775."

These carefully preserved treasures of a mother's heart have a sacred and tender interest. They are a trifle yellow now, and the writers have long since crumbled into dust in the royal mausoleum; but we can with a little imagination picture to ourselves how these, the first letters written by her boys, were received by the loving mother; how she showered kisses on the paper, and showed with pride to Wieland and Minister von Fritsch the firm, decided handwriting of her eldest son.

The difference of character which distinguished the two princes is very clearly marked in these boyish letters. Karl August pours out all the fresh enthusiasm of a youthful mind, delighted with the novelty of the situation in which he finds himself. He is brimming over with high spirits and the enjoyment of the first taste of liberty, and, although his letters show symptoms of the masterful spirit within always ready to assert itself, there is, nevertheless, a generous, frank outpouring of boyish confidence, mingled with affectionate dependence on his mother.

Prince Constantine does not impress the readers of his correspondence so favourably. To be sure it is hard to judge from the hasty, ill-written specimens to hand. He writes seldom and his letters are in a depressed, subdued tone. They are carelessly written and blotted; words are frequently omitted (an expert would say a proof of a disorderly nature). Almost every letter ends with excuses, the refuge of a shallow mind. "Forgive, *chère maman*, this short letter; next time I shall write more, but the weather is so terribly cold that I cannot hold my pen."

Both princes unite in hearty praise of Frau Goethe, the poet's mother. Karl August hopes they do not flatter themselves, when they believe that the kind lady, who seems so very good to live with (and whose eyes resemble those of her son), has some liking for them, as well as they for her. This is prettily put, and at once secured Anna Amalia's interest in the good Frau Aja.[22]

That the difficulties of Knebel's position did not cease with his departure from Weimar, and that they were in a certain sense due to the sensitive nature of the newly appointed tutor, is evident from a complaint that he writes from Strasbourg to his friend and patron, "the highly born and highly gifted Freiherr, Minister von Fritsch." As usual, this lengthy epistle, like numbers written by the same verbose correspondent, runs into four or five pages. We will not, however, trouble ourselves with the wordy compliments and excuses in which Knebel indulges, but go straight to the object of his communication.

"My princes are well primed against me; they have no confidence in me, although I give ample proof that I can be trusted. I tell myself that, as I give no cause for this want of confidence, I should be above caring about it. Nevertheless, heaven only knows how circumstances have occurred, which have thrown certain suspicions on me, and this although I have acted on each occasion in the most upright and sincere manner; and therefore I have now determined for the future to be absolutely silent, and to take no notice of anything. In regard to the Crown Prince I have no complaint to make; he has an honest heart and a fine character, and I am convinced he loves me; and on my part I return his love with my whole heart. His affection makes me endure other drawbacks. After all, people cannot go on hating me for ever. Nevertheless, such undeserved treatment makes me cold, inactive, and, alas! sometimes discontented with myself.

"Prince Constantine, up to these last few days, has given me much dissatisfaction. I have written to Count Görtz and told him frankly that, unless the prince, who is specially in my charge, will give me his full confidence, it will be impossible for me to be of any use to him, and that I could not think of wasting my time in a fruitless undertaking.

"Count Görtz has written to the prince, and given him a long lecture, with the result that he has, during the last few days, drawn closer to me. I hope this is the beginning of better things. I should be grateful if your excellency would find an opportunity to ask her highness the duchess to convey to Count Görtz her approbation of his conduct; but please allow *him* to *think* that I wrote to the gracious duchess on the subject."

There is a postscript to this lengthy epistle which is a proof, if proof were wanting, of the timidity of Knebel's nature, and his consequent unfitness for a post that required a strong character.

"I rely on the prudence of your excellency not to communicate the contents of this letter to any one, or to allow any use to be made of it. I am afraid of Weimar, and I have had good reason to fear its evil tongues. The Crown Prince returns next Wednesday."

The last words of this letter, dated 28 January 1775, touch the outer circle of a subject of great interest to the people of Weimar, and to Anna Amalia especially. The tour of the princes had a double object, so far as Karl August was concerned. He was not only to improve his mind and gather experience of how other princes ruled, but he was to seek a bride. It was undoubtedly early days to talk of marriage to the barely eighteen-year-old prince[23] (he attained his majority in

January 1775, when, according to his father's will, he was to undertake the duties of government), but in the eighteenth century age was reckoned from a different standpoint. It is within the memory of octogenarians of today that women at one time were considered *passé* at twenty-five, and decided old maids at thirty. We have altered this somewhat drastic method of shortening the spring-time of life, and we have likewise raised the position of women by so doing.

At the present time, few, if any, courts in Europe present the terrible spectacle of vice flaunting itself openly, the wife and the mistress having equal rights, and shameless impropriety passing unchallenged by public reproof. The duchess, no doubt, thought that the best way to "steady" (such was the phrase of the day) her son, and give him a taste for family life, was to marry him early. Such a course would likewise ensure the succession, for Prince Constantine was weak, mentally as well as bodily, and it was all-important that there should be an heir as speedily as possible.

Anna Amalia's choice had been made when Karl August was still in the nursery, and his destined bride a baby in her cradle. Since then the powerful Landgräfin of Hesse Darmstadt had died, but this did not interfere with the matter of Karl August's marriage. The princess had been a playfellow of the young prince in childhood, but there had been no meetings of late years. Karl was, therefore, to pay a visit of inspection to Karlsruhe, where the young princess was residing with her sister, the Margravine of Baden. He was to be accompanied by Count Görtz, while Knebel remained at Strasbourg with his pupil Prince Constantine. Count Görtz, whose tenure of office as regarded Karl August was about to expire, was charged with all manner of messages from Anna Amalia, who besought the count to give her speedy and constant news of how the young suitor was progressing.

"Write to me as often as you possibly can," was the anxious mother's request. "Everything that concerns my children interests me." No signs here of a wish to retain in her hands the reins of government, or to keep her son unmarried that she might rule him more easily. Truly to such meanness Anna Amalia's nature could not descend. As she often said, "I am interested in all and everything that concerns my children."

The first letter from Karlsruhe was written by Karl on the day after his arrival. He gives a detailed account of every incident of his journey to Karlsruhe, but on the subject of his meeting with the princess he has little to say, and what he does say is coldly worded.

"Yesterday evening I renewed my acquaintance with the Princess Louise. She has grown much and has become very handsome. During the few minutes in which I had the privilege of seeing her, she struck me as having a good deal of *esprit*, and as possessing a strong character. I shall take every opportunity to see more of her."

Nevertheless weeks went by without much apparent progress being made; there was a royal suitor in the way, but at last he got his *congé*, and Karl writes to his mother in an overflow of spirits.

"The king has said goodbye, and now all will go well. These words are dictated by my heart, dear and excellent mother mine. I implore of you to take care of your precious health for the sake of your son, who loves nothing on earth so much as he does you."

I wonder was Anna Amalia deceived by this outburst of tenderness? Let us hope she was; but one would imagine she read through the lines just as we do, and guessed that it was prompted by the happiness the departure of the king, his rival, had given him, which made him love all the world, and most of all his dear, good confidante and mother, the best of women, except, of course, his beautiful bride to be.

On 19 December 1774 came at last the long-desired news from Karlsruhe to tell the duchess the wish of her heart was fulfilled.

"MADAM AND VERY DEAR MOTHER,

"Penetrated as I am with feelings of love and gratitude for all your goodness, and certain of having your fullest sympathy in this step as well as in any future action of mine, I lose no time in acquainting the most excellent of mothers that I am betrothed to the Princess Louise of Darmstadt. Since you have already approved my choice, I feel sure I shall shortly receive your consent in due form. You may rest assured that nothing can equal my happiness and gratitude. The Princess Louise commissions me to lay her respects at your feet, and to assure you, dearest mother, that she considers herself very fortunate to be allowed to call herself your daughter. I and all the world speak well of your character, which, without doubt, is one of the most estimable to be found, and she is absolutely worthy to belong to you. Her only idea is to make other people happy, and she takes a great interest in my happiness. Be quite satisfied, best of mothers, on my account. I have chosen the one woman in the world who is suitable to me."[24]

Having indulged in these love rhapsodies, the young duke turns to more practical details. He wishes to give his bride a betrothal ring, and is certain that his mother would like the gift to be worthy alike of the donor and the recipient.

"I have been told that the Markgraf of Baden gave his wife a ring which is worth seven thousand gulden, and the one I have placed on her finger temporarily only cost one thousand five hundred thalers; and you will see, dearest mamma, that such an inferior ring is not suitable for the first present I offer to my beautiful bride. With your permission I must also give some presents to the Baroness von Pretlach and the Baroness von Edelsheim, to whom I owe so much; moreover, we have been the guests of von Edelsheim. Farewell, my ever dearest mother. Continue your proofs of love and graciousness to a son whose greatest desire is to be worthy of such a parent.

    "Madam and very dear mother,

        "With all respect to your royal highness,

            "Your very obedient and submissive son and servant,

                "KARL."

Three days later Karl writes again to thank his mother for her ready consent to all his wishes. He assures her he will do exactly as she has told him, and that he will lose no opportunity to tell Princess Louise of her goodness. Then the duchess writes to Görtz on 24 December 1774, and tells him she encloses two letters for her son: one of these he is to read to the princess, the other is for himself. Then there are commissions and presents, and the count has a pretty long list of things to do; but there is a true womanly ring in the following words "You know how tenderly I love my children; you will therefore understand the joy I feel that he has chosen the Princess Louise for his wife. I am disappointed that I am not an eye-witness of the new situation in which my son finds himself. How does he play the lover? Is he very much in love?"

Karl was so much in love that he wanted the marriage to be celebrated at once, but the duchess held to the first plan, that he should visit the French capital and see the world. She gave permission, however, for Prince Constantine to visit Karlsruhe, accompanied by Knebel, and there to make the acquaintance of Klopstock, whose works were highly esteemed by the Landgraf, to whom Knebel read them aloud. Nevertheless, the court etiquette did not allow the composer of the *Messiah* to be received at court, as he was beneath the rank of a Minister of Legation.

This was a painful experience for the somewhat conceited poet, who, when he was seriously ill, had prayers offered that he might be preserved to Germany! Prince Constantine writes to the duchess that everyone in Karlsruhe is making a fuss about Klopstock. But this did not soothe the poet's mortification. He left Karlsruhe in a very bad humour, and without taking leave of the court, and returned to Darmstadt, where no such "ridiculous etiquette" prevented his being present at all court entertainments.

The princes, with Knebel in attendance, returned to Strasbourg in February 1775, where they made close friendships which lasted through their lives. There is a great deal of interest of an old-world character in the letters written home by von Knebel and his charges.

"We have glimpses of a high, intellectual standard, which bridges over all differences of class or station, wealth or poverty, and establishes socialism of a mental character, for which we look elsewhere in vain in this so-called enlightened century."[25]

From Strasbourg the princes and their tutor travelled to Paris, which naturally charmed the young visitors. Karl August, in spite of being separated from his charming Louise, enjoyed himself, as a youth of his age naturally would do. His letters home are a little too historical for a young man visiting the gay French capital for the first time. It is hard to believe 'that he thought of nothing but the deeds of Turenne, Condé, Sully, and other heroes of the Fronde, not forgetting Henry of Navarre. His being in love made him presumably anxious to return to Weimar, where preparations had already begun for the marriage. But of this he says nothing.

"I long," he writes to the duchess, "for the moment when I shall embrace *you*, my beloved mother, again. Although the tranquillity of Weimar will seem strange to me after this gay city, the joy of being with you again will fill my heart with such gladness, that I shall have no room for any regret. I shall be overflowing with happiness."

It was, however, some months before he had this joy, for the princes did not return to Weimar till June 1775, their tour having lasted nine months. They had visited many places and made many friends, but the two principal features of these months of travel were the acquaintance made with Goethe and the engagement of Karl August. The last-named event seems to have drawn the young duke's heart nearer to his mother; as to this we have the testimony of von Fritsch, who, writing to the duchess, tells her that Herr von Stein talks of nothing "but the reverence and devotion the duke feels for the duchess mother"; and then this admirable counsellor points out that since the Crown Prince attained his majority three months ago, and is, in fact, now the reigning duke, "it would be more politic not to fill up any office or place that falls vacant, but to leave them for his appointment later on." Also he advises that the duchess should conduct herself towards her son "more as a friend willing to offer advice than as a mistress who has the right to command." And lastly, he emphasises the *necessity* of concealing her dislike to Görtz.

Amalia (like the sensible woman she could be when not led astray by her affections) received this advice with hearty goodwill. She writes to Fritsch:

"I acknowledge gratefully the many services you have done for me during my regency, and the excellent advice you have given me. Therefore I shall now follow your counsel, and, for my son's sake, as well as for the general good, I shall act towards Görtz with friendly courtesy. But should he attack the persons who have proved their devotion to me, then it would be my duty to show him clearly with whom he has to deal. My son must understand that if he wants me to stand by him in the future, he must reward handsomely those who have served me well. I ask nothing for myself, and I want nothing. My own conscience is my only reward; and I would wish you to believe that my friendship for you will never cease so long as I live.

"AMALIA."

In spite of this amiable resolution, Anna Amalia desired with all her heart that Görtz, whom she looked upon as a dangerous counsellor for her son, should not be placed in any post where his baneful influence could affect her relations with her beloved children. It was in vain that Fritsch preached forbearance and temporising methods. The duchess was too sincere to play willingly a double part. She acknowledged that Görtz deserved recognition for his services towards her son, although it might be that these services were not to her liking, and therefore she was willing to reward what he had done liberally. So far back as 1774 she got this part of the business settled. Writing to Fritsch, July 2nd, 1774, she says:

"The Görtz affair is finally arranged. He accepts a pension of fifteen hundred thalers and the title of first class Geheimerath — Privy Councillor. He wished to play the *rôle* of a disinterested man, who desired to be unfettered by court patronage, but the title of '*Excellency*' tickled his ears so much, that he could not refuse it. Please get the decree of dismissal put in hand at once and let us have done with the business."

But when the draft of the decree was submitted by Fritsch, the royal lady was highly incensed at the flattering terms in which it was couched.

"I find," she writes to the minister, "that there are in the decree two expressions, at least, which imply far too much gratitude on my part, and to which my conscience and sense of honesty prevent me from subscribing my signature. Far from praising his methods of education, I consider that Görtz has ruined my son's character, and has done so from the beginning. I beg you will correct these extravagant expressions and substitute others more in accordance with the truth."

In this letter Anna Amalia shows her dislike to the man, who she considered (and probably with justice) had sown dissension between herself and her well-loved son, and although the rift had not been permanent, still the mother's heart could not forget this wound to her affections or forgive the man who had caused her suffering. Following the precedent set by her late husband in regard to the reward given to his tutor, the duchess issued a decree charging the provinces of Weimar, Eisenach, and Jena, with a parting gift for Count Görtz of 20,000 *thalers*. This tax was paid without a murmur. After doing so much, as she thought, it must have annoyed the duchess to find that these rewards were not in Karl August's opinion sufficient to prove his gratitude towards the man so distasteful to his royal mother. On 12 September 1775, three days after his accession as reigning duke, he sent a rescript, or order, to the chambers, in which he gave to the count a gratification of four thousand thalers as a mark of his gratitude for the fidelity and devotion he had shown to him (Karl August).

CHAPTER V

On 3 September 1775, Anna Amalia, who had not yet completed her thirty-sixth year, laid down her sceptre of office and willingly retired into the shade of private life. For seventeen years she had governed the little duchy committed to her care, with a discretion, prudence, and ability, truly wonderful in so youthful and inexperienced a ruler. Those who had watched her unobtrusive, ever-watchful endeavours to be as harmless as is the dove and not altogether without the cunning of the serpent, were filled with wonder for this young creature, who steered her course in difficult waters to the admiration of all.

During the first years of her reign a whirlwind of misfortune had swept over Germany. There had been a terrible war, in which Weimar, small as was its size, had borne its part; this had been followed by an equally disastrous famine. The conduct of the young duchess under circumstances of extraordinary difficulty was the theme of praise at every court in Europe; her name was honoured wherever it was mentioned. The celebrated Grimm, envoy from Gotha to the Court of France, extolled this "wonderful duchess," in glowing terms:

"The hard reality of the present time turns into the romance of mythology, when we see before us a living representation of the Goddess Minerva, who has taken a human form amongst the romantic woods of Thuringia. She it is whose name shall be for ever immortalised in the annals of Saxony, and who will live in the history of mankind. But greater even than the immortality of history is the respect of contemporaries; and here language itself fails to give an idea of the homage, the reverence, and the love excited by this wonderful princess."

After making due allowance for the German *schwärmerei*, which is conspicuous in this last somewhat laboured compliment, it is impossible to deny to Anna Amalia the praise which is called forth by her admirable administration of the charge left on her hands. Faults she may have had, errors of judgment she possibly made; but when we consider her extreme youth, her naturally gay disposition, her attractive appearance, our wonder grows that, living as she did in an age in which a really virtuous woman was the exception to the general rule, she should have conducted herself in so irreproachable a manner.

Nevertheless, virtuous as she was, she did not escape altogether the shafts of a malicious world. It was a coarse age, and in Weimar the coarseness was accentuated by the roughness of an uneducated, small-minded population.[26] For the rest, there does not seem to have been any ground for the innuendoes and whispers against Anna Amalia, which originated in malicious or idle gossip. Moreover, the duchess's inclinations led her in an altogether different direction. She aspired to be a *bel esprit*, and although not exceptionally gifted as were many of the women of her century, she had a lively imagination, a quick perception and an aptitude for study, in which, now that she had leisure from the cares of governing, she allowed herself to indulge. The study of languages occupied the first place. Her preparations and compositions in English, Italian, Latin, and Greek, both in prose and verse, fill volumes; and her mind expanded and her style gained new vivacity and imagination by writing essays on different artistic subjects or abstruse questions, either scientific or philosophical. She made very fair translations of the Odes of Anacreon and Propertius, and, with the assistance of Wieland, even essayed Aristophanes. Her compositions, short considerations or maxims for daily use, show thoughtfulness and delicacy, and are altogether free from the curse of plagiarism. Her *Gedanken* especially are worthy of notice: Here are a few examples:

"He who wishes to rule others should first understand how to govern himself, and how can a man who is not happy in himself give happiness to others?"

"Contempt for women is the outcome of immorality. Mutual esteem should exist between the sexes; it knits together the bands of social life. Where this is not to be found, the man abandons himself to his savage instincts; becomes self-seeking, and virtue is driven from its rightful position."

Amalia had an agreeable taste for musical composition, as is shown by the little operas she occasionally wrote. From childhood to old age she sought, by learning from different masters and by constant practice, to attain proficiency in painting, but it is best to draw a veil over her efforts in this direction. Although she never was more than a feeble amateur artist, nevertheless the duchess's judgment as to the artistic value of a painting or statue was of value, and often astonished professional judges. She was undoubtedly intelligent in matters of art, and also on most subjects she could say like Leonora:

"I rejoice when clever men do entertain each other
That I can understand their excellent discourse,
And where'er such controversy doth entangle them,
I can follow their devious paths and turnings."

Like Queen Victoria and other intellectual women, the duchess had a distinct gift for governing, and no one with any fairness could dispute that her administration of the duchy during her son's minority had been in every way admirable.

It was, therefore, only natural that she found it difficult to disassociate herself all at once from what had been the absorbing interest of her life for eighteen years. That it would have been wiser for her to have held to her first resolution of non-interference, there is little doubt; and to this conclusion she herself arrived in course of time. But allowance must be made for the anxiety of a mother for a young and inexperienced son, who was running, as she thought, into all manner of danger through evil counsels. The evil counsellor was, of course, her *bête noire*, Görtz, who, in spite of her efforts to thrust him into the shade of retirement by the bribe of the title of Excellency, had executed the old trick, *reculer pour mieux sauter*, and now, like jack-in-the-box, he jumped up as fresh as ever, his former pupil loading him with honours.

At the marriage of the duke it was Görtz who accompanied him to Darmstadt; and the post of court marshal to the young duchess was bestowed upon him, this office bringing him in constant communication with the duke, who took his advice on all points.

Anna Amalia endeavoured to counteract what she considered an unfortunate and malign influence by drawing to the court men of equally strong but more trustworthy character. Here is a letter dated 5 September 1775, addressed to Minister von Fritsch, begging him to be sure to come to the Council meeting to be held the following day, when Statthalter von Dalberg would confer with Karl August on a subject which is not named, but is indicated in the following extract.[27]

"I can tell you nothing definite, only this, that if the Statthalter is not made thoroughly acquainted with the business in all its bearings, I very much fear that Görtz will carry his measure, and then no one will have the courage to tell my son he has made a great blunder."

A private letter from Count Dalberg to Görtz proves that the duchess had grounds to suspect that the quondam governor's influence was not exercised beneficially. This letter bears date 18 July 1775.

"I swear you to secrecy, my dear count, for this is a privileged communication. *Take care what you are about,* for it seems to me that Karl August begins rashly. What is the object of these sudden changes? The report is that he does not get on with his mother, and on more than one occasion I have heard it mentioned that the fault is altogether on his side. This is the more to be regretted, for his mother fulfilled her duty as his guardian well."

As is generally the case, gossip exaggerated the friction which undoubtedly existed between mother and son, the reports that flew about that the duchess had resolved to leave Weimar being absolutely untrue. Those about the Court were well aware that, in spite of a not unnatural and boyish elation at his sudden emancipation, which made him self-assertive and restless at any attempt to control him, the young duke's love and respect for his mother were unshaken by the new position in which he found himself. He was willing not only to ask, but to follow her advice; and in difficult circumstances (many such arose in the first year of his rule) he availed himself gladly of her personal intervention.

So far as the influence of Count Görtz was in question, it was, although he had no prescience of coming downfall, very near its termination. For the rest, the role of court favourite is always a dangerous one to fill, all violent delights being liable to violent endings. Neither was Görtz possessed of a strong enough character to keep the influence he had gained by being a kind and indulgent — perhaps too indulgent — governor. The days for holidays and lollipops were over, and Duke Karl, nearing manhood, saw men and things with the quick perception inherited from Amalia. He required stronger mental food than could be supplied by the flattery and stale maxims of his former guide and friend. At this moment the future of Karl was trembling in the balance of uncertainty; it altogether depended upon the hands into which he would fall.

In October 1775 the count was still in the ascendant, and was chosen by the duke to accompany him to Darmstadt, on the occasion of his marriage to Princess Louise of Hesse Darmstadt. The wedding festivities were of great magnificence. The young pair, after a week of gaieties, left for Weimar, staying on the way at Frankfurt.

There Karl August saw his friend Goethe and introduced him to his beautiful bride, for whom the poet was filled with the most passionate admiration, an admiration which he always continued to express in prose and verse. He gladly accepted the pressing invitation given by the youthful couple to pay a long visit to Weimar; and all the arrangements were made before Karl August parted from his new friend.

The newly married Duchess Louise bases her claims to our attention not on her own merits — for at present her record is little more than a blank sheet of paper — but on the high reputation of her mother, Caroline Henrietta, to whom one of the most intellectual of her own generation had given the title of "The Great Landgräfin." She made her mark in a period which abounded, so to speak, in remarkable women. She united a tender woman's heart to masculine courage, extraordinary judgment and feminine tact. Witness her submission to Landgraf Karl Friedrich, a man of the most singular character. Narrow were the limits in which she had to move, and constant strife marked her life, which passed in one long struggle with the fate to which she was condemned united to a man for whom it was impossible she could care.

In those first years likewise the country was miserably poor, war after war having drained every available resource. She describes in a satirical manner a masked ball which took place in honour of Karl Friedrich's birthday, and which reminds one of a parallel description to be found in the memoirs of Wilhelmina, Margravine of Bayreuth. Caroline found her only pleasure in her visits to the court of Berlin and her intercourse with her "hero" as she called Frederick the Great.[28]

Here, too, as we know, she met our Anna Amalia, with whom she cemented a close alliance. The delightful duchess with her delicate pointed fingers had

more artistic tastes than the strong-minded Landgräfin. The two women, notwithstanding this, and perhaps even in consequence of the contrast, grew attached to
one another, and, out of their mutual liking came the idea of being more closely
connected by the marriage of their children, the great king giving his full consent
that so it should be.

But before this was to happen a stormy time had to be gone through — years of
struggle and poverty, and, worse still for the Landgräfin, of domestic unhappiness,
for the Landgraf Karl Friedrich developed all his bad qualities and gained no
good ones. He can be described as Carlyle's mother described her famous son,
"ill to live with." In fact, Duke Karl must have gone a little further than the sage
of Chelsea, for *his* wife, the Landgräfin, could not live with him — or perhaps it
was he couldn't live with her. Anyway, he decided to remove himself with all his
impedimenta, including his fine stud of horses and splendid dogs, not forgetting
his pages-in-waiting, to Pirmonez, where he pleased himself, leading a military
life which was the one best suited to him. Before his departure he constituted his
wife Regent. This looks like a recognition of her high gifts, as no doubt it was in a
sense, for the Landgraf knew he could trust her with this delegated authority.

Still, when the matter is looked into, the amount of confidence shown was not
so gratifying, and it resolved itself into this, that, although the Landgräfin had the
luxury of being delivered from daily contact with a tyrant, she was still under his
rod; her authority was only nominal; she was not allowed to sign any important
document or issue any decree without the duke's permission. Every day a courier
left for Pirmonez with the papers for the duke's signature and for his orders,
together with a schedule of her daily expenses. She was to undertake no works
for improving the town without his permission; in fact, she was a cipher and at
the same time she had to work as a slave.

A less generous woman than Caroline would have found some way of paying
off a husband who showed so little confidence. The Landgräfin's was, however, a
high-minded nature and had the wisdom to avoid making any scandal. She knew
that pride amounting to madness was the Landgraf's ruling passion, and she was
judicious as well as good-tempered in submitting to the inevitable, and by this
means generally succeeded in getting her own way. Once only did she evade
his orders, in the matter of drawing up the conditions relative to the proposal of
marriage made by the Empress of Russia, regarding an alliance between the future
Czar, and one of the Landgraf's daughters. Here Caroline made use of a woman's
ruse to prevent the ridiculous and inflated proposals of the Landgraf reaching the
Russian Court. For the rest she always kept on terms with her exigeant husband
and wrote to him every day.[29]

At a distance she seems to have had more influence over her strange husband
than at close quarters, and succeeded in inducing him to summon Friedrich
von Moser to Darmstadt in the capacity of Minister. His social reforms caused
widespread astonishment. In the end Moser was dismissed and persecuted. The

Landgräfin, however, believed in him and only in her later days said that he was a traitor. The correspondence between the Landgräfin and the statesman lasted for years, and is a wonderful record — not more wonderful, however, than the immense correspondence of the period. No one who was born in the eighteenth century could escape the craze of the day, letter writing. I know one should be duly grateful that this craze — I can find no other word for it — did exist, but with all my gratitude my surprise still continues. It is well known that the constant scribbling injured both the health and the eyes of our ancestresses, but no medical prohibition had any effect. The Landgräfin's correspondents were highly distinguished, including such men as Grimm, Gellert, Voltaire, and Klopstock, who after a little time made his home at Darmstadt, the Landgräfin delighting to honour the author of the *Messiah*. Wieland also had a share in her regard, and had helped with Lessing and her faithful Ravenell in teaching her to drink deeper of the well of Knowledge. It was Goethe who added the word "Great" to the title Landgräfin; and was it not Wieland who wished that he was for one half-hour lord of the universe, that he might create the good Landgräfin empress of the world?

The more one knows of the Landgräfin, the more one feels convinced that she was a woman of whom too much has not been said, and who deserved the reputation given her by her contemporaries. She was well-read, her reading being not superficial but well digested. Her mind was therefore amply stored with the knowledge of different subjects. There was no showy superficiality about her but a sterling solid basis for an excellent judgment, for she never read for the purpose of saying she had read such and such a book, but because she wished to read it for the improvement of her own mind and in order to make a correct estimate of its merits.

Her remarks on Klopstock's *Messiah* are somewhat surprising, when we remember the popularity the work and the author had both attained. Writing to Zückmantel, she gives her opinion that, taken as a whole, the poem is somewhat dull reading, but that here and there are some beautiful passages. In the same letter she tells him she is sending him Gessner's *Death of Abel*, with which his friends seem well pleased, and she adds:

"I have not yet read Gellert's *Swedish Countess*, but it will give me much pleasure if you will make its acquaintance;" meaning that she is sending him this new book as well.

In one of her letters to the great German scholar Pütter, with whom she had struck up a friendship at Göttingen, she writes:

"You will perhaps recall the wards we interchanged on the occasion when I had the great pleasure to make your personal acquaintance at Göttingen. Our conversation had reference to the desire the Landgraf entertained to induce you to come to Giessen. I shared in this wish before I had the pleasure of knowing you, and the gratification I experienced in conversing with you has much strengthened this desire. Privy Councillor Hesse has orders to confer with you on this subject. It would rejoice me if the proposal made by him should be found sufficiently tempting to induce a man of your distinction to accept our proposal. Everything that is in my power I shall gladly do, in order to procure for Darmstadt such an incomparable benefit as your acceptance of the position would confer.

"Your very affectionate servant,

"CAROLINE VON HESSE."

There is a great charm in Caroline's letters, and in this one especially. Notwithstanding this, it failed to lure the learned Professor Pütter from the time-honoured Göttingen to the more mushroom university of Giessen. The whole of her correspondence is marked by a tone of extraordinary sincerity, which gives one a key to the sort of woman she was.[30]

One is sorry to find this amiable and sensible woman adopting the vagaries of the sentimental school of *Schöngeister* or "Souls," which played a great part in Germany and later on, in a modified form, as the romantic school in France. The sentimentalists, men and women, were full to overflowing of the milk of human kindness — or to use a more appropriate expression — human love. They loved every one: they wept for the sorrows of the whole world: they were full of sensibility of the highest order. Sentimental novels were all the rage, stories by Rousseau and Julie Bondeli being often written in verse. Most young girls read these silly compilations, fancied themselves in love, and often committed all manner of follies. Goethe in his early youth was tinged with a good deal of this sentimentality, and fancied himself the victim of terrible love epidemics.

The queen of sentimentalists was, however, Sophie de la Roche, who in her sentimental love for the world in general was ready to embrace, not metaphorically but actually, every one of her friends, irrespective of their sex. We read of strange doings at the Congress of Sentimentalists which took place in Darmstadt in the spring of 1771. It was largely attended, the meetings being held at Sophie's house, several distinguished sentimentalists being present; amongst them Gleim, then an old man, but addicted to platonic attachments and paternal endearments; the Jacobi brothers, true sentimentalists; also Wieland, then about to leave Darmstadt for Erfurt.[31]

Merck was also a member of this absurd school, and there was a young man named Leuchfering who mixed himself in its concerns. He was twenty-three years of age and held a position of trifling importance in the household of the crown prince of Hesse Darmstadt, whom he likewise accompanied on his travels. Leuchfering was of a curious, fantastic temperament and his sensibility was so excessive that, on hearing any sad or touching news (even though it in no way concerned him or any of his friends) he was apt to weep copiously. He was likewise much given to talking of his own love affairs. He was a poor sort of creature and suited for the part he undertook in the development of the sentimental craze, which, by its foolish doctrines, and especially by means of the pernicious literature[32] it encouraged, and indeed inflated, was the cause of many evils, suicides becoming common. It seems extraordinary that a woman so strong-minded and practical as was the Landgräfin should have put herself at the head of such a movement as this.

To look at her portrait one would say there was not much mock sentiment in the kind, honest eyes and thoroughly practical face. She was nevertheless heart and soul bound up in the fad of the day. She had delightful meetings in the gardens of the palace and all manner of fine high-flown talk. The "souls" had all sorts of names, Urania, and Psyche, etc. One foolish girl had her grave all ready made in her garden, and often shed tears and laid flowers on it. This same sentimental soul — her name was Fräulein von Zeigler — had a pet lamb which she led by a blue ribbon.

Goethe, in the first flush of his youth, came to see Klopstock, who lived under the shadow of the great Landgräfin's protection. Caroline Flachsland, who rejoiced in the spirit name of Psyche, wrote to her lover, Herder:

"Goethe is one of us and a good-natured, merry young man, without much elegance. He is very much taken up with Merck's children, and has a certain something, I cannot say exactly what it is, that reminds me of you, so that I like to see him and to talk to him."

And again Psyche Caroline tells her lover how much Goethe reverences him (Herder). Caroline was a confidante of the Lili episode and was sorry for the poor young man, feeling sure that Lili would never marry beneath her.

One of the last acts of the great Landgräfin was her journey to Russia, accompanied by her three daughters, one of whom was to be the chosen bride of the heir to the empire. This does not seem a very dignified proceeding, but the prize to be won was great, and on these occasions dignity sometimes has to take a back seat. The Landgräfin, however, travelled with great pomp, having a large suite amongst whom figured "friend Merck." A curious incident happened on the journey. One night she was roused out of her sleep by the sudden opening of the door of the *berline* in which she was travelling, and saw a number of faces regarding her curiously by the light of several lanterns. Their disappointment when they saw her wrinkled face amused her, as did their turning their lanterns on the princesses. Their exclamation, "Ah! that one in the left-hand corner, she is the one for us!" explained that this midnight visit was only due to anxiety to see their future empress.

A fleet of three frigates was sent to convoy the royal ladies to St. Petersburg, the Empress Catherine writing:

"I expect you, honoured madame, with impatience, and long to welcome you and your daughters, the princesses; to my court. It will give me happiness to know one whom I esteem so highly, and with all sentiments of regard I am your affectionate cousin,

"CATHERINE."

General Rehbinder was sent with this letter, and accompanied the royal ladies to St. Petersburg and introduced them to Count Orloff, whose house was placed at the Landgräfin's service. On their arrival Orloff told them a lady was waiting anxiously to see them. This turned out to be Catherine. It must have been a strange meeting: the small, insignificant-looking German princess, standing before the queen-like and splendid ruler of the great northern nation with her magnificence, her cruelty, and her unbridled passions, a veritable modern Semiramis.

At the semi-barbarous court the great mental gifts of the Landgräfin were fully recognised, while the charms of her lovely trio of daughters won all hearts. Curiously enough, the words of the rough intruders came true. Princess Wilhelmina, who had occupied the left-hand corner of the *berline*, being the chosen bride of the young bridegroom, Paul. Through all the subsequent *pourparlers* the Landgräfin played the part of the wise, prudent mother, and showed as before-mentioned, a true diplomatic nature, by hurrying on all negotiations, so that everything was signed and concluded before Karl Friedrich's absurd proposals arrived by courier.

The only thing left to be done was to celebrate the marriage, which took place as soon as the consent of the Landgraf arrived; and then the Landgräfin, refusing the invitations of the empress and the entreaties of poor Wilhelmina, who clung to her own people, set forth on her home journey, for she felt that it was a wager between her and King Death. She made the journey despite all obstacles of snowstorms and icebergs, and at last reached Homburg, where she rested a few days with her eldest daughter (married to the grand-duke of Baden), then she turned her steps homeward. She had just finished a letter to her husband describing a cabinet she had bought for her natural history specimens, when she passed away quietly. According to her wish she was buried without any tolling of bells or court ceremonials. Frederick the Great had the following inscription placed upon her tombstone: *Femina sexu ingenio vir* — By sex a woman, in intellect a man.

Her daughter Wilhelmina, for whose advantage she had made the journey which hastened her death, survived her mother barely three years, dying in childbirth, in April 1776.

Of the Landgräfin's daughters (there were five), three were married before her death, one to the Crown Prince of Prussia, another to Prince Paul of Russia, the eldest to the Markgraf of Baden, and, of the two remaining, Louise married Karl August.

The Markgräfin of Baden-Baden was a most accomplished woman. In her early youth she had been elected member of the Fine Arts Academy in Copenhagen; in 1783 the Roman Pastori Arcadi paid her a like honour. Had she lived, she would have gained further distinction for her botanical researches, but she died in Paris, whither she had gone for her health, and where she was occupied in further botanical studies under the guidance of Le Sage and. Lavoisier.

We must now return to the young pair we left at Frankfurt, where, in the first glow of their honeymoon, they had gone to visit Goethe.

This almost ideal marriage, which had been for many years the cherished wish of Anna Amalia, seemed to possess every condition necessary to ensure happiness, the princess being not only gifted with beauty, but of a noble, high-minded character. At first sight, therefore, nothing seemed to be lacking in this union; and yet somehow, at all events in the first years, it failed to ensure the happiness of the wedded pair. In spite of her statuesque loveliness — "an angel in woman's form," Goethe called her — Louise lacked the qualities which were necessary, to enable her to hold the affections of the boyish duke, whose nature though frank and loving, was yet wanting in constancy. His temperament was warm, passionate, frank; hers, reticent, cold, and faithful. She loved her husband with all the strength of her great soul, and yet was incapable of showing her love. She was, however, capable of extraordinary forbearance, self-sacrifice, and virtue.

She had spent two or three years in Russia with her sister, the wife of the Grand Duke Paul; and there she had been trained in the observance of the strictest etiquette, and had been taught to keep all those beneath a certain rank at a distance, as not worthy of her friendship or notice. Any breach of decorum, any want of respect, she resented as an offence; and likewise any lack of dignity in those who were in high position. This stiff, quiet, regular and cold-blooded formality was totally opposed to Karl August's free and easy mode of life; and as a natural consequence their marriage, especially in the early years, was unhappy.

Goethe, who had a passionate admiration for the beauty and the character of the angelic Louise, says: "I looked into her soul, and only that mine was all aglow for her, that glance would have frozen me."

And yet this poor young princess was much to be pitied. Not only was she displeased with the want of etiquette at the court, but she was gravely disappointed in the characters of both her husband and mother-in-law, which failed to accord with her more rigid ideas of what was dignified and proper. She felt hurt and injured in her own self-esteem by what she considered their want of self-respect. At first she remonstrated with her husband in a tone of passionate complaint; but as no steps were taken to change the *laisser aller* that prevailed, the duchess withdrew more and more from the tumultuous gaieties of the court, refusing absolutely to have any share in undignified entertainments, from which every shadow of etiquette was banished.

This withdrawal annoyed the duke, who, after the arrival of Goethe, absented himself sometimes for weeks together. The duchess, who resented this neglect, complained of it in her letters to her sister and intimate friends; and these complaints, from being made the subject of feminine tittle tattle, lost nothing when repeated to others. In this way the first initiative was given to the exaggerated reports, which were afterwards current, of the wild orgies which sometimes took place at Weimar.

Most justifiable were the complaints made by the bride of the lack of comfort in the royal household. She tells her sister that nothing had been prepared for her arrival. There was no palace or castle, for, as we know, the Residenz had been burned down, and in the house chosen by the young duke there was not even a kitchen; everything had to be cooked in the "Red House" and carried across to the duke's residence. The servants and certain court officials, occupied the original Standhaus, where there were also some rooms set apart for guests. In the new building, the duchess's suite of apartments was on the first floor. On the second the duke had his private rooms, and the third was given up to the duchess's first mistress of the robes, *oberhofmeisterin*, and the ladies-in-waiting.

The Countess Wilhelmina Elizabeth Eleonore von Gianini, who occupied the dignified position of *oberhofmeisterin* to the duchess, was a most formal and forbidding person, whose anxiety that neither her own dignity nor that of the royal lady she served should receive any slight was the cause of great amusement to the young Goethe when, later on, he joined the court circle. This same old lady proved anything but amusing to the duke, who from the first detested her and her punctilio. Louise had likewise imported two maids of honour, Fräulein Marianne Henriette von Wollworth, and Louise Adelaide von Waldner-Freudenstein, a pair of starched and dignified pieces of propriety, walking dictionaries of court etiquette, and in the eyes of the dowager duchess most objectionable. The estrangement which from the first moment showed itself between the old and the young duchesses was accentuated when the Duchess Louise, one month after her arrival, appointed Countess Görtz to be one of her ladies-in-waiting.

The duke's gentlemen-in-waiting were the handsome Count Wedel, eighteen years of age, the romantic Einsiedel, brother to the Falstaffian chamberlain of the same name, and Count Werther, a bold rider, who cared for no risk or danger. A hard drinker was the count, and a careless husband to a very pretty wife, about whom and the duke some ripples of scandal were set going. In these early days Louise was much attracted by the sympathetic manners and resigned sadness of Charlotte von Stein, the neglected wife of the Herr von Stein, master of the ceremonies to the duke. The friendship, however, did not last long. "The Stein has too many lovers to suit my wife," said the duke, and this remark applied to most of the ladies of the court.

It must be taken into consideration that the life at Weimar — especially during the early years — of the duchess's married — life — differed considerably from the more elegant courts of Karlsruhe and Darmstadt, as also from the uncivilised, but nevertheless magnificent, court of St. Petersburg. The town of Weimar at the time of Karl August's marriage (although very different from the condition it was in when Amalia was brought there as a bride) was a small, insignificant place; its population, which did not exceed seven thousand souls, was poor, while the town itself looked poverty-stricken. Anna Amalia had done her part in trying to improve such matters as the lighting of the streets and the condition of the houses;

still, even ten years later, Schiller called it *the village of Weimar*, and in comparison he considered Jena a large town. Herder also speaks of "that desert Weimar, half village, half capital." In a geographical annual called *The Traveller*, we read that Weimar was a second-rate place, which could not compare with Jena, either in cleanliness, situation, or in the architecture of the houses.

In 1775 the city walls were still standing. Gates and portcullises gave testimony to times of warfare. Within these walls were six or seven hundred houses containing about seven thousand inhabitants all told. The city gates were strictly guarded, no one could pass through them without leaving his name in the sentinel's book. Even Goethe, favourite as he was known to be, and minister to boot, could not escape this tiresome formality, as is evident from one of his letters to Frau von Stein, directing her to go out *alone* and meet him *outside* the gate, lest their exit together should be inscribed in the book. There was little safety at night in the streets of Weimar, for if you escaped the thieves who were prowling about, you ran the danger of falling into a hole and breaking your leg, the streets being badly lighted, and in some places not lighted at all.

The absence of luxury, or even ordinary comfort, may be gathered from the "Memoirs" of the time. Such necessaries as locks to doors, curtains that could draw, or beds in which one could sleep comfortably, were not to be found all over the Continent, and even in England there was room for improvement in such matters. We read in Wilhelmina of Bayreuth's "Memoirs," her account of the reception she received on her arrival at the Markgraf's (her father-in-law's) palace after her marriage, the want of every comfort necessary, even for an ordinary lady, to say nothing of a king's daughter; and yet how sumptuous were the court toilettes, what laces, what jewels!

Weimar was probably on a better footing than Bayreuth, and if we are to judge by the appointments of the royal residences — Ettersburg, Belvedere, Tiefurt — there is evidence of considerable comfort and even luxury. The Louis Quatorze beds, where a family could have slept (although according to our notions of hygiene eminently unhealthy), are wonderful specimens of ornamentation and carving. So, too, with the toilette appliances. The jugs and basins (in size only fit for a doll's house) are, some of them, of china that would delight the eye of a connoisseur. Nevertheless, in the houses of the middle class and in those of many of the richer merchants the deficiencies were remarkable; chairs and tables were almost universally made of common deal, for not until the close of the eighteenth century did mahogany become general. Looking-glasses were introduced early in the century, but were a luxury of the nobility and richer merchants.

The palace, which is now such an adornment to Weimar, was at this time not yet built; and the duke and duchess inhabited the Fürstenhaus, about which Karl August was always grumbling. Karl August was, as the reader has already gathered, no ordinary character. At fourteen Frederick the Great (his grand uncle) declared that of all the princes he had seen Karl gave the greatest promise; and this promise was realised, although not perhaps in its fullest development. Karl August had many fine qualities, one of the most conspicuous being his keen appreciation of genius.

"It is easy," says a well-known writer, "for a prince to assemble men of talent. It is not easy for him to make them remain beside him in the full employment of their faculties and in reasonable enjoyment of their position. Karl August was the prince who, with the smallest means, produced the greatest results in Germany."[33]

His disposition was overbearing and imperious, his manner often rough and brusque; but his heart was excellent, his courage beyond a doubt. He was a good soldier and a first-rate comrade in the field or in garrison, but somewhat out of his element in foreign courts and drawing-rooms.

And yet there was a poetic enjoyment of nature enshrined under this rough exterior. In a letter of the duke's which has not been printed, he writes to Goethe, then at Jena, saying that he longs to be with him to watch the sunrise and sunset; for in Gotha he cannot see the sun, hidden as it is by the crowd of courtiers, who are so *comme il faut* and know their "fish duty" with such terrible accuracy, that every evening he feels obliged to give himself up to the devil. The delight of this young duke, when not with soldiers, was to be with his dogs; and yet he had a mind full of romance and *schwärmerei*. He would discuss philosophy with Goethe by the hour, talking of lovely things that conquer death.

"Riding across country over rock and stream in manifest peril of his neck, teasing the maids of honour — sometimes carrying this so far as to offend his more stately wife — wandering alone with his dogs or with some joyous companion, seeking excitement in wine and in making love to pretty women, offending in his roughness and wilfulness, though never estranging, his friends — Karl August, though he often grieved his admirers, was with all his errors a genuine and admirable character."

"He was always for progress," writes Goethe to Eckermann. "When anything failed he dismissed it at once from his mind. I often troubled myself how to excuse this or that failure, but he ignored every shortcoming in the cheerfullest way, and always went forward to something new."

In his early youth he showed this steadiness of purpose and fidelity in friendship. That Görtz was rather an unfortunate choice as a tutor does not alter the admiration one feels for the gratitude shown by the youth to the man who had been his friend. It was from Anna Amalia that Karl August had inherited this warm, loving temperament; from his father came something of the weakly constitution. The portrait of him was taken at the age of eighteen, the period when he was released from Count Görtz's tutelage and became his own master for the first time. One can see in the boyish face signs of the strong will, which would have its own way, — sometimes obstinately and unwisely, while the mouth betrays passion of a different order. That he was aware of his own tendencies is shown by a letter, written in his twenty-fourth year, to his brother's tutor, Von Knebel.

"I must restrain my inclination and not allow my heart to follow its own way without rein or bridle. It is very difficult, however, to do this in the unnatural position in which one's life is cast."

These words give a certain insight into the curious mixture of right and wrong, good and evil, that made up the really fine character of Karl August. He was a man, every inch of him, and a good man too, although not quite the angel that the good people of Weimar would have us believe, for Karl August's memory is adored by the inhabitants of that primitive, interesting and altogether charming town. When one reflects on what it must be for a boy of eighteen to be absolute master of himself, to command where he was accustomed to obey, the wonder is not that he makes a total shipwreck, as did poor mad Ludwig of Bavaria, but that he should even make a fair offer at straight steering. Karl August knew that the power was altogether in his hands. He could, had he been so minded, have brought his little duchy in a very short space of time into a pretty state of confusion, especially with his somewhat wild proclivities. He was saved from this by his mother's loving influence, and by his own attachment for Goethe. And although some writers have tried to prove that Goethe's influence was injurious, anyone who reads the story of Goethe's life must (if free from bias) acknowledge that, with occasional exceptions, the poet's influence was for good.

Karl August's principal faults were his rashness and his roughness, his way of expressing himself being sometimes more that of a peasant than a prince. When Goethe's father died, we find him writing in his letter of condolence:

"He is now, a corpse and your mother can at last breathe freely. Malicious tongues say this is about the best march past the old fellow ever did."

It could not be said that he had a taste for low society; nevertheless, he disliked to be in any company where he was obliged to be on his good behaviour. Goethe, who accompanied his friend on a visit to the Court of Brunswick, writes to Frau van Stein:

"Our good duke bores himself to extinction. The strict observance of etiquette which prevails here is not to his liking; he has to go without his beloved pipe of tobacco, and a fairy could confer no greater favour on him than to transform this fine palace into a woodman's cottage." His habits were undoubtedly rough; he was seldom to be seen without a pipe in his mouth, and he loved horses and dogs. He often brought his favourite deerhound into the bedroom of the duchess Louise, who showed her displeasure at this intrusion.

Goethe remarked on this occasion that they were both in the wrong. The duke ought to have left the beast *outside*, but once he had got in, the duchess should have allowed him to stay.

Karl August loved all manner of jokes, and the rougher they were the more to his taste, while he carried his teasing of the court ladies much too far. Goethe, in a letter to Frau von Stein, remarks:

"I am no longer surprised that royalties are so stupid and even silly in their behaviour, when a man like the duke, who has always been surrounded by intelligent men, and whose friends know the usages of Society, at times behaves himself like a ploughboy. He really wishes to do what is just and right, and yet acts in a directly contrary manner. His intelligence and good judgment are surprising, and yet if he does anything good, he immediately does something so stupid that his wax light becomes a farthing rush light."

In *Wilhelm Meister* (into which Goethe has introduced many things which occurred during the first year of his residence at the Court of Weimar, as well as portrayed many of his friends, more or less disguised) the following passage occurs, which undoubtedly is a reproduction of what must have happened to Karl August:—

"The head keeper, soon after the opening of the piece, had lit his pipe and began to take further liberties. His large dogs soon came on the scene. It was true they had been shut up, but managed to find their way to the theatre, and ran on to the stage, where they caused considerable confusion, knocking against the actors and frightening the women. Suddenly they caught sight of their master in the pit, and with one bound leaped across the orchestra to him."

On another occasion, speaking of the duke, he says: "One would love him dearly, were it not that his rude ways alienate his friends, while his rashness makes them indifferent as to what he does." All those who knew Karl August deplored his rash and foolish adventures, which often placed his life in danger, owing to the delicacy of his constitution, which, especially in his early youth, was ill-calculated to withstand the risks to which he exposed himself. It was in vain that his mother entreated, and his doctor ordered, more tranquillity in his manner of life. One might as well think of putting a bridle on an untrained horse. Neither could he, if he would, keep quiet. "He has got St. Vitus's dance in his royal limbs; he can neither sit still himself nor allow any one else to remain still."

Goethe has to confess that although the duke's existence is wrapped up in hunting and shooting, the course of business goes on slowly and surely, and that he takes a willing and painstaking part therein, and now and again does a good stroke of work. "But I don't want or wish to be always set up as a bugbear, and he never asks the others for their opinion, or consults them as to what he should do."

One would think that this deference to his opinion would have been flattering to Geheimerath Goethe, who ought to have been grateful for the friendship of the boyish duke; but Goethe, who was his senior by nearly eight years, was past the season when breaking one's neck seems a trifle, in comparison to the delightful excitement of the risk.

"We were often," he writes, "as near death as men could be, and the death I least desire. I admit that there is excitement in this steeple-chase over hedges, ditches, and graves, through rivers, up mountains, down hills, all day long in the saddle, and at night camping out in the woods under the canopy of heaven. All this frenzy of rush and clatter was more to his mind than his ducal inheritance. He cared little for the dignity, and would have willingly exchanged it for the wild life of a hunter."

Living so much in the open air naturally engendered in the young prince's mind a true love for Nature, which he preserved through his life. There is a refreshing ring in his letter from Gotha (where he was on a visit to the Duke of Coburg) to Goethe.

"Oh! if I could only draw a free breath in the pure morning air and see the sun rise behind the rocks, and watch it go to sleep at night, and have you with me. The castle here is so high and is built on such an ugly plan. It is so full of crawling, servile creatures clad in velvet and silk, that I grow sick and dizzy."

In a letter to his brother's tutor, Knebel, he writes a really poetical description.

"This is my first night of freedom (we shook the dust of Gotha off our shoes this morning). I can breathe freer, for I am far away from the civilised world. A human being was never intended to be a miserable Philistine, working for his daily bread. There is nothing raises the soul like seeing the sun sinking behind the horizon, the stars coming forth. A cool breeze rises . . . the day is done. And this panorama of loveliness is not for us . . . it would go on were we all in space. I will go and bathe with the evening star to light me. . . . The water was cold — it was as if I plunged into the cold night. As I made the first step it was so pure, so clear, so dark. The blood-red moon rose behind the mountain; in the distance I heard Wedel's horn."[34]

There is a touch of romance in this description which is very pleasing.

As a natural consequence this admiration for Nature engendered in the duke's mind a desire to learn something of her secrets; and this search induced an alteration in his manner of life, for the lover of Nature is a hater of lavish display and vain glitter, and is more at ease in simple surroundings. Anyone who would wish to see with his eyes how the young worshipper of Nature followed the teachings of Nature herself, should see the Borkenhaus in the park of Weimar. Small and lowly as it is, Karl August spent there many a night in summer. He slept there quite alone, there being no room for an attendant. He could see across the meadow on the other side of the park the Gartenhaus, where Goethe likewise enjoyed the delight of solitude.

It will be seen from what has been said, that Karl August, despite his faults of temper and his natural roughness, differed from the usual pattern of royal princes, and even from ordinary individuals. And so thought Goethe. who in his old age said to Eckermann:

"Karl August was born a great man; he had a compound nature, and had he lived in the Attic days, the Greeks would have said he had a mixture of god and man and demon. Napoleon, Frederick the Great, Peter the Great, and Karl August have a family resemblance, in so far that no one could oppose them." And then he adds this curious fact: "Everything that I undertook under his direction succeeded, so that in cases where I could not see my road clearly, I had only to consult him, and he instantly hit upon the way to ensure success, and I seldom knew him to fail." He goes on to say: "If the demoniac spirit deserted him, as it often did for the time, and only the human remained, his perceptions were certainly not so clear and, strange to say, everything went wrong."

Whether or not it was in consequence of this dual character, there is undoubted reason to believe that Karl August had extraordinary capacities for being a good ruler. He possessed all the necessary gifts, knew how to give each one his proper place, and was conscientiously desirous to do the best he could for his people and his duchy. He kept his eyes and his ears wide open, and adopted the newest inventions and ideas. He tried to induce Jews to settle in Eisenach, in order that they might establish factories, and he started a sort of bureau, where assistance was given to young men who wished to travel. His desire undoubtedly was to do the best thing possible for his country and people; yet, like all progressive and improving rulers, he found a steady opposition to his philanthropic efforts.

"Out of thousands of people," he writes to Knebel, "there is only a handful who desire, or who have the ambition, to go one step further than the turning point, where they stick fast."

And it was little wonder that the incapacity and rank ingratitude of those he tried so hard to help, should have soured his naturally generous, kindly nature.

Goethe, however, found great fault with the duke's spasmodic efforts "to do right, which always ended in his doing something foolish. God knows will he ever learn that fireworks at midday produce no effect."

Goethe's letters to Frau von Stein, to whom he told his inmost thoughts, show that, although his attachment to Karl August never weakened, yet he grew gradually impatient with his recklessness and extravagance.

"Enthusiastic as he is about what is good and right, he has, notwithstanding, less pleasure in good than in what is improper. It is wonderful how reasonable he can be, what insight he has, how much he knows; and yet when he sets about anything good he must needs begin with something foolish. Unhappily, one sees it lies deep in his nature; he resembles the frog that is made for the water, even although he has lived some time on land." But although Goethe and the duke occasionally fell out, their friendship never really waned. There was often discord between them,[35] as was natural. The duke not having yet exhausted the turbulence of youth, it was only to be expected that, as time went on, a certain coolness should enter into their relations, and although Karl August always addressed his friend with the brotherly "Du," Goethe, after "the first wild weeks," recognised that it would be advisable to adopt another and less familiar address; his letters too became decidedly formal, at times unpleasantly so.

The two great failings of Karl August were his love of good wine and his admiration for pretty women. As he followed Goethe in most things, so he, too, found a second Charlotte Stein; in the Countess Werther von Neunheiligen, who was to him a loving and beloved friend, and who, at all events at first, used her influence to soften the roughness and eccentricities of her friend and admirer.

It was, nevertheless, unfortunate that Countess Werther was not the sort of woman to influence a mind like that of Karl August; and moreover the intimacy began in 1779, when the duke had sown his first crop of wild oats and was settling down to more sensible pursuits. Nevertheless, Goethe, although he more than once speaks contemptuously of the countess, calling her a poor, nervous creature, confesses on one occasion that "she is very useful, and would be more so if the knots in the strand of our duke's nature were of less complicated nature, and the strings not so hard to set going in tune." Goethe himself often found it hard to play upon this curious human instrument.

He writes on one occasion to his confidante, Frau Stein: "He has in the past given me much trouble and annoyance; nevertheless, his naturally fine nature asserts itself, and the best comes to the front, so that he becomes a joy to live with and to work with."

These words from one who had been so intimately connected with him are undoubtedly a tribute to Karl August's character. It is beautifully expressed in the poet's well-known verses. Youth must have its day; we all know this old saying by heart. But what of the holiday spent by the duke and Goethe at the village of Stutzenbach? Although by no means a wild orgy, it was nevertheless unfitting for the position held by both men. They kept a diary of their doings, which Goethe had the prudence to commit to the flames; but it leaked out through Einsiedel's garrulity that Karl August and his minister had not only danced with, but (*geliebelt*) made love to or caressed the peasant girls of the village, who, ignorant of the rank of their partners, behaved after the manner of villagers, and pulled about and played tricks upon their lovers in an altogether rough and unbecoming manner. Goethe in his daily letters to his beloved Charlotte von Stein, tells her all the incidents of this rough flirtation. "The girls," he says, "nicknamed me Mizels."[36]

Dancing was the favourite amusement with the court. In the winter no less than fifteen *redoutes* (public balls) were given, besides balls and small dances at private houses. In the summer open-air dances were the fashion, on a soft carpet of moss or well-cut lawn, with the trees for the background and lights gleaming through the foliage, the band discoursing sweet music.

The duke, too, and his suite rode miles to entertainments given by the nobility, danced all night, and rode back to Weimar in the early hours of the morning. It was a joyous court, this, led by the young duke and his youthful ministers; and in many of the amusements the Duchess Anna Amalia took part.

Wieland, whose innumerable letters are one of the most trustworthy sources of information as to the doings of the gay little court, gives an account of the freedom and absence of stiffness that prevailed there. From the time Goethe became an influential member of the court circle, life was spent more than ever in the open air. Breakfast was often taken on the esplanade before the palace, in presence of a large number of the townsfolk, who stood in a circle looking on and enjoying the witticisms and somewhat broad jests with which the royal circle flavoured the morning meal. Falk relates how Bertuch often gave orders at midnight that the kitchen wagon, with all the *batterie de cuisine*, should be ready to start before dawn, in order to have the *déjeuner* ready, which the duke had invited guests to partake of in the woods. If the destination was further afield the cooks and their assistants had to spend the night in active preparations, baking, roasting, boiling, etc.

The joyous company of, ladies and gentlemen of the court set forth betimes next morning, all on pleasure bent. The still woods would resound with their gay voices. Under the shade of the trees the more romantic wandered arm in arm, enjoying the luxury of a *tête-à-tête*.

"In these moments of freedom," writes Cecilie in the Weimar Album, "a certain *laisser aller* and absence of court etiquette were permitted, ill-natured remarks being discountenanced, and each one was free to follow his or her fancy, there being no inquisitive eyes watching, or malicious tongues reporting, what they did. There were no society papers in those halcyon days, so, without fear of the pen of the scandal collector, Mademoiselle X. and Count M., or Frau von N. and Duke K. A., as the case might be, could wander together through the mazes of the wood, and if under the shelter of the umbrageous trees a lovers' kiss was interchanged, no one was indiscreet enough to hear the sound."

Goethe, in talking later on with Eckermann of his early days in Weimar, acknowledged that "the first years at Weimar were much perplexed by perpetual love affairs." Weimar, indeed, could boast of a number of beautiful and attractive women; women, too, who had mental gifts equal to their beauty. Corona Schröter, for instance, and Amalia Kotzebue. It was, in truth, an altogether ideal surrounding, an intoxicating period, and it was not astonishing that with "youth at the prow and pleasure at the helm," life at Weimar glided down the stream of intoxicating delight. Karl August and Goethe kept the ball rolling, and although one was a husband with a beautiful and charming wife, and the other had the important charge of the interests of the country on his shoulders, neither of these responsibilities was a feather's weight in comparison with the pleasure of the moment.

It must be acknowledged that, amidst the constant stir and excitement, the extravagance, the whispers, the innuendoes, the open scandals, and the secret sins of the little court of Weimar, we turn with a sense of relief to the picture presented by the youthful duchess. Her girlish innocence, her angelic beauty, make a pleasing contrast to the *femmes savantes* and the *beaux esprits* by whom she was surrounded. To be sure Louise was a trifle stiff, not to say starchy; it was for all the world as if one of Holbein's Dutch respectabilities had intruded amongst a gallery of lovely but rather unclothed beauties of Charles II's time. Perhaps it was a tinge of Calvinistic solemnity that kept "the angelic Louise" so far apart from Karl August. Poor young thing! she had a sorrowful and lonely life for many years. It was not altogether the duke's fault, for he was willing enough to love his wife in his own way; but, unfortunately, his fashion of loving and honouring was not precisely to Louise's liking; she had her own ideas as to the holiness of the marriage tie. Neither could she accommodate herself to the manners of the court. She had been educated in a school of strict propriety, such as then prevailed all over Germany. Without the counsels of a mother to show her how to steer her course through the intricacies of her new surroundings, and suddenly brought in contact with a gay, unceremonious *laisser aller*, devoid of all stiffness and ceremonial, where no one appeared to take anything seriously, and where the amusement of the moment seemed to outweigh the more serious issues of life, it was impossible for her to adapt herself to such a subversion of all she had been taught to respect, and equally impossible to attempt to reform such a chaos. She therefore took the middle and rather unwise course, of withdrawing from such amusements as seemed to her wanting in the dignity which should surround one of her exalted position, while at the same time she exacted from her personal attendants, and so far as she could from the court, the observance of that respect and distance which was, in her opinion, the cherished prerogative of those born in the purple.

Now this course of action showed that the duchess was wanting in that flexibility of character which could alone have secured her happiness in the circumstances in which she was placed; and to a man of Karl August's frank, open character, this attitude of silent martyrdom was specially distasteful. He would have infinitely preferred a woman who would, as the saying goes, stand up to him. A passionate, even a teasing, jealous woman he would have understood. A storm, a shower of tears, then lollipops and kisses — that was his idea of a woman's grievance. But the melancholy face, the cold reserve, the absence of complaint — what on earth did it all mean? If the young duke had been passionately in love with his Louise, probably things would have righted themselves sooner than' they did. As it was, long years were to pass before husband and wife got to understand one another. The duchess's nature was so timid that she never allowed anyone, least of all her husband, a glance into her inner nature, and not until they had been married many years did Karl August recognise the superior mental gifts of his wife.

"She is incomprehensible," he wrote to Knebel. "Before her marriage she lived quite alone in the world, without ever finding a human being to realise her ideal of what a friend ought to be, without exercising a single talent which would have softened her nature; she runs the risk of being completely isolated and losing all that grace and amiability which form the principal charm of her sex."

These words are a revelation; in fact they explain the situation, and enable us who read them to understand the barrier which grew up each day like an impassable wall between the young couple. Such situations occur often in novels, and we smile in a superior manner and say: "What ridiculous exaggeration! Quite improbable! A few words would settle the matter in two minutes!" So they would, but it is the saying of the few words that makes the difficulty. It is not well to lay down hard-and-fast rules for the guidance of that most delicate piece of machinery, made by God's own hand, the human heart, with its hopes and fears, its tender throbs, its hopeless misery, its altogether unfathomable cravings and desires. Poor Duchess Louise! she had to fight her battle alone. There seemed to be no help, for she does not appear to have had any female friend at this period, or for some years later; and not even the powerful bond of parental love served to draw the husband and wife nearer together. Anna Amalia, who saw with pain this unhappy state of things, endeavoured to give a helping hand to her daughter-in-law, by establishing more confidential relations between the young pair, but Louise resented any interference from her mother-in-law.

Knebel, who lets us into much that was going on, tells us the first meeting between the two princesses was not productive of very favourable results. This was probably due to coldness of manner on the part of the young duchess — an insurmountable defect which she never was able to conquer. Anna Amalia, who was warm and expansive, was frozen by "this lump of ice"; all the more so, perhaps, because she had shown herself most anxious to secure her as a daughter-in-law. In any case, the characters of the two duchesses were essentially antagonistic. Not in one point only, but in every thought and action, they differed from one another, so that it was impossible for any very warm affection to grow up between them. This must have been a sore disappointment to Anna Amalia, who undoubtedly had worked hard to bring about the marriage.

All contemporary writers on the Court of Weimar mention this want of cordiality between the two duchesses, which had a bad influence on society generally, by encouraging gossip and tending to establish two rival camps. Still, there was no open quarrel, and the Duchess Louise had the good sense to keep on apparently good terms with her husband's mother, while Anna Amalia, who desired to be loved by her son's wife, was only too anxious to avail herself of any opening to thaw the "iceberg," and although she was deeply disappointed that the dream in which she had indulged, of a delightful intimacy with her daughter-in-law, was not to be realised.[37]

Anna Amalia, frank by nature and a decided enemy to all restraint and stiffness, may *sometimes* have erred on the side of too much frivolity. A visitor to Weimar in 1774 describes what he saw at a ball, or *redoute*, given at the City Hall. To his surprise "the duchess remained till the small hours of the morning, most of the company leaving before she did." This easily scandalised gentleman was the one who found fault with the duchess for dancing.

Henrietta von Eggloffstein, in her amusing memoirs, often alludes to the democratic spirit exhibited by the "delightful duchess," who chose her intimate friends, not for either their rank or their riches, but for their mental qualities. (In proof of this we have the close intimacy of thought and affection, which for years continued between her and Frau Aja.)

She did all in her power to induce a better understanding between the duchess and Karl August. She pointed out in a few sensible words to the Duchess Louise, that the course she was pursuing was one that would end by altogether estranging the duke, and that, if she wished to retain his affections, she must conform to the tastes, and study the wishes, of her husband; also that although the gaieties of Weimar might be distasteful to her, she ought not to abstain from occasionally joining in them.

The advice given by a mother-in-law is rarely taken in good part; and it does not appear that the young duchess was any exception to the general rule. "The two duchesses are angry with themselves and with one another," writes Goethe. And, naturally, this coldness between his wife and his mother annoyed Karl August, and drove him further from Louise, who seemed to him to be making an unnecessary fuss. The poor young duchess was the more to be pitied as, from her temperament, she found it hard to make friends in her new surroundings. Everything and every one at the Court of Weimar was so different from what she had been accustomed to. Especially with the women she was not friendly.

"My wife," writes Karl August to Knebel, "lives quite alone, without a single woman friend to whom she can tell her grievances, or with whom indulge in a friendly gossip. Mesdames Stein and Herder, with all their many merits, are too homely or too frivolous for her. My wife," he goes on, "who does not possess a single talent, the exercise of which would help to pass the time, runs a great danger of growing too absorbed in self-contemplation, and of losing the quality of amiability, which is cultivated by intercourse with others."

Fortunately, the necessary female friend was found later on, when, in 1788, an English family, consisting of a father and two daughters, arrived at Weimar to spend a few months. These were the Gores, who became part and parcel of the inner court circle, and whose name is identified with the golden period of the Attic city.

"I have never known my wife," writes the duke to his friend Knebel, "take to anyone as she has done to Emily Gore, and few, here at least, have recognised her fine qualities as this Englishwoman does. This, I trust, may develop into a friendship, that will be of use to both, especially to my wife, who leads so solitary a life without a woman friend. The Gores, too, are very cultured women, and Emily Gore, especially, is full of sympathy; so that she may thaw the ice in that frozen soul. This, I know, should have been my duty, but I have never been able to devote the time necessary to develop my wife's mental qualities. Intercourse with men only is injurious to women. They lose the tender delicacy of their sex, and become in character a mixture of the two sexes, which is by no means to be desired."

That the duchess was conscious of her own shortcomings, is evident from a letter, also to Knebel, written by her in 1805.

"I have studied myself closely, and I have learned to know myself, and this knowledge forces on me the fact, that my existence is powerless to influence others."

The gifted Charlotte von Kalb seems to have had a better insight into the duchess's character. "She was always serene and pleasant, but with her there was no *gaiety of heart*. She suffered in silence, and never allowed herself the luxury of seeking consolation in sorrow. She may have appeared indifferent, but she had a clear perception of what was going on, and her judgment was generally just. There was a general harmony about her, and she was particularly remarkable for a grave and most suitable dignity, and a total absence of exaggeration or levity. Her steadfastness of character was shown in her manner of dress, which never changed with prevailing fashion."

The unhappiness of these first years of married life was no doubt intensified by the disappointment felt in consequence of there being no prospect of an heir to the duchy. This was looked for with the more anxiety as the heir apparent, Prince Constantine, was weak in health and not a desirable successor; and this fact made the people of Weimar and Eisenach doubly anxious for the appearance of an heir in the direct line. When at last the wished-for child made its appearance, the joy was clouded by Providence sending a princess. This check to the loyalty of the good citizens of Weimar was, however, removed in 1783, when the duchess gratified her husband and the people by giving birth to the much-desired prince.

From this time the relations between the young husband and wife entered on a much happier footing; the querulousness which had tinged the angelic Louise's sweet nature disappeared, and as she showed Karl August more of her real nature, he grew to lean upon her judgment and to prize her love. "There was between them and throughout their lives a real and noble friendship."

One word more. Great stress is laid by some writers on the intimacy which existed between Goethe and the duke, especially in the early years of his married life, the first wild weeks at Weimar being always brought forward in proof of the poet's bad influence over the young duke. Goethe, however, quickly tired of these extravagances, while his admiration for the beauty and character of the "Angel Louise" would have led him to throw the weight of his influence over the duke in her favour.

"Louise is an angel," he had written, in the early days of the betrothal of the young duchess. "Only the twinkling stars saw me pick up some flowers that she had worn on her breast, and put them away in my letter case, where many of the secrets of my heart are treasured."

CHAPTER VI

To Goethe the duke's invitation to Weimar had come at a moment when the natural love of change, which is, present always in youth, was accentuated by the termination of the "Lili" episode, which had plunged him into one of his tenderly melancholy moods. To this was added the strong liking, which he already had begun to entertain for the duke (a liking which was fully returned), while his admiration for the duchess's ideal beauty stirred the easily moved pulses of his heart. He was all eagerness for the visit. His mother always ready to second any plan of her beloved son, got ready his wardrobe; while *der alte* Goethe, a practised grumbler and a Radical to boot, looked askance at this friendship between his son and one of the scented and powdered aristocracy, to whom he bore an undying dislike. This dislike was accentuated by the recent fall of Voltaire from his high state as the intimate friend of Frederick the Great. In the end, however, the old man's opposition (which to say the truth was more grumble than reality) was got over, and, when the duke's letter of reminder arrived, all was settled. The duke had left at Strasbourg one of his gentlemen-in-waiting, Herr von Kalb; he was to wait there until a landau ordered by Karl August should be finished, and then come on to Frankfurt, where he would call for Goethe and bring him to Weimar. Goethe accordingly made all his preparations, said farewell to his friends, and packed up his belongings, including his finished, half-finished, and just-begun compositions, together with his own library, etc. All this showed that he contemplated a long visit; but probably he did not intend to stay a lifetime, as proved to be the case.

The day appointed for the journey arrived; but the evening came, the night closed in, and no landau, and no von Kalb appeared. Eight, nine, ten days followed, and still no one came, no one wrote. It was a distressing position, and young Goethe repented, both that he had been so hasty in packing, and so frank in telling his movements. It is amusing to read how this great mind could not resist a feeling of youthful shame, at being made the subject of a practical joke on the part of his friend Karl August. This was his father's view; the elder Goethe, being a republican at heart and a rich burgher to boot, held the poor and proud nobility in the greatest contempt. He was all anxiety to get his son safely away from those fine friends, who had treated him in so scurvy a manner, and was very free with his money (a somewhat rare event), encouraging his son to travel in Italy. Goethe, however, decided that he would go to Heidelberg, where he had a pleasant time, stopping in the house of a certain Fräulein Delph, who had been a confidante of his love for Lili. This confidence did not prevent him from engaging in a warm flirtation with Fräulein Buchwitz, the daughter of one of the best families in Heidelberg. He had serious thoughts of marrying her, and entering the service of the Elector of Mannheim; but this plan and Fräulein Buchwitz likewise were forgotten when, one evening on his return to his apartment, he saw lying on his bed a letter. It was from Frankfurt, and announced the arrival of von Kalb at last.

And now, how simple was the explanation, and how fortunate it was that mortification had not led him into the service of the Elector of Mannheim, and an uncongenial marriage.

"The expected one had waited for the new carriage day after day, hour by hour, as we waited day after day for him; then he had gone by Mannheim to Frankfurt, and there to his horror found that I had left. He had in all haste despatched an 'Estafette' with his hastily written letter, and implored me to come to Frankfurt at once, and not to put him to the shame of returning to Weimar without me. My grave hostess, Fräulein Delph, now came, and, when she heard I was contemplating departure, she made a scene, which I at last put an end to by sending my servant to order a post chaise. Then she would listen to nothing I said, but did all in her power to hinder me from packing. The trunks were carried down and placed in the chaise; all was ready; the postillion cracked his whip to show he was impatient to start. I extricated myself from her grasp, but still she tried to hold on to me. I cried out in the words of Egmont: 'Not a step further, for, see, the chariot of the sun awaits us; it holds our destiny, its wild steeds tear at the bridle. Let us hold on like grim death, for now we swerve to the right, now to the left, rushing over stones, rocks, and precipices, tumbling, crashing, rushing on wildly. Where we go none can tell.'"[38]

Poor Fräulein Buchwitz! We can imagine the scene that took place when Fräulein Delph had to announce next morning that the handsome lover and probable husband had vanished in the night time. Well, there is nothing new in the story, and poor Buchwitz had, doubtless, to console herself with another admirer. History, however, says nothing thereof.

While the poor damsel wept, the irresponsible Goethe was speeding back to Frankfurt, and, in spite of his father, who made a great scene, he carried his point, abandoned his journey to Italy, and set off that same evening with Von Kalb in the historic landau.

The travellers arrived at Weimar on 7 November 1775. No lodging having been provided for Goethe, he gladly accepted the hospitality offered by von Kalb's father, who held the post of President of the Chamber, and lived in the Topfel Market. There were two pretty sisters of Kalb's, one of whom, Charlotte (afterwards of the *bas bleu* coterie), was sufficiently pretty, charming and *spirituelle* to be made love to. Goethe's reputation, however, as a lady-killer had gone before him, and Charlotte was duly warned by her brother; but it does not appear that the warning had much effect.

On the day of his arrival Wieland was invited to dinner, in order to smooth over the little difference which had arisen the previous year, 1774, in consequence of Goethe's satirical attack on him in his humorous farce, *Gods, Heroes, and Wieland.*[39]

Wieland, writing to a friend (8 November) says:

"Goethe has arrived. How can I describe to you this *splendid* young man, or convey in a few words how my heart went out to him? I sat next to him at table, and since then I can think of nothing else. My mind is *full* of Goethe as a dewdrop is of the morning sun." Then he goes on to say: "This wonderful creature will, I think, remain longer with us than he first intended, and if it is so decreed that Weimar is ever to take a first place in the world of art and literature, it will be through Goethe's presence amongst us."

In the evening the royalties gave what was called a *free redoute*, that is a ball at the public rooms, for which the duke paid all expenses; and here the new arrival made his first appearance. Everyone of distinction, including the duke and the two duchesses, was present, from anxiety to see the celebrated writer of *Werther*.

The next day he was invited to dine at the Fürstenhaus, but as he was only a burgher's son he could not dine at the royal table. A seat was provided for him at a second table. This unavoidable slight was amply made up for by the reception he met later on from all the rank and fashion of Weimar. The ladies without exception desired to be presented to him, and he was introduced by Einsiedel, the chamberlain, to a crowd of lovely women.

Wolfgang Goethe's appearance at the period when he first appeared in Weimar was very striking. Only twenty-six years of age, he was tall and elegant in figure, with a wonderfully captivating air and manner — that is, when it pleased him to make a good impression. His forehead was high, his nose long, his lips full; his brilliant black eyes — wonderful eyes they were, in which much of his beauty lay — could at times be sad, loving, irresistible, at other moments haughty, bold, delightfully humorous; or, if his anger were roused, they could dart forth lightning and annihilating glances. Added to this, he possessed a full measure of bodily strength, was skilful in all manly exercises, and brimming over with the wildest and most youthful spirits. He was full of teasing tricks and inexhaustible nonsense, while the shafts of his ridicule and the keenness of his wit never flagged. Life had so far been for him a playground; he knew little or nothing of its graver issues. Everything smiled on him, and, with the exception of some love episodes, such as parting from Lili and the marriage of Lotte, he had never known a sorrow.

The appearance of this remarkable and handsome youth, the cool nonchalance, bordering almost on impertinence, of his manner, together with the superior air of genius which made itself felt, took the court of Weimar altogether by surprise; it carried them completely away. On *his* side he tells us he found himself in a strange company of people making up, as it were, a family party; not only highly born but highly educated people, whose tastes were all for art and literature, and who loved the art and literature of their own country. He was particularly struck by the youth of the court and the complete absence of strict etiquette that prevailed elsewhere; this freedom was due to the slackening by the Duchess Anna Amalia of those strict rules, which hedged in and regulated the courts of Europe in the eighteenth century.

Although Goethe was at Weimar in the character of the duke's guest only, his powerful personality soon made itself felt. Almost without an effort he assumed the role of leader, and gave, as it were, the tone to all that was going on in the court circle; and this superiority he maintained for years.

"Like a star which for some time has been hidden behind the clouds, he shoots forth refulgent," writes Knebel. "Every one hangs on his words, especially the ladies. He has a great deal of the spirit and manner which distinguishes his books, and this makes him doubly attractive." Knebel adds: "He is dressed *à la* Werther and many follow his example."

This was only a straw that showed the way the wind blew; but it was nevertheless a flattering compliment, that all the men of fashion in Weimar should have appeared in the fashion of the character Werther, in blue coats with brass buttons, yellow waistcoats, leather breeches, and top boots — the last being an extraordinary innovation, as heretofore it had been *de rigueur*, especially when ladies were present, that men should wear white silk stockings and shoes, boots being only permissible in bad weather. It was true that Karl August led the way, and perhaps the only exception was Wieland, who told Goethe that he was too old for such mummeries.

The first few weeks of Goethe's visit were spent in a wild tumult of gaiety, which went on "from early dawn until midnight." There were boar hunts, skating and sleighing parties, with and without masks; suppers and dances winding up the day's enjoyment. There was much talk about all that was going on, which was only natural in a small capital where the court circle was the cynosure of all eyes. The fierce light that beats upon a throne becomes under these circumstances a kind of searchlight. Under Goethe's guidance some of the members of the young duke's court indulged in pranks that made the townspeople open their eyes with amazement. Bertuch, Goethe, and Einsiedel set the example, sometimes changing clothes with tramps and beggars and realising a good wallet full of groschen. Another of these senseless jokes was for Goethe and Karl August to stand for hours in the market-place in Jena, cracking sledge whips for a wager. "Imagine," says Lewes, "a duke and a poet thus engaged!" In this way Goethe nearly put out one of his eyes.

Goethe, who describes himself as, up to this time, suffering from the separation from his beloved Lili, began now to feel a new emotion rising in his heart. Under its influence he writes to a female friend:

"At last I am beginning to flirt again, which is a sign of improvement. Love-making is, under such circumstances, the only palliative for suffering like mine. I tell lies and swear constancy to every pretty girl I meet, and I have the faculty of believing for the moment that every word I say is true."

It was on a visit he paid to the Steins at their country place, Kochberg, that the revival began to take place, although he could not bear the dullness of the place in which this fair creature lived. He forgot her, however, in the distraction of a delightful visit to Erfurt, the district over which Herr von Dalberg presided. With him and Wieland he spent three delightful days in the house of a certain Frau von Keller, whose daughter was the original of Wieland's Psyche.

Also, he pays devoted court to the two duchesses. The young Louise is to him "an angelic vision"; he treasures a rose that falls from her dress, and is deeply vexed that her statue-like coldness will not kindle into some warmth for that good fellow, her husband. The superior intellect of Anna Amalia he at once recognised, and her *gaieté de cœur* charms him. The boiling point is reached when the two Stolbergs, old friends of Goethe, arrive at Weimar, and the fun grows fast and furious. Being noble, they can sit at the ducal table, one on each side of the newly married duchess.

"She is an excellent woman, has the sense of an angel as well as the face of one, and in spite of her outward coldness, she has the warmest and best heart in the world." So writes Fritz von Stolberg to his sister, the Countess Bernstorf, who later on became lady-in-waiting and proved an acquisition. Stolberg adds, "*Engel Luischen* is angelic. The dowager duchess is a very pretty woman, not more than thirty-six. She is clever and dignified, her eyes full of kindness, very unlike some royal persons who wrap themselves up in a cloak of dignity. She is charming in conversation, talks well, has a very fine wit and knows how to say a pleasant thing in the best possible manner. Prince Constantine is a very good fellow. A certain Frau von Stein, wife to the master of the horse, is a pretty little person. We are on a very pleasant footing at her house: it suits us admirably, and they seem to like us."

Here is another account in which the dowager duchess figures.

"The duke and the *Statthalter* of Erfurt,[40] an excellent fellow, with Goethe, and several of the suite, came to dine with us. When we had finished all the good things, the door suddenly was opened, and lo, and behold! who should come in but the duchess dowager and the Frau von Stein, both looking very majestic. They carried each a sword three feet in length, which they had taken out of the armoury, and they came, if you please, to knight us all. We fell in with the joke and kept our seats with great gravity, while the two ladies went round the table laying the sword on each man's shoulder, which they did very prettily. After the table was cleared we played at blind court.[41] Fritz (von Stolberg) is fascinated by the deformed little Göchhausen, whose liveliness and good-heartedness animates her whole being to the tips of her fingers."

When the two young men left Weimar, the elder one carried in his pocket his appointment as gentleman-in-waiting to the duke; but, as we already know, he was not allowed to accept the post.

The sledge parties, which took place by torchlight, were a source of great gossip amongst the townsfolk, who, of course, were not allowed to share in these amusements. The Hussars (the duke's own regiment) had to stand for hours holding the torches, there being no other method of giving light. This, however, did not scandalise the public mind so much as the dances given on the ice, in which the dancers were all masked, the masks being of the most hideous description — in fact, a sort of revival of the ancient satiric masks. In addition to these revels there were the amusements in which Karl August took special delight; such as races, and hunts at breakneck speed, pig-sticking, and the mad midnight rides, [42] jumping ditches, stone walls, everything that came in the way, regardless of danger to life and limb.

"We are somewhat mad here," Goethe writes to Merck, "and play the devil's game." Wieland, although still enraptured with the splendid youth of the stranger, is obliged to acknowledge that some of his doings are outrageous. All ceremony was abolished between Goethe and Karl August. They called one another by the brotherly "Du"; each confided to the other the inmost secrets of his heart. Goethe seems to have been carried away by the novelty of the position in which he found himself. He was most to blame. Writing to Knebel, who was at Tiefurt, Goethe announces that his friends, the Stolbergs, and Karl August are "coming next day." "We shall be seven in all," he writes, "the most extraordinary party that ever sat round a dinner table. Make no fuss about us, and treat us with no ceremony." [43]

There was considerable gossip about these lawless feasts, where drinking and carousing was carried beyond the ordinary limits recognised in a lax age. At one of these feasts, given in the Fürstenhaus (under Bertuch's supervision), [44] the proceedings began by all the glasses being thrown out of the window. They were replaced by skulls which were brought from an adjacent churchyard. Fritz Stolberg, holding one of these skulls in his hand, made a pathetic funeral oration on the cranium of a true German, whose health was drunk in bumpers.

The noise made by these orgies, especially after the arrival of the Stolbergs, travelled far and near, and, no doubt, they lost nothing in enormity from the different additions made by the gossips. Klopstock, who knew the reputation of these men, thought it his duty to write to Goethe a most characteristic letter of remonstrance and good advice, in which he with an astonishing lack of *savoir faire*, introduces the name of the Duchess Louise.

"The duchess," he says, "is almost masculine in her power of self-control, therefore she will suffer in silence and hide her sorrow. But this grief will eat into her heart and will wear her down. Goethe, think of it! the *heart of Louise* is sore with grief."

It must be acknowledged that for anyone to write *unauthorised* in such language of a matter so sacred as the relations between the duke and his wife, passed the limits of ordinary interference, and we are not surprised that Goethe's answer should be cold and concise.

"Pray for the future, dear Klopstock, spare us such letters; they do no good, and are quite superfluous. What answer can I make? None. For either I must cry *peccavi* like a schoolboy, frame some sophistical excuse, or, like an honest fellow, defend myself. I might have a mixture of all three, which would go nearest to the truth, and what use would it be? Therefore, let us have no more about this matter. You may believe me that, if I were to attend to all such warnings and read all the letters of gratuitous advice sent me, I would not have a moment to myself. The duke was for a moment grieved that this one came from Klopstock, for he loves and respects you. For the rest, we hope to see Stolberg. We are not worse, and, please God, not better than when he last saw us.

"GOETHE."

In great wrath Klopstock replied:

"You are not deserving of the *great* proof I gave you of my friendship. It was great because I, unasked and most unwillingly, mixed myself up in a matter which did not personally concern me; and since you throw away 'all such letters and refuse to listen to gratuitous advice' (I quote your own words) you have as a matter of course thrown away mine. I therefore beg to tell you that you are quite unworthy of the proof I gave you of my friendship. Stolberg shall not return to you if words of mine can prevent him, or, rather, if he listens to his own conscience."

These letters give us an idea of the reports that were circulating as to the reputation of the Court of Weimar, and enable us to realise how Goethe's character suffered in consequence.[45] Count Görtz, who was naturally jealous of the newcomer's influence over Karl August, painted him in the blackest colours, as did also his coadjutor in Erfurt, Count Dalberg, although the latter was on terms of confidential friendship with both the duke and Goethe.

"We hear strange tales of this singular man," writes Merck to the bookseller Nicolai; "a book could be written upon all his follies and mad pranks. These have all been confided to me by his own townspeople in Frankfurt, and for three miles round they talk of nothing else. If it were all true what they say — which it is not, God be thanked! — he would long since have forfeited his rights as a citizen, but there is not an iota of truth in these tales. He is full of high spirits, but quite incapable of any wickedness."

All these evil reports got about through people writing to one another and talking to one another, — in fact, gossiping by pen and word of mouth, as we gossip now-a-days, though now not nearly so much by letter (I wish we did, and there would be a chance of good memoirs in the distant future) as over tea-cups in the afternoon.

There was a certain gentleman by name Claudius, who lived in Darmstadt. He writes to Herder, that — "there are funny reports from Weimar." I am at a loss, I confess, to discover the object of this remark, or why it should be quoted by German writers, it is so very indefinite; and why connect it with Goethe? Zimmermann, however, who writes from Hanover, is much clearer, and dots his i's and crosses his t's when he sends a piece of scandal. "We have here now," he says, "a certain Herr and Frau von Verlepsch; the last-named is full of gossip about Weimar. If all is true that she relates, it is enough to make one's hair stand on end." He then goes on to communicate some particulars which have come to him through a lady, Goethe's *most intimate friend*. We can easily guess that this friend was Frau von Stein, wife to Herr von Stein, who was Karl August's gentleman-in-waiting. This lady, years before, had excited in Zimmermann a tender interest, of the same platonic character as her later friendship with Goethe. I cannot think Frau von Stein acted loyally in writing as she did to her old admirer of her new friend, but one has only to look at her face and see what sort of woman she was. Her letter, however, although interesting as a pen portrait, is not very reliable.

"Goethe," she says, "has caused a social earthquake here. It will require all his genius to restore the chaos to order. It is quite certain that he has excellent intentions, but he is too young and too inexperienced to manage such an imbroglio. However, we must wait for the end. Meantime all our happiness here has disappeared; our court is no longer what it was — a ruler discontented with himself and with all the world, every day imperilling his life, having only a minimum of bodily strength to rely on, a brother still more weakened, a disappointed mother, a discontented wife — a *tout ensemble* of excellent people who do not suit one another, and are therefore an unhappy family."

Zimmermann considers that his fair correspondent takes rather too lenient a view of the situation, her leniency being prompted by her partiality for the chief offender. He knows that the Duchess Louise complains bitterly to her sister at Karlsruhe of the neglect of Karl August; still the doctor himself takes a lenient view of Goethe, who perhaps deserves "praise instead of curses," and in any case genius like his is not to be trammelled by the law that governs inferior mortals.

This letter of Zimmermann's has a certain importance, as it strikes the keynote of the whole situation. Jealousy, that most common of all vices, was at work in poor Louise's heart. When she wrote her complaints to Karlsruhe one would sympathise to a certain extent with the young wife, but for the fact that we know how Goethe admired "the angel Louise." Later on she found this out and recognised that she had no warmer friend. But the baser form of jealousy, that which does not spring from wounded affection, but from an envious nature which grudges that those who merit success should receive their proper reward, now took possession of the hearts of nobles and courtiers. They had seized every opportunity to make much of the handsome, witty, clever guest of the duke, in order to curry favour with Karl August by so doing. They supposed that the stranger was only a bird of passage, who could not interfere with their plans and projects.

But later the courtiers began to look with distrust and jealousy on the close friendship between the newcomer and the duke. There was no talk of his visit coming to a close. Their spirits were somewhat cheered when Goethe, whose poetic temperament was beginning to weary of the constant scenes of dissipation, "the masking, skating, hunting, drinking and dicing," grew impatient for the serenity of solitude; he felt a longing to escape from the *hot air* of society, and to enjoy the company of simple country folk, so he went on a solitary excursion to Waldeck. He was speedily recalled by the duke, who found life dull without the companionship of his new friend.

His return was not welcome to his enemies, who were hoping that some fortuitous circumstance would put an end to the new friendship; but in this they were doomed to disappointment. His absence had made Karl August only eager to secure the constant presence of his friend. Soon it was observed that a change had taken place in both young men; there was no more of the unbridled orgies of the first wild weeks. Goethe had drained the cup of pleasure to the lees, and now his magnificent intellect craved for a wider sphere. He would be a ruler of men.

But here it must be owned we are, in reading his biographies, confronted with a strange fact, for which no explanation at all satisfactory can be offered. What was the powerful charm that attracted and, as it were, bound Goethe in a life-long embrace to this insignificant little town, situated in the far-away Thuringian mountains? He, who could have made a figure in the great theatre of the world, to be content with so narrow a circle! It was not altogether his newly born friendship for Karl August (although this was a genuine sentiment on his part), neither was it any newly awakened interest in Weimar itself, nor any tender feeling towards a woman (that was to come later). It was, in the first place, the power, which was a remarkable feature of Goethe's character, of conquering all obstacles that might present themselves under new circumstances, and having once mastered the situation, he found it impossible to detach himself again from the spot where he had, as it were, taken root, and in a short time he became part and parcel of the place. Perhaps the best explanation of the problem is to be found in Goethe's own words: "My situation here is advantageous enough, and the Duchy of Weimar and Eisenach is a stage upon which I can experiment as to my capacity for playing my part on a larger platform." That he never sought that larger platform, but lived and died in Weimar, is a matter of history.

It seems, on looking at the subject from different points of view, that Goethe was by no means unprepared for the position offered to him by Karl August. So far back as the meeting at Mainz, offers had been made to him, and the journey to Weimar was not only to make a friendly visit, but also to reconnoitre the "*terrain.*" The duke, who every day grew more attached to his new friend, pressed him constantly to accept some post in the administration; and so early as 1776 Goethe wrote to his friends at Frankfurt: "You will soon hear that I have begun to make a figure on the *theatrum mundi*." He was, in fact, a member of Karl August's Privy Council (Geheimerath) long before he received the title, Wieland tells us, adding, — "Goethe will never get away from here; Karl August can neither swim nor wade without his help."

We must now return to Goethe and the political crisis. Much as the young politician was tempted by ambition and pressed by his royal friend, he would not bind himself to any decided action before he had thoroughly learned the work that lay before him. Hence came the apparently sudden fit of devotion to work, which showed itself by constant presence at the council meetings, no one understanding what brought him there. If one could have looked into his mind, one would have seen that he was trying with all the strength of his will to find some way in which to reconcile his acceptance of office as royal adviser with that freedom of opinion which he held to be every true man's, and especially every poet's, birthright.

"Freedom of opinion and a competency are to be the first conditions of the new arrangements," he explains to Merck; a fact that is proved by the agreement between the duke and the young Goethe, which von Kalb brought to Frankfurt for the approval of the parents, for it was necessary, by the laws of Germany, that their written consent should be obtained. The declaration or proposal made by Karl August contains some remarkable passages, if we take into account that the writer was only nineteen years of age.

"When a man of such genius as Goethe diverts his extraordinary talents into a different and unaccustomed channel, he is not misusing his great gifts, and as to the fallacy put forward that, through his entering public life deserving statesmen were thrust aside and contemned, I deny this emphatically. My resolve was taken on the day I succeeded to the position I hold, that I should never bestow the post of ministerial adviser — a post which brings the holder thereof into such close contact with myself, and which is so intimately connected for good or evil with the interests of the people — upon any but a person in whom I could place absolute confidence, and this confidence I feel I can bestow on Dr. Goethe."

That this declaration, or protocol, which goes into close details unnecessary to reproduce, was the unassisted product of the young duke's mind, is hard to credit, and there are turns of expression which would be to some undoubted evidence of the influence of an older and more able man.

Moreover, there is ample evidence in the letters and papers in the Goethe *archiv* to prove that, from the first day when Knebel introduced the two princes to Goethe, the personality of the great German writer took hold of Karl August, who was attracted, not so much by the appearance of this "splendid young man" as by his wonderful mental powers, which, as it were, dominated and electrified the young duke.

The influence once gained lasted (with slight checks now and again) the lifetime of the duke. On his side Goethe must be credited with sincerity of purpose. His influence in no way resembled that possessed over King Louis of Bavaria by Wagner, whose aim, at least in the beginning, was to secure for himself the light and luxury for which he craved. Goethe's influence was elevating, not deteriorating. We know from his writings that in the very early days of Goethe's visit to Weimar, in the midst of a whirlpool of amusements, the two friends, duke and poet, whose united ages did not amount, to forty-seven years, had long and earnest conversations on the subjects of administration and practical government, and plans, which later came to fruition, were sketched for the advancement of science and the amelioration of the poorer classes.

Goethe often expressed to his intimate friends his joy that the duke held the same opinions on many subjects as he did. He was full of hope that, later on, he could mould the mind of his friend, and bring him to see the evils that abounded in every part of the administration; he cherished the hope that Karl August would prove an ideal ruler, that Weimar, emancipated from the burdens laid upon it by bad laws and weak government, would become a typical example of peace and prosperity.

There can be little doubt that something of the changes about to be made had filtered out through different channels and had filled the minds of those already in office with dismay, while the general feeling was one of indignation that a burgher's son from Frankfurt should push his way into the select circle reserved for the ancient nobility of Thuringia.

Knowing the value set upon titles by these aristocrats, Karl August conferred the dignity of the ennobling "Von" on his friend, an honour which cannot have been greatly prized by the son of a staunch republican, who was himself before all things democratic. It was Anna Amalia who induced the young poet to accept the honour, which failed to make "*a Goethe*" acceptable to a "*contemptible and brainless nobility*." The brainless nobility, however, were right in scenting danger, the conferring of the title being only the prelude to fresh honours for the plebeian Frankfürter.

Soon came the announcement that Dr. Von Goethe had been made Geheimerath, or Minister, with a seat in the Privy Council and a salary of one thousand two hundred thalers yearly. "This stranger, a poet by profession, twenty-six years of age, who drew the duke into all manner of dissipation and who danced at fairs with the village girls! Shameful! Intolerable! Scandalous!" shrieked the hysterical courtiers. Even Minister von Fritsch lost his sedate dignity, and for once forgot himself so far as to show his inner feelings of jealousy and discontent.

In an angry letter to Anna Amalia he pours out his indignation: "Are old men who have served the country well and given their best abilities to Your Royal Highness, to walk after this Tasso Goethe?"

It was in answer to this that Karl August wrote his well-known and most generous defence of his friend, "in whose honour and honesty he had unalterable and everlasting faith."

On this Fritsch wrote to the duke tendering his resignation.

"The man who enjoys the honourable and distinguished position of Minister must naturally be in constant communication with your person, and in evidence at your court. How could I fill such a post; I who possess no courtier-like polish, whose manners are rough and tinged with a gravity that makes me appear unbending and deficient in those graces which are necessary for a courtier? I cannot help thinking that both my character and my increasing years render me quite unfit to occupy my present office about your highness, and I beg you to receive my resignation."

Karl August showed the minister's letter to his mother, and asked her to soothe Minister von Fritsch's little fit of temper. Amalia, therefore, wrote a letter well calculated to throw oil on the troubled waters:

"Is it possible that you would desert my son at the moment when he has most need of you? And are your reasons for so doing worthy of you? I think not. You are prejudiced against Goethe, whom you know only through false and mischievous reports. You understand well how my every thought is centred upon my son, and how it has always been my strongest desire, and still continues to be my one ambition, that he should have about him men capable of teaching him how to govern the country and people committed to his care. If I believed that Goethe, instead of possessing such qualities, was one of those crawling creatures who only think of their own advantage, I should be the first to use my influence against him. I will say nothing to you of his talents, of his genius; but, apart from them, the opinions he holds should teach him to do his best to make others happy. But let us talk no more of Goethe, but of you, and let me tell you that *your religion* and *your conscience* alike forbid you to desert your prince. Look for a moment into yourself. I am sure, indeed I know, that you are grateful. I beseech you to show your gratitude now and also your affection for me by not deserting my son at this moment, and under these circumstances I ask you to do this as much for your own sake as for that of my son.

"I am, with the sincerest regard,

"Your sincere friend,

"AMALIA."

Who could read such a letter as this and remain deaf to such sweet womanly words? Fritsch continued to act the part of a faithful friend and adviser to Karl August for twenty-four years. It is somewhat surprising (and decidedly unusual) to find that Fritsch, who had been in the ministry since Karl August's birth, should have settled down comfortably with "Tasso Goethe," and is a distinct proof of the cleverness with which Goethe managed to steer clear of the different shoals that beset a man raised suddenly to so high a position. The Goethe *archiv* possesses a portfolio containing the correspondence between Goethe and Fritsch which extends over many years, and is of the most friendly character.

Karl August showed his gratitude to his old friend and minister, by giving him a grant of fifteen hundred thalers; in this manner the danger of a split in the cabinet was dexterously averted. There still remained Count Görtz, the duke's former governor, whose influence, as we know, had been supreme. Of late, however, a change had come over Karl August, who no longer saw through Görtz's spectacles. As was only natural, the former governor was loath to lose his power.

Goethe's influence was much too strong for Görtz to contend with, and soon we hear of his tendering his resignation, and withdrawing from the court into private life. Later he took office under Prussia.

The famous French politician, Talleyrand, when in any perplexity, quoted the well-known proverb *Cherchez la femme* and acting on this we shall now seek the woman whose hand helped to steer the course of Goethe's future life. No one can say it was a bad course; it led to much intellectual progress; it made Weimar the centre of all that was most distinguished in art and literature; it brought to perfection the gifts of men like Herder, Wieland, Schiller, besides others of less mark. And yet all this was brought about by the influence of one woman — by no means a woman of intellectual power, but a woman well adapted to charm and fascinate such a nature as Goethe's.

This woman was Charlotte von Stein. It was undoubtedly her influence which made of the great poet a truly great man. He ceased his habit of flirting, now with one now with another, and rested peacefully (at least for a few years), content with his love for Charlotte although she was considerably his senior. Sometimes, during the first months of their intimacy, his letters were of the warmest; but the lady understood how to administer a douche of cold water, if her lover went too far. He wrote to her daily, sometimes twice a day, and when away, invariably sent an *estafette* with his daily letter. Truly his constancy was admirable. Still, it must be remembered that there was a husband.

The Master of the Horse,[46] however, was well acquainted with the character of his Charlotte, and never for a moment had any fear lest she should be carried away by a gust of passion, to forget that she was his wife, and the mother of his son, who was ten years old when Goethe became a friend of the family. For many years Fritz was to him like his own son, and lived altogether with him. A recent writer, commenting on this curious episode, says that this love-story, as it existed between the years 1776 to 1786, is almost a poetic idyll.

Charlotte Ernestine von Schardt, was born in December 1742. As the daughter of Schardt, the then master of the ceremonies, she had grown up in the court circle, at that time presided over by the beautiful Charlotte of Bayreuth, who had married the eccentric, half-crazy Duke of Saxe-Weimar. Even in her childhood Charlotte Schardt was sentimentally inclined, and we are told preferred "gazing at the stars to playing with her doll." As she grew up she developed a strain of romanticism — a feature of the age, which was cultivated as a sort of religion by some high-strung romanticists. Her education tended likewise in the direction of sentimentalism, so did her whole air and manner. Beautiful she was not, in the strict sense of the word, but her sad eyes, large and lustrous, looked out on the world with the appealing expression of one who sought rest somewhere, but could not find her heart's desire. Her whole air was that of one ever seeking and always misunderstood. Like the other members of her family, as soon as she was of proper age, a place was found for her at the court.

Charlotte, who was one of many sisters, most of whom had found husbands in the court circle, was early trained to the duties of lady-in-waiting. She could read aloud, play the harpsichord, sing in a tender voice sad music, which suited her sad eyes, and she understood well how to flatter and how to flirt. In an incredibly short space of time she attracted one of the best *partis* of the court circle, namely, Gottlieb Ernst Josias Friedrich von Stein, who was sprung from a noble house. As in those days girls had little chance of marrying the lover of their choice, Charlotte, without murmuring, agreed to accept the first suitor that came in her way, and was married off hand to a man for whom she not only felt no love, but later grew to dislike. Seven children were born to her, of whom several died, and her health suffering in consequence, she went to the baths of Pyrmont, where she met Zimmermann, who for a short period occupied the position later filled by Goethe. In fact, it was this first platonic friend who directed her attention to the rising genius, by advising her to read *Götz von Berlichingen*. She corresponded for years with Zimmermann, and expressed to him her admiration for Werther and, his sorrows. Her husband, when he visited Frankfurt with Count Görtz, made the young poet's acquaintance, but previous to this we find Zimmerman writing to his dear fragile friend:

"Wherever I have been lately (and I have visited amongst other places, Frankfurt and Geneva), I have taken the opportunity to mention your name."

This rather curious method of puffing was evidently done at the fair Stein's suggestion, or, at all events, it was pleasing to her to be so advertised. But the *friend* goes further.

"At Strasbourg I met Goethe (who was returning from Switzerland, where he had been travelling with the Stolbergs), and showed him amidst a hundred other silhouettes, the one you sent me of yourself. He wrote underneath: 'It would be a wonderful spectacle to watch how the world is mirrored in this soul, which can only form its judgments through the medium of love, for its only guide is tenderness.'" (This was a very bad shot, for of all the cold-blooded flirts this Charlotte was one.) "Never," continues friend Zimmermann, "was there a better piece of character reading from a silhouette, and you, gracious lady, must acknowledge the truth of the words. I stopped during my stay at Frankfurt with the old Goethe. The son is one of the most extraordinary and the most gifted of geniuses that have been produced here below. He tells me that he will without doubt visit Weimar. And you will bear in mind that all I told him at Strasbourg about you kept him awake three whole nights!"

These hundred silhouettes were intended for Lavater's great work on physiognomy; also to demonstrate how far the features of the face corresponded with the character. Goethe wrote for Lavater under the silhouette of Charlotte von Stein: "Firmness, courteous persistence in one course, amiable, agreeable, submissive; naïve, very self-complacent, and fond of talking of herself; benevolent and true-hearted; conquers generally by tears."

We are at liberty to draw our own conclusions as to how much Zimmermann's revelations of what he knew of the fair Stein's character had to do with Goethe's wonderful skill in physiognomy.

It was only natural that all this talk induced Charlotte's attention to fix itself upon the young reader of her character. She had accompanied the Duchess Amalia, when she went to Ilmenau to meet the two princes on their return from their tour, and she heard the account they had given of the young poet, of whom they and Knebel never ceased talking. Also the Duchess Louise, who had made Goethe's acquaintance, spoke to her dear Charlotte of this wonderful young man, whose tender regard for herself she had (with a woman's quick perception) doubtless noticed. She may have felt the interest even a good wife sometimes cannot help feeling towards one who has to fight against an unfortunate attachment to herself. And so it was that before Wolfgang came to Weimar these two women were interested in him, talked of him to one another, and looked forward to his arrival.

During the first years of this strange friendship Goethe went to Charlotte every day, and some of his letters are burning with love, others exceedingly prosaic. Here is a slight selection taken at haphazard: "Good morning. Here is asparagus. How were you yesterday? Philip baked me a cake, and thereupon wrapped up in my blue cloak, I laid myself upon a dry corner of the terrace and slept amid thunder, lightning, and rain, so gloriously that my bed was afterwards quite disagreeable." Again he writes: "Thanks for the breakfast. I send you something in return. Last night I slept on the terrace wrapped in my blue cloak, awoke three times at twelve, two, and four, and each time there was a new splendour in the heavens."

Of course there are others of a much warmer character — and occasionally there are explosions of jealousy, for Frau von Stein had a choice of admirers. Von Knebel, who in later years seems to have burned his elderly wings fluttering round the lady, describes her as a sweet excellent woman, for whom nature supplies the want of passion which she does not comprehend. And again he finds in conversations with Frau von Stein the greatest *nourishment* (a curious expression). He assures his sister the dear woman is "absolutely *free* from any kind of coquetry, is well educated, and has a decided knowledge of art," from which we may assume with certainty that she had admired his, Knebel's, feeble water colours.

There can be no doubt, however, of the strict propriety of her conduct, and through it she kept her hold on her admirers' affections for many years.

The daily correspondence between Charlotte and her admirer is one of the most extraordinary on record, and has its counterpart in Merimée's letters to his unknown fair one.

Charlotte von Stein will live in story so long as the great genius of Goethe continues to fascinate those who study his wonderful masterpieces. The singular charm exerted by this woman, who possessed neither the attractions of youth nor of extraordinary beauty, and whose intelligence was but second-rate, must, however, remain a mystery. "Frau von Stein wearies me with her talk of what she knows nothing about," says Anna Amalia, and from what contemporary writers tell there seems to have been good ground for the complaint. Goethe himself found it hard to explain the power this woman eight years his senior exercised over him.

"I can only explain," he writes to Wieland, "the power she exercises over me, by the theory of the transmigration of souls. Yes, we were, we must have been, formerly man and wife. Now, I can find no name for us."

The curious comments of Charlotte's son, Frederick von Stein, form one of the strangest features of this remarkable history. The correspondence, he remarks, between his mother and Goethe, while it proves that emotions, even dangerous in their warmth, were not far distant from their intercourse, also serves to place in a still stronger light the virtue and prudence of a woman who, while keeping her young, gifted and ardent lover within the limits of *strict reserve*, contrived to console him in all his trials, both mental and material, by her sincere sympathy as well as by her soothing protestations of sincere and lasting friendship. German writers speak with enthusiasm of this tender, poetical love idyll, which lasted in its first fervour for ten long years. It received its first blow when Goethe went on his visit to Italy, the correspondence dwindling to letters once a week. When he married Christiane Vulpius, the tender idyllic Charlotte let the mask drop, and abused him like a fishwife.

The house where Charlotte von Stein lived practically alone (for her son tells us that his father came only once a week to visit his family) is a large stone-fronted mansion — such as house agents love to describe by the term "residential." It now makes one of four or five handsome houses, but in the days when Charlotte lived there it stood alone in a large garden with magnificent trees, which formed a sort of curtain between Charlotte and Wolfgang, whose little house in the park was within twenty minutes' walk.

The great beauty of Weimar was, and still is, its lovely park, than which there can be nothing in nature more beautiful. Once seen it can never be forgotten, for it recalls hours and even days of exquisite enjoyment. Anyone who has wandered through its sunny walks and winding shades, watching its changing beauties, from the fullness of summer to the lovely tints of autumn, then deepening again into winter, will easily understand how Goethe could have been content to live in so small a city which had, beside its *nest* of friends, so charming a park. It was, indeed, mainly his own creation, and filled a large space in his life. The walks in the park are so numerous that it is difficult to make a choice, but I own to a predilection for the pleasant stroll which begins by crossing the bridge over the Stern which leads away from the palace. Here we have some magnificent trees, splendid giants which look upon us miserable pigmies with the silent contempt of their long experience. We walk humbly under their protection from the burning sun till we come to Goethe's Garden-house, where he lived for seven years.

A little further on, in one of the loveliest spots, "made picturesque" by the grouping of the trees, chief among which is the brilliant mountain ash "with berries red as coral hanging in clusters," stands the Borkenhaus (Bark House), which was erected by Goethe for a *fête* of the duchess, and which later was often occupied by the duke, who was attracted by the situation of this retreat, resting as it does against a moss-covered rock. Its solitude engenders the dreamy sensation of past and present mingling together, a feeling which is here intensified by the flowing waters of the Ilm, as they run their lazy and rather useless course close by.

The park was the scene of many of those open-air *fêtes* organised by Goethe for the gratification of his patron and friend, Karl August, and also as a homage to the Duchess Louise, for whom he had an enthusiastic and chivalrous admiration. The Luisen-Klause or (Louise's Hermitage), which later went by the name of the Borkenhaus, was a tribute to the lady of his devotion. Goethe wished to honour the duchess's birthday, on 25 August 1778, by an open-air *fête* in the park, in which a dramatic representation was to be included; some nights before a great storm arose, in consequence of which the Ilm overflowed its banks and destroyed all chance of an open-air performance.

Nothing daunted, Goethe, without saying a word of his purpose, set to work, and put workmen to hollow out a portion of the overhanging crag. Three days and nights were occupied in this task, which escaped the notice of the tattling Weimarites; and, lo and behold! there suddenly appeared as if by enchantment a charming moss-covered cottage with two windows and a little charming wooden balcony, with a stone staircase leading up to it. Here the duchess and all the court were received by Goethe as Pater Decorator, surrounded by a body of monks. The guests were then conducted into the first room, "where saucers of *kalzbeer*" were offered to them, which they drank with iron spoons. Suddenly music was heard; a door at the back flew open and disclosed a splendid banquet.

Goethe delighted in these festivals, which were much to the taste of the duke and duchess. Duke Karl was very partial to the little Borkenhaus, which was soon made into a cosy nook. A shady row of trees concealed it from general observation. By means of a bell the cottage was brought into communication with the arsenal, where troops were quartered; and when this was done a bedroom was added for the use of Karl August.

At the Borkenhaus the duke often received his ministers, and here he spent many pleasant hours with Goethe and other intimate friends. From the roof of the Borkenhaus Goethe's tiny hut or cottage was visible. To this tiny dwelling-house the poet, when he first came to Weimar, took an extraordinary fancy. It was not the dwelling itself, so much as the lovely but neglected garden, which was to the poetic mind of the young man a joy for ever. He must possess it or die. The only obstacle in the way was that it already belonged to Bertuch, who had been for years keeper of the duke's privy purse. To Bertuch Karl August said: "I must have your garden; I cannot help it, for Goethe wants to have it; he says he cannot live without it." Bertuch, in true courtier fashion made no protest, and in return for his complaisance received some land elsewhere. This story, however, which has been repeated in a dozen biographies, is contradicted by a recent writer, and the contradiction is supported by an entry in Bertuch's account book: "1,294 thaler 16 groschen for the purchase of the garden, bought for the hon^{ble} Minister of Legations, Herr von Goethe."[47]

The situation of Goethe's that was simply perfect. The town, although so close, was completely shut out from view by the thick growing trees — it was a perfect solitude, and yet there were now and again tokens that the giddy world was close at hand. The church bells ringing out, or the music from the barracks, or the screaming of the peacocks in the park.

The joy of his life Goethe calls his little garden. He cultivated it himself with the help of Philip, his man-servant. Entries in his diary, which it would take too long to quote here, are full of his joy and content with the duke's present.

Goethe lived in this house for seven years. He loved its solitude, and when he wished the luxury of being undisturbed, he locked "all the gates of the lodges which led from the town so that," Wieland complains, "no one can get at him except by the aid of picklocks and crowbars." Here the duke came often, sitting up till late in the night in earnest discussion, often sleeping on the sofa instead of going home. Here both duke and duchess would come to dine in the most simple, unpretending way, the whole banquet on one occasion consisting, as we learn from a casual expression in the Stein correspondence, of some cold meat and soup.

He often had visits from Anna Amalia and the Frau von Stein. The latter took great interest apparently in the study of botany; she, however, never came unattended. Either her husband was of the party or her children, or sometimes her brother, and her two friends the Iltens.

Anna Amalia, when she visited Goethe's garden, sometimes remained the whole afternoon. "The Duchess Amalia and the prince were in excellent humour," writes Goethe in his diary, "and I offered so much hospitality that, when they were all gone, I was glad to eat a bit of cold meat and to talk with Philip about his world and my world. And now I am tired and shall go to bed, and I hope to sleep till I awake refreshed. Goodnight. It is near eleven o'clock. I have drawn the plan of an English garden. It is a grand sensation to be alone with nature;[48] tomorrow morning it will be lovely."

In 1794 Karl August, after his return from his tour in Italy, erected a more ambitious residence in the park. This was the Römische Haus (Roman Villa), which was begun in 1794 and finished 1799. It was called by the people of Weimar "the house over the cold kitchen." In structure it is in a semi-Italian style of architecture, and is ornamented by many statues, copies from those in the Roman palaces.

Karl August was buried here by his own desire.

CHAPTER VII

Anna Amalia's interference in the affair of Fritsch's retirement was her last political act. From the time that Goethe became minister, Karl August turned altogether to him for advice. The duchess, who had the highest opinion of Goethe's capacity for administration, was well pleased to see her son in such safe hands, and with great wisdom abstained from all interference. For the rest, she had long desired to be freed from state affairs, and to have leisure for the intellectual and artistic pursuits which were more to her taste than politics or public business, which latter she had undertaken in the interest of her son. Already, when in the flower of her youth, she had shown a marked taste for retirement, in order to devote herself to the study of the great lessons which nature teaches to those who are willing to learn. And now that she was free from the trammels of government, she arranged a plan of life which, although it was not that of a recluse, gave her ample time to gratify her love of art and to drink deeper of the great well of knowledge; for Amalia had a large mind, ready to embrace all subjects which had to do with nature in its very widest sense. Nor was her life by any means retired or solitary.

A woman of her energetic disposition, and gifted as she was with social qualities of a high order, and a capacity for enjoying life to the fullest extent, was not likely to hide her light under a bushel. On the contrary, she collected round her a circle of men and women whose names are a sufficient indication of their claim to a high place in literature and art, and of this gifted circle she was the moving spirit. No one knew better than Anna Amalia how to hold this wonderful collection of savants and wits together, and how to make each one contribute his or her part in a constant and delightful interchange of social gifts. The only circle which could approach to the Weimar *coterie* was the gathering of men and women, remarkable in their different capacities, which assembled at Luxemburg in the early part of the last century, under the guidance of the gifted Sophie Charlotte of Prussia,

It will be remembered that, at the time the Residenz Schloss was consumed by fire, Minister von Fritsch offered his newly built mansion[49] which stood at the corner of the Esplanade, to his royal mistress as a dower house. This offer Anna Amalia accepted, and until her death occupied the "Casa Santa," which was the name given by Wieland to the *Witthumshaus*. It is a commodious and handsome residence; there is a broad staircase and a wide corridor, which leads to the principal sitting-rooms, and a spacious reception salon, on the walls of which hang the portraits of the members of the royal families of Brunswick and of Berlin. This apartment opens into the red sitting-room, which takes its name from the colour of the rich damask hangings and furniture. Here the duchess held her symposium — or rather one should say her round table — not of strong Arthurian knights, but of highly intellectual men and women. This circle generally assembled on a Friday evening.

The importance of the social influence exercised by the personality of Anna Amalia must not be forgotten, when we consider the wonderful galaxy of distinguished men and women who were drawn to Weimar, and gave to the little duchy the name of the Modern Athens. We have seen how, during the childhood and boyhood of her children, Anna Amalia directed all the energies of her mind to the task of fulfilling her duty as regent and mother, and how she surrounded her sons with men of superior intellect, Wieland, as we know, being one of the first arrivals. When his task of education was finished, it was again Anna Amalia who settled upon him a pension of one thousand thalers, on condition that he should make Weimar his home, it being specially agreeable to the duchess to have a man of his intellect near her, ready to help her with her studies, and she extended to him the friendliest and, in a measure, patronising kindness.

That the duchess had a somewhat uncertain, and occasionally violent, temper is made evident by a curious letter, to be found in Wieland's correspondence with Merck. It was written during the first month of Merck's early acquaintance with Anna Amalia. The beginning is missing, and therefore we are left ignorant of the reason why it was written, whether it was a friendly warning or an outburst of one of Wieland's occasional fits of bilious jealousy, or perhaps an answer to some enquiries made by Merck, in consequence of something which had happened either to offend him or put him on his guard.

The letter, is dated Weimar, August 1778.

"You know as well as I do that at times the darkest shadows surround the brightest constellations, and this fact makes it more difficult for me to analyse a character which is Rembrandt-like in its lights and shadows. Basta! you are aware, or should be aware by this time, that no one — yourself not excepted — loves this dear woman better than I do: therefore I will ask you to make allowance for the faults and human failings of the persons who surround the duchess. I have often been driven *nearly* mad by all that goes on, but there are moments when no human being could keep their senses in such a perpetual up and down of ill-humour, impatience, uncertainty, and pettiness, which is enough to destroy any character. I know well what I had to endure in the years '73 to '75. Meanwhile every word we both have said of the dear woman is true. You have noted as well as I the Rembrandt and Guido-like shades that come across the blue firmament;

but the longer I exist, the more I am filled with respect even for the black patches, which at one time disfigured to my short vision the always pleasing tableau presented by such a life, and the longer I live the more I am convinced that, *telle qu'elle est*, she is one of the most delightful and splendid mixtures of human, womanly and royal qualities that has been on this earth of ours."

On another occasion he writes:

"The duchess expects a letter from you, and I shall say no more except that, if you will pen a few lines that will only take ten minutes or so to write, you will not only please the duchess but do a kindness to those who have to live with her, who will have a better time. The moral which I wish to draw is pretty plain."

It is evident from these remarks that Merck had been subjected to a little touch of the duchess's temper inherited from Grandpapa William of Prussia. Anna Amalia was no angel, as her flatterers would have us believe; she was a woman, with a woman's faults, sharp in temper, sometimes hysterical, often unjust, but always lovable, always true to her friends with a fidelity beyond praise, and in most cases she met with faithful service.

Wieland was, however, very spasmodic in his friendships. He was of an amiable, loving nature, attaching himself to those who showed him kindness, but growing jealous and angry if they exhibited a preference for any other friend. Writing to Merck, for whom he had a warm regard, he says:

"If it should come to pass that I am no longer capable of forming fresh attachments, I should still preserve my love for Goethe and for you, and I trust in God that my heart will never grow cold or incapable of loving you both."

These words were written in the year 1775, soon after Goethe had come to Weimar, and two years later his affection for Goethe seems unchanged, for to the same correspondent he writes:

"Lately I have spent two delightful days in Goethe's company. He and I have had to make up our minds to be painted by Rath May for the good pleasure of the Duchess of Würtemberg. Goethe sat in the forenoon and afternoon and begged me, as 'Serenissimus' was absent, to bear him company, and, for the improvement of his mind and mine, to read him something out of 'Oberon.' Luckily, it so chanced that this generally excitable individual happened to be on this occasion in his most receptive humour, and was as easily amused as a girl of sixteen. Never, in all the days of my life, have I seen anyone so pleased with another man's work as he was with 'Oberon' all through, but especially with the five song's wherein Hyon acquits himself verbatim of the emperor's commission. It was a real *jouissance* for me, as you can well imagine, especially as a few days later he confessed that not perhaps for three years would he be again in the same condition of receptivity or openness of mind for an *opus hujus furfuris et farinæ.*"

In considering the circle of great men who were drawn to Weimar, principally by the presence there of Goethe, one cannot fail to notice the tact and generosity displayed by the poet towards those who, he thought, were battling against evil

I. Anna Amalia in her younger years as Duchess of Saxe-Weimar

2. Ernest Constantine, Duke of Saxe-Weimar, 1754-58

3. Prince Karl August when a child

4. The Schloss, the residence of the dukes

Left: **5.** Christoph Martin Wieland

Below: **6.** The ducal palace, built between 1789 and 1803

Above: **7.** A view of Weimar, 1784

Right: **8.** Karl Ludwig von Knebel

9. The house in Frankfurt where Wolfgang Goethe was born

10. Portrait of Caroline, Landgräfin of Hesse Darmstadt

Above: **11.** Goethe playing with
Merck's children, Merck is standing
by the window

Right: **12.** Fraülein Ziegler

13. At the Tivoli, Rome, 1789. From the left, artist Johann Georg Schütz, Johann Gottfried Herder, Anna Amalia, Luise von Göchhausen, Angelika Kaufmann, Johan Friedrich Reiffenstein, Friedrich Hildebrand of Einsiedel, Maximilian von Verschaffelt and Antonio Zucci

Right: **14.** Goethe and Karl August in their "Sturmperiode" in the park

Below: **15.** The Borkenhaus (bark house)

16. The bridge leading to the Borkenhaus in the park

17. The Monument to Genius in the park

Right: **18.** The Schiller Bank in the park

Below: **19.** The Tempel Herrenhaus in the park

20. A waterfall in the park by Georg Melchior Kraus

21. An idealised rustic scene in the park by Georg Melchior Kraus

Above: **22.** The Ilm in the park by Georg Melchior Kraus

Right: **23.** Gottfried Herder

Above: **24.** Wieland's house in Weimar

Left: **25.** Sophie de la Roche

Right: **26.** Fredrick Hildebrand, Freiherr von Einsiedel

Below: **27.** Anna Amalia's Round Table in the Witthums Palais

28. Anna Amalia portrait by Johann
Friedrich August Tischbein

29. Angelica Kaufmann,
a self-portrait

Right: **30.** Anna Amalia,
a portrait by
Angelica Kaufmann, 1788

Below: **31.** Tiefurt

32. Charles Gore, 17 July 1793, by Georg Melchior Kraus

33. Eliza Gore

34. Emily Gore

35. Goethe and Corona Schröter in "Orestes" and "Iphigenia"

36. Corona Schröter with Goethe and Karl August

Above: **37.** The Newest Thing from *Plundersweilern*, by Goethe, with Goethe on stilts

Right: **38.** Corona Schröter

39. Silhouette of Goethe

40. Prince Constantine, the second son of Ernestine Constantine and Anna Amilia

41. A scene from *The Fisher Maiden* drawn by Georg Melchior Kraus

42. The old theatre at Weimar, built 1779 and destroyed by fire in 1825

Above: **43.** The 1830 theatre, replaced in 1908.

Left: **44.** Portrait of Goethe's mother, Frau Aja

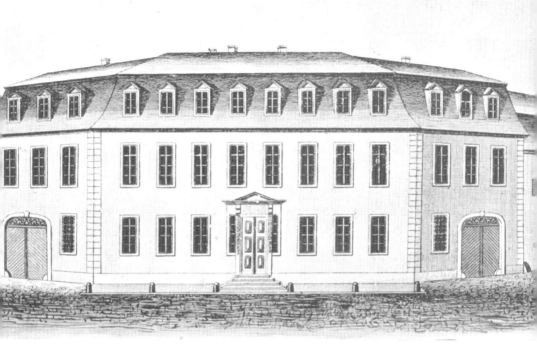

45. View of Goethe's house on the Frauen Platz as it was in 1781.

46. View of Goethe's House, 1901

47. Portrait of Goethe by
Angelica Kaufmann, 1787

48. Portrait of Wolfgang
Heribert Dalberg

49. Karl August Böttiger

50. A group of Weimar's celebrities: 1 Goethe; 2 Schiller; 3 Weiland; 4 Klopstock; 5 Lessing; 6 Herder.

51. Portrait of Duchess Louise of Saxe-Weimar-Eisenach, created Grand Duchess in 1814

52. Karl August in the park with his
dogs, 1828

53. Karl Friedrich, 1783-1853, the son
of Karl August and Louise

54. The legitimate children of Karl August and Duchess Louise of Saxe-Weimar-Eisenach; Karl Friedrich, the future Grand Duke, Karoline Louise and Karl Bernhard

55. Portrait of Goethe, 1802

56. The grand ducal library

57. Theobald von Oer 1807-1885: The Weimar Court of the Muses

fortune. The case of Herder is specially noticeable. Goethe had met, as the reader may remember, at Darmstadt a number of the Sentimentalists, amongst them the pretty and fascinating Caroline Flachsland, then engaged to Herder, whose wife she shortly after became. Herder was already known to Goethe by reputation — these two causes moved the generous mind of the more prosperous minister to extend a helping hand to the less fortunate Herder, and an invitation to come as Court Chaplain to Weimar was despatched to him at Buckeberg. It should not have lessened Herder's feelings of gratitude that his timely offer came from his wife's acquaintance. Herder's was, however, a strangely crooked nature; his experience of life, his ill-health, poverty, and partial blindness had soured his temper, and given him a distrust of everything, even of good fortune.

Gottfried Herder was the son of a pious cantor and teacher in a girls' school at Möhringen. When only twelve years old his eyes became so affected that blindness seemed inevitable. A Russian surgeon offered to cure him of the disease, if he would promise to become an oculist. This agreement was entered into, and Herder went to St. Petersburg. Fortunately, at the first operation he witnessed in the hospital he fainted, so he was sent back to his own country with the advice that, as surgery had failed, he had better try theology. This he did, keeping, however, an open mind as to Church matters. This was quite consistent with the spirit of the time, and his broad views advanced him in the calling he had adopted. His promotion was rapid. In 1764 we find him assistant teacher at the school attached to the Cathedral of Riga, and in an incredibly short time he became *Hof Prediger* — court preacher, or chaplain. He did not remain long at Riga. For the moment he abandoned his religious vocation, and, although he was offered immediate preferment, he accepted instead the post of tutor to the Princes of Holstein, who were about to make the grand tour. He travelled with them to Italy and France. At Strasbourg, his eyes again becoming affected, he had to resign his post and remain under medical care. But this apparent trial led to good fortune, for here he met Wolfgang Goethe, who was the instrument of bringing him, as we know, to Weimar.

This was in 1776. He had just received the distinguished honour of a call to the great university of Göttingen, as professor of theology — a high distinction. Before, however, he could accept the post, the King of Hanover (who had his doubts as to some of Herder's views being too broad) made it a condition that he should go through what was called a *collegium*, or examination, before being installed in his chair. Herder refused, being upheld in his determination not to submit to what he considered an indignity, by the fact that he had in his pocket Goethe's lately received letter of invitation to come to Weimar as court preacher. In it there was no talk of sound views or broad views, everything at Weimar tending towards freedom of life and freedom of opinion.

That we should not look a gift horse in the mouth is a useful proverb which applies to many things. If Weimar was to be a second Athens, it must enjoy an

Athenian liberty of opinion. So said friend Goethe, and Duke Karl agreed with him. Herder was officiating at Buckeberg when the invitation came to him. He had not given satisfaction to his congregation, who severely criticised his preaching; they felt he was no ordinary man, and they disliked him (as small minds do) for his superiority. As a preacher, it was true, that he lacked strength; they would have preferred what is called "a death and judgment" sermon, well sprinkled with brimstone. Herder's pale, dark face, his small, insignificant figure, his delicate appearance, were not imposing, neither were his postures nor delivery in any way striking or impressive; his listeners were never touched, and "left the church as cold as they came in." In a small room, on the contrary, both his appearance and his delivery produced an excellent impression. He made, however, one good friend in the great lady Gräfin of the neighbourhood, who became his constant benefactress. She it was who helped the helpless Herder to put the miserable parsonage into a decent condition for the reception of his bride, Caroline Flachsland, who at last had summoned courage to ask him when the long engagement was to be put an end to. Poor golden-headed Caroline — called by the Sentimentalists Psyche — had suffered enough under her brother-in-law's roof to desire a home of her own.

"A respectable old clergyman married us," writes Caroline; "all my relations were present, and the evening was beautiful. We felt it was God's blessing that was given to us; the love of my dear brothers and sisters, the sweetness of the May day, the beauty of the starry night, seemed to come as a heavenly gift with the blessing of God upon our union."

Five months later, in October, 1776, Herder and his bride left Buckeberg to take up their residence in Weimar. Soon, however, clouds began to gather. From the first there was little *rapprochement* between Goethe and Herder, the latter feeling an ungenerous dislike to the man who had patronised him — for so his distorted mind viewed Goethe's kindly act. Naturally disgusted, although not surprised, at this phase of human nature, Goethe was quite willing to fall in with Herder's wish to stand aloof from his benefactor. This fact, however, did not prevent Wieland from entertaining jealous fears lest the new arrival should supersede him in Goethe's affection. This fear increased as time went on, and when Herder had been a year in his office, we find Wieland complaining bitterly to Merck.

"Goethe and Herder are, for me, as if they were not here. As to the first named — ah! when I remember the hours I used to spend in delightful conversation with him, time flying as we talked! — and now, whether it is in consequence of the (as I shall always think) unfortunate circumstances in which he is placed, or has placed himself, his genius seems almost entirely to have left him, his imagination is clouded. Instead of the brilliant emanations which, like sparks, irradiated from every look and every word, he is now enveloped in a *political frost*. He is always kind and *harmless*, but he is absorbed in the contemplation of his own importance, and there is no approaching him. For the rest, we meet seldom. At the same time there is no quarrel between us. On the contrary, I am convinced of my love for him.

"As for Herder, everything that you prophesied as to him has come true, word for word. For particulars I must wait until we meet, as, please God, we shall soon. In one word, what has happened was to be expected, and I have at last (seeing that in his eminence's eyes everything I did was set down to weakness of mind, or feeble character) withdrawn the stream of my benevolence and have retired into my shell. The man is impossible; he is like a thundercloud, full of electricity. From afar the meteor makes a fine impression, but may the devil keep me from close proximity with such a volcano. No one is more ready than I am to acknowledge the genius, goodness, excellence — in fact, all the good qualities, mental and spiritual — which a man may be possessed of, and likewise to agree that in comparison I am only as a farthing rush light, but for the life of me I cannot endure to see a man so penetrated with the consciousness of his own worth; and truly he must be at bottom a poor creature to find satisfaction in teasing and spying on others; for my part I should like to put the Pyrenees between me and such a fellow."

Herder, through ill-health and the hard fight he had with misfortune, was undoubtedly difficult to live with, and, therefore, not an agreeable addition to the circle at Weimar, where everyone was in such close touch with the others; a man who, like Herder, was perpetually nursing a grievance against some one, became an incubus. It was true, in Herder's case, that, all through his life, he had lacked the acknowledgment which, *after his death*, was lavishly given to his great, undoubted genius. Many men have had to suffer from this neglect while the public lavishes appreciation upon the favourite of the moment. The Herders, both husband and wife, were singularly wanting in gratitude, as is evinced in their correspondence with one another.

Anna Amalia, took the most benevolent interest in the struggles of a man of genius like Herder, who was cursed with poverty. The letters of Caroline Herder teem with grateful thanks for her constant gifts to help the family. Now it is a present of fur caps for the children, or a comfortable shawl for herself. 20 January 1779, she writes in great delight over "the lovely piece of cloth which has just gone to the tailor's to be made into a coat for my son Gottfried, who, so soon as it is ready, will wait on your grace to show himself."

It is pleasant to find in Wieland a different disposition from Herder's. When, in 1777, he received the offer of a most tempting and lucrative appointment at Gotha, he writes to Merck:

"The advantages should be great indeed to compensate me for the life of tranquillity, ease, and affection, I enjoy here. . . . The royal family are about the best people in the world; they are well intentioned towards me, no one presses me; they ask so little of me that I am really ashamed to eat their bread and do exactly as I like. Their highnesses in Gotha are well disposed towards me, and if any misfortune were to happen *here*, there is nothing would suit me better. But now I am content; I sit under the shade of the trees in my garden in which, last autumn, I planted one hundred and ten apple, pear, and cherry trees; and I ask you, would it not be a hard trial not to eat the *fruit* out of my *own orchard*, and would it not be foolish of me when I am happy in my obscurity (*Qui bene latent*, etc.) to plunge into *mare infidum?*"

Anna Amalia had a very tender regard for "der alte Wieland," and a deep respect for his great gifts. All the same, she could not resist an occasional laugh at his expense, especially at the constant increase in his family. Writing to her uncle, Frederick the Great, she says:

"Danischwende (composer of the famous Golden Mirror') is again a happy father. I am sure the constant accouchements of his wife, and of the *Merkür* (the newspaper he edited), will be at last too much for him. He seems to enjoy them both, however, so one can say nothing. Everyone to his fancy."

But although she jested in this manner she was, in fact, a generous friend to the Wieland household, always ready to help when need arose in the ever-increasing family.

For the Duchess Louise, Wieland had an enthusiastic admiration, which was partly due to his having spent his early years at Darmstadt. The homage paid to his great gifts by the great Landgräfin and by the town of Darmstadt was very grateful to Wieland, who, until his "Oberon" drew all eyes on him, had been put in the shade by the younger genius, Goethe.

As this chapter is specially concerned with the Weimar circle, in 1776–1780, I do not think it will be thought amiss if I include Johann Friedrich Merck, who was constantly associated with Weimar, and especially with Anna Amalia. Merck was *l'ami de tout le monde*. "I.M.," Karl August calls him; "Friend Merck," was Anna Amalia's term in addressing him. A most delightful companion, cicerone, adviser as to all matters of art, and, moreover, pleasant as a companion, and to be relied on as a friend — not a bad record to leave behind.

Merck's parentage was not distinguished; he was the son of an apothecary in Darmstadt, and received an excellent education at Göttingen. He married early in life, after a passionate wooing, Louise Francesca Charbonnier, whose name shows her French descent. In the year 1767, he settled in Darmstadt, where he held several good appointments. He was versatile and clever, but wanted strength of mind and steadiness of purpose. His married life was not happy, although all accounts agree that the fault did not lie with the beautiful and highly gifted Francesca. One of his singularities was to take up his residence at Kassel, where he spent many months, during which time he wrote the most loving and despairing letters to his wife, all the time refusing to return to her. He was likewise much given to adoring the ladies of Darmstadt, and was much spoken of for his devotion to Caroline Flachsland, whose sister was married to Merck's intimate friend, Councillor Hesse.

Merck was a man of studious habits and remarkable judgment upon all matters of taste, his knowledge on such points having been perfected by constant travel all over Europe. His opinion in all branches of art, ancient and modern, was eagerly sought by collectors of *objets d'art*. In addition to his undoubted experience in such matters, Merck was a delightful companion, being endowed with the qualities which make for social success (these, let it be noted, are generally natural, not acquired gifts). He was admitted to the friendship of many royal persons. As we already know, he accompanied the Landgräfin Caroline Henrietta to Russia, on the occasion of her daughter Wilhelmina's marriage to Duke Paul, afterwards Czar. We shall meet with him, acting as cicerone to Anna Amalia on one of her tours. From an intellectual standpoint Merck was held in high estimation; besides being a constant contributor to the *Merkür*, he wrote on art and artists, while his opinion and judgment was eagerly sought by writers like Herder and Wieland. Over the "young poet," who had risen like a giant amongst poets, Merck exercised a judicious influence. Goethe, indeed, in his early days, relied altogether on his friend's judgment. How short and to the point is the following keen criticism as to the proper aim of all writing:—

"Thy endeavour, as always, is in the one direction, to give to the *realities* of life a poetic setting; whereas other writers commit the stupidity of *investing* a situation which is *purely imaginary* with a poetic halo which is utterly incongruous, and therefore leaves the reader *unconvinced*, this being a fatal as well as a stupid piece of nonsense."

Wieland, who cherished in his capacious heart a tender attachment for "that excellent Merck," writes to him on one occasion: "When thou hast given thy opinion without pique or bias of any sort; it would be indeed a foolish man who would refuse to submit his judgment to thine, or would venture to appeal to another judge." And on another occasion Wieland bursts out with a protestation: "Rather than be unfaithful to thee, I would strangle my wife and my children: of this thou may'st be convinced."

Anna Amalia made Merck's acquaintance in Frankfurt in 1778. In July of this year the duchess, accompanied by her lady-in-waiting, the sprightly Göchhausen, and her gentleman-in-waiting, von Einsiedel, made an excursion into the Rhine provinces to study art and to enjoy herself, both of which intentions she fulfilled in the most satisfactory manner. She visited Düsseldorf, and at Münster made one of the "mystic circle" which gathered round the Princess Galitzin; in Coblenz likewise she made acquaintance with Wieland's lifelong friend, Frau de la Roche,[50] and in Frankfurt met for the first time Goethe's mother. From that meeting began the intimate friendship which for years continued between the duchess and Frau Aja.

Einsiedel writes to Knebel, "Of Goethe's mother I can only tell you that she surpasses all you have said of her. At her house we met Merck, who since then has been our travelling companion: Without doubt he is one of the most remarkable men that I have ever known; he possesses social gifts in advance of anyone either you or I are acquainted with. The pleasure the duchess finds in his society adds much to our general content." He adds: "Merck is a great authority on all artistic matters, and knows more about such things than the rogues of artists do."

This letter set the tongues of gossips in Weimar wagging. The duchess had caught a new "lion" and was bringing him back in her train. Whereupon speculations began, as to whether the lion (Goethe), who had been in possession more than three years, would be turned out, or whether he would maintain his position, and overthrow the new pet (Merck) whom the duchess was bringing with her.

As a matter of fact the duchess arrived from her tour on 1 August 1778 without the "new pet," who preferred to return to his own home "to dream over the happy hours he had spent in her gracious presence, and to give thanks to Fate, who for once had bestowed upon a poor wretch like him (Merck) four weeks of golden days." Very nicely put, friend Merck.

Anna Amalia answered this effusion in a very pretty letter.

"Your honest gratitude for the pleasant moments we spent in agreeable converse or in looking at the lovely Rhineland, is very flattering to me; and I can in return assure you that you contributed considerably to my enjoyment. I feel grateful for the opportunity given to me of knowing one who possesses as you do a firm belief in truth and goodness, and who with a true faith and courage submits himself to the will of Providence. Farewell, and do not forget your promise to come to us soon. My son will be glad to see you, and you may be sure of the unchangeable regard of your friend,

"AMALIA."

The princess accompanied this letter with a very handsome gift of money, which Merck,
protesting all the time he did not deserve such liberality, accepted; and from this period he seems to have taken upon himself the office of agent in the matter of buying *objets d'art* and such like for his gracious lady, acquitting himself with his usual judgment and spending a wonderfully small amount of money. This self-imposed office led to a correspondence carried on through many years. During this correspondence good friend Merck occasionally overstepped the proper reserve, which, according to our ideas should exist between a royal lady and her "man of business," for so we must consider Merck.

From his original signature "humble slave" he becomes after a short time "humble servant," and the tone of the letters is that of an impetuous young man writing to a friend or comrade. The duchess, however, was endowed with the dignified courtesy which was a marked characteristic of the *grande dame* of the eighteenth century, and passed over these slight indiscretions with the *savoir faire* of a true aristocrat, remaining on friendly terms with that "excellent Merck."

As we have said, the duchess's excursion to the Rhineland came to an end on 1 August 1778, and that inveterate but delightful letter-writer, Wieland, writes on the 2nd of August to Merck:[51]

"The duchess arrived yesterday evening. She had a wonderful reception — triumph and kettledrums, with great demonstrations from the faithful and devoted citizens on her return. Of course, I only saluted the court *en passant*, but I am to behold her today at her toilette. The people here say that the duchess has picked up a new *bel esprit*, and brought him back in her train. He rejoices, they tell me, in the name of 'Marks,'[52] and you can imagine what fun can be got out of this unfortunate appellation; although in this position much would depend on the personal appearance of the bearer.

You can understand that this has given rise to much joking over the 'Marksen' past and present, (fortunately for me my years and appearance put me '*hors de jeu et de combat*' and there was much curiosity to see if the new marrow-bone would put the nose of the one who has been ruling the roost for the last three years out of joint, or if the latter would maintain his position in the first rank.

"In fact, to understand the gist of the tittle-tattle you should be familiar with the undercurrent of popular feeling, that is, the hatred that prevails here against anyone who belongs to the circle of wits and *beaux esprits* and what a d———d medley of confused notions this name conveys to the unenlightened. For the rest you cannot imagine what a distinguished place you fill in the esteem of Duchess Amalia. Nothing affords me more gratification than to hear commendation bestowed upon those whom I love and esteem, and I can give you every assurance of Anna Amalia's friendship. I am commissioned to give you a thousand compliments, and that her Durchlaucht (Highness) counts on the fulfilment of your promise to spend some weeks here in the coming winter. She told me that she had grown so accustomed to see you, that she misses you *at every turn* — in short, you have won her esteem, and you may be sure I seized the opportunity to repeat to her grace all your praises of her and how you were devoted to her body and soul."

From this time a great friendship existed between Merck, the duchess, and those of her suite who had been Merck's travelling companions. His name is continually turning up in the voluminous correspondence of the Duchess, Thusnelda, and others. He seems to have been a general favourite and his visits were anxiously looked for. The duchess, who corresponded with the good Merck at great length on the subject of art also gave him news of the court.

In one of her letters she complains bitterly of the report which has been spread everywhere that her tour had a political object. "The gossips here insist upon my little pleasure trip being an invention of the cabinet. This has very much annoyed Einsiedel, Kraus, and Thusnelda, who are indignant at having to descend from their dignified position of "connoisseurs" to the rearguard of court officials. The Stein," she adds, "makes me shiver with her talk of Rembrandt and Vandyck." She concludes by asking friend Merck to buy her a wine cooler, and encloses a bank order (for Amalia was singularly honest in all money dealings). She adds a request that Goethe may not hear of this piece of extravagance. "It might give him a fit," she writes, "seeing that Rath Goethe grows miserly in his old age."

In another letter she writes pleasantly:

"I was on the point of sending you an epistle charged with gall and wormwood when yours, four pages long, reached me. This softened my wrath somewhat, but not sufficiently to silence me as to the prostitution of your valuable time, running about here and there as you do. As I understand, you now keep company with publicans and sinners. I was obliged to send messengers to all the encyclopædists, booksellers, and political Satans in Frankfurt, in search of you. All that was wanting was the Darmstadt trumpeters whose noise still rings in my ear. They would have made fine noise drumming out the War Counsellor Merck — and all this in vain. Set out at once, you unclean spirit, and may good angels send us back our good old Merck, heartily welcome always to us."

Amalia's friendship must have cheered the latter portion of Merck's life, which ended in the terrible gloom of insanity. He could still find pleasure in her letters and in such kind words as "Farewell, my dear old Merck, keep well and never forget you have a friend in Amalia."

CHAPTER VIII

Twice a week the dowager-duchess dined with her son at the court table. On Sundays there was high festival, when the officers on guard, the ladies of court, as also the gentlemen, could dine if they chose. On Wednesdays guests could only come by invitation. The dowager-duchess had a public reception at the Witthums-haus every Thursday, at which the newly married pair and the court were always present, while her private and more literary circle generally met on Fridays.

Anna Amalia's general circle (it was often supplemented by guests or chance visitors to Weimar) included her personal suite. Her ladies were Frau von Stein, lady-in-waiting, and Fräulein von Göchhausen, or Thusnelda, the name by which she was generally known; the one remarkable for her beauty and her lovers, the other for her plainness and her wit. He who knows the heart of woman cannot be sure that Göchhausen would not have sacrificed her wit for Charlotte's beauty; and who can say that she would have been wrong? We know that a statesman and writer of reputation —Disraeli, no less — said, if given the choice, he would elect to be a beautiful woman up to the age of twenty-five.

Poor Göchhausen was deformed and small of stature; her mortification at her want of height was increased by a whim of the duchess, who christened her tiny maid-of-honour, Thusnelda, after the woman whom all Germany honoured for her *gigantic* stature, while Wieland gave her the name of the Gnomide. Thusnelda the second could not well be offended at this joke, for she herself was given to the bestowal of nicknames — in fact, every sort of joke was to her fancy. She indulged in tricks of all kinds, and took it in good part when others retaliated in the same manner, although the jokes played upon her by Karl August and Goethe sometimes passed the limits of a friendly jest.

Small in stature, frail in body, by no means pretty, Thusnelda was full of *esprit*, extremely witty, well-educated (according to the high standard of education in her day), and possessed of natural gifts which imparted to her conversation a delightful freshness. She spoke three languages with fluency, so that her conversational powers were not limited to her native tongue. It is curious how this gift of conversing well seems to be no longer necessary, and if one may use a vulgar expression, there is a decided "slump" in good talkers. Where and why has this delightful gift disappeared? Will it ever come back? Or is it that, being a plant of delicate nurture, an exotic, in fact, difficult to rear and requiring delicate and peculiar handling, it has died out for the want of congenial soil?

The gift of conversing — by this of course is meant talking, not gossiping — is by no means confined to the French (although possessed by some French men and women in an extraordinary degree). Some of the best conversationalists of the nineteenth century were Germans or Russians, notably, Madame de Staël and Madame de Krudener. The salon of Anna Amalia may be said to have been the parent of the salons of 1801, and the quality of the talk was quite up to the standard of the later period. How, could it be otherwise, when such intellectual giants were of the company? Fancy a table round which sat Goethe, Herder, Wieland, Gleim (occasionally), and the lesser lights, Knebel, Einsiedel, and Merck! The list could be considerably extended.

The women, too, bore their share bravely, for Duchess Anna Amalia talked with "much elegance," as was natural to one of her race. Fräulein Göchhausen was sprightly and *tant soit peu* audacious; Charlotte von Stein appreciative; Charlotte von Kalb satirical and clever; Amalia von Kotzebue trenchant; Henrietta von Eggloffstein amusing; the Englishwomen who later joined the circle were pleasant, and occasional strangers added their quota to the general whole. Amalia was, however, careful to keep the standard of conversation up to a certain level. A good conversationalist herself (as most foreigners are), she understood that too much talk is apt to degenerate into mere dribble; therefore she made a rule that there should be intervals of reading aloud, and hence someone — it might be Knebel, or perhaps the amiable Einsiedel — set the ball rolling by reading aloud some new poem or essay which had appeared in the *Merkür*, or some *jeu d'esprit* from one of the wits, or a poem written by Knebel or Einsiedel, both of whom had a pretty talent for verse-making.

Soon sparkling witticisms began to circulate; there was an interchange of repartee; the shrill laugh of Fräulein Göchhausen mingled with the cooing softness of Charlotte von Stein, and the Fräulein von Göchhausen and the Baroness von Stein were not the only ladies who had a reputation for wit and beauty. Amongst the numbers whose names appear in memoirs and letters of the period, the first places for agreeable manners, full of that charm which characterised the *grande dame* of the eighteenth century, must be given to clever Frau von Eggloffstein and the pretty Henrietta von Eggloffstein, whose memoirs of the time in which she lived are such pleasant reading; to the highly cultivated Amalia von Imhoff, painter and poetess; to Countess Bernstoff, sister to the Count von Stolberg; to Fräulein von Wolfskeil, and to Fräulein Marie Oertel; this last named was an especial favourite by reason of her cleverness and her readiness to fill a gap when this was needed, either in conversation or in whatever might be going on. The personal appearance of Fräulein Marie was in itself so provocative of fun and good humour, that her extreme plainness was soon forgiven, especially by men, with whom she was extremely popular.

Amongst the men the first place must be accorded to Friedrich von Einsiedel, the duke's chamberlain, who, from his amiable disposition, received the name of L'Ami, or "friend of his friends." Einsiedel had from his boyhood served about the court, having been in the days of the regency one of Anna Amalia's pages, in which character he had played many a boyish prank, and it must be owned he made anything but a dignified Chamberlain, many of his adventures having a Falstaffian ring. He could indeed have claimed like that worthy, that he was not only witty himself, but the cause of wit in others. The strange fits of absence of mind which occasionally seized upon him, and during which his purse or hat could be taken from him without his being aware of it, gave rise to numerous tricks which helped to dispel the *ennui* that, despite the presence of the great geniuses who made their home in the little capital, was apt to fall upon the courtiers. Henrietta von Eggloffstein, in her memoirs, gives an amusing anecdote of Einsiedel.

"On the birthday of the reigning Duchess Louise, Einsiedel was to conduct nine young ladies, dressed as the Muses, to the presence of the duchess, there to recite a poem with congratulations on the auspicious occasion. Arrived at the palace he found, when in the presence of the duchess, that he had forgotten the poem. The Muses in indignation surrounded him and, half in fun, seized him by his coat tails and dragged him here and there, from side to side, each one joining in the chorus of abuse showered upon him for his negligence. The scene was truly comic, the duchess joining in the general laughter which was excited by the spectacle presented by the unfortunate Einsiedel, his yellow wig dragged to one side and displaying his jovial face, from which the mask had fallen off."[53]

Einsiedel, however, must have possessed qualities of a higher order than mere harmless fun and good humour, else he could not have enjoyed an intimate friendship with men of the high standard of Herder and Schiller. "Einsiedel is an excellent, unaffected man," writes the latter to his friend Korner, "and is far from being devoid of talent." He is sometimes confounded with his brother, also in the duke's service as gentleman-in-waiting, and who, being of a gay, dissipated character, got into some discreditable adventures; one of these, his marriage with Countess von Wertheim, is so singular as to deserve mention. This lady, who was one of the court circle had agreed to desert her husband and children and country for love of the handsome gentleman-in-waiting.

This is, unfortunately, not a new experience in the world's history; but the countess's manner of loosening the matrimonial bond was certainly novel, and undoubtedly showed she had some regard for her husband's feelings. This lady had a constitutional tendency to fall into swoons which lasted some time. She took advantage of this weakness to feign death; her ruse succeeded, and she was laid out as really dead. With the assistance of a maid she rose up in the middle of the night and made her escape to her lover. A wooden figure wrapped up in her grave-clothes was buried in the family vault. Einsiedel took his fair one to Africa, where he had gold mines. Both of them soon wearied of their banishment and returned to Germany.

We can imagine the astonishment and indignation of the deceived husband and family, on seeing the resuscitation of one whom they supposed to be dead. In the eighteenth century, however, great leniency was shown in regard to such episodes, foreign courts, and especially those of Germany, possessing a very low standard of morals. Take, for example, the debased condition of the Court of the Electors of Hanover, while at Würtemberg, Dresden, and Berlin a like condition of open immorality existed. The Court of Weimar does not present such an infamous record. Nevertheless, general laxity prevailed, and there was a strong flavour of the unhealthy French school mingled with the romance and sentiment which is at the bottom of the German character.

As for the pair whose story has been told, and about whose future my readers may be curious, a legal separation was obtained for the (supposed) corpse, and Countess von Wertheim was legally married to the duke's gentleman-in-waiting, who lived to the ripe age of seventy.

Karl Ludwig von Knebel was born on 20 November 1744. His father held different posts, having been at one time chancellor, then ambassador to Regensburg, finally *geheimerath* in Anspach, to which province he belonged by right of inheritance. Karl had excellent teachers both in Regensburg and Anspach; he enjoyed study but detested the law for which his father destined him. Finally, seeing there was no use in further opposition, the *geheimerath* gave his consent and Knebel was allowed to enter on a military career. He served for ten years very respectably, but without making a military reputation. From the time he retired into private life he devoted himself altogether to the Muses, and here again his devotion met with a small return. He never received any particular favour from the mistress he courted so assiduously.

Meantime, his position, as tutor to Prince Constantine and travelling companion to Karl August, brought him in contact with all those most distinguished in art, literature, and politics. Knebel, as we know, accompanied Prince Karl on his first visit to Frankfurt, where the memorable meeting with Goethe took place. Later on he had some experience of the court of Karlsruhe, and of the duchess's father, the odd Landgraf. Karl Friedrich who was given to taking fancies, in obedience to the strange law of contrasts which so often governs likings, especially with quick-blooded persons, became possessed by one of his sudden whimsical friendships, the object being the unfortunate Knebel. Knebel soon discovered that this prefer-ence drew upon him the eyes of the whole court, which, urged by insane jealousy of all the tokens of friendship lavished on him by the Landgraf, made the rest of his tour with the young princes exceedingly unpleasant.

The princes felt they had been overshadowed by their tutor, especially as Görtz, who from the first had taken a jealous dislike to Knebel, did all in his power to insinuate that that officer had his own reasons for the manner in which he had behaved. And what was even worse to a man of Knebel's shy character, he made him a butt for all his coarse pleasantries.

One of these took a form most disagreeable to a man of Knebel's retiring disposition. It appeared that Knebel, who up to this had guarded strictly the doors of his inner citadel against the attacks of the fair ladies of Weimar, had been suddenly surprised and his citadel had been captured by a fair markswoman in Karlsruhe, who, unconsciously or with malice prepense, had winged her arrow straight at the gallant major's breast. The fair markswoman was a certain court lady — by name Fräulein von Göchhausen, otherwise Thusnelda, who was at this time acting as maid-of-honour to the Markgräfin of Baden. Knebel mentions her in his diary; but with the reticence one could expect from one of his retiring character, he specially remarks that, *for a woman*, she had a wonderful sense of morality! It was not this quality that attracted him, however, neither was it her beauty, although he extols her appearance, love, we must suppose, making him blind to her deformity. Her wit it was that penetrated poor Knebel's heart. It does not appear that he ever told his love. He was poor, and on that account was shy of asking any woman to share his small fortune; this secret, however, oozed out.

The jests levelled at him and the lady of his thoughts, were exquisite torture to a man of Knebel's character. He mentions this love passage of his in his diary, but in so guarded a manner that there is nothing worth repeating. Apart from this episode, 'Knebel's life story was almost tragic. Not indeed, in the sense that it contained startling or terrible events, but rather that kind of tragedy which underlies the lives of many, unknown even to their best and nearest friends. His letters to the sister who loved him so devotedly give us the key to the whole story. Nature had given him a fine appearance, an excellent heart, a good understanding; he was clever and well-educated, literary in his tastes, a good soldier. He had, however, the faults of youth; he was excitable and obstinate and was no courtier, hence he never got on — he could neither favour nor flatter, and his poverty prevented him from joining in the amusements of the court, especially the gambling, which went on pretty freely at the duke's house. The suffering caused to Knebel, by having to run the risk of losing a few shillings, to him a sum of importance, is piteous.

"My soul," he writes to his sister, "suffers, but never so much as when I am in the gay world of the court; then I am miserable." And again, "Since October we play here two or three times a week. I have won a few groschen, but on most occasions I have lost several thalers. This is an infamous method of losing money and in no way suited to people of our means." He had a morbid manner of looking at everything. When friends suggested his making use of a pleasant talent he had for writing he said: "What should I write about that is not either too late or too soon for this generation?"

In the same way when an heiress showed herself favourable towards him he writes to his sister: "Providence intended us to be poor, and therefore gave us a certain limpness, which is opposed to success in any, but especially in this direction."

Karl August, with his active and self-reliant mind, grew weary of this same limpness, and showed his desire to be rid of his old friend so plainly that Knebel retired to Jena, bitterly disappointed that he had not been given a post in the administration. His sister Henrietta was a replica of her brother, having the same miserable self-distrust and self-consciousness, which made the lives of both brother and sister miserable. Her brother considered her a highly gifted and altogether remarkable woman, whereas she was an ordinary and not particularly interesting character. Knebel's brother Max, who was a source of great trouble all through his life, in the end committed suicide. After this calamity matters brightened. The duchess Louise entrusted the wonderful Henrietta with the education of the Princess Caroline (who seems to have lived with her governess), and Anna Amalia married Knebel to the charming singer, Fräulein von Rudorf.

Heinrich Meyer, the artist largely patronised by Karl August and Goethe, had much simplicity combined with a reserve of dry humour, which made him a most amusing narrator.

Count Karl Brühl, afterwards manager of the Court Theatre at Berlin, paid visits to Weimar lasting for months, and may be counted as forming one of the duchess's circle. Brühl, whose musical talent was remarkable, was also a fine declaimer of poetry, and being a man of all-round talent, was always made welcome, bringing as he did the freshest news of all artistic and literary novelties.

To these names we must add that of Bertuch, the comptroller of Karl August's household, Ridel and the brothers Fritsch, Herr von Seckendorf, and Baron von Wolfskeil, gentleman-inwaiting to Karl August. Herder and Goethe occasionally looked in, and Wieland was a constant visitor to the Witthumshaus; later came Schiller and Jean Paul Richter.

That amiable artist, Kraus, has handed down the principal members of Anna Amalia's circle, in the well-known picture, which hangs in the grand-ducal library, and is in itself a lasting testimony to the duchess's excellent taste.[54]

Here we have the principal members of Amalia's circle as they sat round the table on a certain Friday and were sketched by the young artist. Amalia is painting, her brush in her hand, a smile on her pleasant face (this portrait produces a more favourable impression of the duchess than does the well-known portrait so generally put forward), as she listens to Einsiedel, who, in his uniform of gentleman-in-waiting, is reading aloud, probably one of his own "little things."

Goethe, who is sitting beside him, is almost effaced; one sees the back of his *perruque*, with the pigtail tied with a black bow. The very pretty woman next to him is Henriette von Fritsch (wife to one of Minister von Fritsch's sons), who held the post of lady-in-waiting to Anna Amalia. Her neighbour in the corner is Hinrich Meyer. Seated, next to the duchess is Elizabeth Gore,[55] the elder of the two English ladies who with their father, Charles Gore, made Weimar their home. On the other side of the table is her sister Emily, dressed in black, with a wonderful hat and an air of being somebody. Beside her sits clever little Fräulein Göchhausen, a satirical smile on her Jewish face. Behind her looms the great personality of His Eminence Herder, his hand on the back of Göchhausen's chair and his large face staring with an intense expression which conveys more of wonder than admiration.

The merits of the picture, which is a large one, are diminished by its being reduced to the necessary dimensions for our present purpose. It should be seen in its entirety.

As we look at this interesting picture, the question arises: "How would such a society meet in the present day?" The experiment has been tried and has always failed — the wits at Holland House and fore house were an approach, but Macaulay has given testimony as to the want of success that attended these receptions.

During the winter season Fräulein von Göchhausen's Saturday breakfasts were, next to Anna Amalia's Fridays, a favourite entertainment. As a matter of fact they were more popular than the Fridays of the gracious lady, for the reason that there was more freedom and less *gêne*. Thusnelda, being a popular little woman, had the best of good company, with savants, pretty women, and fashionable men; while each invited guest, out of friendship for the kind little hostess, did his or her best to make them a brilliant success. One cannot help noticing, as a dispassionate onlooker, free from bias and prejudice, that Thusnelda's breakfasts were, on the whole, better organised than were Anna Amalia's round-table afternoons.

People were more at their ease than under the eye of the duchess (kindly as her glance might be); consequently there was less effort and more spontaneous wit. The lesser stars, who were often crushed by the magnitude of the greater lights, could shine with their own effulgence; and yet it is not to be supposed that the company gathered at Thusnelda's were not learned men and women. Böttiger once read a tragedy by Sophocles, the different parts being distributed amongst the company. On another occasion a question was set which was to be answered at the following Saturday breakfast, and the answer being satisfactory, a second trial was made.

"What did Schiller mean by his *Mädchen aus der Fremde*?"

The Countess von Eggloffstein (not Henrietta, who was her sister-in-law) sang the poem. Her commanding figure, her inspired face, with the brilliant eyes full of life and spirituality, carried conviction to the minds of the listeners, who with one voice agreed with the singer that the *Mädchen* was poetry.

Music often lent its charm to Thusnelda's *réunions*. Wölff, the Kapellmeister, was a pianoforte player of repute, and Hummel, *the* composer of the day, played at many of these gatherings, while Corona Schröter was occasionally persuaded to let her charming voice be heard.

Another house which "received" was that of the Eggloffsteins. Here on Sunday afternoons all Weimar came, especially during the short days of winter, when picnics and outings were impossible. The company, which was of the best, occasionally stayed so late, being either engaged in learned discussions or sometimes in silly gossip (for all the world of Weimar was not learned), that the afternoon became evening and, as the discourse was not half ended, these chosen friends remained for supper and often into the small hours of the morning.

Gleim, who, being on a visit at Weimar, was invited to one of the duchess's Fridays, tells this story:

"I brought in my pocket a copy of the just published 'Göttingen Musenalmanach,' and at the duchess's request I read from it to the assembly. Whilst I was still reading a young man came in, whom I hardly looked at. He had spurs to his boots, I noticed, and wore a short, green hunting coat. He sat down amongst the listeners — he was exactly opposite to me — and listened very attentively. Except that he had wonderful black eyes, his appearance did not make any impression on me. However, it was fated that I should make nearer acquaintance with him. During a pause in my reading several persons began to discuss the book, one praising it and others finding fault. The young sportsman, as I thought he was, got up from his seat and, addressing me in a most courteous manner, proposed that he should relieve me, as I must be fatigued with reading aloud, by taking my place for a short time. I could not refuse so courteous a proposal, and handed him the volume.

"But, Apollo and the Nine Muses! what did I hear? At first it was some mild stanzas, but then came an avalanche of wild imaginings that were not in the 'Almanach,' bits of Burger's and Stolberg's poems that would never have had a place in the volume he held in his hand. Once it actually seemed to me as if Satan had taken hold bodily of the reader, and I almost expected to see his Satanic Majesty appear before me. The poems this man, or demon, read, were delivered in a voice that was capable of expressing every modulation, every note of the human gamut, while he mixed up in a strange jumble, without confusion of text, hexameters, iambics, and doggerel. And as he poured out this stream of romance with the greatest gravity, it seemed as if he had a sort of mission to fulfil. How wondrous was the humour of his extraordinary imaginations! glimpses of the wonderful, the marvellous, the all-enchanting, scattered thoughts of such infinite beauty, that the authors to whom he ascribed them might have thanked heaven on their knees, if they could have had such wonderful imaginings.

"So soon as the joke got bruited about, the whole company were filled with delight. They all gathered round, and to each one present the poet gave a few lines. I was lightly reproved for setting up to be a Meacænas to all young poets, artists, and scholars. I was praised on one hand, ridiculed on the other. He compared me wittily enough in a short fable in doggerel verse to an unusually patient turkey hen, who sits upon eggs which are not her own, and who on one occasion tried to hatch an egg made of chalk. At this I called out to Wieland, who was sitting opposite to me at the table: 'That is either Goethe or the devil!' And he answered me in the affirmative, adding: 'He has got the devil inside of him today, who is trying to get out on one side or the other: so take my advice; don't go too near him.'"

CHAPTER IX

For persons in private life to amuse themselves with dramatic performances is a very old custom, and one which carries us back to past centuries, when in most towns of note there existed an amateur theatre, in which members of society were at once the performers and the spectators. The universities favoured this practice, and the students performed on a private stage the classical masterpieces of the Greek and Roman writers, as well as light modern comedies.

Always anxious for progress, Anna Amalia in 1771 had invited the famous dramatic company, got together by Seiler, to come to Weimar (which was beginning to be known, in a small way compared with its later reputation, as the home of art and artists). Wieland tells us that Anna Amalia was thoroughly convinced that a well-ordered theatre can do a great work, in the intellectual improvement and general refinement of a nation.

He adds that this estimable princess, "Not alone desires by this means to amuse the minds of the upper class and give to men whose time is occupied in business matters an agreeable relaxation from their labours, but she also desires to reach the poorer and less educated classes, and to give to them the same opportunities, which are the right of those in a superior station of life; and there-fore Weimar enjoys a privilege not known to other capitals in Germany, that of having theatrical performances for which there is nothing to pay, while the moral effect upon all who take part is equally remarkable. The author is encouraged to work for a theatre where the excellent training of the actors is a security that his composition will receive full justice. Likewise the literature of Germany, the taste and the reputation of the country, all gain by this step, and are raised to a higher platform." He adds: "Surely the name of Amalia deserves to be written in the book of the Muses for the beneficent protection accorded by her to every branch of knowledge, by which mankind in general has benefited largely."

So far Wieland. His words were prophetic. The theatre of Weimar attracted numbers of actors, singers, artists, and a school of music grew up, which was placed under the conduct of an Italian artist named Schweizer. By the wish of the duchess, Wieland wrote his *Aurora* and *Alceste* as a basis for German opera. Like all innovations, this new departure caused an outcry. An opera in the unmusical language which Charles the Fifth had declared was only fit for horses![56]

In spite of the existing prejudice, Wieland's experiment in writing *Alceste* succeeded so well that with one voice the nation called upon the celebrated musician, Glück, inviting him to do honour to the poem by marrying such exquisite verse to equally beautiful music. Unfortunately, so far as Weimar was in question, a check was momentarily placed upon active co-operation in dramatic and musical affairs. The reader will remember that when the Residenz Schloss was burned in 1774, the theatre, which was in the castle, was likewise consumed. As there was no theatre, and no funds to build a new one, Seiler and his company returned to Brunswick, from whence they had come on Anna Amalia's invitation. Weimar was therefore left destitute of all theatrical excitement. Occasionally a strolling company passing by stayed a few weeks, setting up an apology for a theatre under canvas; and even to meagre attempts like these the patronage of the court was freely given.

This condition of affairs was, however, soon to change. In 1775 two events took place — Karl August married and Wolfgang Goethe came to Weimar.

The newly married duchess had from her childhood been accustomed to look upon music and the drama as a necessary part of the day's amusement. Like many other foreign towns, Darmstadt had its theatre, with its regular company of actors. That Weimar should be so destitute was a matter of astonishment to Louise. Goethe, too, had that love of the stage and everything connected with the drama that is generally to be met with in young ardent minds, to whom the very air of the theatre — the peculiar aroma of "saw-dust" as Charles Matthews was wont to call it — is a sort of ambrosia.[57]

Goethe, accustomed at Frankfurt (where there was a fine theatre and a good company) to spend his evenings at his favourite amusement, felt, like the duchess; completely at a loss what to do with himself. The duke commiserated both his wife and his friend, and confessed that he, too, was in a similar position. "But," he said, "without a theatre and without actors, how is the deficiency to be supplied? "The fertile mind of Goethe found an answer to this question. "Let us find the place," he said, "and take possession of it, and the company is ready made." And so it proved.

Anna Amalia's resourceful mind was very helpful in smoothing over difficulties, and soon a miniature theatre was arranged under her management, first in the *Fürstenhaus*, or ducal residence, and later on in the *Redoute* on the esplanade. This little theatre was certainly not ambitious. In breadth the stage was not more than eleven feet. Some of the scenery painted for the Residenz theatre had been saved from the fire, and of this several beautifully painted scenes by Kraus could be made available. For the necessary expenses a subscription was started. Anna Amalia subscribed out of her private purse eighty-eight thalers, and for the cost of lighting she agreed to give ten thalers for every representation, Karl

August contributing a like amount. The small scale on which the plays had to be produced in no way hindered the enjoyment of the spectators, or interfered with the success of the amateur performances in this *bijou* theatre.

Just at this period private theatricals were more the rage than they are at present; for nowadays amateurs have at last learned that they do not compare very favourably with well-trained professional performers. But in the latter portion of the eighteenth century the distinction between the amateur and the professional was less marked; for the reason that the stage was on a far lower level, and really good actors were rare. "In Berlin, Dresden, Frankfurt, Augsburg, Nüremberg, and Fulda, there were celebrated amateur companies. In Würtemburg for a long time a noble company put on sock and buskin; in Eisenach prince and court joined in the sport. Even the universities, which in earlier times had, from religious feeling, denounced the drama, now forgot their antagonism, and in Vienna, Halle, Göttingen, and Jena allowed the students to have private stages."

I find from contemporary sources that the amateur company of Weimar was considered superior to all others. It had its poets, its composers, its scene-painters, its critics, and its costumiers; it embodied a company of which even the recruits were ready-made actors. Anyone who showed talent for any particular branch, whether singing, dancing, or love-making, was at once seized upon and made to join the *corps dramatique*.

Anna Amalia, the duke, Prince Constantine, and the ladies and gentlemen of the Court, were all willing to take a part at the shortest notice, and devoted their very best energies to the performance of the most insignificant *rôles*. The rehearsals were supervised by Goethe and Von Seckendorf, an admirable comedian. The regular company, which, however, was constantly being added to, consisted of Karl August, Prince Constantine, Knebel, Einsiedel, Bode, Musäus, Seckendorf, Bertuch, Kranz, and Goethe. Eckhoff, an actor permanently engaged at Gotha, came over occasionally to play what are called "guest parts."[58] The women were Duchess Anna Amalia, Corona Schröter, Amalia von Kotzebue, Madame Wolf, Fräulein von Göchhausen, and others.

The front seats were reserved for the court officials, privy councillors, etc. After that places were allotted to the general public. There was no paying for tickets, but it would appear that the *dramatis personæ* contributed to the expenses, although it is not positively stated that such was the case. Still, we are told that the first year's performances paid all the expenses, but that, as the next year's were on a grander scale, the duke had to give assistance, and that he generously defrayed the cost of the scenery, dresses, and lighting. Bertuch, the comptroller of the duke's household, was likewise the theatrical paymaster; and we read of his shaking his head solemnly at having to pay a hundred thalers (£15) for the cost of one performance. This does not seem a large sum from our point of view, but as these entertainments were of constant occurrence, they constituted a somewhat expensive amusement. When the plays were performed outside of Weimar, the duke had no share in the expenses, which were generally borne by the Duchess Amalia.

When we look back over the one hundred and thirty years, or so, which have passed since the amateur theatre of Weimar was the sole institution of its kind that the inhabitants of Weimar and Jena possessed, we are struck by the fidelity with which history repeats itself. Here we have a set of amateurs — with few exceptions — taking upon themselves the office of well-trained actors, confident in their own strength, and venturing to range themselves on the same platform with actors educated to the stage, What cool audacity! What absurd vanity! you may exclaim. This, however, would be a mistaken verdict, based; probably, on what we all have suffered from the vanity of the present-day amateur, who, unable as he is to carry his stick properly or walk the stage naturally, yet considers himself quite the equal of any well-trained actor. We see examples of this absurd self-conceit every day, and often suffer in pocket from our friends' crass vanity.

This was not the case with the amateurs of 1776. It was a part of education in the eighteenth century, especially in Germany, where intellectual cultivation had attained such a relatively high standard, for young persons in good positions who had no idea of making the stage a profession, to learn how to declaim, and how to walk, moving the different members of the body, — head, arm, hand, and foot, as Nature had intended they should be moved. They were, in fact, taught to do these small things after the manner of the stage. This was principally the case at public schools, where the students gave a performance once a year. And when I use the word taught, I do not mean to convey the perfunctory sort of teaching given in schools of the present day, with the arm sawing the air, and articulation much on a par with that of a Hyde Park orator, but a school of oratory wherein each pupil was taught the art of declaiming. We also have to remember, in connection with the excellence of these Weimar Thespians, that, in consequence of the long-continued wars, most of the public theatres had been closed, and that the large towns relied for their theatrical amusements on the amateur playhouse.

As I have before remarked, amateur theatres of great excellence were scattered all over Germany. The acting at the Weimar theatre was good all round. Goethe, who was passionately fond of acting, was, especially in the beginning, too violent in his delivery, and at all times his movements were too stiff. In 1776 he had become director, Karl August resigning in his favour. As Wolfgang could do nothing by halves, the wonder is how he found time to attend so many different undertakings — political, artistic, and social.

There is no doubt that, from the time the management of the theatre came into his hands, a great advance was made in theatrical matters; the quality of the acting was improved, and likewise the choice of pieces differed from the somewhat old-fashioned selections of Anna Amalia, who was at first associated with the duke in the theatrical management. Goethe was firm and rather autocratic in his sway, allowing no outside interference with his orders, which had to be strictly followed.

No neglect was permitted, and the smallest item or the most insignificant part had to be studied and rehearsed, with as much care as if the success of the whole play depended on its proper performance.

That there was much opposition to these strict rules is easy to imagine; and the difficulties he had to encounter were only to be surmounted by a man of his determined will. Some of the troubles of a stage-manager's life can be gathered from Goethe's "Little Notes." When his charming play, *Die Mitschuldigen* (The Culprits), was in rehearsal, he had considerable difficulty with Einsiedel, who finally resigned his part; but not until Goethe had written to him: "I swear you will do it well, if only you will put your mind to it. I don't know what I shall do. The others play well, but I have absolutely no one to take the part of Söller; and I know that you will play it admirably. Perhaps I will call to see you today."

Again he writes more earnestly Einsiedel, I beg and beseech that you will fix your stupid mind on your part. The others are first-rate.

Tomorrow I could rehearse with you alone, and on Saturday with the rest. Monday at the theatre, and Tuesday or Wednesday the performance."

It is evident from the following playbill that Einsiedel remained fixed in his stupidity, and was therefore replaced in the part of Söller by Bertuch.

DIE MITSCHULDIGEN

Alceste	GOETHE
Söller	BERTUCH
Der Wirth	MUSÄUS
Sophie	CORONA SCHRÖTER

Another play, written by Goethe specially for the company, was *Die Geschwister* (The Brother and Sister) written in three evenings, and inspired it was said, by the love of the sweet eyes of Amalia von Kotzebue, sister of the dramatist, who was at this time only a youth. He says in his memoirs: "Goethe had at that time written his charming piece, *Die Geschwister.*[59] It was performed at the amateur theatre in Weimar, Goethe playing William and my sister, Marianne, while to me — yes, to me — was allotted the part of Postillion." Goethe threw his whole strength into his performances of *Alceste*, a part which had a certain analogy to the position in which he stood to Frau von Stein. Nevertheless, the argus eyes of the court gossips noticed that his embraces of Marianne were of a more affectionate character than is usual with fraternal embraces. Probably he had a *mauvais quart d'heure* with his Charlotte later on.

Frau von Stein seems to have had no talent for the stage, or perhaps she imagined it was not in keeping with the *rôle* of the neglected wife, which she had assumed. Still, it seems extraordinary that Goethe did not press her to join the "troupe"; for it would have been delightful to have been her instructor, as he had been to many a *débutante*.

Wolfgang and the duke were always on the lookout for new recruits, either in the town, amongst the court set, or in the neighbourhood; and any pretty girl or handsome young fellow was sure to be enlisted in the duke's company. There were rehearsals almost every day of either an opera or a play, so that these so-called amateurs had to work as hard as professionals, without any reward beyond the honour of being included in so fashionable an undertaking. Besides, to the young people there was a delightful novelty in playing at being actors and actresses.

Those who have ever taken part in such amusements will readily understand the pleasurable excitement of this almost feverish life, with its triumphs and its failures, its squabbles and its intense excitement, the rehearsals and the pleasant suppers, the flirtations and the lovemaking. Oh, it is a pleasant time, this time of play-acting; and the Weimar theatricals were pretty much the same as the performances that you and I have assisted at, for human nature has not altered much since those days, although perhaps we have grown less outwardly proper than were our grandmothers, and less *hardi* than were our grandfathers; who, if report tells truth, were somewhat audacious in their love-making. Be that as it may, the Weimar theatricals were exceedingly popular, and the fame of the fun which they afforded — and, not least, the opportunities given for flirtation — all fanned the flame and added to their popularity.

The company was in truth a distinguished one. The dowager duchess, the reigning duke, and Prince Constantine were often included in the caste, likewise the first officials of the court, statesmen, ministers, generals, and military men of all ranks in the service, pages, and private individuals. The acting was good all round. Goethe, who was passionately fond of the stage, made an interesting lover, but, as before stated was, especially in the beginning, too violent, and at all times his movements were stiff for example, as Alceste in *Die Mitschuldigen*, as Orestes in *Iphigenia* and as Belcour in *The West Indian*. Moreover he was what is called in theatrical slang "a bad study"; that is to say he could not or would not learn his part, but trusted to his power of extemporising. This is a fault common to most amateur actors, and one which would not be tolerated in professionals, who would soon hear of it if they did not give their proper "cue."

But so far as Goethe is in question, one is surprised, not so much that he occasionally forgot his words, but that he ever remembered them, seeing that his memory was charged with such a multiplicity of different subjects. Not only was he actor and stage manager (nothing being done without his personal supervision or written directions), but he also composed most of the pieces which were acted, the music, when it took the shape of operetta, being contributed by Sigmund von Seckendorf, who had much musical talent.

Kapellmeister Wolf, an excellent musician (his wife had been a *prima donna* of the second order of merit), likewise composed excellently well; and there was later a remarkable addition in the musician Schubart. Sometimes the duchess herself, who, as we already know, had much taste for music, contributed a song or two.

She also wrote an operetta, *Erwin and Elmira*, to which Goethe added two songs. This was performed in 1777 with much success. It did not, however, attain more than a *succès d'estime*, nor did its composer desire for it a more extended arena.

Amongst the theatrical company at Weimar, there were two women who would have been remarkable at any period for their beauty and their talent. These were the two celebrated singers, Fräulein von Fach — Corona Schröter[60] — and Fräulein Louise von Rüdorf. The first of these ladies deserves special mention. Corona Elizabeth Wilhelmina Schröter was born in 1750 at Guben, and was trained for the stage at Leipzig by Hiller, whose wife was Corona's godmother. She sang when only fourteen with Mara at the Leipzig concerts, and there Goethe, then in his student days, got to know the charming young girl musician, who was surrounded by admirers. When she was sixteen, Müller, one of the Leipzig burgomasters, wanted to marry her, but his offer was refused. Later, a rich nobleman, already provided with a wife and family, of which appendages he said not a word, enticed the youthful Corona to meet him at Dresden, promising to marry her there. Fortunately, on her arrival, she was informed of his true position, and returned to Leipzig without seeing him. Another lover was Körner (best known as Schiller's friend). In 1787, Schiller, writing to Körner says:

"Her figure and the remains of a beautiful face are a complete justification of your infatuation for this gifted woman. What must she have been when forty years have taken so little from her charm?"

Corona's beauty lay principally in her Junoesque figure and wonderful grace, charms which, however, do not always resist the advances of time, so well as they did in her case. Goethe, who saw her in 1776 when she was at the zenith of her successful career, wrote to Frau von Stein: "The Schröter is an angel. If only Providence would send me such a wife, I would leave you in peace." A cast of the actress's beautiful hand can be seen amongst the treasures collected in the *Goethehaus* at Weimar, and one of his best poems (on Mieding's death) is dedicated to the actress. Corona, or Krone as Goethe called her, had every charm that could chain the affections of a man like Wolfgang. That she in a measure sacrificed a great career, to live in the comparative shade of so small a town as Weimar, is undoubted evidence that she regarded Goethe with a tender feeling. She sang exquisitely and was an excellent musician, her compositions being very harmonious and pleasing. On the stage her walk and every motion were full of nobility and grace. Although in her declamation she was apt to be somewhat too emphatic, her movements were perfectly under her control.

After she had been for many years a member of the amateur company of Weimar, she left the stage and became a *kammersängerin*, making her home altogether in Weimar, where she had many warm friends. In 1818 she died at Ilmenau, regretted by all who had known her.

Another charming singer was Fräulein von Rüdorf, who later on became Major von Knebel's wife. She had a beautiful voice of great flexibility, joined to wonderful purity and freshness of tone, and had been well trained in the Berlin Academy. It was quite by accident, however, that she became a professional singer; but having made a success in the leading part in the *Mondkäse*, she remained as a permanent member of the company. She sang roles such as Zerlina in *Don Giovanni*, Marguerite of Valois, and in *Richard Cœur de Lion*. On her marriage she left the stage, and accepted a post in the household of the Duchess Amalia, where she was also much esteemed as a private singer. She was still living in 1840, having lost her husband as well as her beloved patroness. She is often mentioned in Wieland's letters as the pretty Rüdelchen.

Goethe, Einsiedel, Seckendorf, Knebel, Bertuch, and Musäus all wrote for the amateur stage. Many of their works have been lost, but mention is made of most of them in the *Tiefurter Journal*.

Kraus, a very clever artist, undertook the painting of the scenery and the decoration of the stage, together with the control of the supers and carpenters, a rather arduous task. The name of Mieding, the first-rate machinist of the company, has been made immortal by Goethe's well-known lines.

With such exceptional management, and with a company endowed with many exceptional gifts, the amateur stage of Weimar could not fail to win a reputation unique in Europe, and one which has lived to the present day. To those who have had experience of the difficulties of managing an amateur company, due to the susceptibility, jealousy, and abnormal vanity of each individual, it seems an almost incredible fact that it should have existed for so many years without some terrible upheaval. Nevertheless, it is "a colossal truth" that, amongst this remarkable assemblage of talent, geniality and complete absence of anything like squabbles were a marked feature. For the rest, the arrangements were thoroughly original. For instance, there was the unique idea of having two companies, one for French the other for German plays, both of which were on the same footing and equally well looked after. The stage, being movable, was changed with the company that played.

It would seem, however, that a more distinct necessity for two companies arose from the same cause that often prevails under our present-day management. The Weimar actors received so many invitations to visit outlying provinces, that it was absolutely necessary to increase the *dramatis personæ*. These noble vagrants, thoughtless, extravagant, jovial, true Thespians at heart, in a right merry spirit, as Thusnelda describes, were ready to pack up bag and baggage and travel over hill and dale, from one hunting lodge, country seat, or distant town to another, from Ettersburg to Tiefurt, Belvedere, or further afield to Dornburg, Jena, Ilmenau, Erfurt, Rudolfstadt, and even as far as Leipzig. The actors had thus the advantage of a new public, and so avoided the terrible pitfall of always acting to the same audience, which in the long run is destructive of all individuality in an actor. The fresh surroundings and different circumstances in which the company found themselves were of immense service in giving confidence to new recruits, and correcting those mannerisms which are often the result of always playing before the same audience of friendly admirers. The efforts necessary to overcome the strangeness, the disadvantages and the obstacles which of necessity occurred in these Bohemian experiences, were of infinite value, and tended to form an altogether stronger type of actor than those now trained as it were in the more tender nursery at home.

It was, however, in Weimar itself and in its immediate neighbourhood that the dramatic life, under the immediate influence of Goethe, reached its highest point.

On the French stage the parts best played were by President von Lyncker, whose forte was *Mantellrollen* (old men's parts), Stallmeister von Stein, who had been many years in France, Count Puthus, and Einsiedel, who had the air of a *petit maître* especially in his young days, and was admirable as a forward page, etc. Goethe wavered between the romantic and the humorous *rôles*. Von Knebel was always the dignified father, or the offended husband, or the selfsacrificing somebody. The personality of Professor Musäus was laughter-provoking, even if he never spoke, and he was a good comic actor to boot.[61] Einsiedel preferred the *rôle* of lover, in which, however, he was not so popular as Goethe. Karl August also, and Prince Constantine, were constantly in the cast. The duke seems to have had certain gifts; at all events, he acted well enough *for a duke*, and was of course applauded accordingly. Prince Constantine was, I think, only once entrusted with an important part, that of Pylades in Goethe's *Iphigenia*, and played it only *once*, Karl August afterwards taking his place. Neither does Anna Amalia (who must have first place among the lady players) appear to have made any success beyond that accorded to her by esteem. One comes to this conclusion from the absence of all remark. Even Frau Rath Goethe fails to contribute one of her "honest, uncontrollable outbursts" of admiration. So, I think we must conclude that the *dear woman's* gifts did not lie in this direction. We may, however, be pretty sure that she never discovered the fact. Fräulein Göchhausen played the sprightly waiting-maid, and coquetted with the wicked French nobleman, who wanted to run away with her mistress. We know the sort of part. She varied it occasionally by taking that of a governess, but at all times she was clever and amusing, and it pains one to hear that some unfeeling people laughed at her deformity.

Mention must be made of the children's plays which occasionally took place, and which were admirably put on the stage. In one of these, called the *Edelknabe* (Noble Boy), young von Lyncker played the principal *rôle*, that of the prince was given to von Contes, who atterwards became president, while the part of the mother was taken by Frau Bonda, *kammerfrau* to the duchess. Young von Lyncker acted so well, that Anne Amalia promised him a watch set with turquoises, similar to one she had lent him for the performance; the little actor was also invited to the next ball at the *Redoute*.

The number of pieces produced at the Weimar Theatre is astonishing, and most of them were written by this wonderful circle of poets, writers, and geniuses. Einsiedel had a nice turn for comedies, most of them after the school of Louis XIV. He likewise adapted some of Molière's comedies. Knebel, who was always ponderous, wrote for the theatre, but imported so much of his gravity as to be wearisome. Goethe and, later, Schiller wrote some of their finest plays for the Weimar stage. Mention has already been made of the *Mitschuldigen* and *Die Geschwister*, both by Goethe. Other pieces came later on.

The West Indian, by Cumberland, appears in the theatrical repertory. It seems strange to read of Karl August playing Major O'Flaherty, Eckhoff the Father, and Goethe Belcour, the last named being dressed in a white coat with silver lace, blue silk vest, and blue silk knee-breeches, in which costume he said to have looked superb.

In January 1777 a new piece, called *Lila*, was played, its principal merit being the large sum spent in producing it — 7,516 thalers, an enormous sum even for the present day. Oefer, Anna Amalia's instructor in drawing, made exorbitant charges for painting the scenery, while the dresses cost seventy thalers apiece. In a letter written by Goethe to Bertuch, he says: "I must give the chief conductor of the orchestra a *douceur*, for he worked hard; also the town musicians must have something; therefore send Seckendorf forty-two thalers to distribute amongst them. G."

Amusements must be paid for, but we cannot be surprised that the poorer population grumbled at the extravagance of the court.

In 1778 Goethe's restless genius took a new departure. He tells his Charlotte that he has written a new play for the birthday of the Duchess Louise.

"It is a piece of nonsense, a comic opera — no less — full of folly and fun, an you please. If Seckendorf will set the rhymes to music that will fit them, we shall give it in winter time." And to Merck he writes, asking him, "What do you think of my new departure? You will say I am riding the demon of parody to death. Think of all the actors you know who lend themselves best to caricature. You will see at my mother's a sketch of the dresses, from a drawing by Kraus."

The real facts, however, were that the new piece, which was called *The Triumph of Sentimentality*, was written when Goethe was suffering keenly from an unfortunate consequence of his sentimental teaching in the *Sorrows of Werther*. A young girl committed suicide by throwing herself into the river Ilm. It seemed she had been deserted by her lover. In her pocket was a copy of the *Sorrows of Werther*. The body was taken to the house of Frau von Stein, as the nearest to the place where the misfortune occurred, and every effort made to restore life. Goethe remained all day trying to console the wretched parents. The incident distressed him deeply and added strength to his crusade against Wertherism and sentimentality, which he now exhibited in the most ridiculous light.

The hero of the piece is a prince, who lives for nothing but sentiment and serenades. He adores nature — in books, or as one sees it on the stage. Sunrise is lovely, but it breaks one's sleep; morning air, too, is often chilly, so he prefers remaining in bed. He, therefore, has a mechanical device made, a sort of travelling diorama, wherein trees, rocks, mountains, rivers, woods, in short, everything necessary for a romantic situation, could be presented at a moment's notice. Then the prince falls in love, but he wishes to be in love without having to submit to a woman's caprice or ruinous exactions; therefore a doll; he thinks, will answer the purpose as well. So one is made for him of life-size, and dressed in the same clothes as the woman he admires. To it he makes the most extravagant love. The real woman (Corona Schröter) appears, but he will have none of her and prefers his dolly; thus sentimentality triumphs.[62]

It has been justly said that, "National wit is scarcely amenable to criticism. What the German thinks exquisitely ludicrous is to a Frenchman or Englishman often of mediocre mirthfulness."

The cost of producing this piece came to three hundred and ninety-eight thalers, the chief item of expense being the dresses, which were unusually handsome. Corona Schröter's cost sixty thalers. The scenery and accessories were, on the other hand, very moderate. A painted moon was only one thaler, the doll's wig two thalers, and her stuffing only seven groschen.

This piece makes dull reading now, but when it was originally played at Weimar, Böttiger[63] tells us it was full of "exquisite fooling." "Coarse it was," he adds, "and most personal." This latter quality is naturally lost on readers of today. The satire was declared equal to that of Aristophanes, the spectators seeing themselves as in a mirror. At the end the doll was ripped open, and out fell a multitude of books which were then the rage, amongst them "Waldemar" and "Werther." The piece was interspersed with ballets, music, and comical changes of scene, so that what now reads as a dull farce was then a delightful extravaganza, bubbling over throughout with the same farcical spirit as is shown in the *Marktschreier of Plundersweilern*, full of the most scathing sarcasms, and ridiculing the author's own works as well as those of Wieland and Jacobi.

For the rest, the methods resorted to in these parodies were decidedly in the worst taste. Every person who had any peculiarity, or whose life contained any adventure which lent itself to burlesque, was introduced into the piece, the unfortunate original being present, a fact which — of course — increased the fun. It must be granted that Goethe in no way spared himself, *Werther* and his sentimentality being, as we have seen, made supremely ridiculous. By so doing, he thought he earned the right to burlesque others, and, as the duke appeared to thoroughly enjoy this "pillory of wit," no one ventured to say a word against what was undoubtedly a breach of good manners. Moreover, a man of Goethe's genius should have been above "burlesquing," which is not a refined amusement, especially when carried so far as to ridicule publicly a work like Wieland's *Alceste*. There was a general feeling of disapprobation when the famous farewell of Alceste to Ahmet, "Weep not, thou idol of my soul! "was accompanied by the sound of the posthorn. Wieland, who was present, gave a loud cry and left the theatre. Everyone present felt that a man of his age and position should not have been exposed to so public an insult.

In *Orpheus and Eurydice*, composed by Seckendorf, Wieland's *Alceste* was again chosen as a subject for burlesque, and yet, strange to say, Anna Amalia lent her countenance to this insult to her old friend by playing the part of Eurydice, Seckendorf taking that of Orpheus, who is represented as an Italian improvisator who has come to demand the release of his beloved from the shadowy kingdom below the earth. The other characters were played by Bode, Countess Bernstorff, and Herr Seidler. The performance was strictly private, only twelve persons being present.

Goethe wrote to Frau Stein of this affair: "We have made merry over Wieland's masterpiece; after all one must be foolish sometimes, and we are no worse than the generality of mankind."

Wieland did not see the matter in this light. Writing to Merck he expresses himself in strong terms: — What gives me pain," he says, "is that every blackguard trick that takes place at Weimar or at Ettersburg is made known, God knows how, to the world at large. You'll therefore soon hear of the honour done to me at Ettersburg; namely that in a farce called *Orpheus and Eurydice*, the song:

"'Weep not, thou idol of my soul!'"

was parodied in the most ridiculous manner you can well imagine, and threw the large audience into shouts of laughter — this is how we treat our friends here. The unclean spirit of *polissonnerie*[64] and ridicule of everything most sacred, which has for a long time prevailed in the higher circles, supersedes all feelings of decency, all ideas of fitness of place and season, all delicacy, all modesty, and deadens all shame. I confess I am weary of it; I believe, however, the intention is to disgust me, and so drive me into the *sottise* of leaving."

Goethe at this time writes in his dairy: "We are committing all sorts of follies here." It would seem, indeed, as if the demon of discord had entered into his mind. A few days before the Wieland episode, an equally unpleasant incident took place in the trial of Jacobi, for writing a novel called *Waldemar*. The two brothers Jacobi belonged to the Sentimentalist school, and were intimate with the literary set of Weimar. The younger brother had written *Waldemar* which was read out to a select circle, seated under an oak tree at Ettersburg.

The reading over, judgment was pronounced and sentence passed. Then Goethe ascended the tree, and to punish the writer and to give a warning to others, the book was nailed to the tree by its cover, the leaves fluttering in the wind, to the great delight of all who saw it. Jacobi,[65] when he heard of this trial and sentence, was indignant, and let Goethe hear of his anger. Goethe answered through a friend that the whole matter was to him unpleasant, the book eminently so, and that he could not resist the temptation to turn it into a burlesque, particularly the close, where "Waldemar" is fetched by the devil, etc. The Duchess Anna Amalia had a printing press of her own at Ettersburg, and on this a copy of a revised *Waldemar* was printed, with woodcuts and some "alterations." The duchess-dowager sent Merck a copy of this skit, saying: "If this venture pleases the public, a new volume will shortly follow."

We turn with relief from the spectacle of genius descending to buffoonery to welcome *Iphigenia*, one of Goethe's finest dramas, but one which was not finished without many struggles and much grief of heart, which at times amounted almost to despair. His letters to his friends, and especially to Frau von Stein, tell the story of what a poet can suffer in the effort to realise the dream of his poetic nature, especially in the heated atmosphere of court life, which was so adverse to the lofty theme which filled his mind, and which as yet he could not bring forth.

Lest his conception of the high-souled Grecian maiden should fail in its intention, he took flight. He writes from Dornburg, 10 March 1779, after a few days' residence there:

"The piece is coming into shape, its limbs begin to work. I live with the men of this place. I eat and drink, joke sometimes, but am hardly conscious of what I am about. My interior life follows another and very different road. Now I have a faint hope that I may make my escape between eleven and twelve tonight from Apolda."

Again he writes to Knebel, to whom was entrusted the part of Thoas:

"Excellent old man, I must confess I am a perambulating poet. If only I could get two or three quiet days to myself in the dear little castle at Dornburg, I should get finished in no time. Of such good luck I see no chance at present. This evening the noise made by two dogs has nearly driven me wild. Neither threats nor *pourboires* to their owners will get them silenced."

In March he writes to Frau Stein: "It is useless, the thing is accursed!"

And again, the same day, to Knebel, he complains bitterly of the uselessness of his efforts. On the 7th there seems no salvation anywhere, "and I am tormented grievously by one scene in particular. I think if only I could get a good start, the rest would follow at a swinging pace."

From Büttstadt he writes more cheerfully, and from Allstadt comes the news that the first three acts are ready. On the 13th, he writes to Knebel:

"See Prince Constantine alone (he was to play Pylades), read him over his part quietly, and give him some hints how it is to be played."

On 16 March 1779 he goes away again to Ilmenau with the determination not to return until the piece is finished. He wrote the fourth act in one day, sitting on the Schwalben rock at Ilmenau; and on the 28th, the drama was finished.

On 6 April 1779, (in Easter week), the first performance of Iphigenia took place. The caste was as follows:

Orestes[66]	....	GOETHE
Pylades	....	PRINCE CONSTANTINE[67]
Thoas	....	KNEBEL
Arkas	....	SEIDLER
Iphigenia	....	CORONA SCHRÖTER

"Never shall I forget," exclaims Dr. Hufeland, "the impression Goethe made as Orestes in his Grecian costume. One might have fancied him Apollo. Never before had there been seen such union of physical and intellectual beauty in one man." His acting, nevertheless, according to his biographer, had the defects of most amateurs, being impetuous and yet stiff, exaggerated and yet cold. He had other faults which have been mentioned before, but in spite of his defects he managed to charm his audience, and there is no doubt in humorous parts he was equal to the best professional actor of his day. Anna Amalia writes to Frau Goethe, to thank her for some little present, and sends her a copy of *Iphigenia*.

"WEIMAR, 1779

"DEAR GOOD MOTHER,

"I am in receipt of two letters from you and also the boxes of biscuits, for which I thank you heartily. What you tell me of the marriage of La Roche's daughter[68] is incomprehensible. I have shown your letter to Doctor Wolf, but his residence at court has taught him fine manners, so he neither ground his teeth nor cursed under his breath, but shrugged his shoulders at the lamentable history. We are all curious to learn the name of the man to whom poor Louise is to be sacrificed. The proverb which says, 'Judge me by my words but not by my actions,' applies to these Sentimentalists, who have no hearts. The third festival has passed off well, and Thusnelda will send you a full account. It has been again repeated and with great applause. I must send you the whole score of Iphigenia, that you may judge for yourself what a fine work it is.

"You wish, dear mother, to know who has cut out my silhouette. [69] It is the work of your son, who first drew it and gave it to his faithful Philip who cut it out. That is the whole riddle.[70]

Towards the end of May I expect Merck at Ettersburg. Ah, mother, dear mother, I am sure you guess my thoughts. How is it with the old father? Give him many greetings from me.

"Good-bye, best of mothers, keep me in your thoughts and think of me often.
"Your friend,
        "AMALIA."

In the beginning of the year 1778, the dramatic company received a new recruit by the arrival of Countess Bernstorff,[71] whose niece had married Frau von Stein's brother (von Schardt). The countess, who had lately been left a widow, was accompanied by her man of business, Bode.[72]

"The day of your departure," writes Anna Amalia to Merck, "came the Countess von Bernstorff with Bode, and they are both here now. You know well all the reports that are spread about us, and to keep up our reputation of eccentricity we made both the countess and Bode pass their examination, she in acting and Bode as dramatic author. I send you herewith a prologue and some songs, etc., written by him. Bode has likewise rearranged an old French piece called *La Gouvernante*. He played the Gouvernante excellently, and Wedel made a very amusing lover. Geheimerath Schardt was his servant, while the Countess Bernstorff, Thusnelda, myself, and the little Schardt, were the pupils of the governess, who in the end took herself off and left her charges to do as they liked. This was kept very quiet, and one afternoon when we were all ready, I invited my children and the Duchess, Seckendorf, and Goethe to come out, and we played our little piece with great *éclat.*"

On another occasion Bode was acting in a piece called *The Imprisoned Maiden*, a piece of American extraction, dealing with a castle that surrendered to women's wiles. Bode was the commandant of the besieging army and Commander Braun defended the castle. Bode, who was an enormous man, both in height and breadth, could not find a costume large enough to fit him, and was therefore stitched into fleshings. When the sound of the battle going on outside reached him in his tent, he rose up from his couch, but — well, to put it gently, the sewing had given way; therefore the curtain had to be lowered.

Also in the after-piece, *The Jealous Husband*, there was another misfortune. The part of the lover was to be played by Einsiedel, who fell ill shortly before the performance began, and his place was taken by the before-named Commander Braun, who learned his part and got Einsiedel to coach him, so that it went fairly well, especially as there was a good prompter, who promised to keep his attention on the new recruit. All went smoothly till the scene in which the lovers are surprised by the jealous husband, who is hidden behind a curtain and has to rush out when he gets his cue. This word was utterly forgotten by Braun, who was stricken with a terrible attack of stage fright. He stuttered and stuttered. The husband waited in vain.

At last, seeing there was no alternative, Bertuch (who played the part of the jealous husband) rushed forth from his concealment, sword in hand, to take his life and so make an end of it. The captain, however, was too upset to grasp this idea, and absolutely refused to be killed. In vain Bertuch whispered in his ear: "In the devil's name why don't you die?" Nothing would restore common sense to the distracted actor. Finally Goethe, out of all patience, called out in a stentorian voice: "If he won't die like a brave man, let him die like a coward! Stab him in the back!" But even this did not restore the nerves of the victim to stage fright; he still continued stuttering, while Bertuch, stealing behind him, gave him a tremendous shove, which precipitated him on to the stage, where he lay helpless, and was borne away on a shutter amidst peals of laughter from the audience.

It had long been promised that Merck should come to Weimar in the spring of 1779:

"The duchess is counting the hours till you come," writes kind-hearted Wieland to his friend; and then he adds, "I must really scold you for not having sent an answer to her kind invitation. You are always preaching to us that we are not sufficiently attentive to our Gracious Princess, and, as St. Paul says, behold you are now the castaway. You know, and the duchess knows also, that we are all quite silly about you, and that you can treat us as a beauty treats her lovers. Goodbye. It is to me vexatious that when you are so near I have still to write."

Wieland's affection for his friends was a beautiful trait in his character, which for the rest appears to have been as sincere as it was loving. And yet what a Voltairean curve there is in the thin lips!

Merck's visit was highly satisfactory. He was the friend of everyone, the two duchesses being included in the number of his admirers, and although this made things somewhat difficult, he managed to steer safely through, his long experience of courts naturally being in his favour.

Merck's visit over, things suddenly took a disagreeable turn. These things happen everywhere. We all know what dark days are, and it is not unpleasant to hear that royalties have to endure these changes of *temperature* as well as their subjects. Again it is Wieland who gives us a peep at Anna Amalia, who is now at Ettersburg.

"There is nothing but scraping of fiddles, blowing of cornopeans, and piping of whistles; it is enough to make the little angels in heaven sing Alleluias. It is a good thing for the dear woman that she loves all the Muses collectively."

Belvedere, Ettersburg, and Tiefurt are the country seats of the ducal family, the two last being more intimately connected with the Weimar stage. Anna Amalia resided at either one or the other during the summer and autumn seasons. Ettersburg, about an hour and a half distant from Weimar, is charmingly situated on the north side of the Ettersburg. The air there possesses that vivifying quality which is especially characteristic of the Thuringian mountains. It is a commodious but by no means palatial residence. There is a beautiful hall and a charming dining-room with a delightful gallery, where the musicians play. There are some fine pictures, and *objets d'art* in great abundance. The rooms are shown where certain royalties slept at different times; Napoleon and Alexander, Czar of Russia, who were at Erfurt in 1808, hunted in the forest of Ettersburg, and lunched with Karl August under the shade of one of the magnificent linden trees.

The room is likewise shown where Schiller wrote one of the scenes of his *Maria Stuart*, and where he and Goethe worked together — it is pleasant to think that these two great men were free from the usual literary jealousy. It is therefore plain that Ettersburg has its associations, irrespective of the highly carved bedsteads in which a whole family might sleep comfortably, and which divers great personages occupied on certain occasions recorded in the guidebooks.

I confess I felt more impressed when I stood in the large room, now an armoury, where Anna Amalia and her *beaux esprits* strutted their brief hour on their mimic stage: But even here the association is more with the theatre in the wood. The great beauty of Ettersburg lies in the woods which surround it, and stretch away for miles. In the autumn of the year great *battues* are now held in these woods, where in Anna Amalia's time the ladies and gentlemen of her suite amused themselves with picnics, walking parties, and all the different diversions with which a number of young and lively people turn the summer into one long holiday. Best of all, in the very centre of this delicious solitude, in the very heart of the wood, did the dear romantic nature of Anna Amalia conceive the idea of erecting a pastoral stage, whereon pastoral plays could be played. The Arcadian playhouse, as designed by this delightful duchess, is today pointed out to visitors.

It is easy to note the traces of the fairy ring, which was made in the thick vegetation by the cutting away of undergrowth and the clipping of overlapping branches. A regular wall of bushes, cut to the proper, height, formed a partition between actors and spectators, while the natural advantages of the spot furnished a background of trees, and a carpet of green moss over which rugs were thrown, and which made decoration easy.

Look for a moment, I pray you, at that lovely copper beech, whose branches make so delicious a shade to the weary eyes of the zealous sightseer. Look well at its massive stem; you see there what knits us who live in the present to the far-away past, and to those fair ones, whose airy figures flitted through the shady woods, whose gay voices resounded from point to point, lending to this charming solitude life and animation. We seem to see this gay company, when in the glee of their hearts they laughingly inscribed, or had writ for them, those names which you and I are looking at. They will last as long as the old trees stand — though they who wrote have passed their centenary we know not where!

It must be confessed that the names are written in a very up-and-down fashion, scrawled as children would scrawl them over the bark of the old tree. Von Falk, Knebel, and Wieland are together; a little further on a shaky hand has written Schiller, Lyncker, and Bertuch. Then we have the names of Einsiedel and Fräulein Göschhausen, and at a little distance those of Princess Caroline, the daughter of Duchess Louise and Karl August, and of Karl Alexander the late grand duke!

To return to the theatricals at Ettersburg, the wildest ebullitions of fun and humour were allowed. Here Goethe's political *Puppenspiel* was produced in honour of Anna Amalia's birthday, but it was not a surprise entertainment, for we are told the duchess got it up and worked hard to have it ready for the occasion.

In October 1776 Wieland writes to Merck: "The duchess is arranging to have Goethe's *Puppenspiel* at her next *fête*. Everyone is busy; Kranz with the orchestra, and Kraus with the scenery. For the last fourteen days all hands have been at work, and nearly all day, at Ettersburg. Goethe comes occasionally to see how the work is getting on, and the duchess is everywhere the life and soul of the whole thing; she keeps the ball rolling, and works away with her whole mind and with all her strength. I pretend to see nothing of what is going on until all is ready. This is a harmless mystification which always takes place on these occasions, and to which I submit with the best grace possible. Certainly half the court and a good many of the townsfolk play in the piece. For instance, Fräulein von Wöllwärth is the ginger-bread girl, the Schröter plays the Tyrolese, and Madame Wolf Queen Esther. I would give a gold piece that you were here to see the fun, but if you did come you would have to join the company. Goethe will have it that you will be here when the nightingales sing, and by that time he will have completed all the improvements he is making on this side of the Ilm, and which, between you and me, will cost a pretty penny. There will be a row in the Chamber when the bill comes in, but the improvements have changed this side of Weimar into an Elysium."

With one of Thusnelda's lifelike touches she paints the whole scene. "With the blessing of God we played in the new theatre Einsiedel's version of *Le Medecin Malgrè Lui*, and afterwards Goethe's *Jahrmarkt von Plundersweilern*, which was received with great applause by the distinguished audience. We have been three weeks hard at work, the smell of paint and the noise of hammers making a pleasant diversion; our duchess, Dr. Wolf[73] Kraus, etc., tumbling over one another in their eagerness to get all finished in time." She goes on to say that Einsiedel's translation of Molière's play, which was the curtain-raiser, was admirably played, Einsiedel making a first-rate Sganarelle. Goethe was Léandre, and the Duke, Valère. This, however, was only the prologue to the event of the night, Goethe's admirable farce or *Puppenspiel*, in which he played three parts, as will be seen by the accompanying bill, which was sent by the Fräulein to Goethe's mother.

Doktor	VON EINSIEDEL
Marktschreier (Town-crier)	GOETHE
Ahasuerus	MUSÄUS
Esther	MADAME WOLF
Hamann	GOETHE
Mardochai	GOETHE
Tyrolean peasant	CORONA SCHRÖTER
Pfefferkuchenmädchen (gingerbread seller)	FRÄULEIN VON WÖLLWÄRTH
Office porter	BERTUCH
Wife to the porter	DEM. PROBST
Tyrolean	VON SECKENDORF
Native of Nüremberg	SCHALLING
Carriage greaser	VON LYNCKER
Captain of the Gypsies	STEINHART

Gypsy boy	SEIDLER
Peasant	STEINHART
Wife to the same	MADAME STEINHART
Milk maid	DEM. NEUHAUS
Savoyard with Marmot	VON LYNCKER,
Savoyard with Marmot	VON TODTENWARDT
Butcher	VON STAFF
Pork butcher	VON LUCK (Kammerherr)
Governess	FRÄULEIN THUSNELDA — i.e., V. GÖCHHAUSEN
Demoiselle	FRÄULEIN VON KOPPENFELS
Parson	KRAUS
Sausage man	AULHORN
Shadow	AULHORN

The audience included, in, addition to the two duchesses the Crown Princess of Brunswick, who enjoyed the drollery of the farce immensely. A banquet followed, and then, to quote again from Fräulein Göchhausen: "Their high and mighties (with the exception of our duchess) took their departure, while we, the *pack of comedians*, enjoyed ourselves at a ball specially given *for us*, which lasted till daylight made us ashamed of our revels." The *Jahrmarkt* was the first of the series of "masked plays" (or pantomimes more rightly) which became so popular. These nonsense plays, as Goethe called them, were not always in the best taste. They originated in Goethe's visit to Darmstadt in 1777. Goethe's mother writes to Anna Amalia, 1778:

"How I should have enjoyed being present at the *Jahrmarkt von Plundersweilern*[74] and to hear who played in it. Fräulein Thusnelda has graciously promised to send me a full account."

On 4 November 1778 Anna Amalia replies:

"Thusnelda is sending you an elaborate account of the *fête* I gave on my birthday. Friend Wolf managed everything for me, and das *Jahrmarkt* went off splendidly. Your son sends you the score of the play as it was acted, and you will also receive a picture, the joint work of Kraus, Wolf, and myself. It is the portrait of Seckendorf as the street beggar, and is a contribution to the Weimar apartment. I am getting the songs I wrote for the piece arranged for the piano, and so soon as they are ready, you shall have them.

"Think of me as your friend,
"AMALIA."

Frau Aja, in sending back the picture (it was only lent for a few days), describes the effect it produced on Merck:

"GRACIOUS PRINCESS,

I return you the Masterpiece. It would be impossible to describe the pleasure and joy it gave me, and all those who have seen it, but I must tell you about Merck. He arrived punctually at 12 o'clock. The company to meet him were Bolling and Riese. We lunched well, and then I brought Merck to see the picture. He was amazed. I did not let him touch it, and when I saw him take out his handkerchief and rub in a corner, I just carried it away to another room. At Ahasuerus, Hamann, and Mardochai we all laughed heartily, also at the caricature of Herr Wolf with the silhouette in his hand." There is a great charm in these letters of Frau Goethe's, the charm of simplicity. She makes no effort at being anything but herself, and even the friendship of a duchess did not upset her mental equilibrium.[75]

At Ettersburg the open-air performances were constantly given by torchlight. In this manner were performed Einsiedel's operetta, *The Robbers*, also *The Gypsies*, in which Goethe collaborated with Einsiedel. (In this last a good deal was borrowed from *Götz von Berlichingen*.)

Another curious conceit of Goethe's was to write a piece after the manner of Aristophanes, in which a number of persons represented different birds, being dressed in the actual feathers of the bird they represented. They could move their heads and stretch out their wings and agitate their tails: the owls and the horned owls could roll their eyes. Wieland writes to Merck:

"We have had a strange performance at Ettersburg (in the open air), which, being well executed, had the most ludicrous effect. In addition to the intense enjoyment afforded by this Aristophanic comedy to the duke and the dowager duchess, it was pleasant to see that Goethe, in spite of all the tormenting cares of his ministerial life, was able to enjoy himself like a boy. He was in excellent humour."

He adds that Corona Schröter spoke the epilogue, in which the well-known phrase so often quoted was heard for the first time: "The unspoilt favourite of the Graces."

For the birthday of Karl August, in 1782, the Duchess Amalia held high festival at Ettersburg, and a theatrical representation of the *Judgment of Paris* was given. This piece has been lost or stolen, like many others written for the private theatres of Ettersburg and Tiefurt by Goethe, such as *The Women of the Venusberg*, and *The Ratcatcher of Hamlyn*, of which only the well-known, "Ratcatcher's Song" has been preserved.

The Gypsies, a joint composition of Einsiedel and Goethe, referred to above, was beautifully represented. The performance took place after a hunt which had been given by the duke at Ettersburg, and the dowager duchess had invited a number of guests to witness the open-air theatricals. The carriages with the invited guests arrived at the moment that Karl August and his party in their hunting-dress were riding into the courtyard; the dowager duchess clapped her hands; immediately on this signal a rocket went up in the woods, and like lightning a blaze of light illumined the dark shadowy trees. On the arm of her son, Anna Amalia led the way through the illuminated park, followed by guests, till they reached the theatre which Nature had formed in the woods, with thick-growing bushes for scenery. Here they found a gypsy encampment with a bright fire of sticks, upon which a kettle was boiling gypsy fashion. The zither sounded; gypsies arrive with packets of stolen goods; there is great joy. The gypsy captain, Adolar, was played by Goethe; Helarin, the heroine, by Corona Schröter. There is an oil painting at Ettersburg which represents this scene. It is by the indefatigable Kraus, who has handed down so much that recalls this golden period of Weimar.

CHAPTER X

Situated in the quiet valley of the Ilm, where the river narrows as it runs through the mountain paths, surrounded with the greenest of meadows, embosomed in a forest of umbrageous trees, Tiefurt, so far as the house is in question, is a disappointment. One has read so much of all that went on there, that the modest country house, or rather old-fashioned farmhouse, is something of a shock. Tiefurt was originally built as a residence for the overseer or superintendent of the large farms appertaining to the estate, which now contributes a goodly portion of the ducal revenues. The situation was, however, so much to Anna Amalia's liking, its solitude so complete, its old-fashioned simplicity so attractive, that, without spending money to transform it into a royal residence, and so spoil the charm that she found in its simplicity, the duchess did merely what was necessary to make it suitable for Prince Constantine and his tutor, von Knebel.

The Becken bridge was left standing, and resting-places were made in the solitude of the far-stretching woods, rustic bridges spanned the running river, statues ornamented the grounds; while behind the house the large and beautiful park extended for miles. Walks of great length can be taken under the shade of the spreading trees, and the pedestrian of today at almost every step comes on some memento of the days when Tiefurt was the scene of joyous gatherings.

To Tiefurt, (after Prince Constantine ceased to reside here), Anna Amalia was wont to come in summer time, and here the fashionable society of Weimar spent many a summer's day, their gay voices resounding through the woods. The names of the fair ladies who walked here with their lovers are — many of them — carved, as at Ettersburg, on the bark of the noble trees. Memorials to artists, singers, men distinguished in various paths of life, are set up in out-of-the-way places. A moss-covered arbour on the banks of the Ilm is dedicated as a sort of temple to the goddess Thalia. In a lovely nook, shaded by the over-hanging branches of the trees, on a bank of moss over which in summer-time grows a profusion of roses, is erected a statue to Mozart. He carries a lyre of colossal size, and on either side are the masks of comedy and tragedy with cloak and stave. The white stone rising out of the soft green moss is truly artistic, while the ever-flowing Ilm running at the foot of the altar chants an eternal song of praise.

I have said that the exterior of Tiefurt is disappointing, but if this feeling exists, it is amply compensated by the interest of the interior. Here we come in touch, as it were, with those who lived there: and as we walk through the quaint old house, the feeling of their actual presence follows us as we move through the rooms they once inhabited, touch the inanimate objects they used, and make comments on their mode of life.

Everything remains as it was when Anna Amalia and her circle spent the summer days in this sweet spot. Here, in a little cell or nook, so small as only to hold a table and chair, Goethe was wont to write when on a visit. The inkstand and the letter book which he used, still lie on the table, which is placed at a window overlooking the wooded landscape. Goethe loved Tiefurt with its tranquil silence. He came here often, staying for weeks at a time. His taste was of great help to the duchess in arranging her new hobby, especially in the hanging of the pictures which cover the walls at Tiefurt. These are of different standards of excellence. Many are copies of Italian masters, made during Amalia's visit to Rome in 1788, by Bury and other artists. There are some originals by Angelica Kaufmann and Tischbein, one by Sir Joshua Reynolds of Lady Waldegrave, afterwards Duchess of Gloucester, and a portrait of Lady Coventry; also one of Lady Hamilton. The cabinets of china show beautiful specimens of Sévres and Meissen, one tea-service being the gift of Frederick the Great to his dear niece.

As in most houses of the period, these valuable specimens are mixed up with a "congattory" of rubbish such as ladies then delighted to collect about them. Copies of paintings done in tentstitch, framed and glazed, fans with Chinese figures pasted on cardboard, or cardboard pricked and worked in silk, and collections of shells were a great feature, as were also chairs worked in tent-stitch. Very charming is the model of a stage and theatre. One of these Goethe always had made for each piece that was acted at the theatre of Weimar.

In the dining-room there is a wonderful sideboard, one side of which is an enormous winecooler. In the duchess's sitting-room, which is a good-sized apartment, everything remains as it was when she occupied it. In this room there are two beautiful marble busts, one of her lady-in-waiting, Charlotte von Stein, another of Goethe, by Gulanor. There is also a wonderful collection of silhouettes, then so much the fashion; those of Karl August and Frau von Stein were cut by Goethe.

In the August of 1780, Anna Amalia had to make a journey to Brunswick to take a last farewell of her father, who died shortly after her arrival. His death grieved her much. From the time of her marriage he had associated himself closely with her and her affairs, and during her regency his advice had been of the utmost service. She therefore was much affected by this breaking of the tender tie between parent and child. She would never feel young again. Weimar and Ettersburg seemed too bright and gay for her present mood; Tiefurt, with its shady walks and extreme quiet, seemed more suited to her melancholy thoughts; so to Tiefurt she came rusticating. Constantine and his tutor, Knebel, had lived here for three years. The prince was now making the grand tour. We have of late lost sight of Prince Constantine; he has only shown himself occasionally, taking part in a hunt or theatricals, in which latter he did not distinguish himself. You can see from his portrait that he was a poor, feeble creature, weak in body and not strong mentally, for which his accident of birth was in a measure accountable. Tiresome as a child, troublesome as a boy, he retained these disagreeable qualities, and as he grew to man's estate developed a fund of eccentricity as well. Knebel, who was his tutor for years, does not seem to have possessed the firmness of character required in dealing with so curious a nature. In vain he endeavoured to infuse into his pupil's mind some higher instincts than those which led him to court the society of ballet dancers, and to drink with common louts at country inns; Constantine smiled the flickering smile we see in his portrait, and "pulled his young moustache."

There was no rousing him, for the reason that he had no taste, no ambition, no military instinct. He was indifferent to everything except hanging about the green-room of a theatre. This taste soon landed him in an entanglement with a second-rate actress, which was the cause of so much talk and scandal, that the duke, to get him out of the way, arranged that he should travel with Knebel. The young prince, however, refused to go, unless he had the companion he wished, and as his choice was Hofrath Albrecht, stepson to the Abbé Jerusalem, no exception could be taken. Albrecht, though a clever and excellent man, proved a somewhat dull companion, so that Constantine found his own selection a greater bore than even Knebel, and as soon as he reached Paris shook off his guardian, and plunged into all the dissipation of the most dissipated capital in Europe. From Paris he went to London, where he resided for several years, returning at last to Weimar, where he was received as the prodigal son. He resided in Weimar until 1802, when he died at the age of forty-four. When Anna Amalia came to spend the summer of 1780 at Tiefurt he was still abroad, and this was another source of anxiety to the duchess, who had always loved *son petit Constantin*. Wieland, who had a tender nature, was anxious about the dear woman, "who is here, with Thusnelda as her only companion. Her lady-of-honour, Frau von Stein, has gone to cool her hot blood at the waters of Pyrmont; there is no company, two servants forming the whole of the establishment."

This quiet life, without a master of the ceremonies or a casino, suited Anna Amalia's present frame of mind admirably. "One can study in peace," she writes in August to Merck.

Another attraction which Tiefurt possessed for Anna Amalia was that here, more than at any other of the royal residences, she could regulate her life as she pleased. She loved to spend the spring and summer days in this dear retreat, where she was free from the state and ceremony which hedged in life at Weimar, under the rule of Duchess Louise.

Soon after she had risen, Anna Amalia, in her morning gown, her still beautiful hair tucked carelessly away under a large straw hat, went to feed her pets, the much-prized English hens, and her pretty cooing doves. Then there were other animals to be noticed besides these special favourites. When this duty was over, the duchess strolled leisurely, her book in her hand, to her favourite seat in the park. Here she loitered, sometimes reading, more often thinking, until the sound of a bell warned her that it was time to return to the house and get ready for the midday meal.

Her toilette did not occupy much time, and while her maid arranged her hair the letters which had come were read. Her lady-in-waiting (generally Fräulein Göchhausen) and Einsiedel dined with her, and occasionally there were strangers. Wieland was a constant guest, for Anna Amalia, who had a sincere regard for the now elderly philosopher, had given him a tiny residence in the park, where in the later years of his life he came every spring, and in this peaceful retreat wrote his later works. After dinner the duchess retired, and the rest of the household amused themselves until the bell sounded tea time. If the weather was fine tea was taken out of doors, a convenient plan in view of the number of people who usually came in the afternoon to visit the duchess. Tea was served under the shade of the trees. As everyone knew that Anna Amalia detested stiffness and undue ceremony, the guests were quite at their ease and natural; and the woods resounded with gay voices, and the air was filled with the sound of laughter; the younger portion of the guests playing games, running races, all in the most joyous spirit. Those, however, who, either through disposition or advancing years, had no taste for such frivolity, were in no way required to exert themselves, but could sit quiet, either absorbed in contemplation or conversing with their neighbours. "Above all things let us have no social martyrs," Anna Amalia would say; "this is Liberty Hall."

It was, however, when the day with its cares and its amusements was over, and the stillness of evening had hushed the stir and bustle which had reigned in the afternoon, that the most enjoyable time was at hand. Then, those who formed the intimate circle gathered in the drawing-room, where the time was spent either in music, which Anna Amalia loved passionately, or in turning over the pages of some new book; and if anything was to be read aloud it was entrusted to Fräulein Göchhausen, while the other ladies worked at a large frame, in which was stretched a piece of tapestry intended by Anna Amalia as a present for her son. If the weather was unfavourable for an evening stroll, the duchess played a game with Wieland, or perhaps he would propose to read aloud one of his manuscripts, which he had brought in his pocket. Then woe to any unreflecting person who was not properly attentive, or who ventured to whisper or make an interruption of any kind; the irascible author would burst into an angry tirade, put his paper back in his pocket and retire into his shell, where he remained unmoved alike by the most abject apologies from the offending party, or by Anna Amalia's soothing words until the appearance of the supper tray, when the clouds cleared away and a most enjoyable interchange of thought on every subject followed.

At such moments Anna Amalia was at her best. She showed the rich stores of her mind, not ostentatiously or with the air of a bluestocking, but talked with much simplicity upon all subjects from the highest philosophy to some *jeu d'esprit*, which she appreciated with all the quickness of an intelligent nature. Her reminiscences, of remarkable people she had met and episodes of her life, were of the deepest interest. Neither was she always in this mood. Amalia was, like all sensitive people, very responsive to her surroundings, and an uncongenial element among those about her produced the effect that a breath of cold air has on a musical instrument, it put her out of tune — or perhaps out of harmony would be the better expression.

Yet, in regard to the life at Tiefurt or elsewhere, it is not for a moment to be supposed that it was Elysium. A state of Elysium cannot be expected to exist where men and women are in daily contact. Philosophers they might be, but the proverb, which tells us that, if we "Scratch the Russian, etc.," applied here as elsewhere: we might exemplify this by an Eastern proverb, "Where there is much light there are many shadows." Goethe has demonstrated this in his Rembrandtesque effects, and such effects can be made on the human canvas. The highly gifted men and women who formed such a remarkable circle in Weimar, were apt, even at Anna Amalia's evening reception, to fall into discussions in which their uncontrolled passions often made them forget the presence of their hostess and her ladies. "Wieland's ill-humoured criticism, Herder's biting persiflage, Knebel's uncontrollable temper, and above all Goethe's dictatorial manner, each of these acting upon one another often caused such an explosion as required all Amalia's powers of soothing to restore even a semblance of tranquillity."

Having arranged to spend a portion of the year at Tiefurt, Anna Amalia made herself acquainted with her surroundings, and, as was her custom, strove to render all the people round her happy and content, in which endeavour she was seconded by Frau Aja, than whom none understood better how to help in such a work.

Wieland, writing to Merck, gives us a picture of life at Tiefurt. "Our dear good Duchess Amalia is rusticating here since Prince Constantine has gone to travel. I circulate between my writing desk, my garden, and Tiefurt. . . . You may be sure that nothing short of some very rough treatment on your part (which I have no reason to expect) will ever put an end to her friendship for you, which is true and sincere. She is really one of the best women on God's earth, and I doubt very much whether, in her position of life, you will find another with such a heart and head, or one with whom people of our station in life can associate, and yet preserve the right to their own individual opinions. For my part, I should be the most ungrateful wretch between heaven and earth, if I could forget all the kindness she has shown me and mine, and how she has assisted in making the happiness of my life. I assure you that I have no idea how I should survive this dear princess, if I live to my seventieth year."

Amalia's disposition was so instinct with life and the desire for progress, that she infused the same qualities into those about her.

Wieland in 1782. acknowledges that "Up to now the dowager duchess has been our great helper; without her Weimar would ere now have sunk into as insignificant, wearisome and soulannihilating a nest as any in Germany."

Wieland was evidently in a bad temper with the duke and his *Geheimerath* when he gave vent to this ebullition; not that I am disparaging the effect of Anna Amalia's judicious help and always ready sympathy: she had her own troubles and made head against them bravely, finding, as she tells us, in music a veritable angel of consolation in hours which otherwise would have been dreary.

"It is a cordial for the black vapours," she writes to Knebel, "and it is written in the Bible that King Saul drove away black melancholy with musical instruments. You must not think, however, dear Knebel, that I am in Saul's condition of mind."

Writing to Knebel after her return from Worlitz (from whence she brought a new plan for improving the grounds at Tiefurt, by growing yew and laurel hedges) she says:

"Hardly have I arrived here when I am full of beginning my new plans. My poor Tiefurt is astonished at my grand ideas, and indeed my hands are full. I took the Bosquet, which was in a terrible condition, in hand, and have brought it to so good a state that neither fauns nor nymphs need now be ashamed to take up their residence there."

Of course, Amalia had the usual feminine craze of the period for writing those long, crossed and sometimes recrossed letters, written in palest ink on quarto paper, which was folded in four and sealed with red or black wax. They were all kept carefully in their cases; and well that it was so, for what a fund of interest we of the present day have found in these dusty boxes; how the publication of their contents have upset all we have learned in our youth as to Mary Queen of Scots and many others, and what delightful reading they have been. There are no such letter-writers nowadays, and most people tear up their letters, so there will be no turning out of tin boxes for the benefit of succeeding generations.

"On 11 August 1781," Wieland writes, "the Weimar circle, Goethe included, came here for the Harvest Festival, and on the 12th there was also an entertainment for the country folk."

On 16 August 1781 the following announcement appeared. It brings us in touch with what Anna Amalia called her little joke.

"A society of learned men, artists, poets, and politicians of both sexes, have joined together with the view of bringing out a new periodical, in which all that is noteworthy in the politics, wit, talent, and intellect of this remarkable age is to be laid before a select public.

"The title of this proposed publication is to be *The Journal or Diary of Tieffurth*, and it is intended that it shall resemble as closely as possible the well-known and popular *Journal de Paris*, with this difference, that, instead of being a daily issue, it will appear but once a week. The copies can be either bought for ready money (nothing less than a gold coin will be taken), or in return for MS. contributions, The first number will appear at the end of the present week.

"TIEFURT, August 15th, 1781."[76]

The author of this flourish (which Merck ridiculed with fine irony) was Einsiedel, who had just returned from Karlsbad. He occupied the post of editor, his secretary being "The Gnomide," otherwise Fräulein Göchhausen, who proved an excellent assistant, with her "mobile pen" and her very reliable qualities.

"Whether the idea of the journal was first broached on the day of the Harvest Festival, or, as I rather think," writes Herr Suphan, "on a previous date, it belongs to the plans for cultivating constant cheerfulness, which the duchess Anna Amalia desired to promote."

"It is a little joke of mine for passing the summer." These are the words with which she introduces the parcel of the journal which she sends to Frau Aja in the beginning of November. "It has succeeded so well," she goes on, "that we are to continue it, and perhaps what I send you will give you some pleasant moments."

This statement is confirmed word for word in a letter written by Goethe to his mother two years later, sending her a large parcel of the journal. "This weekly journal was begun by way of a joke, when the duchess dowager was living last year at Tiefurt" (he is wrong in the date), "and since then has been continued. There are some excellent things in it, and you will find it well worth looking through."

"It was started for the amusement of a literary circle," says the editor of Herder's *Fragmentary Papers*. In this collection, published in 1785, were several of Herder's contributions, which had not appeared in the original collection. Likewise we learn that in the imaginary conversations between Theomo and Demoder, "Theomo" was Caroline Herder and "Demoder" Herder.

Herder's folk-songs were received with delight, also his letters on theology and Hebrew poetry. A still warmer reception was given to his "Ideas on the Philosophy of the History of Mankind," 1785. Musäus contributed his legendary or fairy tales in 1782, Wieland who was busy editing the *Merkür*, and writing his *Oberon*, also contributed some excellent translations.

The *Tiefurter Journal* had declared its intention of following in the track of the *Journal de Paris* which had been founded ten years previously, and had a high reputation. The French journal appeared every Sunday, four pages large quarto. "One can still read this excellent paper with pleasure. Besides the astronomical charts and the Exchange news which it regularly included, there was a regular staff of contributors who provided well-written articles upon such subjects as botany, medicine, engravings, administration, and public matters. There were likewise announcements of family events, and small instalments of fashionable news."

The advertisement of the *Tiefurter Journal* specially mentioned that the contributors were to be of both sexes. Weimar had always extended recognition to women writers, and in the celebrated circle of Sentimentalists, women like the Landgräfin of Hesse, Sophie de la Roche, etc., were highly considered. Henrietta von Egloffstein, who came to Weimar in 1787, alludes to the extraordinary intellectual force of the women. "They head the regiment," she says, "but they do not overstep due limits."

To the *Tiefurter Journal* Anna Amalia, we are told, contributed the somewhat lengthy and decidedly dull tale of "Cupid and Psyche." She translated it with the assistance of Wieland from the Italian. The Gnomide writes to Knebel on St. Martin's Day 1783, sending him a copy of the journal, which she says is especially good.

"The poem 'Remembrance' is by the little Schardt, and the 'Alphabet of Love' by Emilia von Werthern. The rest of the number is from Herder's pen." Caroline Herder was also a contributor, but Sophie von Schardt's little poem excited Goethe's admiration. He writes to Knebel:

"There is a poem called 'Remembrance' in the current number of the journal. Do you know who wrote it?"

In this small circle and under the veil of anonymity, several poetesses, shrinking from publicity (for we are dealing with a period, when for a woman, especially in the days of her youth, to seek publicity was an offence against propriety), made their first debut in literature by means of some poem or tale.

Herr Suphan gives as an example of the expansion of mind — Fräulein Göchhausen's letters to Knebel. One especially he tells us he has often quoted. In it she refers to the difficulty of expressing one's thoughts in writing.

"The letters seem so cold and inanimate, as contrasted with the image presented to the mind. Ach, Gott! for one evening here with you, sitting by the fire in your little corner room. Through the window we can see the branches of the poplar trees waving, and the long yellow meadow grass flying like lightning through the bushes. Ah! for such an evening now. I would throw all my letter paper into the fire, and make a great flame in the chimney, which would burn brightly."

I wish space allowed me to quote Herr Suphan's interesting account of the Court of Weimar at this period; also of the passion then existing for everything French. At the court of Berlin no other language was permitted, and some German writers, wishing to please the great Frederick, wrote in this borrowed tongue. To the credit of our Weimar circle of *litterateurs*, they never adopted this fashion, and it was due to the great personality of Goethe and his fidelity to his own tongue, that this degrading practice was abandoned throughout Germany.

In a letter of Villoison's to Knebel, written on 22 May 1782, he records the impressions he received during the first weeks of his stay at the Court of Weimar. "Nothing can equal the intelligence and the genius of Madame la Duchesse Mère, or her amiability, her affability, and her kindness. Mademoiselle Göchhausen has much grace, delicacy, and a beautiful mind. Mesdames Stein and Schardt are serious and deep thinkers. But what a court it is! so full of intellectuality and knowledge, and yet so artistic. The great ladies of the court instruct their children in painting." He concludes with this trite remark on the reigning Duchess Louise: "She is as anxious to conceal the extent of her knowledge as others are to display it."

Anna Amalia could not help giving a sly dig at this all-round admirer. She writes to Knebel,

"But *I also* am a Princess *full of genius.* What do you think of that? "Nevertheless, Villoison (whom Karl August thought to be an honest man) was quite sincere in his praises of this wonderful court. An unknown visitor to Weimar in 1784, said to be a Hanoverian count, and who was received at court, is even more enthusiastic than the French visitor. Herr Suphan does not for lack of space quote all this count said, but he makes special mention of Countess von Werthern for her charm of manner, natural, unrestrained, courteous and amusing. But this, he adds, is the "tone" at Weimar, and it "was in the company of such women that Goethe, Herder, and Wieland took delight."

"The journal has now appeared in medium quarto size. It is the celebrated *Tiefurter Journal.*"

In these words Anna Amalia, who is jubilant over the news, sends Knebel a copy. The duchess was in good spirits, but this had nothing to do with the success of the journal of which, to speak frankly, beyond the circle of contributors and their friends (who were not of much use financially), the sale was extremely small. There were Goethe's mother and his Zurich friend, Bade Schulthess, but for these foreigners special copies had to be prepared.

As a commercial speculation the *Tiefurter Journal* was not satisfactory, the outlay being in excess of the receipts; but it was never meant to be a source of profit, it was Anna Amalia's "joke," and as such had succeeded *á ravir.* On the other hand, it cost something to produce, and the sale was practically *nil.* Wieland made some mild jokes over the financial embarrassments of the editor.

"The times are hard," writes Thusnelda, and Wieland (Merkür) amuses himself by twitting the much-worried editor. "I have heard nothing from you of late," he says maliciously.

Karl August communicates to Merck his ideas on the subject, October 1782. "We have nothing but bad news from Tiefurt. The report is that the amateurs, connoisseurs, and men of letters have grown rotten, and the odour is so bad that one can smell it thirty miles away." This was a side thrust at Darmstadt as well as Tiefurt. Certain dates and letters, together with Knebel's diary, have established the fact, not known till 1896, that the *Tiefurter Journal* ran its course for three years, 1781-84. Sometimes it was issued monthly in place of weekly.

There were of course (as in all amateur undertakings) certain irregularities, as, for example, when, in 1781, a fearful epidemic of influenza swept over Weimar. Moreover, the dowager duchess's absences, on visits and the like, caused interruptions; for, not only was she the moving spirit, but she also took with her the editor, Einsiedel, and the secretary, Fräulein Göchhausen. September and October 1782 she spent at Dessau, and in the autumn of 1783 she stayed for six weeks at the Court of Brunswick with her brother, the reigning duke. On her return the journal was resumed.

The beginning of the last year of the journal was remarkable for the excellence of the contributions. Towards the end, however, a marked decadence set in, when apparently Einsiedel was the only "moving spirit." "It was a bad sign," says Herr Suphan, "that his prize questions, which he started in No. 35, evidently with a view to arouse interest, met with no replies." The number printed on the last issue is 49, but it would seem that there were only 47 issues of the journal. The collapse of this undertaking was much to be regretted, but it only furnishes another instance of how necessary it is in all such enterprises to have a professional manager, who understands the work of editing, pushing and making things go.

Amongst the contributors to the journal was Karl August, who wrote various pieces, amongst others an account of the birth, life, and death of Minerva, as shown in the shadow play which he highly commends. Goethe in the beginning wrote some beautiful odes, but latterly, having so much on hand, he seems to have given up contributing. Many of the charades and short poems were written by Prince Augustus of Gotha, who had a pleasing talent for verse-making. One of the best stories is "Der Ritter Eckbert." Of this Knebel writes: "If we only knew the writer, we would present him with a vote of thanks for thus holding up human nature as in a magic glass." As a humorous piece, Seckendorf's "Incident in the life of Herr von Giks Zrun Gakelstein" is very diverting. It is much in the manner of the *Ingoldsby Legends*, and possibly suggested them. Anna Amalia wrote some pretty verses and Einsiedel was a constant contributor; at the close he appears to have been the only one.

A great feature of the journal was the prize questions. One of those propounded was "How can a set of people who have nothing to do avoid *ennui*?" The answers which are given are clever and witty. At the close of the three years people had grown tired of the questions, and Einsiedel confesses that when he propounded one he received no answers.

CHAPTER XI

Tiefurt being a small house, there was not sufficient accommodation for Anna Amalia's personal suite, to say nothing of the guests which her hospitable nature rendered a necessity. Her ingenuity, however, was equal to the occasion. The guest rooms originally were few, but some of them were large. These were divided into two, and where it was practicable a third room was likewise partitioned off, this being only a tiny compartment, merely capable of holding a small bed and table. Recesses were made in the passages by curtains which could be let down, and here the ladies-in-waiting could entertain a friend in private with a cup of tea.

Fräulein Göchhausen had a small bedroom to herself, and here a very unkind trick was played upon her by Goethe, in which I regret to say Anna Amalia took part; but, as before mentioned, practical joking had become a regrettable feature of court society. The joke in question was, considering the delicate physique of Thusnelda, decidedly ill-advised. Fräulein Göchhausen was on a certain day despatched to Weimar to execute commissions for the duchess. These occupied her till late in the evening, when she returned to Tiefurt.

Meantime her absence had been made use of by the duchess and Goethe to have the door of Thusnelda's bedroom taken off its hinges, and the space, which was a very narrow one, filled up and paper pasted over. When poor Fräulein Göchhausen returned every one was in bed, a light being left as usual in the hall. But as she ascended the staircase the light was blown out, as she thought by a gust of wind. It was very dark, so she put her hands on the wall and groped her way, seeking the door of her room, but could find nothing of the sort — it was all one flat surface.

Thusnelda was puzzled, and thought she must be on the wrong side somehow. It suddenly occurred to her to fetch the maid who slept on this landing, but she found that the maid's bed was empty. Again Thusnelda groped with both hands along the surface of the wall, but no door could she find. She called out — no answer. She screamed — no one came. Strangely enough, although she was accustomed to have tricks played upon her, and in her turn played many a trick on others, the idea never occurred to her that she was the victim of a practical joke. At last she lost all control of herself and in her excitement grew hysterical, when, apparently by accident, someone came with a light, and conducted the poor worn-out Thusnelda to a room that had been provisionally got ready for her.

Another joke was perpetrated by Anna Amalia on a large scale, and the fact that Goethe was included amongst the number of the hoaxed would point to Thusnelda having suggested the trick, which was not quite after the duchess's manner. A select party, including the *Geheimerath*, were invited to dinner, and as the duchess's cook was excellent and her wines of the best, all her invitations were gladly accepted. When the covers were removed a splendid feast met the gaze of the guests; everything that was in season was on the table, but, when they tried to eat — good heavens! the coveted dainties were only painted imitations! It was a true Barmecides' banquet. The select party of *litterateurs* and counsellors tried to laugh, but their faces betrayed their disappointment and indignation. Fortunately, it was only momentary, for in an adjoining room another repast was ready to console the deluded guests. We do not hear how Goethe liked being tricked in this way, but we may be sure Fräulein Göchhausen's shrill laugh was not wanting.

The dinner of wood just as it was served a hundred and twenty years ago, is one of the curiosities of Tiefurt. It can be seen in the old kitchen, and is one of the attractions to tourists.

Tiefurt, like Ettersburg, has also a close connection with the history of the stage of Weimar, of which I have in the preceding chapter essayed, with the help of the best German authorities; to give my readers a short account. It was in the year 1781 that the dramatic life of Tiefurt was called into existence by the indefatigable duchess. At first there was a divergence of opinion as to the prospect of success in starting a theatre similar to that at Ettersburg, and so many contrary opinions were given as to where it should be, in case it was decided to have one, that Anna Amalia, tired of the discussion, gave up the idea, and contented herself with what was called in jest the Academy of Music. The members of the Academy included such musicians as Corona Schröter and Fräulein von Rudorf; also the best musical amateurs in Weimar joined this so-called academy, which held its meetings at the *Witthumshaus*, music being only the pretext for a good deal of fun and flirtation.

When the hot days of August came the musical jesters grew somewhat limp; everyone pined for open-air amusements, and Anna Amalia, who was always a promoter of healthy pleasures, revived the idea of an open-air theatre at Tiefurt, where she intended to pass the summer. This idea being warmly seconded, the first thing was to choose the site for the theatre. This was soon done, the lovely woods having many secluded spots, where nature had provided an amphitheatre suitable to the purpose. One of these, called *La Petite Coulisse*, was unanimously chosen, and it was agreed that the first performance should be given in honour of Goethe's birthday, on 18 August.

The piece chosen was *Minerva's Birth, Life, and Actions*, written by Sigismund von Seckendorf, a play well suited to the natural advantages of the open-air stage.

Minerva's birth was, as we know, peculiar, and it would strike us as being somewhat difficult to represent. The piece was, however, of the kind called *ombres palpilantes*, as distinguished from the *ombres chinoises* which were merely shadows thrown by means of a magic lantern across a screen. The *ombres palpitantes* were, as the name imports, *breathing* or "palpitating" shadows. In other words, the reflection of the *actors and actresses* was thrown on the sheet or screen, with all their movements and gestures, which corresponded with the words they spoke. In some instances there may have been a diaphanous screen, through which the actors were seen.

This form of shadow play was very popular, having been introduced by Duke George of Meiningen. Corona Schröter excelled in it by means of her graceful attitudes.

I will not fatigue my readers with an account of Minerva's adventures, which are told at length in the *Tiefurter Journal*, but merely refer to the final tableau, when, in a silver cloud or halo, appeared the name of "Goethe," to which a gold crown was presented by Minerva, (personated by Corona Schröter), followed by Apollo, who offered his lyre, and the Nine Muses garlands of flowers, while in the sky appeared the words "Iphigenia" and "Faust," surrounded by a golden halo.

Thus was the open-air stage at Tiefurt consecrated to the Muses, and from this time it became the birthplace of many new developments, one strong point of interest being that here was produced an altogether new conception of *Faust* taken from the original Saga, or myth. Another favourite shadow play was *Midas*.

For Tiefurt, Goethe wrote "A Wood and Water Piece," called *The Fisher Maiden*, the music for which was composed by Corona Schröter, whose setting of the *Erl King* was much admired, the *Erl King* being one of the characters introduced into the piece. The place chosen was on the banks of the Ilm near the bridge, which was illuminated by countless torches and lamps. A number of fishermen's huts were erected on the bank, and fishermen's boats, nets, and other implements connected with their trade were scattered about the shore. The cottage of Dörnchen (Corona Schröter) is in flames; the fishermen assemble from all parts; a flotilla of boats appears simultaneously on the river, while the whole scene becomes ablaze with light, which is as suddenly extinguished, everything being left in darkness till the end of the piece, when the stage is again bathed in light. This effect of light and shade was very striking. "The beautiful evening, the music and the illumination," writes Thusnelda, "made an enchanting spectacle."

Unfortunately, the crowd of spectators who gathered on the wooden bridge to see the illuminations, was too much for so slight a support, and the bridge broke. There were, however, no fatalities; everyone took the diversion in good part and laughed at what was a joke, but might have been a tragedy. The great charm of these open-air plays lay in the effect of the light and shade produced by the illuminations and the dark green of the background.

If one might venture to criticise so distinguished a company as the Weimar actors, we might complain of the excessive number of performances, to say nothing of the expense, which was entirely defrayed from the private purse of the duke and Anna Amalia. There must have been great danger of wearying the audience by too frequent entertainments. *Reculer pour mieux sauter* is an excellent motto to be observed in most things. Naturally this observation would not apply in the case of masterpieces by Goethe; it may be doubted whether these were always done full justice to. We have, however, in this matter to bow to the verdict of those who witnessed these amateur performances, albeit their judgment may have been warped by friendship, and in some instances probably influenced by the position of the actors.

Goethe's nonsense pieces were always delightful, and, as a rule, the company were equal to the rendering of these. The same welcome, however, was not accorded to the pieces written by Knebel, or to those adapted by Einsiedel and Seckendorf.

Goethe's penetration grasped the fact that one may grow weary of even the choicest wit, and that novelty is an absolute craving of humanity. He therefore looked about for something new and in this year (1781) introduced masques, the first being given on the festival of the Three Kings, which is the German equivalent for our Twelfth Day. There was a brilliant gathering at court, including the Prince of Meiningen. "Epiphania," an ode to Christmas, by Goethe, was sung by three singers in costume, Corona Schröter representing the first king. Her song began: "I am the first and the wisest, and likewise the most beautiful." This masque having mightily pleased "the High and Mighties," a second took place, on 30 January, in honour of the Duchess Louise's birthday, and as *l'appetit vient en mangeant*, so the wish for novelty made society eager for another. Accordingly we hear of preparations for a splendid masque called "Winter," which was given in the *Redoute* on 16 February. Herr von Stein was a splendid figure as "Winter," Frau von Stein appeared as "Night," and Goethe as "Sleep."

Soon, however, the languor which had for the moment been banished by the new excitement, reappeared. Anna Amalia writes to Knebel, December 1781: "I am like a driver, who is for ever whipping his horses to get them out of the mud, into which they and the cart are for ever slipping, but alas! they will stand stock still and no efforts are of avail. There is much talk of new plays, comedies, etc., but nothing definite is arranged. I have settled that the Weimar Theatre shall open on November 24th, with a shadow play, which will represent the story of King Midas. What other novelties may follow I cannot at present tell you."

The ever popular story of King Midas seems to have done well, but still the cloud does not appear to have passed away, for in this same month, 1782, we find Karl August writing: "Here everything seems to be out of joint. Goethe looks pale and bilious, and does not know what to be at." And Goethe also complains to his friend Merck: "Since the beginning of the year there has been a constant round of theatricals and *redoutes*. I am thoroughly sick of continually turning the axle, and my soul wearies of this and many other matters." Also Fräulein von Göchhausen pipes her little complaint. She, too, is weary (as well she may have been, and with more reason than the somewhat spoilt author). Listen to poor Thusnelda. "Plays, balls, masques, *redoutes*, etc., all succeed one another in the race for amusement, and friend Goethe has handed his gold chain of office to another shepherd, who has arranged for the birthday of the duchess Louise a new ballet, with a charming story and interludes of songs and dances, concluding with a wonderful ballet."

Three days before the performance the stage manager, Mieding, died. Goethe's beautiful poem, entitled "Mieding's Death," appeared in the *Tiefurter Journal*.

"Goethe is very busy," writes Fräulein von Göchhausen; "he has finished *Egmont* and is now writing *Tasso*." This love of work was a symptom that the round of amusement, which was sapping his best energies, was about to come to an end. Signs and tokens of weariness were showing themselves likewise in the duke. Meantime the building of a regular theatre in Weimar began to be talked about amongst the amateurs. This idea, at first merely a subject of conversation, developed later into the theatre, which, under the management of Goethe and Schiller, earned a world-wide fame. But this is looking rather far ahead.

The first step which led to the grand result was, as is often the case, taken by an outsider, a certain Herr Hauptmann, who filled the office of master of the hounds in the duke's household. He was supposed to be wealthy and was fond of speculating, and as a speculation started building a large hall suitable for *redoutes* or other amusements. There was a garden at the back, where on summer evenings open-air entertainments and illuminations after the pattern of Vauxhall could take place. Hauptmann found his building expensive, and to defray the charges borrowed large sums from the duke's treasury on the house itself, which, as it soon appeared that the builder was in bad circumstances, fell a bargain to Karl August, who was the largest creditor. Soon all the necessary arrangements were made. Here Anna Amalia had a fine room, where in the winter season the plays, which were now a feature of Weimar society, could be given. The *redoutes* could be held in the same apartment. The seats and barriers were movable, so were the stage and the pit: a fine hall was then left where everyone could dance till morning.

Following the inevitable law of change, the amateur company which had done such good work began to fall away. In 1784 a troop of German comedians were invited to come to Weimar under the management of Bellomo. This was a deathblow to the amateurs, and was much deplored by the dowager duchess. She writes sorrowfully: "Every one here is asleep." She was, however, a woman of resource, and speedily found her consolation in studying Greek.

Clouds now began to darken the horizon of Weimar, and threw their shadows over Amalia's life. She was disappointed that, do what she would, the *rapprochement* she wished for did not come to pass between her and her daughter-in-law, who, although always respectful towards her husband's mother, still kept outside the barrier she had erected between herself and Anna Amalia. "A lump of ice that there is no thawing," was the verdict of our genial duchess. Neither were the relations between the royal couple very satisfactory; their disappointment in the matter of the wished-for heir embittered matters.

Goethe too was troubled about many things. That he had lost much of his popularity affected him little, for he could be well satisfied with the tangible advantages he had received; in addition to the dignity of *Geheimerath* conferred upon him by Karl August, the Emperor Joseph II ennobled him in 1781. Karl August was afraid to break the news of this dignity to the burgher's son, and it was Anna Amalia who undertook to inform Goethe of the honour conferred on him. His biographer says: "As he had been six years at court without a patent of nobility, he may have felt the *necessity* as rather an insult." This was not, however, the view taken by the nobility of Weimar and Eisenach, who regarded the bestowal of this honour on the son of a Frankfurt citizen as a scandalous outrage on their privileges. "The hatred of people here;" writes Wieland, "against our Goethe, who has done no one any harm, has risen to such a height since he has been made *Geheimerath*, that it borders on fury."

The duke, however, paid no heed to the opposition. He was more than ever "the friend of his friend," and Goethe repaid his confidence. It was Goethe who suggested, in view of various complications which now arose, and which have nothing to do with our narrative, that a short absence would cut the root of the evil, and Karl August eagerly grasped at the suggestion. The court, and even Anna Amalia, supposed that a visit to Frankfurt and Kassel was to be the extent of the journey. Karl August writes to Anna Amalia from Frankfurt 19 September 1779:

"Best of mothers, I am writing from Goethe's house, where I am staying. Goethe's mother is a splendid woman, I rejoice to be with her. Nothing particular since I wrote. Everything goes well. Last night there were some wonderful Northern Lights."

The arrival of the travellers at Rath Goethe's house in Frankfurt is delightfully told by Frau Aja, in one of her letters to Anna Amalia.[77]

"FRANKFURT,
September 24th, 1779.

"Our gracious and best prince (Karl August) got out of his carriage a few doors up the street. (This on purpose to surprise us.) He opened the door of the house noiselessly, and came into the blue drawing-room. Now imagine me, Frau Aja, sitting at the round table, when the door suddenly opens and, in a second, Haschelhans' (i.e., Goethe's) arms are round my neck, the duke standing in a corner so as not to interfere with a mother's joy; and there he remained until Frau Aja, almost intoxicated with joy, and hardly knowing what she was doing, greeted her good prince as well as she was able, and also the handsome Wedel, who took his share in the universal joy. Then came the entrance of the father. I feared the joy of seeing his son would kill him, and even to this very day on which his highness has left us, he is not quite himself. Neither am I much to speak of. Your highness can well imagine what the joy of these days has been. Merck came, and acquitted himself on the whole well; but he can never leave his cloak of Mephistopheles at home, he is so accustomed to wear it. Against the usual custom, but in accordance with the duke's wish, there was no prince or princess at supper."

She then gives an account of the different entertainments which the duke and Goethe attended, and then goes on:[78]

"Dearest princess, pardon this cold letter, which, in consideration of the subject, is dry and short. It is impossible for me to make it better. I feel all day as if I were drunk with joy. I am delirious, and not until I come back to real life will my senses return to me. Until then Frau Aja entreats your highness to have patience with her. We have no other thought but our present joy, and the thought that, although they are leaving us, they will return, and then the joy will fill my heart again. God grant they return happy and well, then shall they drink the best Rhine wine in splendid tumblers specially ordered. If your highness only knew how often I think of you with tears of joy in my eyes, how often I speak of you, how often Frau Aja blesses the day when the best of princesses gave to her beloved country such a ruler as Karl August. When she thinks of all this and much more, Frau Aja can only go into a corner and let the joy of her heart express itself in happy, happy tears. And all I know and feel is that the best of all princesses has given to us ineffable joy. This is only a little sketch of days which, to quote Werther, God spares to His saints, that they may take their burden again on their shoulders and tramp about the world with it, the remembrance of the happy hours allowed to them making it light to carry.

"Now, most august princess, keep us in your gracious memory. The father commends himself to you, and Frau Aja will live and die,

"Your Royal Highness's

"Obedient and most humble servant,

"K. E. GOETHE."

Soon Karl August writes to Anna Amalia:

"What will you say? Instead of going tomorrow to Düsseldorf, as we had arranged, we are starting for Switzerland.[79] This will displease you a little, but I hope not much; and soon you will rejoice with us. I have enjoyed myself here. I think I have astonished Goethe's mother, but I like her and I think she likes me. Merck is here; he will ride a day's journey with us. There are beautiful pictures here for sale. I have perpetrated a little folly to the tune of only a hundred ducats."

From a subsequent letter from Merck to the duchess we learn that the duke and Goethe spent *four days* with Frau Rathin. That was a pretty long visit, and so Merck insinuates. "The old man (Goethe's father) is simply incorrigible," he writes to Anna Amalia; "his manners are too bad. Imagine that when the duke lodged for four days in his house, he never gave his wife one penny more house money than usual. This man is Goethe's father and Frau Aja's husband! The other day he was chuckling over the thought that it was not he who advanced the duke the money for the oil paintings he purchased here. I believe if he had done so, he would not have closed his eyes in sleep. I cannot understand why God allows such human beings to live. I trust your highness will excuse my gossip. I feel as if I were at Ettersburg, sitting under the large lantern, in the act of taking something to eat from the servant and from the *kammerherr* something to drink.

> "With the deepest respect,
>
> "Your Highness's humble servant,
>
> "J. MERCK."

I don't know if my readers will agree with me, in thinking that Merck's gossip was well-intentioned, so far as Frau Aja's interests were in question. The duchess at this time took no notice of the strong hint she had received, but that she told the duke is evident from the fact that he sent money later on to Merck for Frau Aja.

Meantime the travellers had crossed the frontier to Switzerland. There were only the duke, Goethe, and Wedel. They had the lightest of trunks, and the strictest incognito was observed. Goethe separated for a day from his companions to pay a visit to Sesenheim. "There I found," he writes to Frau von Stein, "the family I left eight years ago, and was welcomed in the most friendly manner."

In his letters to Frau von Stein, a great portion of which were afterwards published as *Letters from Switzerland*, the reader will find an account of his ride through Switzerland. The effect upon the duke's mental and bodily condition was wonderful, nature and the open-air life producing the most salutary effects. Goethe arranged a meeting with his old friend Lavater; he describes the almost angelic tranquillity of the old man's life. "There is a sense of repose and aloofness from all the pressure of life." He (Goethe) was so impressed by the successful result of this meeting, and the beneficial consequences that he felt confident would result from Lavater's conversations with the duke, that he resolved to erect a monument to Lavater in Weimar; and writing to him after his return, he says: "You know how useful from many points of view this journey has been to the duke, and how from this a fresh start will be made, not alone in his, but in all our lives. I shall commemorate this happy event by erecting a memorial to the worker of the cure."

Anna Amalia, likewise, when she saw the change in her son, erected a temple in his honour.

There is no doubt the long conversations Karl August had with the philosopher on all subjects were of infinite benefit to his character, and greatly helped to form his judgment, which was apt to be led astray. From this time the faults of his education were not so apparent, and as time sobered the impetuosity of youth, his undoubtedly remarkable character developed. Unfortunately, the roughness was never quite eliminated. Goethe likewise benefited by contact with a mind superior in many ways to his own. It was noticed on his return that the "haughty exclusiveness and reserve, in which the new *Geheimerath* had wrapped himself," were considerably lessened, and although exalted, he knew he was still a man, not a god."

The travellers, who had been now absent four months, returned home by way of Karlsruhe and Darmstadt. According to Merck's account, Karl August and Goethe created a *furore* at Stuttgart, where the duke insisted on going to court. Great difficulty was experienced in getting proper dresses to appear in. While here they visited the Military Academy. Amongst the students who came up to receive three prizes was a delicate, almost sickly youth of twenty, who kissed the coat of the reigning duke in an awkward manner, his nervousness being, as he afterwards narrated, due to the presence of Goethe; for this youth was Karl Schiller, who had failed to get a prize for German composition.

Karl August,[80] on his return to Frankfurt again took up his residence with Goethe's parents. We are told "he paid liberal attention to Frau Aja's good old wine and privately sent her a sum of money to compensate her for the expenses of the visit." Therefore Merck's intervention was manifestly effective. But one would have supposed the Geheimerath's mother would have been too proud to receive payment from her son's guest.

Back in Weimar, things resumed their former course, only with a difference. Goethe has begun to think of *Wilhelm Meister* and the study of science. Theatricals still keep their hold; "they remain amongst the few things in which he still has the pleasure of a child and an artist." In great delight Wieland writes to Merck of the new order of things. Progress is the order of the day (August 1780); no less than three newspapers are in the field: Jägemann's *Italian Magazine*, Bertuch's *Spanish Magazine*,[81] and Wieland's *Merkür*, a very interesting production of a different order of merit from the two first named.

The *Merkür* was a review in small compass, but took a high place in literature by reason of its contributors, who included Wieland, Herder, Merck, Bode, Boteler, etc. — in fact, all the leading men of letters in Germany. Wieland, the editor, was indefatigable in his efforts to keep the standard up to the proper level. He wrote much for the *Merkür*, mostly in prose, his *Danischwende* running through two or three volumes. His correspondence with Merck is full of this "beloved child," for whose benefit he is always urging Merck to send him copy. Wieland, whose affectionate nature never allowed him to bear malice long, makes a pleasant contrast to the sensitive, fault-finding Herder, and his sharp-tongued but excellent little wife.

The constant bickerings of the alumni and the amount of soothing the susceptibility of the contributors required was only what one would expect from a society of geniuses. Karl August, whose manners were somewhat rough-and-ready, often offended unintentionally. The Duchess Louise, good woman as she was and anxious to be all that was kind, lacked (as many of us do) the capability of showing what she felt. She was, as it were, frozen, and it took time and sorrow to melt the ice that had gathered round her heart. The gift of sympathy (a gift that changes the whole surface of life) is accorded to only a few. I mean by the word sympathy, not the well-worn expressions with which we are all familiar in the conventional letter of condolence. Sympathy requires no words, no high-flown phrases out of the *Complete Letter-writer*; it is a sort of magnetic current which, without the need of words, communicates itself to the sufferer. "I too have dwelt in Arcadia, I too have lost all that makes life worth having. . . weep out your sorrow in my arms."

Anna Amalia possessed this gift of sympathy in the highest degree; the touch of her hand, the look in her eyes, the tender, motherly manner, were irresistible. Every man, woman, and child felt that here was a friend. It mattered not from what cause they suffered, whether by their own or someone else's fault, she was ready to console, and no poor soul ever went away without feeling its trouble lightened. The sorrows of genius (unacknowledged genius) she was always ready to soothe, if she could.

When misfortune came upon an over-burdened wife or husband, she gave material help of the most useful kind, and for mental trouble she was always ready with the truest, the most consoling sympathy. Many an afternoon when she might have wished to be otherwise occupied, did she listen to Wieland's lamentations, over the difficulty he found in expressing himself in verse, how it took him three hours to write one strophe, "turning and twisting the thing in my brain." His letters to Merck and others fill one with compassion, for we know how much depended on the success of his work. It is pleasant to know that it did succeed, beyond expectation. Goethe sent him a gold crown as a symbol of his congratulations (1780), and the duke, who knew what hard work it had been for the already heavily-weighted poet to accomplish his task, sent him words of kind congratulation. *Oberon* lives to this day — immortalised by Weber, it is true, but of itself a lovely poem and dear to every German heart.

In November 1781 Anna Amalia writes to Frau Aja, to tell her that Goethe had at last recognised the necessity of having a residence suitable to his position.

"Weimar,
November 23rd, 1781.

"DEAREST FRAU AJA,

"I have the pleasure to announce to you that your beloved Häschelhans[82] has graciously made up his mind to hire a house in the town.[83] He will not come into possession till next Easter, because the lease of the present tenant does not expire till then. In the meantime, dear mother, *we have won half the battle*, and it is well that he has come so far. As he has behaved so well, I have promised to give him some of the furniture. Dear mother, will you be so kind as to choose some chintz for covering sofas and chairs, and send me the patterns and the prices asked?"

Then she goes on to tell her friend how delighted "old Wieland is with the present sent him by Frau Goethe and how he exclaimed: 'What a woman! She is the ornament of her sex!' — and to this I answer: Amen. . . .

"Our Wolf sends you a thousand greetings. He is well and in good spirits."

The year 1783 opened brightly; the birth of the long desired prince filled all hearts with joy, and gave to the duke the steadiness and serious purpose which had hitherto been wanting.

The baptismal ceremony took place on 5 February 1783, and we can imagine the joy of the people of Weimar, who, like the good people they were, took a lively interest in everything that concerned the dear ducal family. "Herder preached," says Wieland, "like a god," and Wieland's Cantata was set to music by Kapellmeister Wolf, and was sung on the occasion. There were torchlight processions and barrels of beer, and every man drank as much as he could, and a good deal more than he ought. But then it was their duty to drink on this auspicious occasion. Every poet in Weimar, and there were a round dozen (taking the lesser lights with the stars) thought it his or her duty to write a birthday ode, there being one remarkable exception. His biographer draws the attention of his readers to the great generosity displayed by Goethe in not entering the list. "It could not be attributed to want of affection; but he who had been ever ready with ballet, opera, or poem, to honour the birthday of the two duchesses must have felt that now, when all the other Weimar writers were pouring in their offerings, he ought not to throw the weight of his position in the scale against theirs. Had the worst of the offerings been his, it would have been prized as the highest."

There is a touch of the condescension of the giant to the pigmy in this his overstrained generosity, which could not have been pleasing to the author of *Oberon*, or even to such minor poets as Einsiedel and Knebel.

The young father in his elation at the happy event writes a delightful letter to Merck.

"Your congratulations are in the right key, for if there be any good dispositions in me they have hitherto wanted a fixed point; but now there is a firm hook upon which I can hang my pictures. With the help of Goethe and good luck I will, for the future, paint in such a manner that, if possible, the next generation shall say, 'Ah! he too was a painter.'"

It is pleasant to record that these words were not merely due to the effervescence of youthful happiness which has attained its wish; it was a firm resolve, to which during his life the duke adhered.

We know from Goethe's correspondence with Charlotte von Stein that there were occasional rifts in the close friendship between Goethe and Karl August. The difference in their ages, although not sufficient to prevent intimacy, yet made Goethe impatient with faults and weaknesses, into which some few years previous he himself would have been betrayed. Writing to his Charlotte, he complains that the duke, "Enthusiastic as he is for good, always begins by doing something foolish; he is like the frog, he is made for the water, even when he has lived some time on land." Goethe refused to accompany the duke to Dresden, the latter's behaviour when on the Swiss tour having irritated his more refined instincts, and the letter of refusal he desires Frau von Stein to read. "If you think right, send it to the duke, or speak to him if you think it wiser, only do not spare him. I only wish to be quiet and to let him know with whom he has to deal. You may tell him also that I have declared to you that I will never travel with him again. Do this in your own prudent, gentle way."

The threat, however, was not fulfilled, and, whether owing to the lady's mediation or some other cause, a reconciliation took place. But soon there came another temporary disagreement. Again he writes to his confidante: "The duchess is a truly good and amiable woman. The duke is a good creature, and one could heartily love him, if he did not spoil everything by his schoolboy manners, and wear out one's patience through placing his life in danger by his reckless exploits. I have grown quite callous to the possibility of my dearest friend breaking his neck, arms, or legs."

"These occasional outbreaks," his biographer says, "made no permanent effect on the longstanding friendship between the duke and Goethe, the latter's generosity and friendship asserting itself, in spite of passing fits of ill-humour." "The duke," he writes, "is guilty of many follies which I willingly excuse, considering my own."

Karl August was no ordinary character, and as time went on he displayed an amount of good sense and courage, which were of inestimable service in the evil times that overshadowed the coming years. He possessed a superabundant activity, was unceasing in his efforts to improve the condition of his subjects, and his tastes were simple, like those of Goethe. He had, in fact, in many points a strong resemblance to his friend. He lacked, however, "the quality which never allowed Goethe, except in his wildest moments, to overstep limits; he wanted the tenderness and chivalry which made the poet so universally acceptable to women."

His manners were rough, and he was more at ease dining with his officers than in a ladies' drawing-room, even in that of Duchess Louise. The etiquette of court life always bored him, and it was, therefore, as far as possible, dispensed with at the court of Weimar. But all these were mere specks on the surface of a truly fine character. Karl August was in many ways a *great man*; that he was not altogether great, was in a measure due to his early training. His attachment to Goethe, who was about eight years his senior, was that of a younger brother to his elder. There were moments of dissatisfaction and occasional quarrels, but a friendship practically unbroken for fifty years is a record creditable to both, and is undoubtedly uncommon.

Goethe, in his later years, speaking to Eckermann on his friendship for the duke, said: "For more than half a century I have been connected in the closest relations with the grand duke, and for half a century have striven and toiled with him; but I should not be speaking truth, were I to say that I could name a single day on which the duke had not his thoughts busied with something to be devised and effected for the good of the country, something calculated to better the condition of each individual in it. As to himself personally, what has his princely state given him but a burden and a task? Is his dwelling, is his dress, or his table, more sumptuously provided than that of any private man in easy circumstances?"

And Merck adds his quota of praise: "The duke," he says, "has a character firm as iron. I tell you sincerely (he is writing to Nicolai) that he is most worthy of respect, and one of the cleverest men that I have ever known."

In 1786 a general feeling of unrest seems to have seized upon the circle at Weimar: occupations, pleasures, friends, and surroundings — all and everything seemed out of joint.

Knebel had started for a long journey to the south; Merck was gone to Holland, to make an exhaustive search into questions of natural history. The letters of the travellers, their meeting old friends and interesting adventures, all raised in the mind of Anna Amalia a desire for change, a wish to see other countries, and Rome especially. Karl August, too, was constantly absent, partly from his natural inclination for travel, and partly in consequence of political complications, which necessitated visits to the Courts of Austria and Berlin. In addition to these political affairs, the duke was anxious to procure for Prince Constantine a military position in Saxony, which he thought might steady the prince, whose conduct was not by any means satisfactory. He took counsel on this point with his uncle, the Duke of Brunswick, and for this purpose paid a visit to Brunswick, from which visit he returned much impressed by the great qualities of the duke, who had lately succeeded Duke Karl.

The following year his military duties took him to Berlin, where Frederick the Great was slowly wearing out. Karl August writes to his mother: "The light which was failing has sent forth a flash of its former brilliancy, but a sudden blaze often heralds total darkness." This opinion proved correct, but before the total eclipse came to pass Frederick the Great had an opportunity to do his favourite niece a favour. Prince Constantine, who had ever been a thorn in the side of the ducal family, had infringed all military rules by leaving his post of duty during the manoeuvres at Schlesien.

Karl August presented a letter from his mother to the king, in which Anna Amalia in the most touching manner entreated his forgiveness for this breach of discipline on the part of her son Constantine. On this, the last occasion he was to have of doing his niece a kindness, Frederick did not fail, and Constantine was pardoned.

A few weeks later Frederick, writing to Anna Amalia, remarks that he was sorry Prince Constantine had not presented himself at his (the king's) levée "and given me the opportunity of speaking to him, which I would have gladly done for your sake." He concludes:"If I were not so old, I would go to Weimar that I might have the happiness of embracing you, my dear niece, again. As it is, you may always believe that, absent or present, I am ever tenderly attached to you, my very dear niece.

"Your faithful uncle and friend,
"FRIEDRICH."

The last letter Anna Amalia received from her celebrated relative is not in his handwriting, only his name is signed by him, with a trembling hand. It is dated 20 January 1786.

"MY DEAR LADY AND NIECE,
"If I could follow the wish of my heart, I would accept your invitation and come to Weimar to spend some days with you. But your highness knows full well that higher duties than my own pleasure keep me here, and the cares that press upon me will not allow me to be absent from Berlin. There is, therefore, nothing left for us, but to renew from time to time the intercourse which has been to me throughout the later years of my life a source of true enjoyment.

"I am, my dear niece,
"Your Royal Highness's good uncle,
"FRIEDRICH."

The sense of duty which chained the weary king to the service of his country cost him his life. He died in August 1786. Anna Amalia who was ill at the time of the king's death, was much overcome by the news, and it was probably owing to the shock to her nerves that the incident occurred to which Karl August alludes in the following letter, dated three days after Frederick the Great's death.

"The strange apparition which you mention, my dearest mother, as having appeared to you, has greatly excited my curiosity. Could you not arrange for the ghostly visitant to remain until my return? joking apart, I imagine that it so happened that you and Thusnelda heard a groan, which came God knows how. This caused your nerves to be on the stretch, and in your case especially, in consequence of your recent illness and the atmospheric pressure, your nervous system was in the highest degree impressionable to any species of delusion or phantom of the imagination. In my opinion the whole thing was a delusion, and I am strengthened in this opinion by the fact that Thusnelda, who is in good health and not suffering from nerve prostration as you are, saw nothing. So far as the groan went, perhaps we shall come to the bottom of this mystery. All the same, I should like to penetrate the veil that hangs over the land of spirits.[84] It is very fortunate that your health has not suffered from the fright. I hope however, this will teach you that the evening air is not fit for you, and that in future you will take more care of yourself."

A longing for change succeeded to the depression felt by the dowager-duchess. It was some time, however, before her wish could be realised.

A hundred and twenty years ago, people did not decide over night that they would go to Paris or Rome next morning; it was a matter of very serious consideration and meant a large outlay of money for travelling carriages, post-horses, couriers, and the like. Geheimerath von Goethe was, however, a rich man, and these little matters were not of importance. His health was giving uneasiness, and when he accompanied the duke to Karlsbad in the autumn of 1786, he found no difficulty in getting his permission to travel for a year: indeed, his words were "for an indefinite period." He added that he felt it necessary for his intellectual health, that he should lose himself in a world where he was unknown. But what about his dear Charlotte, who was left behind in such cavalier fashion? Well, she had her letters — not every day, but as often as an imperfect postal system would allow. The letters (with necessary omissions) were later given to the public under the title of *Travels in Italy*.

It was indeed high time for Goethe to breathe the fresh air of larger cities than little Weimar, where his gigantic personality was growing oppressive, even to himself. His ten years' residence in the Modern Athens had been a blank as far as literary progress was concerned; his great gifts had been more or less frittered away in the getting up of plays and entertainments. It was true that, during the last year, he had withdrawn himself more from the frivolities of society, and in the solitude of his garden house had written a good portion of *Wilhelm Meister*. This was the first note heralding a healthy revival, to which his visit to Italy gave the final touches. The tranquillity of his life, the absence of the daily official pressure and the social treadmill, acted beneficially on his nerves, which had been continually at high tension, while to a mind so receptive of the beauties of nature and the treasures of art, it was, as it were, a new birth to be able to live thus in the ancient capital of Italy, to visit its antiquities under the guidance of Reiffenstein, and study with Wincklemann its ancient philosophy.

"It is a jubilee of joy," he writes to his mother, on 17 November 1786; "a miracle, that the desire of your soul and the longing of my youth have at last been accomplished."

The first letter of Goethe to Anna Amalia is dated 23 December 1786.

"I have been wishing for some time to give your highness some news of myself and of my residence in Rome, but I can hardly hope to write anything worthy of interesting you, for the traveller can rarely convey to others (in writing especially) his sensations, on finding himself in the very spot where his heart and his imagination have wandered for years. I have now finished my first hasty survey of Rome. I am acquainted with the town, its situation, its ruins, villas, palaces, galleries, and museums. With such abundance of material the mind, the imagination, the heart, are all fully occupied, but when one has to consider these things from the standard of their actual worth as matters of art, not to consider them from the effect they have made upon us, but from their individual merit, then the task becomes more difficult, and we feel that it would take time to fully grasp all we have to learn.

"Being determined to neglect nothing that can add to my first enjoyment, I have visited the ruins with an antiquarian,[85] the other works of art with different artists, and I have come to the conclusion that it would take a lifetime of mental activity to grasp in full extent all that is to be learned here; and here I have come to the conclusion that it is easier and more satisfactory to study the secrets of nature than the mysteries of art. The smallest product of nature has in itself the necessary power of production, and we have only to use our eyes to be assured of this. A work of art, on the other hand, owes its perfection to the outside; it is created by the artist, who seldom, if ever, realises his ideal, so bound is he by certain laws, which are indispensable to the nature of art and are not so plain or so easy to follow as the laws of nature. The works of art are, in fact, limited by tradition; the works of nature are God's outspoken word.

"I shall never forget the words you spoke to me at our last meeting, nor the pain it gave me not to acquaint you with my determination. I trust on my return I shall find in your highness an equally gracious and amicable princess.

"Your humble servant,
"GOETHE."

Anna Amalia was much pleased with this letter, and in her friendly way sent it to some of the Weimar circle. Herder had the first view of it, and in his usual fashion thinks only of himself. "Why should the pope and his monks possess this land of milk and honey, where the laurel hedges and the lemon-trees are in blossom, while we live here *behind the church* in a dense fog?"

Knebel, who is in Switzerland, hears of the letter (probably through Thusnelda), and writes to ask that he may have a look at it, promising to send it back safely. Merck also applies. So Anna Amalia promises to say a word to Frau Rath, who has the extracts from Goethe's letters to Karl August, which the duke had sent her, and Frau Rath writes to her dear duchess:

"Every wish of your highness is for me an eleventh commandment. Friend Merck shall have the two letters (more than these I have not had), but I much doubt whether he will find anything in them to make fun of after his fashion. To me they have been a great comfort. I am rejoiced, because at last this greatest desire of his life has been accomplished. From his early youth the thought of Rome filled his mind, and my joy is great; for I know what he feels, now that he is in presence of the masterpieces of antiquity, will be an enjoyment for all the rest of his life; likewise for his friends who will share his enjoyment, for he possesses the gift of reproducing what he has seen in a vivid and convincing manner. May God bring him back to us sound and safe, then my wishes shall be fulfilled."

CHAPTER XII

The many cares which had pressed upon Anna Amalia during the last few years, the death of her father, Duke Karl, the illness of her brother, the distress of mind she suffered in regard to Prince Constantine — all of these things, although borne with fortitude and apparent calm, had preyed deeply upon the affectionate nature of the duchess, and now resulted in a severe illness, which caused grave fears of her life. The anxiety and distress this gave rise to, not alone in Weimar itself, but in every part of the duchy and amongst foreign nations, was a gratifying tribute to the merits of our duchess. There was universal joy when Doctor Hufeland, the court physician, issued more favourable bulletins, and a slow convalescence was followed by recovery.

Nevertheless, Anna Amalia's constitution was enfeebled, and a total change to the warmth of the sunny south was deemed absolutely necessary to restore her mental and bodily activity. The first date fixed was the autumn of 1787, but Goethe discountenanced this plan, on the ground that the invalid would not reap so much benefit from the change of temperature as if she came in the spring, which in Italy is so enchanting and so reviving to one exhausted by illness. So it was arranged, and Anna Amalia gave herself up to the delights of anticipation. The very thought seems to have restored her strength, and scattered the cobwebs of melancholy, which had for a time dimmed her natural gaiety.

"I must tell you a wonderful piece of news," she writes to Merck in the beginning of the year 1788 — "I have settled that this year I shall make a journey to Italy. Is not this a bold flight? The very thought that my desire is to be accomplished, and that I am to see with my own eyes that beautiful land, fills me with happiness. I believe Italy is to us what the river Lethe was to the Ancients. There one's youth is renewed and everything the disagreeables one has to encounter and the rest — are all forgotten and one becomes an altogether new person. I hope, dear Merck, you will give your blessing to my journey."

In the spring of 1788 the preparations were begun. The undertaking was surrounded with many difficulties. To the people of Weimar the idea of their dear duchess making such a journey seemed actually flying in the face of Providence, and in their distress they had recourse to Minister von Fritsch, begging of him to lay before her their petition — their earnest petition — that she would abandon a project so fraught with danger. The minister promised to lay their wishes before the duchess, and he did so in one of his long-winded epistles, which we will take the liberty to condense.

"The honest burghers of Weimar are trembling at the dangers to which your highness will be exposed in the long journey you contemplate. Their distress at your late dangerous illness was great, but greater far is their present anxiety at the idea of a journey to a country where the climate is anything but healthy, and might prove injurious to your precious health. These good people say nothing of another powerful reason against your absence — that it will be injurious to the trade and manufactures of the town, which benefit largely by your highness's presence. I will do them the justice to say I believe this has nothing to do with their anxiety." (Then why mention it, good Master Fritsch, unless you wish to benefit the town?) He ends with the hope that the duchess will weigh the matter well before she makes a decision.

The duchess complied with this last request; she sent no answer for five days, during which time we must suppose she was considering what her faithful burghers had, through her excellent friend Minister von Fritsch, put before her. Then, as the result of her cogitations she sent through Minister von Fritsch a very pretty letter to her kind friends, thanking them for their anxiety but adhering to her intention of going to Italy, which she assured them was absolutely necessary for her health, which she trusted, with the blessing of God, would be fully restored, and that, if the Almighty permitted, she would return to her good friends and live amongst them for the rest of the time allotted to her. So it was settled; nor was it indeed probable that the duchess would have given way to such old-fashioned ideas; that obstinate little chin of hers was indicative of a steady purpose. Minister von Fritsch ought to have known this, and we may be pretty sure got a rating for placing his dear duchess in so unpleasant a position. If Anna Amalia's temper was quick, her anger never lasted long, and, doubtless, Fritsch was soon forgiven.

Meanwhile another party had set out for Rome, in which was included Herder, whose grumble as to the fogs behind the church had, we must suppose, reached the ears of Statthalter von Dalberg, who was on the point of starting for Rome, and who now invited Herder to accompany him as a guest, all his expenses to be defrayed. In this act of kindness Dalberg was influenced as much by his wish to be of use to his friend (he had known Herder many years) as by his desire to secure a third person to break the awkwardness of a *tête-à-tête* journey with a lady, who, although she was related to him by some cousinly ramification, would be, he thought, rather a trying companion. The lady in question was the wife of Sigismund von Seckendorf, whose name has been previously mentioned in connection with the stage of Weimar, as a fair actor and an excellent playwright.

Before coming to Weimar he had lived some years at the court of the Markgraf of Bayreuth and Anspach (the successor to Wilhelmina's Markgraf), where he had filled the post of minister. Unfortunately, he was not to the taste of the Margravine (Lady Craven), and in consequence had to leave Bayreuth. He was a handsome man, his manners and everything about him bespoke the gentleman. His wife, on the contrary, although a cousin of Dalberg's, was not of the *grand monde*, and as it appeared had nothing of a lady about her. She did not join the party till they reached Innsbrück, and up to this Herder had enjoyed himself much.

But now everything was to change. Herder's adventures, although most unpleasant for himself, are very entertaining. The lady, who from the first took a dislike to him, made herself most disagreeable. He fancied she despised him because he was poor. It was not fancy, however, but unpleasant reality, when she insisted on taking one side of the large berline to herself and making the others uncomfortable. After a little Dalberg fell quite under her spell and did everything she liked. At Bolzano Herder met Kayser, one of Anna Amalia's travelling party. He told Herder that they had started on August 15th, but that he found it impossible to travel with the suite, and so Anna Amalia gave him the money to find his way back to Switzerland. Herder's spirits revived at the prospect of seeing the duchess in Rome, as his situation was growing everyday more uncomfortable. Dalberg and his fair friend having now become close allies, Herder realised the truth of the proverb about two being company. The lady, having taken a dislike to him, influenced Dalberg against him, and he found the only way to get on was to pay his share of the expenses. When he arrived in Rome he got away from his uncongenial companions and hired a lodging for himself, where at all events he was at peace, and free from the lady's insults. But there was the lodging to pay for and the living, and there was the family at home. "All the money I have goes in food," he says piteously. "If one only had money one could live pleasantly — not that things are dear here, but I have so little." His wife, pretty Caroline Flachsland, does her best to console him. "In the end," she writes, "the few thalers you spend won't make much difference in our year's income."

But then the income was such a pittance. Caroline had hard work to keep house on it; but she writes most cheerfully of all that is going on in Weimar, where everyone is most kind to her, especially Goethe who is back in Weimar and settled in the new house in the Frauenplatz. She gives an account of an evening at Goethe's, whose conduct she describes as odd.

"There were few people, the Stein, Schardt, Imhoff, and myself. We all hoped that, with so few, he would be himself, but soon the door opened and in came Frau von Wortel and her children, and also Voigt. We were ill at ease, and a little after seven came away. Frau von Schardt told me that, yesterday at the dancing picnic, he wouldn't speak a word to any woman of position, but danced and made love to all the girls, kissing their hands and going on with every kind of nonsense. In short, he does not want to have anything to say to his old friends." She adds: "His going on with the girls in this manner did not please the duke, who was present." Again: "The duke was at Goethe's on Saturday; he enquired for you and told me to ask you, had you no leisure to send a line to your friends, or was your time better occupied in writing tender letters to your wife. I excused you as well as I could, and I think he was satisfied, he was so friendly. Since then I have not seen him."

Caroline was evidently much taken up with Goethe, she is for ever bringing in his name, and he grew very attentive, often coming to see her and talk over Herder's affairs and his bad treatment by Dalberg.

It is amusing to read through the lines the growing jealousy of Herder, who dislikes to be "talked over" by his wife and her friend. Especially wroth is he with Caroline for showing his letters to his intimate friend. "Have I not repeatedly told you not to do so?" he writes. "Now I command you." Caroline, however, who had not very much penetration, evidently did not guess the cause of this outburst, and continued to quote Goethe's opinion on every subject. Of serio-comic interest is the correspondence between husband and wife, as to his paying attention to his dress, the buying of a new silk gown for evening wear, and the price he has to pay; she makes imploring requests that he will not wear soiled neckties and that above all he must be sure to get the new silk gown. The affair of the gown occupies much space in the correspondence between husband and wife and has quite a Vicar of Wakefield flavour, in all of which Caroline Herder's goodness of heart comes out well. But once Anna Amalia (who was ever good to the Herder family) arrived in Rome, Caroline's troubles were at an end. A place was reserved for Herder at the duchess's table, and kindly Thusnelda looked after him in any difficulty.

On 10 August 1788, Amalia started on her journey, which was to last till the summer of 1790. In the previous winter Goethe had brought from Rome a young Italian named Collina, who was now about to return to his own country and it was proposed that he should act as guide on the journey to Italy. For some reason, probably out of a kind desire on the duchess's part to benefit him, Kayser the artist, was substituted for Goethe's Italian; this proved a mistake.

The duchess's travelling companions, in addition to Kayser, were Einsiedel as gentleman-in-waiting, and Thusnelda as lady-in-waiting. Amalia made the same resolution as Goethe, to hold aloof from society, but she was of too social a nature to keep to this determination, and for this reason her tour was eminently successful. We hear of the travellers from another party, who had started shortly after the duchess.

Anna Amalia and her companions arrived at Verona on 3 September 1788, the journey thither occupying nineteen days. But what a journey! very different from rushing through at breakneck, *grande vitesse* speed, seeing hardly anything of the lovely panorama of mountains, valleys, and lakes. Listen to Thusnelda's graphic description (in a letter to Wieland):

"Imagine yourself in a narrow mountain pass, the end of which seems to dissolve into clouds, the mountain's top covered with snow and ice, out of which there seems no possible outlet. All round, the eye sees nothing but high mountain peaks reaching heavenward, tumbling waterfalls which draw the mountains closer to us: every quarter of an hour we pass pictures of the crucifixion, representations of accidents, carriages upset, or legends of the saints whose miraculous intercession has saved men from certain death. The art of these representations is of the rudest kind, and makes a curious contrast to Nature's handiwork which is here seen in perfection. By degrees the mountain scenery with its splendour and immensity gives place to the loveliest of smiling landscape. Here is nothing but hill and dale; vineyards stretch as far as the eye can reach; it is the land of fruitfulness and plenty. At nine o'clock yesterday evening we arrived here, where the duchess intends remaining some time." The duchess adds these few lines:

"My dear old man, I write these few lines to show you you are in my thoughts. For myself I feel like the holy souls in Elysium. I trust all goes well with you. AMALIA."

To Goethe Anna Amalia writes at more length.

"Verona.

"At last I am within the gates of Italy, so long my promised land. Last night I arrived at Verona in excellent health and spirits." She then gives an account of Kayser's conduct. "At Regensburg he got into bad humour, but when I spoke to him he complained of being ill, and we begged him to keep himself quiet and look after his health. At Innsbrück he got another fit of ill-temper and wanted to leave, but Einsiedel reasoned with him and he stayed till we arrived at Bolzano, where he insisted on leaving, although Einsiedel pointed out to him that so far he had not had occasion to be of any use to me, and that he ought to do some service before he left. I spoke to him and asked him to come as far as Milan, but he would not, so I gave him money for his return journey and he is gone. We are now in the hands of Collina, who so far has been satisfactory. We have had an excellent journey; the weather is splendid, we are in excellent health and spirits."

These letters, which in the usual manner were handed from one to another of the select circle of Weimar, gave universal satisfaction, Karl August taking care it should be made known to the people generally that their dear duchess had made a prosperous journey. Meantime the blank caused by the absence of the travellers was in a measure filled by the return of Goethe, who appears to have somewhat cut short his tour. His absence from Rome was a great loss to the duchess, but he did his best to make up by constant letters of advice and by introductions to all his friends.

It was Herder who received Anna Amalia on her arrival in Rome, 4 October 1788. Thusnelda tells us that after he had poured out all his grievances and had recovered from a fit of ill-temper and overwrought nerves, he became very agreeable and lived with the duchess as one of the family. His letters to Weimar are filled with amazement at the duchess's never-flagging activity and excellent spirits. In Rome she lived as a private individual, under the name of the Countess Alstedt, but was treated with all the respect due to her high position.

"Everyone here," writes Herder, "says that no royal visitor has ever received more, if so much, honour as is shown to our duchess." The Italians were delighted with the good humour, the gaiety, the wonderful intelligence and the charm of manner possessed by the duchess, whose capacity for making friends was never so clearly shown as in this Italian tour. Everywhere she went it was the same story, and it cannot be said that this popularity was due either to her position or her wealth, minor German royalties being held in small estimation, while English millionaires and Russian princes scattered gold as if it were copper. Anna Amalia's popularity was all the more gratifying that it was due to her personality. The duchess was thoroughly happy; the largeness of the life as compared with the littleness which was a necessary condition of a small circle like that of Weimar, was delightful to one who had an open mind on every subject; and her circle of friends growing daily larger, she became a centre, round which gathered every sort and condition of political, artistic, intellectual, religious, and non-religious men and women.

Thusnelda sends Wieland a sort of diary of what they are doing and the friends they have made.

"The mornings with few exceptions are devoted to sight-seeing and art, and every day we see something new. I prefer the Museums, the Pantheon, and St. Peter's, which one could visit over and over again. On these pilgrimages we are accompanied by Herder and Reiffenstein.[86] We go out at ten o'clock and return before two. Both gentlemen dine with us, also occasionally some one of our new acquaintances, and there is then conversation which would, I know, please you; and how it would gratify me if you were here! After dinner we either take a siesta or, if very fine, a walk to some remarkable place. Rome is full of charming walks. We all meet at the tea-table and are sure to have several of our acquaintance. The theatres are not open yet, but there are concerts. This is our usual life, though some days in the week the duchess is obliged to receive the *grand monde*; but this is the only break.

"The duchess never dines out of her own house (on account of her health, all ministerial dinners and evening parties are forbidden); the only exception she makes is for the Cardinal Boncompagni (State secretary), Cardinal Bernis, and the Spanish Ambassador, Azara, the same who published Mengs' works. These dinners are very interesting, for the reason that these three men belong to the best and most interesting circle in Rome. Cardinal Bernis comes almost every second evening to the duchess, and despite his seventy years of age, is the very best company that you can imagine. He is so clever and has seen so much of the world, and of the best of everything, both in his own country and elsewhere. He knew Voltaire and Fontenelle, and other great lights, and relates pleasant anecdotes of that period.

"The duchess is at home only to a select few in the evening (if she allowed free entrée, half the society in Rome would put in an appearance). The cardinal sometimes is accompanied by most interesting and agreeable people, and from seven o'clock, I assure you, the company is often of the very best. At some of the large conversaziones where all Rome comes pouring in, there are often three hundred people present. To these the duchess goes seldom — perhaps once a week, never oftener. As the people here have shown, especially for Romans, the most extraordinary civility to the duchess, the consequence is *par contre-coup* that I have much to do; nevertheless, I have never been so well and have enjoyed myself exceedingly. The Holy Father (as you are aware) is a handsome man, and it gives me pleasure to look on his face. Our dear princess sends you a great many greetings and thanks for your last letters, and will soon write to you."

"Herder," she says, in another letter," is in excellent form, enjoying life. He is very good and constant to us, and comes mostly every day to dine. He goes out a good deal, and has a fine silk gown for festivities. He and the old sea-lion (Reiffenstein) get on admirably. Our artists are Bury, Schütz, and Verschappel; these are standing dishes, but others come occasionally. Bury is a nice fellow and my favourite; he reminds me of Fritzchen (the young von Stein)."

Thusnelda's graphic pen paints in a few words the novel effect to her of the Italian climate. "In Italy we learn what the originals of the sun and moon are like. In Germany we have only copies." By degrees Anna Amalia finds it impossible to keep to her rule of not going to receptions; she has to accept some invitations to the royal palace. "The duchess enjoys it," writes Thusnelda, "and everyone says there never was a German princess in Rome so popular as our duchess. She is treated by everyone with more than courtesy; it is devotion. The Vatican even extends a friendly welcome; she received three places for the ceremonials on St. Peter's day and for all the processions, etc."

The Abbé Ceruti, introduces Anna Amalia to the Arcadian Academy, where there is a great deal of speech-making and talk of science. But the highest dignitaries, too, interest themselves about Amalia. She is sent the best seats for ceremonies in the Sistine Chapel in the Vatican, as well as the places for the ceremonies in St. Peter's; and still more, the Holy Father is ready to grant an audience to the gifted duchess.

"Tomorrow," writes Thusnelda," is the great day, when the duchess is to be presented to the pope. She has received such favours from the Vatican that this is necessary, and it will be looked upon as a compliment on her side as much as on his. She will be received by the pope alone; her lady-in-waiting even will not attend her, and the interview will take place with closed doors, the attendants remaining in the ante-chamber. When the duchess's interview is over, I am to be presented by the Princess Santa Croce, a favour which has never before been shown to persons of my position."

Of the proceedings on the day she tells us: "At five o'clock we drove to call for Princess Santa Croce, and then proceeded to the Vatican. We were first brought to Cardinal Braschi's apartments, where several cardinals and monsignors were assembled to do honour to the duchess. Towards six o'clock we went to the pope. The Swiss Guard presented arms and several ceremonies were gone through. We mounted a steep staircase and passed through a number of rooms. The duchess went by herself to the pope, and her audience lasted half an hour. After the duchess, Einsiedel and I were presented. Then we returned through many rooms and across the garden by torchlight." Amalia also writes her account of the reception. "On the evening of November 23rd, I was presented to the pope. It was a theatrical and comical scene; it was for all the world as if I were being led away to some secret tribunal. When we returned home we made great fun of the many comical situations."

Amalia was a stiff-necked Lutheran, and her pride was in arms at having to bend to the head of the more ancient Church; but setting aside these Lutheran prejudices, she was liberal-minded. Her judgments of character or personality were never influenced by religious bias, as for example when later on she got to know intimately Archbishop Capecelatro, one of the ideal and saintly priests of the Catholic Church, she writes: "How happy should I be, had I always near me men like this bishop, free from self-seeking, full of intelligence, and gently drawing the heart towards God." Later on, and in order to see Capecelatro again, she travelled to Apulia to take leave of him.

Thusnelda says: "The parting for ever from such a man as the archbishop of Tarent is a kind of anticipated death."

CHAPTER XIII

Another close bond of friendship, which was knit during this time, was with the artist Angelica Kaufmann Zucchi. Angelica has long since descended from the position she once held. But in 1788, and for fifty years later, great prices were given for her work.

Drawn together by their common admiration for Goethe and their love of art, the two women became dear friends. In one of his first letters to the duchess, Goethe strikes the keynote of this friendship: "You have seen Madame Angelica by this time, and this excellent woman must from many different points be interesting to you;" and the duchess immediately responds:

"I go to Angelica as often as I can, and she comes to me; she is in every way *eine herzliebe frau*.[87] Next Friday I am to sit to her for my portrait, certainly not as a model, but I wish to have something of hers. Old Zucchi has given me some of his drawings."

The first letter Angelica writes to Goethe after the duchess's arrival is in a joyous tone. It begins: "Do you know, my dear friend, that I am coming to Weimar? Have you ever dreamt of such a thing? Her excellency, the duchess, has invited, in the most cordial manner, good Rath Reiffenstein, Zucchi, and me, either to accompany her back or to follow her. Fräulein von Göchhausen and Herder were present and added their entreaties. Was it possible to refuse such a gracious proposal? The promise has been given *if circumstances permit*. Blessed Weimar, which, since it has given me the joy of knowing you, I have so often envied, and to which my thoughts fly so constantly, shall I really see it, and see *you there*? Oh, most beautiful dream, and still I hope that, even before this journey comes off, we may see you in Rome. That the duchess has shown herself so gracious to me, I have to thank you for, my best and dear friend.

"This gracious princess honours me with a visit constantly, and she allows me to go to her. We often speak of you, and then what joy fills my soul. A few evenings ago her highness visited the museum, attended by her whole suite, that is, Herr Baron von Dalberg, Frau von Seckendorf, Herr Herder, etc.; Zucchi and I had also the honour of attending her. It was quite a festival for me. Nevertheless, there was something wanting to make me perfectly content. Your name was repeated in the hall of the Muses, but I looked about me and only saw you in spirit. When we all stood before the Apollo, someone proposed that we should offer a prayer to the god. Herr Herder said we should each ask for something. My prayer to Apollo was that he would inspire you to come to Rome. Oh, that my wish may be granted; but it must be *before* I go to Weimar.

"The duchess's circle is exceedingly pleasant, and what a kindly dear creature is Fräulein von Göchhausen. So intelligent and so lively, and she does everything so well. The Duchess seems quite satisfied. The weather is beautiful; everything looks to the best advantage. Madame von Seckendorf desires to be remembered to you. I am glad that you like the title page. Herr Rath is sending the design, perhaps tomorrow, with other things to you. I hear much in praise of your *Tasso*. I am rejoicing over the hope you have given me, that you may still read it to me. It is a consolation for much, May Apollo strengthen you in this good purpose. I thank you meanwhile for having thought of me.

★ ★ ★ ★ ★

"Zucchi and I often talk of you, but alas! that is not the same as being with you. All, the happy time; the dear Sundays, which I will think of as long as I live. Her highness, the duchess, seems to wish that I should paint her portrait. Next week I shall have the honour to commence it. I hope my work will please. I have just finished the two Shakespearian pictures.[88] A mass of things are waiting for me to begin. One after the other they will gradually get finished. It is all well so long as health lasts; but on that score I cannot complain at present. I am anxious about you, and trust you take care of yourself.

"The other day I chanced on a good specimen of an Intaglio, cut in "Hiuzint,"[89] which I rather fancy. I send you an impression, which I hope may reach you safely. The stone is very fine, and cut in a masterly manner in my judgment, only I have a doubt on account of the subject, because under the four antiques there seems to be the head of a philosopher. A word from you will settle this matter and be a guide for me in the future.

"I am glad that you like your present situation, and that you have time to prosecute your work. May you live always happy and content, and if you have an idle moment, think of me. Farewell, best of friends.

"A. K."[90]

In several of the duchess's letters to Goethe there is most kind mention of Angelica. "I have sat twice," she says, "to Angelica, and the picture promises to be a splendid success. The last time I sat, Herder read for us your poems. The good Angelica was so inspired, that the portrait seemed to grow under her fingers." And again Herder writes: "Angelica is a lovely Madonna; only she lives in herself and feeds upon her own branches." Fräulein von Göchhausen also gives her meed of praise: "Angelica has such a beautiful soul; there are few like her, and out of love for her one grows better when near her. She loves the duchess, and yesterday she wept tears of sorrow at the thought that our quiet evenings were over. We cheer her up with talking of her visit to Weimar, and so try to dispel the melancholy, which hangs about a farewell."

Einsiedel writes to Goethe, 15 November 1788: "I have delayed writing until I could tell you something definite as to our plans. Nearly four weeks have been occupied in visiting Roma Antica, and since the beginning of this month we occupy ourselves with Roma Moderna. But the great world has latterly taken complete possession of us. The duchess receives much more attention than we ever expected and far more than is usually paid to royalties; but if the duchess consulted her own interest she would not stay here much longer, for it requires close attention, and is very fatiguing to receive all these advances in the proper manner."

(The duty of replying to invitations, leaving cards, etc., devolved on Einsiedel as chamberlain; hence the complaint.)

"There appears to be no other way of cutting short this whirligig, and resuming our free and tranquil mode of life. Although the duchess excuses herself from all large dinners and entertainments on the plea of her health, she says she cannot refuse such things as conversaziones, little dinners, and the like, and in this way our circle of acquaintances is growing larger every day. . . . She is flattered at the wish of everyone here to make her stay pleasant, only I doubt her being able to continue the exertion it involves, and the constant attention which is necessary in order to give each person the attention he considers due to his position. The advice of Cardinal Bernis is invaluable, and Santa Croce helps us with his experience of society in Rome.

"The duchess's plan is now to go to Naples in January — that is earlier than she intended — and to live there quietly which she has quite given up doing here. Reiffenstein will accompany us to Naples, which is a great relief to my mind, otherwise I should have had to search for another antiquarian mentor. Farewell.

"Yours,

"EINSIEDEL."

Very amusing is the ill-humour which breathes through every line of this letter. Einsiedel was evidently not lying on a bed of roses. The duchess was probably a little thoughtless, as people are apt to be when in a whirl. There was no doubt she enjoyed the excitement of the perpetual *va-et-vient*, and the homage she received was pleasing to her.

In all the whirl of sight-seeing and amidst the rush of visitors and entertainments, the duchess never forgot those she had left at home, and to her household and old retainers she wrote at regular intervals. Here is a letter, full of kindly words to old Kogeln, who had been many years in her service.

"DEAR OLD KOGELN,

"Your note and good wishes for my birthday gave me much pleasure. Take great care of yourself and keep well, so that on my return I may find you in good health. Give my greetings to Piper[91] and tell her to give the maids a good kiss from me. I am very well and take great care of myself. Adieu, dear Kogeln: Fräulein Göchhausen sends you her remembrances,

"AMALIE."

The duchess writes to Knebel in the same affectionate tone, but more intimately:

"One would think, dear Knebel, that it would be the easiest thing possible to write letters from Rome, and yet nothing is more certain that it is very hard to accomplish. Imagine for yourself what it would be to sit at a splendidly covered board, and have a stomach that will digest all that is provided. Well, this is my condition. The enjoyment here is great, for one is surrounded with the most perfectly beautiful things the world can produce. Dear Knebel, would I could transport you here, and lead you into the temple of the Muses, where Apollo is surrounded by the Nine: he plays upon the lyre; his whole being is harmony. We hear his melodious song, it fills the mind, and one's soul is full of harmony. Herder has written some lovely lines, which show that the right spirit has entered his soul. These stanzas of his have the ring of true art. Read them attentively and you will have an idea of this lovely work of art."[92] Then she goes on to tell Knebel "that the sweet little verses he had sent Goethe were read to Madame Angelica while she was painting my portrait, or rather I should say the tableau she makes of me, which is full of poetry." Knebel answers in a tone of affected gaiety, assumed in order to conceal the depression he feels at the general outlook, which, politically, was undoubtedly bad; moreover, learning, according to the pessimistic major, was likewise declining.

The winter of 1788-9 was one of extraordinary severity, experienced all over Europe. Rome was no exception, and the cold was doubly felt as there were no appliances for keeping out draughts or heating the enormous rooms.

Thusnelda writes to Goethe: "We are trying to keep up the illusion that we are in a warm climate, but it is a pretence; the truth is, we are as cold here as you are in Weimar, with far fewer facilities for defending ourselves against the biting wind, which penetrates through our weak defences. There is no talk now of expeditions, or running here and there; we sit at home and long for a good fire. The duchess is leaving for Naples in the hope that Vesuvius may warm her frozen body; a curious result of coming to Italy. We shall resume our unfinished sight-seeing on our return, as the duchess has taken a villa for the spring situated on the Trinità de Monte, said to be the healthiest part in Rome and quite close to Angelica."

Herder corroborates Thusnelda's report of the weather. "It is merciless weather here," he writes to Goethe. "Everyone who is not accustomed to it is out of spirits and discontented, except our duchess, who is always well content and in good spirits. The pope sent her a present yesterday." He goes on to say that Anna Amalia is much taken up with music, and has here the very best. "Besides the concerts given by Bernis, Ruspoldi has had four, at which we had the most lovely music, as he had the very best musicians."

Herder then proceeds to unfold a project of his, which he entreats Goethe to carry out — "For you know," he says, "better than I do what a change our duchess will feel when she returns to Weimar and finds so little to attract her. Could you not form a musical society which could perform those concerted pieces she loves so well, and also have supervision over the theatre, get a good opera company, etc.? I spoke of this to Einsiedel, who quite agreed that it would be an excellent thing, if only it could be arranged. Think over this and do the best, otherwise I very much fear she will feel leaving here greatly, for she has so many occupations and is made so much of, while in Weimar there is nothing for her to do.

"On the other hand, I have not very pleasant impressions of my stay here. Everything has been more or less of a disappointment. At all events, my experience, although bought dearly enough, will be of use. I will look well, and on all sides, before I take such a journey again. However, I am determined not to walk in your footsteps and return home "indifferent to all human beings," which would be more unpleasant for me than for you, since I have no art world wherein to find consolation for the extinction of present joys. I may truly say I have *never* felt so cold in my appreciation of art as since I have seen the beginning, the growth, and the finish, as they are here demonstrated before one's eyes.

"Perhaps I am influenced by the fact that "poor Tom's a-cold." I am literally frozen, and when one is frozen through and through, one can neither speak nor think nor feel, one can scarcely see or hear, and least of all learn how to speak. If ever I reach home again I will get you to tell me what you saw and what I *didn't* see. I shall keep my mouth shut. I fear — I very much fear — that you no longer care for Germany, whereas I have travelled to Rome to become a true German, and if I could I would colonise this country with Germans. If I ever get back and ever get warm again, I will write a treatise entitled 'Rome in the Year of Our Lord 1789,' and I hope I may be able to put this plan into execution.

"Farewell, dear friend. My fingers are too cold to hold the pen; my heart is frozen and my soul is an icicle. Farewell! Give my greetings to the duke and duchess, and to anyone who may perchance remember me.

"HERDER."

That Herder exaggerated slightly, if not *the cold*, the moral depression from which he was suffering, is shown in a letter of Fräulein Göchhausen. "Herder goes with us to Naples. He seems to wish to attach himself to us. That is what I always wished he would do; *he is in good spirits*, has many acquaintances, enjoys himself, and is very popular!"

The duchess also writes long letters to Goethe and to Wieland, to whom she gives an account of her visit to the museum in the Vatican by torchlight, and poor old Wieland is in raptures.

"Indeed, your highness cannot conceive the benefit you confer on a poor deserted old man by writing to him such delightful letters, one of which is of more value to him than all the epistles in the world, from those of Phalaris to those of St. Paul inclusive. Your highness will probably consider this comparison as one of those florid compliments in which such a well-known courtier as I am would be likely to indulge, and, out of an excess of modesty, you may refuse to believe that your little notes could compare in importance with the letters of Cicero to Atticus or St. Paul to the Corinthians. Still, it is none the less true that the aforesaid little scribbles have more interest for me, and give me the most agreeable sensations by which my frozen heart revives from the dejection produced by the gloom of November and the absence of my princess. But the knowledge that you are well and happy, and that in the midst of a circle, which naturally tends to banish thoughts of the past and recollections of the absent, you should have remembered your old friend, whose life is now nothing but a memory of the past — this, I say, shows such a good heart, that I feel consoled to think that I shall never be quite forgotten."

Some people may think this the letter of a courtier, but to me it seems to have a ring of real, sincere affection. "Der alte Wieland" (and yet he was not an old man, according to the present age standard) was of an affectionate nature, and very sensitive to kindness; he followed with the deepest interest every incident of the duchess's tour, and was enthusiastic about Cicero and the Roman Senators. Fräulein Göchhausen declared he knew more than all the *cognoscenti* in Rome, as was proved by his translation of Horace, and his notes on the Satires and Epistles, which the travellers studied most diligently.

The duchess and her party (including Herder) arrived in Naples on 14 January 1789. On 3 February 1789 we have Thusnelda writing in rapturous delight to Wieland:"Oh, dear friend, what a country is this! Truly the land of milk and honey. Climate, vegetation, people, all and everything is wonderful. A third enchantment is music, for Naples is the birthplace of music. We have here a collection of better voices than all Italy can produce, Marchesini excepted. In Paesiello's opera *Cato* there are three magnificent singers, Bariti, the prima donna, David, the tenor, and Crescentini, the first tenor; all the rest would have been considered with us firstrate artists, but their light is eclipsed by the three just named.

"Paesiello is a very pleasant man, and his face at once conveys the impression that the world treats him well. He comes to the duchess on evenings when there is no opera; he plays and sings for her his operas. The Archbishop of Tarento, Capecelatro, is also here; he is an excellent man — Herder thinks much of him — and is quite different from our bishops. He and the duchess are friends; he is intellectual, artistic, and talented. We have also made acquaintance with Abbé

Fortis, a worthy and interesting man. The duchess does not go into society here, but she receives some of the best people."

When the severe weather had passed the duchess and her suite returned, on 20 February 1789 to Rome, fortunately in time for the ceremonies of Holy Week.

Fräulein Göchhausen writes to Wieland, on 17 March 1789:

"You know all about the ceremonies which take place during Holy Week in the Sistine Chapel much better than I do, who have seen them. Can anyone forget the strains of the *Miserere* by Allegri and Palestrina, and the devotion of the kneeling multitude, the processions of the cross, with pope, cardinals, bishops, etc., all singing hymns; the lighting of the church; the illumination of the cross? On Good Friday the pope and the cardinals on their knees in the middle of St. Peter's, the thousands of human beings, and the magical effect of the sudden change from gloom and darkness to the brilliant illumination of the enormous building, the blessing given by the holy father after High Mass on Easter Sunday from the balcony of St. Peter's to the multitude gathered to receive it — all these magnificent ceremonials are impossible to describe."

Thusnelda's description of the *Miserere* is worth noting:

"The *Miserere*, sung by thirty voices, does not sound like singing or instrumentation, or harmony of any sort, but it is a union of the best portion of these three units which presents the most celestial — I should call it harmony — ever heard on earth. Truly an angelic choir." She describes the pope's blessing in the same enraptured terms, and the extraordinary silence of the immense multitude of sixty thousand people on their knees, while the one figure standing, as it were, "between heaven and earth," gave the blessing. "Then the cannons thundered and the bells rang out. It was as if the whole earth were making festival."

At the end of the letter she says: "We see our Angelica (Kaufmann) almost every day; her garden is only separated by a little mount from ours. She generally spends with us every evening that we are at home; she is an excellent woman. Our beloved duchess is well and happy. She sends you a thousand remembrances and good wishes, and I am to tell you that, if only you and a few more of her prized friends were here, she would be as happy as anyone could be on this terrestrial globe of ours. We all look forward to seeing you again as one of our pleasantest prospects, and I assure you that, in spite of all our enjoyments here (and *I* certainly have never had in my life so many pleasures as since I came here), the thought of our return to Weimar and the pleasure of seeing again my own little room is constantly present to my mind. When will that be? I hope sooner than your incredulity believes.

"The duchess wishes to return to beautiful Partenope (Naples) once more, to see it in all its beauty at the best season; therefore she has settled on remaining this summer in Italy. This is the advice of all who know the country; they recommend the sea air as making the heat more bearable; but we all hope to return in the autumn. Herder desires me to give you his remembrances. You will soon see him.

His Penelope and little Telemachus are the syrens which draw away our Ulysses, and he dares not, though he fain would, be deaf to their song."

Herder left Rome on 14 May 1789, in spite of all the efforts made by the duchess to induce him to come to Naples. In these efforts she was assisted by Madame Angelica, who, to speak the unvarnished truth, had set up one of her "friendships" with Herder. This otherwise estimable woman had one fault, — admitted by her biographers — *vanity beyond that of most women*, which induced her to accept homage, especially the homage of men of genius. It was a perfectly harmless vanity and not calculated to arouse any jealousy in the mind of Zucchi (who, for the rest, knew the excellence of Angelica's beautiful character).

The correspondence with Herder is interesting, as showing the singular influence Angelica exerted over men's minds, even at an age when such influence is supposed to cease; and likewise as giving an insight into her life, and confirming the testimony of Goethe that she was hard put to it to provide money for the household. 'Zucchi was undoubtedly avaricious, as the future disclosed. He was saving his own money and spending hers, hardly earned as it was.

"Der alte Zucchi ist geizig," [93] writes the Duchess Amalia in one of her letters, and Herder alludes several times to Angelica as a victim sacrificed in every way to the greed of her father and husband.

It will be remembered that the German philosopher arrived in Rome after Goethe had left it. He came in the company of Baron von Dalberg and Frau von Seckendorf, travelling at the charges of the baron, and the story of his many discomforts and his final rupture with his friend has been already told. One of his first visits was paid to Angelica, and he gives his impressions of her in a letter to his wife:—

"ROME,
"*September* 21st.

"I have just been to Angelica; she is a delicate, tender soul, artistic to her finger-tips, extraordinarily simple, *without any bodily charm*, but extremely interesting. Her principal attraction is her simplicity and extreme purity; she reminds me of a Madonna, or a little dove. Alas! for art and for the world generally, she is growing old. She lives retired in an ideal world, which she shares with the little birds and the flowers. Poor old Zucchi is a good sort of man in his own way; he resembles a Venetian nobleman in a comedy."

By-and-by he grows more eloquent:

"These last few weeks have been purified and brightened by my friendship with Angelica. Oh! what torments might I have spared myself had I only known earlier this noble creature, who lives shy and retired as a heavenly being. Since my return from Naples, I have drawn nearer to her, and *she is dearer* to me than all else in Rome. I am so happy with her; she, on her side, regards me with the *deepest reverence*,[94] while of thee she speaks tenderly and with a certain timidity. She looks upon thee as one of the *happiest of women*. The impression this gifted creature has made upon my mind is indelible; it will last my whole life, for she is utterly devoid of envy, free from vanity, and incapable of insincerity. She knows not what meanness is, and, although she is perhaps the most cultivated woman in Europe, is full of the sweetest humility and the most angelic innocence. I tell thee all this, my own, because I know that from thee I need hide nothing, and because thou wilt rejoice with me that after my bitter months of solitude, I have found this pearl, or rather lily, which heaven has vouchsafed to me as a blessing and reward. It is in this light that I regard her."

Caroline Herder was no doubt an amiable woman and an excellent wife; her letters prove this; but she must have been sorely tried when post after post brought her rhapsodies of this sort over the perfections of another woman. Here is another when the friendship had considerably advanced.

"Rome,
"*April* 1st.

"Angelica sends thee a tender souvenir — it came on Easter Day; a little ring, which I am to put on thy finger, and with it now I seal this letter. On this side of the Alps I may look on it as mine own, and on my return give it to thee from thy sister. No one knows of this little present except the good Reiffenstein, who ordered it for her. It is, indeed, a faithful symbol of her pure, tender soul, for truly friendship and love are one. So she represents her sweet soul as a tiny sparrow resting upon a branch of myrtle, a type that our union shall exist, absent or present. *Say nothing of this to anyone*, but take the remembrance as it is meant, in good part. A purer, more exquisite creature does not exist on earth. Like to a pious victim, she has all her life been sacrificed to her art, for it she has lived and still lives; now she is nearly fifty years old, and it is still the same.

"She loves me with a warm affection, and I love and honour her as a saint. Do not, however, believe, my dearest wife, that my affection for her would keep me one day longer in Rome than it is right for me to remain. Angelica would be the first to advise me to go, if she saw me inclined to stay, for, with all her tenderness, she has a strong and almost masculine mind. Therefore, it is that I reckon so strongly upon her sympathy, and see such a wonderful dispensation in this friendship. I regard it as the germ of far more in the future, and neither time nor absence shall interrupt it. It is, I think, a reward for my undertaking this journey, a panacea for all I have undergone, and thou also, my dearest, must look upon it from this point of view. The birth of this friendship has awakened in me a tardy prudence and a resolution to live henceforth for thee and my dear ones, for now I feel more strengthened in good than I have ever been."

In a letter dated 20 April 1789 he makes allusions to Angelica's lonely life, unblessed by children, and adds: "But she is, indeed, an angel of a woman, and her goodness sets the balance right between me and others of her sex, who have served me ill. She has the activity of a man, and has done more than fifty men would have done in the time. In goodness of heart she is a celestial being. I gave her thy kiss as it stood in thy letter, *without transferring it to her lips*. Once I did kiss her on the forehead, and once she unexpectedly seized my hand and would press it to her lips. *There*, that is all between us! I thank my God that He allowed me to know this pure soul, and that through her I carry away one pleasant memory from Rome. She is with us constantly, sometimes with the duchess, who loves her on account of her great modesty. I am with her every moment I can spare. She came unexpectedly to Frascati, and I do not know if she will also come to Tivoli.

"Thou must love Angelica for my sake, for she deserves it, the strangely tender, loving soul; she knows thee, and we speak of thee often, and then she says softly she esteems thee to be very happy. The story which you heard from Frau von Stein[95] is false, although I myself do not know the true history of the affair. Once she began to tell it to me, but her grief at the recollection would not let her finish. Take the letter she sends thee kindly; she is not strong in words, but in deeds a most honest soul. English and Italian she speaks and writes beautifully. German is to her almost a strange language[96] Her best wishes accompany me when I go, and her friendship *for us both* will last as long as we live. This is the confession of my heart's feelings while in Rome, written only for thee, for I must and always shall write to thee what fills my heart."

This ingenuous confession of his inmost feelings, together with the kissing passages, did not altogether please Madame Herder. She writes to her husband that she feels like Ariadne deserted by Theseus, and urges his return to his home and family. Herder's answer is an amusing lucubration intended to calm any little jealousy that may have arisen in his wife's mind, and impress upon her Angelica's friendship for *her*.

"I count Angelica amongst my true friends. In years, she *is much older than I am*, and she is more a spiritual than a corporeal being. She is, however, a true heart, there are few like her, and through hearing constantly of thee from me, she loves thee also. So in every way she is worthy of being joined to us by a close bond of friendship. She often says to me that the whole happiness of her life depends upon the continuance of this bond; that she would wish to die now, since she has (though truly for but such a short time) seen and known me; it is to her as a dream.

"I write to thee, my dearest, everything, because it is my habit so to do. Thou knowest that these words of hers do not make me vain, but rather humble. I look upon the friendship of this dear and noble woman as a gift that heaven has sent me, which has turned me from all else, and in a theoretic manner has elevated my thoughts and exalted my whole being, for she charms the mind, purifies and softens it, and is a good, tender creature. Do love her for my sake, dearest; she is so good, and her life is not happy. For the remainder of our poor lives we must do all things to please this willing victim to art. She sends you a thousand greetings. I told her yesterday when I saw her for a few moments, that this day would be the anniversary of our wedding-day, and so, if it be possible, I am to go to her this evening, and we will bear you and the children in remembrance."

In the postscript to this same letter, he adds the following:—

"When I went this evening to Angelica, she with infinite grace slipped into my hand a little gold chain as a remembrance of today; she said it was for us both. She is in every way a sweet, angelic and pure woman. Thou must promise an eternal friendship to her, and with me render thanks to heaven who has given her to me to know and to love."

On 9 May 1789, Herder writes to his Caroline an account of an expedition to Tivoli, to which Madame Angelica came unexpectedly.

"Her silent, modest grace;" he says, "gives the tone to the company she is amongst; like a chord of music she is in harmony with all. Oh, what an exquisite nature is hers — a nature like to thine own, my dear one; like thee, she makes no claim upon our admiration, but it is full of sympathy and tender feeling for others. I leave Rome content, now that I have been to Tivoli."

Then he goes on about Caroline's journey to Carlsbad, and concludes as follows:—

"My best and dearest, do not constrain thyself, if thou wouldst prefer to remain at home. Thou hast received by this time my letter, and wilt know how best to decide. It was thy remark as to feeling like 'Ariadne' which gave rise to the idea in my mind. But fear not. Where could I go but to thee? Everything draws me to thee, and thou wilt no longer find me rough and fierce, but gentle, tender, forbearing. Oh, I have learned, if I never knew it before, what I have in thee. Also, fear nothing from the Angelica friendship. She is the best woman in the world; the most thoroughly honest; besides, her mind and mine are turned to other things. As I have many times repeated, she is truly modest; she honours thee as a sort of divinity, and loves me in a spiritual manner. She greets thee affectionately, and thou canst receive this greeting from *my hand*. She is in truth an angel. At Tivoli her silhouette was taken, which I shall send you in my next,"

His next is the last of this remarkable series of letters.

"*May* 13*th*, 1789.

"Well then, in God's name, my trunk is packed. All is ready; tomorrow I leave Rome for Pisa. I am well, and, all things considered, have had a time in Rome of which few strangers can boast.

*   *   *   *   *

"Angelica, who is dear and good beyond all expression, greets thee cordially, and sends thee her silhouette. Take it with feelings of love and kindness. The angel has made me during these last weeks inexpressibly happy. I would I had known her earlier: the good, excellent, tender, beautiful soul. She likes me as much as I do her; our friendship will grow stronger year by year, for it is founded upon the purest esteem and love. So too, must thou, if thou wilt please me, take her cordially to thy heart. Thou wilt do so when thou knowest her better, the tender, loving creature. The duchess esteems her highly; so do all who come in contact with her, for she lives and acts as a beneficent being. Today I dine with her, and tomorrow we take our last drive together. May Heaven bless and preserve this sweet woman! Farewell, my good soul, no longer to be a desolate Ariadne. Farewell! think joyfully of my return. I am far happier than I deserve to be."

Herder's hopes as to the continuance of this friendship do not seem to have been realised. Whether Madame Herder, as a wife sometimes does, put her foot down upon the intimacy founded upon the "purest lines of love and esteem," or whether Herder himself, with the erratic nature of a genius, grew tired of his worship of this beneficent being, does not appear. The letters which he may have written shared the same fate as those of Goethe. The only one quoted by Angelica's biographer is written in a cold strain, very unlike his former rapturous expressions. In his case it is evident that, contrary to the poet's assertion, absence did not make his heart grow fonder. All through this curious correspondence of Herder's, allowance, however, must be made for the nature of the poet-philosopher, which was high-strung, sensitive and altogether Teutonic. His *seelen-sentimentalität* meant very little, certainly nothing dangerous. Yet it cannot be disputed that the friendship and admiration of such men as Herder and Goethe is a rare testimony to the worth and attractions of Angelica.

During all this time Anna Amalia had done her best to reassure the absent "Ariadne," as we may see from the following letter:—

"Rome,
"*March* 1st, 1789.

"To CAROLINE HERDER,

"As I know well that your dear second self writes regularly to his better-half and tells her all about himself and also about us and what we are doing, I have not been in a hurry to write to you, but waited, dear Frau Herder, until now. I must write now to tell you that I have won a victory (a small one) over Herder. It is true he will not acknowledge it, for a strong man does not like to be conquered by a weak woman; nevertheless, it is a fact.

"In the beginning I did all that was possible to draw him away from his philosophy and to make him one of us. All in vain, it was not to be done. I grew angry at last, and I acknowledge that I did tempt him with the charms of lovely Partenope[97] as set against his dry study of philosophy. She caressed him, called him her favourite son. Our philosopher smiled, he grew more lively, he returned the tenderness shown him; then cold wisdom stepped in, and, growing jealous of Partenope, tried to overcome her attractions by throwing cold water on his enthusiasm for her rival, who in her turn flattered at her conquest, sought in every way to secure him. She called to her help a veritable syren,[98] a beautiful enchantress, who, through her form, her voice, her enchanting attitudes, the very perfection of Greek art, fairly enraptured him.

"Wisdom's dry teaching, philosophy itself, was forgotten; an electric spark touched his heart and filled it with a new sensation; his whole being thrilled with a new sense of life, joy, and blessedness; it was a new creation. Philosophy, however, did not desert him; she made a fierce attack on him, and, alas! won the victory." The duchess adds that Herder will not remain in Rome much longer, "His thoughts and looks are all directed to the north, where all his dear ones are. You can be quite easy about your husband's future, the gods wish him well; he will return to you with a faithful heart and a contented spirit.

"Think of me sometimes and greet the children for me.

"AMALIA."

To Knebel, Anna Amalia writes, beginning her letter with an allusion to the classics:

"In Virgil's 'Æneid' you will find an accurate description of what is now before my eyes; and how I wish you were with me to contemplate its wonders!"[99] She goes on to say that, "Poor old Herder is getting better since he came to live with us; he is called here 'The Archbishop,' and I am congratulated on having so distinguished a man in my suite. He is very popular, especially with the ladies — nevertheless, his dear little wife has nothing to fear, for he is as faithful to her as a general superintendent."[100] She does not quite understand whether Wieland is in joke or earnest when he writes that he is coming with bag and baggage, children included, to Naples, "Where a humble existence with good health would be better than the wealth of Crœsus in the bleak Thuringian mountains." Anna Amalia answered this outburst with the ironical observation that she did not think he would relish living amongst the "Lazzaroni."

Herder writes of his home-coming 16 July 1789:

"On the 9th of this month I arrived in Weimar, at two o'clock in the morning. There was nothing to greet me, but the most lovely moon an one side of the heavens, and on the other the first gleam of the rising sun. In my house all was ready for me, only I had no key and I was obliged to wait while my wife let her lover escape into the garden by the back door. When I got in there was great joy amongst the big and the little. Since then I have been playing the *rôle* of the idol Baal. I eat, drink, sleep, and talk. The German wine and food suit me well after my journey of two months. Further than this I can do nothing. Laziness is the product of a residence in Italy, which I prophesy even your highness will on your return experience. One feels like a pendulum, which has been constantly swinging, but now only vibrates in oneself. The whole journey seems to me like a dream from which I have wakened. A pleasant dream it was, and your highness is the central figure of my dream, the good fairy who made it pleasant. Dreams have made up much of my life, and the dream has often been better than the reality. So it appears to me now. To *me* — but your highness has better dreams than I have."

CHAPTER XIV

Two days before Herder wrote this letter to the duchess, and quite unknown to him, Europe was shaken to its centre by the news of the terrible events taking place in France. The spirit of revolt, which had long been seething in the minds of the French nation, had now burst forth, and the first torch of what was to prove a universal conflagration was kindled at the storming of the Bastille. Soon France was the scene of disorder and pillage. The poor-spirited Louis XVI, unable to grapple with such a situation, made matters worse by his ill-timed concessions, and drifted helplessly to his doom. One does not feel so much compassion for this *roi fainéant* as for his high-spirited queen; but the terrible tragedy, which was later to fill Europe with dismay, was in 1789 in its first chapter.

All thinking minds viewed the prospect with dismay. Not alone France, but Europe generally was ripe for the coming war; it needed only a match to ignite the powder-horn and cause an universal explosion. The King of Prussia, in view of the gloomy seven years' campaign of Frederick the Great, felt himself constrained to threaten Austria with war, if that country meddled with France: not that the Emperor Joseph II had any idea of burning his fingers by trying to help his relatives. The general feeling of the country was decidedly against fighting. Moreover, the revolutionary spirit did not go beyond a good deal of talk, as in the case of the Stolbergs, Jacobys, and Frau Rathin Goethe, who was a republican of a mild order. Klopstock and Kant were bound to make some demonstration, but their cry of — "Liberty and Equality" was intellectual rather than political. Wieland, who was so little a supporter of despots as to have hardly raised his hat to Frederick the Great, sent a cosmopolitan address to the National Assembly. Herder was also more for than against the Revolution. But it was only skin-deep with these two men and they soon awoke from their patriotic semi-revolutionary dreams when they witnessed the results.

Meanwhile Amalia was still at Naples, where she received a letter from Knebel, dated 3 August 1789, eulogising the proceedings in France, which he declares will now be the first nation in Europe. Its action, he considers, "a proof of greatness of mind and sympathy with the general good, and this alone is sufficient to make

France the *first of nations*. History cannot offer a finer example. That is what Italy will never learn, and therefore I beg your highness to return to us with your heart unchanged."

The answer of the duchess shows how much more clear-sighted was her judgment of the situation.

"NAPLES,
"*September* 16th, 1789.

"I do not pretend to predict the consequences of the French Revolution, or give any judgment upon the matter. I think one can apply to the present situation the words of a certain Grecian Senator who said to Solon: '*Chez vous les sages discutent et les fous décident.*' Up to the present it is nothing but anarchy; whether any good can come of it time must decide. Several French refugees, princes with families, are expected here."

Also Karl August writes to his mother from Eisenach, where both he and Goethe have been making improvements.

"What do you say to the French Revolution? I would give much (you know I am a lover of new institutions) to have been an eye-witness of this incomprehensible and wonderful upheaval. I hope that your return will produce a revolution here. I look forward to this, and to seeing you in renewed health and spirits."

Karl August did not expect much good to follow from the Revolution, for the reason that the French nation was "so devoid of morality"; and writing from Aschersleben to the Duchess Anna Amalia, on 27 September 1789, he says: "We have serpents round us from which we can only be delivered by the sword. Nevertheless, I am rejoiced that my dear mother is returning to us." And then he touches on a delicate subject in a manner that gives the reader a high opinion of his sense and good feeling.

"If the misunderstandings which were a source of trouble to you should again arise, you must try to remember that no human being can alter his peculiarities, or even appreciably soften them, and that to accomplish such a transformation would be the work of a lifetime. Will you promise me (as I am now a man of ripe years and considerable experience) to give me for the future your full confidence, and if you have grievances to complain of, confide them to me, who love you better than anyone, and who, being so nearly connected with you am more likely to be interested? I give you my solemn promise that the first time you complain of any grievance, the matter shall be most carefully investigated, in order that anything displeasing to you may be rectified, and, if necessary for your comfort, the cause shall be removed. Of course it is understood that the trouble must be one arising from some condition of circumstances or surroundings which can be altered.

"Let us, dear mother, for the future talk over these matters together. The obstacles to your comfort will disappear, and we shall be able to form a correct judgment as to what are mere trifles not worth considering, and what are inevitable necessities which must be accepted. In this way I trust the rest of our lives may pass contentedly."

We are left in the dark as to how Anna Amalia received this affectionate and sensible advice. Neither do we know what was the exact subject of the text; but we can form a guess. That both duchesses were estimable and amiable women did not affect the issue, but no doubt the friction was intensified by the tittle-tattle of the court and the carrying of stories.

For the rest, the moment was approaching when, in the face of a universal calamity, both women recognised the good qualities of each other.

This was, however, in the distance. Anna Amalia was still in Naples. "Our beloved princess," writes Thusnelda to Wieland, "sends you a thousand good wishes, is well and is loved and admired by everyone. The queen will not hear of our leaving, but our duchess is getting anxious to return, and the conflict is giving her pain. For my part," she adds, "I wish I could forget that I must leave this lovely spot." And again, writing on 17 November 1789 she repeats: "I am quite ashamed that my heart is so bound up in this place and this delightful people." In another letter she describes an expedition made by the duchess along the coast of the Adriatic, during which they slept in a Venetian monastery. Here a crowd assembled and begged for an audience of the duchess, and on this being granted there came forward a number of poets, each of whom recited extempore verses. Scenes like this were pleasing to Anna Amalia's somewhat romantic temperament; they endeared Italy to her, and made her reluctant to quit a land, where poetry and sentiment were the keynote of every life.

Meantime changes were going on in Weimar. One of these which had to do with Herder had greatly interested the duchess. In July 1789 Herder had received a call to the University of Göttingen as Professor, being allowed to make his own conditions. This was flattering. At the same time it involved leaving Weimar, to which he was bound by so many ties, which he could not bear to break. On this subject, Goethe writes to Anna Amalia: "Herder has a wife and children, and he cannot sacrifice their interests to his own inclinations." Anna Amalia quite sees this, and so does Karl August, for Goethe, writing to the duchess, tells her the duke has been generous, but still there was a difficulty remaining, the education of the boy. Will the duchess charge herself with this? And the duchess gladly agreed, and so the matter was settled. Herder remained at Weimar, with the official rank of consistorial vice-president and a salary of four hundred thalers a year. Caroline Herder was quite content with this high-sounding title and increased means. She declared that having already lived in Weimar thirteen years, and having on the whole received more good than bad treatment, she would be loath to quit it.

This was not very warm acknowledgment, but poor Caroline, on the other hand, was worn out with the anxiety as to how the affair would turn. She did not want to leave Weimar, and she was too weary to express herself prettily, and Anna

Amalia understood. Later on, in October, the "vice-president's" lady has quite recovered her spirits and writes very warmly and gratefully to the duchess. After expressing her gratitude she goes on: "Goethe and Herder spend one evening in every week together, but they never speak of Italy. This is agreed upon, for the reason that it is too painful. From the same cause they defer asking any questions until the return of their royal patroness." Then she adds that she has grown "very old" and cannot replace to Herder the fascination which so attracted him in Italy: (This is an allusion to the Angelica episode.)

Herder sends the duchess a birthday ode, and Karl August felicitates his mother on what is to him the most loved and honoured day of the year. Wieland contributes a somewhat maudlin poem, full of "loving and longing," and, in return for all these good wishes, Anna Amalia writes the good news that she looks forward to being back in Weimar in March. But again there is delay. Brother Frederick Augustus of Brunswick has lost his wife, and Anna Amalia persuades him to come to Italy, "the Lethe of all sorrow, where one grows young again." The arrival of the Brunswick relations naturally detains the loving sister, and the people in Weimar shake their heads, while Karl August grows somewhat testy. "There is a time for all things," he says, "and it is time my mother returned to Weimar."

A wilful woman generally has her own way, and, in spite of all efforts to move her, the new year, 1790, found Anna Amalia still at Naples. How could she tear herself away from this enchanting land, where even Vesuvius honoured her by a slight eruption? "It was majestic. Never in my life have I experienced such a sensation;" writes the duchess; and Fraülein Göchhausen adds: "Was there ever such a country? Here we have summer — lemons, pinks, roses, and jasmine, all growing in our garden." It seemed a pity to leave all this brightness and return to the dreary cold north.

Herder touches on this in a letter to the duchess, 25 January 1790: "Memory is perhaps the purest of enjoyments, and as such lasts the longest; therefore I feel convinced that your highness will imitate the philosophy of the guest, who rose from the banquet leaving much of the feast untouched. Yes, I feel convinced you will return to us happy and content."

As a matter of fact, the preacher of this excellent doctrine did not practise it; but this is not extraordinary, being a common phase of human frailty. Herder's health was, moreover, giving anxiety to his friends; he was captious and discontented, and a coldness had arisen between him and Goethe, certainly through no fault of the latter. The appointment of Schiller, on Goethe's recommendation, to be Professor of History at Jena, had probably roused Herder's jealousy. He loudly declared he was not going to be "a dupe" any longer. The Göttingen appointment had, however, soothed his bad temper, which for the rest was partly due to his illness.

At Easter 1790 Goethe set out for Venice, where he was to await the duchess and her party, and conduct them to Weimar. He had, however, a long wait, for still the duchess delayed, making one excuse after the other, while Goethe, who had many reasons for wishing to get home again, distracted his mind by making an excursion into the Tyrol.[101]

Finally, on 2 May 1790, the duchess and her suite arrived in Venice, where she spent some weeks, nominally resting after her journey from Rome, but in reality enjoying the last glimpse she would have of Italy. "You must remember," she writes to her brother, "that from my sixteenth year I have lived for others, and it is only since I came to Italy that I have lived for myself."

But her holiday, like all pleasant experiences, came to an end at last, and after she had exhausted every possible excuse for delay, she with much grief of heart set out for Weimar under the escort of Goethe. Leaving Venice on 22 May 1790, they arrived in Nuremberg on 9 June, where Knebel met his beloved patroness, and on 18 June 1790, she reached Weimar again.

Many of us have experienced the flatness which oppresses one, on returning to the monotony of everyday life after a season of rest from domestic cares. Remembrance of the pleasanter scenes we have quitted makes the dullness of the old routine all the more difficult to bear. Neither had Anna Amalia the joy of meeting her son, which would have compensated her mother's heart for much. Karl August was on military duty in Prussia. The outlook was gloomy and all nations were preparing for what seemed looming in the near future. Nor was the social atmosphere at Weimar more satisfactory. Much had happened during Anna Amalia's absence, and a general discontent and dullness had succeeded to the former gaiety of the little capital. Nor was Amalia herself free from a feeling of discontent.

"Since my return to Thuringia," she writes to Knebel, on 3 August 1790, "I am not in my usual spirits. It seems to me as if I had been asleep, and that my dream was one of delightful days which I had spent in lovely Italy; but I have wakened to the prose of everyday life and my sweet dream is gone from me."

Soon, however, the duchess roused herself, and returning to her former habits of study, drew round her a circle such as Weimar alone could offer. Writing from Belvedere to her constant correspondent Knebel, she says:

> "BELVEDERE,
> "*August*, 1790.

"I am busy forming a circle. Herder, Wieland, and Goethe always come to me. I have invited Herder to stay here to make use of the water of the well, which is a natural spa. Goethe unfortunately must go to the duke in Silesia. I trust, as there is now peace, that my son will come at the end of August. I have little August Herder with me, and he is an amusing, bright little fellow. I am arranging the art treasures I brought home from Italy; they form quite a little museum. Thus I live — in the enjoyment of the past, and seek as far as in my power lies to share this enjoyment with others."

In November 1791 she again writes from the Witthums Palais, Weimar:

"I have been settled here for some days now. The leaves have begun to fall and I can see nothing of my beloved hills but naked trees, which do not form the prettiest background to Nature's stage. In the town it is not much better, but I occupy myself in arranging my Italian curios and so keep my mind occupied. Dear Knebel, kindly inform me which of the best cut stones, in your opinion, are the most valuable. I should like impressions, either in sealing-wax or sulphur." She goes on to say she has been to Erfurt, where the national assembly had been held. "My son Constantine," she adds, "has been with me for some days, and I find him much improved in every particular. The reports from his commanding officer, too, are satisfactory."

Amalia's correspondence at this period is wanting in its usual brightness. She was evidently feeling the change from the glorious sunshine and pleasant life in Italy. The general outlook was likewise depressing. There were rumours in the air which portended evil; a reaction against crowned heads and authority was agitating the oppressed lower class, and the restless demon of war was stirring up the different nationalities. Both Anna Amalia's sons were with the Prussian camp in Silesia, whither Goethe had also gone in July to join the duke, who told him that, instead of stones and flowers, he would see the field sown with troops.

Goethe, who was no soldier, compensated himself for the *ennui* he suffered, by studying the different families of "the stones and flowers." He lived like a hermit in the camp, and began to write an essay on the development of animals, and also a comic opera.

The Duchess Amalia, meantime, tried to distract her thoughts from the dark shadows that were gathering in every direction, by her usual panacea, occupation. She set about collecting from her journals and letters the most interesting extracts and observations on men and things. These, when put in order, she submitted to Herder for his opinion. Herder highly approved, only making some objection to a letter of Einsiedel's. For each portion of the letters sent him by Amalia, Herder had nothing but praise to give, to which he added his desire that others besides himself should be equally favoured.

Anna Amalia, however, like many amateurs, was not always inclined to finish what she had begun, but ever eager to start something afresh. We hear nothing more, therefore, of "the letters," but find her next engaged in reading the German classics as a help to translating Wieland's *Dialogues with the gods*, into Italian (1791?). This, having first submitted it to Jägemann, the principal librarian of the grand ducal library, she sent with a friendly greeting to her lady friends in Italy.

If Goethe had put into execution his idea of publishing his Italian travels, the duchess would have undertaken the translation. The dedication of Goethe's Venetian epigrams shows how deeply he was touched by this offer. But, to the annoyance of the Duchess Amalia and all his friends, Goethe, at this period of his life, was absorbed in scientific studies, thus leaving unemployed those higher mental gifts, which had been given him to use, not to bury. It is a curious freak of men of genius often to be met with, that, in place of concentrating themselves on the development of one particular talent, they wander over the whole field of literature, art, and science, turning themselves, as it were, into walking encyclopaedias. Surely this is a mistake. As it happened, Goethe lived long enough to complete most of his works, but had he died earlier, *Wilhelm Meister* would have been left unfinished while he was making his experiments in osteology.

In 1791 Anna Amalia and Herder tormented him into resuming the ever-delightful *Wilhelm*, but he soon relinquished it for the study of dry bones, and his friends, including the two duchesses, began to be seriously alarmed, lest this great work should never be completed. At this period he lived retired, going nowhere, and was altogether absorbed in his scientific studies, which both Anna Amalia and Herder called "time wasted over old bones." The value of these studies could not, however, be lessened by any irreverent gibes.

Meanwhile a new star had risen in the poetic firmament, and its first rays lighted up Weimar. I refer to Schiller, than whom a more thoroughly interesting personality, or a more high-souled and romantic poet, has never lived. The long struggle of Schiller's life is most pathetic. Mention has already been made of the school, or college "speech day" at which the young and delicate student received in Goethe's presence the prizes he had gained. Goethe was now forty-five, and Schiller thirty-five, a pale, sickly-looking man, poorly dressed and poorly fed. The composer of *Don Carlos* and *Wallenstein*, had to support life by translations for which he only received a miserable sum, not enough to feed him.

His life is sad to read, and the inroads made on his constitution by want of proper nourishment enfeebled him. He died, at a comparatively early age, and in the last years of his life he could only write under the fillip of constant draughts of champagne. He had not yet written *Wallenstein* when he first came to Weimar, where we get a glimpse of him from Henrietta von Eggloffstein. It was at the Witthums Palais. "A brilliant gathering was collected: Goethe, Wieland, Herder, Knebel were there, and in the middle, talking to Anna Amalia, stood the poet Schiller, quiet and collected, with eyes clear as the moon over which no stormy clouds would ever pass."

Not alone did he resemble the tranquil moon in his quiet demeanour, but also in the modest manner in which he retired when the fiery planet of the day (Goethe) took his place. Yet Goethe was very good to Schiller. He got for him the appointment at Jena, which relieved him from all financial worries. Truly, as Goethe's biographer says: "The history of literature presents nothing comparable to the friendship of Goethe and Schiller." Naturally antagonistic to one another, the tenderness shown on one side towards the man who bore, in his whole appearance, the traces of the bitter struggle he had gone through, and the gratitude felt by the other for the protecting, almost fatherly, interest evinced towards him — these two feelings completely stamped out all the lower instincts of jealous rivalry.

Of course, the public did its best to sow discord, instead of following Goethe's advice, and rejoicing that it had "two such poets to boast of." There was the usual crying up of one against the other. Schiller, whose modesty was one of his many charms, confessed his inferiority. "Compared with Goethe, I am but a poetical bungler," he writes to Körner. Each had his admirers, Goethe being more appreciated by men, while Schiller's delicacy of touch, his tender love passages, etc., gained him the love of women. There was also a total absence of the freedom of thought and language, which made Goethe not suitable for "the young person."

From the time Schiller came to Weimar he shared with Goethe the directorship of the theatre, where many of his plays were produced. Schiller's death took place in the spring of 1805. Goethe at this time was so ill that it was feared he too might die. He was just recovering when, in April, Schiller's death caused him a relapse. "The half of my existence is gone from me," he wrote to Zelter. "My diary is a blank — the white pages intimate the blank in my life. In those days I took no interest in anything."

CHAPTER XV

In 1790 the position of the French royal family, together with the wave of revolution passing over Europe, alarmed all thinking minds. European statesmen dreaded the consequences of this first step, which might end in universal anarchy. An alliance was formed between Austria, Prussia, and Russia, with the result that the King of Prussia undertook to despatch an army of five columns to the Rhine. Prussia demanded from the different countries free transport and provisions for the troops at the usual rate of payment. Such payment was, however, not to be made until after the conclusion of the war.

The Duchy of Weimar was thus placed in a most difficult position, since an enormous body of troops, made still larger by the, to us, incomprehensible addition of a crowd of camp-followers, women and children, with servants, and numbers of dogs, who were attached to each battalion, required to be fed at the expense of the country. Moreover, Karl August, being a general in the Prussian Army, Weimar had to furnish a certain contingent of troops with all necessary equipment. The duke thought that this equipment and the transport of troops to Silesia would prove only a pleasure trip, and would not mean war, since the Emperor Leopold wished for peace, and so did Russia; he imagined that the proposed mobilisation was only meant to intimidate the revolutionists.

With this sanguine outlook the duke at the end of July 1792 left Weimar for Koblentz, where the general air of gaiety convinced him that there was not much danger of a serious war. The town was full of French *émigrés* and French princes, — teeming with gratitude to their allies. These affected a contemptuous tone in speaking of "ces misérables" as they called the *sansculottes*. This was part of the fool's paradise the royalists lived in, although it may be doubted if they really held the optimistic views they made pretence of. Meantime there was feasting and carousing in Cologne. The Archbishop of Trier entertained the princes and commanders of the Prussian army of rescue, the allies pledged one another in bumpers of the archbishop's choicest wine; the declaration made by the King of Prussia that Paris, the seat of all evil, should be erased from its place amongst the capitals of Europe was received with enthusiasm. This exploit was evidently considered a foregone conclusion.

On 3 August 1792, Karl August writes:"The news we get of the treatment the royal prisoners, and especially the king, receive, grows each day more alarming. It is not a newspaper lie, but an actual fact, that a portion of the Tuileries has been consumed by fire, and that the king's life is in the utmost danger. The residue of the Swiss guard have been put to death, and even amongst the people there has been considerable slaughter."

The Prussian troops had now set out on their march. We are told that Hogarth would have found innumerable subjects for his pencil, in the scenes which took place on the route; as, for instance, when the welcome accorded in different towns to the hungry, wearied soldiers took the form of wreaths of roses to crown their martial brows, or it might be of a sacerdotal blessing on their arms. Fortunately there were always excellent and thoughtful women to be found, who gave the exhausted soldiers fresh water to cool their burning thirst. But after all, water is not very satisfying.

Anna Amalia, meantime, had written to Karl August's secretary Weyland at the Camp Rübenach, July 1792, and requested him to send her news of the duke as often as possible; and as these letters from Rübenach, as well as the correspondence between the duke and his mother, are preserved in the archives at Weimar, we can follow almost every step of this heartrending campaign, and obtain a realistic picture of this terrible chapter in the world's history. The sufferings of the Prussian army, from the highest official or royal prince, down to the scavengers, were terrible, and were borne with wonderful fortitude. Ill-fed inefficiently clothed, the men had to make long marches in the rainy season, when the whole country was like a wet sponge.

According to Weyland's account, discomfort on the march was less trying than the *ennui* of the long halt, which under the circumstances had to be made. Karl August, who persisted in looking upon the war as a joke, summoned Goethe to the camp, where he arrived on 17 August 1792, a few days after the capitulation of Longwy. The duke had a long story to tell his friend of all the hardships and privations he and his soldiers had endured. Goethe, who was eminently a man of peace, had no interest in the cause for which he was obliged to live, even temporarily, in a damp atmosphere, with no prospect but sheets of rain streaming continuously over the camp. Karl August, whose tent was like a small lake, had taken refuge in his "equipage," where he had reserved a dry seat for his friend.

Out of this swamp the army was at last delivered and arrived at Verdun, from which place Karl August wrote to his mother. This letter shows that the duke had ceased to regard the war as a matter of child's play.

"LOUVEMONT, BEFORE VERDUN,
"*October 12th*, '92.

"You have, my dearest mother, my warmest thanks for your recollection of my birthday. I trust I may be spared to spend a few more anniversaries contentedly with you, and where the thunders of war shall be silent, for, to speak frankly, it is a terrible spectacle. I will say nothing of our experiences, but leave all that to Weyland. In the first place, I cannot get near the writing desk, because the tent itself is almost under water, and the floor is saturated. I must try and get a little room where I can write. All the Cavalry Generals are ill, with the exception of General Cunibe von Kalbreuth, who is detached. I also am one of the few generals who can still get about. I am in excellent health. I can only say that we must make haste to finish the campaign, as we are convinced that there is no chance of such a thing as a counter-revolution, or of a junction with the soldiers, and we are in a strange country, surrounded by enemies, where everyone wishes us evil.

"Also, in view of this accursed weather, which makes it too risky to attempt a communication with our powder magazines, it would be foolish to risk a battle, which, even supposing we won, would not advance us much, as, although we might kill a lot of these fellows, their places would be at once taken by others; and in the meantime the enemy has secured the most advantageous positions, from which it would be hard to dislodge them. Besides, it is impossible to secure fresh artillery and cavalry remounts, considering how far we are from headquarters.

"We have, in fact, given ourselves away, and must now face the fact that we cannot hold Verdun, because the country will not supply sufficient forage. We shall have to retreat upon Longwy, and retire to the fortress of Capen, there to watch the course of events. Probably some sort of *accommodement* will be arranged. I think this is likely, because the French are constantly declaring they are not *our* enemies, and only wish to be at war with Austria, of which nation they speak in an insulting manner, but are anxious to be our allies. They spare *us* in every way they can and do us no injury.

"A second campaign is not to be thought of, as everyone sees that war is not possible; it has done no good and has decimated our army through illness, while the horses too are crippled: all this from the want of provisions and the dearness of everything. In fact, the health of the fine troops we brought here is utterly ruined, and they could hardly hold their own against the enemy in the field.

"Spain in the meantime is getting ready, but the French army has advanced into Savoy and has already taken Chambéry. Our army has endured without a murmur, as much as human nature, can, of all kinds of hardship, and up to the present we have had only twenty deserters, but our sick list is eight thousand, and there are over one thousand disabled horses. There have also been many deaths among the sick. I hope that our winter quarters will be quiet enough to enable me to return home, which I ardently desire to do, and that by next spring the war will be over. Give my best remembrances to all about you, and with loving farewell,

        "C. A. H. SA."[102]

"I have sent Goethe to Longwy. During the last nine days he has had to do without his 'equipage,' and has had no bed to sleep in."

Karl August saw clearly that the campaign was doomed, and that nothing but disaster could result from this organised effort. He longed to be back in Weimar, instead of following this wild goose expedition to Paris. Still, like a true soldier, he set his whole mind on doing the best possible under adverse circumstances. Prince Constantine, on the other hand, was fretting and fuming at his enforced absence from the scene of action. He wrote to his mother from Querfurth, on 3 December 1792, of his desire to join the Prussian Army.

"I hope soon to have the good fortune to quit this quiet corner of Saxony, where one can only watch the great struggle going on through a telescope."

In a short time this good fortune came to Constantine. He took part in the siege of Metz, at a time when certain diplomatic transactions were causing considerable excitement. These negotiations ended in the different members of the German Confederation or Reich, agreeing to join the emperor in the war against France. Goethe, who from the beginning of the struggle had accompanied the duke in his self-sacrificing efforts in the cause of the empire against France, found himself in a by no means unpleasant position. So far he had nothing to complain of, and was content. While the army invested Metz he corrected his "Reineke Fuchs," composed short essays and poems, and lived as pleasantly as he could amongst the Rhine students. He sent pleasant accounts of his military experiences to Herder, while Karl August, who was deeply impressed by the lamentable issue of this deplorable war, wrote in very different terms:

"How differently people judge, who are not eye-witnesses of this misery! A sort of stupor has come over me; 'my mind seems to be standing still.' I am incapable of forming a clear judgment as to whether our part in this deplorable mess is for good or evil."

While this condition of affairs prevailed in the political world, a sudden and terrible affliction fell upon Anna Amalia, whose maternal heart was already wrung by fears concerning the safety of her children. On 6 September 1793 Prince Constantine died. The cause of his death was mysterious. It was given out as being due to typhus fever, then prevalent in the camp at Metz, but there were whispers of a quarrel and a duel. All through his life the prince had been a cause of anxiety to his family, especially to his mother, his strong will, which was allied to a weak constitution, not making a harmonious combination.

Some of his escapades have already been mentioned, but of late years he had grown wiser, and it was hoped had sown his last crop of wild oats. In any case, mothers are proverbially most attached to the child who gives the most trouble, and Anna Amalia had undoubtedly a weakness for *son petit Constantin*. In any case, now that the grave had closed over his faults, they received that condonation generally extended to the failings of the dead. "He was a good fellow," everyone said, "and his own worst enemy," etc., etc. We all know the stock observations made on such occasions. Meanwhile Karl August, whose heart was undoubtedly in the right place, was deeply concerned for his mother, who he knew would mourn her "scapegrace." He wrote to the Duchess Louise, asking her to break the news as gently as possible, and for some days could not find courage to write to his mother about their "common loss." One cannot but admire the great tenderness with which he expresses himself.

"I am expecting with the greatest anxiety news of your health, which I am afraid has suffered from this sudden blow. I wrote to my wife to break it to you. God grant it may have no bad effect. I trust all my friends are doing their utmost to help you to support this trial. Everyone here has the greatest sympathy for us in our affliction. Your brother, who desires to be remembered to you, was much shocked at the melancholy accident; the accompanying letter from the king shows how much his majesty feels our loss. May your guardian angel, and the Consoler of all who suffer, strengthen and comfort you. This is my sincerest wish and hope. Here everything remains as it was. I am 'on leave' with the Duke of Brunswick, for there was nothing to do where I was, nothing to see and nothing to hear; and even here, with the exception of the society of the duke, your brother, everything is quiet enough. I have written today to Goethe to tell him the details of our misfortune.[103] I am in good health. Think of me and try to find consolation with those who are devoted to you."

Anna Amalia was guided by her son's advice, and, for the rest, she was of too strong — I would almost say too masculine — a character to abandon herself to undue grief, or what are called womanish tears. After the first shock she exhibited much fortitude and resignation, which is shown in her letter to her favourite brother, Frederick Augustus.

"TIEFURT,
"*September 15th, '93.*

"You have a good heart, dear Fritz, and I know you feel for a mother's grief, who has suddenly been plunged into terrible sorrow. You will sympathise with me, for oh! I have now only *one son*, and every day I fear to hear bad news of him. God grant that I may be spared this. I pray Him to lead Karl's heart in the ways of peace, so that he can without dishonour follow thy example. This is now my only desire on earth."

Karl August's wishes corresponded with those of the Duchess Amalia, in so far as he wished to return to his duchy, where his presence had become most necessary after an absence of eighteen months. He asked the King of Prussia for a furlough of twelve weeks, which was granted. The joy of this meeting softened the bitter grief of the mother's heart, since she must have felt that, while Providence left her one child, she dared not venture to question the dispensation which had afflicted her. As a proof of her determination to conquer her own feelings, she went to console her faithful Einsiedel for the death of his uncle, and while she was in Jena she put off her departure for two days in order to be present at a comedy which the students had got up for her amusement. Her son had then been only four weeks dead.

The duchess in her hour of sorrow experienced the truth of the saying: "As you sow you shall reap." Those who are hard to others seldom meet with much sympathy when their own turn comes. Anna Amalia was to reap a rich harvest from good deeds she had sown; not alone her faithful attendants, but every one in Weimar, tried to show sympathy as they best could, in the sorrow which had fallen on their loved princess. Goethe tells Jacobi: "Being somewhat of a help in the hour of need, I have done much to distract the stricken duchess." Her faithful old Wieland was unremitting in his efforts to turn the direction of Anna Amalia's thoughts, while Thusnelda was, like a second self, feeling the sorrow as if it were her very own.

These are all testimonies to the love which Anna Amalia's constant kindness had inspired in those who had received benefits at her hands. This tenderness for her sorrow, joined to the ever efficacious effect of time in healing the wounds of the heart, by degrees softened the first bitterness of Amalia's grief. She resumed her favourite occupations, although, as was only natural, she was no longer the pivot upon which all literary movement turned. Still, her sympathy for all endeavours made in the field of poetry, philosophy, or literature was as keen as ever; she took the most intelligent interest in all that was going on, saw with pleasure the growing friendship between Goethe and Schiller, while, on the other side, Herder and Wieland drew closer together. That friction of any kind was now totally absent from the court circle of celebrated men was due in a great measure to the gentle influence of the dowager duchess, which she exercised in an unmistakable manner over Herder, Wieland, and Goethe.

After Constantine's death Anna Amalia resided altogether at Tiefurt, rarely coming to the Witthumshaus. So far back as 1782 she had placed in the grounds of Tiefurt the busts of three of her favourite poets, with inscriptions written for her by Villoison.

She now wished to erect a tablet to those who were no longer amongst the living and to Prince Constantine first of all. She writes to Knebel July 1796: "I received the enclosed yesterday, but too late to thank you, which I do now with most grateful feelings. I would like the first line, namely: 'In the vale where thou the early spring didst enjoy' to be set up. According to my feelings for those who are dead and those who are left behind, the simpler it is the better. Without first consulting Goethe, who does not seem to wish to have anything to do with such things, I beg of you to have it engraved in large letters on the monument. There must be no mistakes, for that is very objectionable, so will you see to this before you give it to the stonemason to cut on the tablet."

In 1798 the circle at Weimar received an agreeable addition in Jean Paul Richter, better known in those days by the name of "Hesperus," which he had adopted as a pseudonym. He was altogether different from the men of genius hitherto congregated in the modern Athens, who had passed from manhood to old age in these Attic shades, and who undoubtedly (probably from the narrow sphere in which they lived) possessed a wonderfully high opinion of themselves. Jean Paul had, however, no reason to complain of his reception. Herder, especially, was much drawn to him; so, too, Anna Amalia, who was charmed with the simplicity, naïveté, and singularity, which characterised the stranger. We find Herder writing in his usually flowery manner, that Heaven had sent him a treasure, "which I dare not hope to keep." As it turned out, he did preserve his treasure, and had the happiness of seeing Jean Paul daily for some years.

Goethe received the newcomer politely, but without any absurd demonstrativeness. Meantime, Jean Paul wrote to his friend Otto: "It was with apprehension amounting almost to terror that I entered the abode of Goethe. Everyone in Weimar depicted him as cold and indifferent to all earthly things. Madame von Kalb told me he no longer admired anything, not even his own works. Every word, she said, 'that drops from his lips is an icicle, especially to strangers, whom he is with difficulty persuaded to admit to his presence.' His house impressed me; it is the only one in Weimar built in the Italian style. From the very staircase it is a museum of statues and pictures. . . . The god at length appeared; he was cold, expressed himself only in monosyllables, and without the slightest emphasis.

"'Tell him,' said Knebel, 'that the French have just entered Rome.' 'Hum!' replied the god. In person he is bony, his physiognomy full of fire, his look a sun. At length our conversation on the arts and on the opinion of the public, perhaps also the champagne, animated him, and then at length I felt I was with Goethe. His language is not flowery or brilliant, like that of Herder; it is incisive, calm and resolute. He concluded by reading, or rather I should say acting, one of his own unpublished poems, a composition truly sublime."

After this, the flames of his heart pierced the crust of ice; he pressed the hand of Jean Paul, who, in his enthusiasm exclaims: "No, there is nobody like Goethe! We must be friends."

This expectation, as readers of Jean Paul are aware, was not realised; the two men were diametrically opposed on every point. Goethe wrote to Schiller his opinion, that "Richter's love of truth and wish for self-improvement have impressed me in his favour, but the social man is a sort of theoretical man, and I doubt if he will approach us in a practical manner." Schiller's opinion of Richter is not given, but Richter thought Schiller "stony." Jean Paul stayed in Weimar three years, living in a very retired manner, much occupied with his studies and not mixing much with his literary *confrères*. He often came to the Duchess Amalia, who had a warm liking for this interesting and retiring man. Here is a prettily worded letter of thanks for some flowers sent to him by Anna Amalia:

"The lovely roses your highness presented to me were as delightful as an evening spent with the giver, only more surprising. . . . I cannot give expression to my thanks, or to my pleasure. I trust that the flowers of poetry, I hope shortly to lay at your Highness's feet, may give you a tithe of the pleasure that I have felt in contemplating these children of the past summer, and which they will continue to give me while they last."

Anna Amalia, who had not lost her elegant gift for letter-writing, answers:

"Friendship often attaches more value to the gift of a friend than it deserves. You, dear Herr Richter, have woven a charming wreath out of the few flowers I sent you. They had no other value than that they expressed my estimation of the virtue and talents for which you are distinguished, and the esteem with which I am

"Always your friend,
"AMALIA."

CHAPTER XVI

It is not always the case that age softens instead of hardening the character, which, as we often see, grows peevish and fractious under the burden of added years and increasing infirmity. With Anna Amalia there was no sign of this disagreeable metamorphosis. On the contrary, as years advanced, her heart seemed to be purified; her self-love decreased, her affectionate care for others increased; her thoughts centred on her old friends, and her desire was to make everyone round her happy. With such a nature the approach of that dread enemy, old age brings no fears in its train, and even death itself has no terrors.

The duchess took great interest in Knebel's marriage with one of her favourites, the charming singer, Louise von Rüdorf, whose name has been before mentioned. This marriage, which took place in 1798, did not promise to turn out a happy one. Fräulein Rüdorf, or Rüdelchen, which was the duchess's pet name for the bride, was still a young woman, although no longer in her first youth, while Knebel, as we know, was a well-seasoned old bachelor, who had made love to half Weimar, including Emily Gore and Fräulein Göchhausen. The happiness of such a marriage was indeed doubtful, and Anna Amalia, who took great interest in both parties and especially in Rüdelchen, had grave misgivings.

A wedding, however, appeals to everyone, and Anna Amalia and the court generally were stirred by this event. The wedding breakfast was given by the duchess, and the happy pair retired to Ilmenau, where Knebel's sister, who was *gouvernante* to the Princess Caroline, lived. Both Knebel and this sister of his, who figures largely in his cumbersome volume of recollections, were a pair of nervous, irritable creatures, without any backbone; always grumbling, self-upbraiding, and weakly whining over their ill-luck in being poor, and consequently not considered as they felt they deserved to be.

As a rule, everything goes wrong with persons of this infirm character, and we are not surprised that all the ills of job fell upon Knebel, who could neither persuade Karl August nor Prince Constantine to provide for him, or induce his father to give him money, or even take proper care of his brother Max, who, being a lunatic, eventually committed suicide. The marriage with Rüdelchen was another mistake, one which Anna Amalia with her knowledge of life felt certain would be far from happy.

A few months later, in October 1798, we find the duchess writing to the bride, evidently in answer to her complaints of her husband's conduct.

"It is his vanity which makes him do such foolish things, and you must consult a medical man of the place in regard to what you have noticed, and tell him to pay attention to these symptoms, especially if he is more violent at the change of the moon: perhaps he cannot help it."

Again, on 29 April 1799, the duchess writes to her favourite:

"Thank you, dear Rüdelchen, for the beautiful roses; they gave me increased pleasure from your saying you had gathered them yourself. I lose no time in telling you the pleasure they give me. It surprises me that any one can remain in Ilmenau in this weather. About my music, I think it will be very good."

This remark referred to the duchess's *Thoughts on Music,* a little volume she had put together, and of which Herder writes, June 1799, that it had filled him with sweet harmonious thoughts, and that he closed the book with a musical chord sounding in his ear. Also Kapellmeister Krantz, so closely associated with the amateur theatre, is full of praise of this later composition of the duchess's, and Anna Amalia's kind heart being responsive to old memories, she exerted her influence and, through Haydn, got Kranz a good appointment at Stuttgart. "But now all is over with my music," says kind-hearted Anna Amalia.

On 16 February 1801, Anna Amalia's mother, Philippina Charlotte, Duchess of Brunswick, died. We know her well, through the sparkling pages written by her sister Wilhelmina, mentioned already, who married the Markgraf of Bayreuth. Both Wilhelmina and Philippina Charlotte were sisters to Frederick the Great. A more detestable character than this same Duchess of Brunswick did not exist. She cared for none of her children, and she especially disliked Anna Amalia, because she had wished for a prince instead of a princess. In her will she gave full effect to her dislike, leaving Anna Amalia but a trifling legacy, while the largest share of her property was bequeathed to Augusta Dorothea, abbess of Gandersheim. The closing words of her will were an entreaty that there should be no dispute over it, but that each one should take the share left him or her with a good grace. Anna Amalia followed this injunction, and although she was the eldest daughter, she submitted to the injustice which her mother had always shown her, and continued to show, even on her deathbed.

Death seemed now to be continually knocking at Amalia's door. In her circle of friends the gaps were frequent. At the end of this year 1801 Wieland lost his excellent wife, and the duchess grieved for the sorrow that had fallen on her old friend. She wished, so soon as the weather grew milder, that he should come and stay with her at Tiefurt. No one knew better than the duchess how to console those who were in sorrow, and we find Wieland writing, in June 1802: "Since the beginning of this month I am with our good duchess at that Elysium,

Tiefurt, where (for a person in her station) she shows me the most unexampled tenderness, attention, esteem, and friendship, does everything that is possible to cheer and comfort me, and to make me forget that my Alceste has left me for ever. I try to seem content and happy, but it is only seeming. I cannot *forget*; but to please this best of princesses I do my best, and also to please her I try to work, of course with many interruptions and very slowly. In the morning I continue my translation of 'Euripides.'"

Wieland now sold his little property at Ostmannstadt, where he had buried his Alceste, and had arranged when his time came to be buried with her. This done, he settled himself permanently in his house in Weimar. It was close to Anna Amalia's garden which occupied the large space now covered by Schiller's Strasse. It was a beautiful garden of large extent, laid out with the straight walks and beds of flowers then in fashion. There was ornamental water, fine shady trees, etc. To this enchanted garden Wieland begged he might have a key; he was sure his honoured princess would allow an old man, on the brink of the grave and broken down with grief, this privilege. And kind-hearted Amalia agreed, although it may be well imagined it was not quite agreeable to her to give him this right of way.[104]

Still the death-roll goes on, recalling to recollection the wonderful tale written by Doctor Johnson, wherein one Mirza saw as in a vision a large concourse of people passing across a broad ditch; occasionally one dropped in, but the rest were in such a hurry, they took no heed; and so it went on till none were left. The next victim was Herder, who died in December 1803. He was not yet sixty. Light, Love, Life, were the three stars of his existence. His death caused deep sorrow, not alone in the court circle and amongst his friends, but amongst the poor, who loved to hear those simple sermons of his, delivered with wonderful eloquence, that had gained for him a reputation which equalled, although from a different standpoint, his extraordinary erudition and poetical gifts. Few men possessed greater virtues than Herder, or more lofty aspirations. Unfortunately, his uncertain temper and morbidly sensitive nature made him, if not ill to live with. To be perpetually taking offence where none is intended, or twisting an innocent observation into an intentional insult is a decidedly unpleasant form of genius. Someone said Herder was like an instrument of exquisite tone, in which, by some fault of mechanism, a slight but oft-recurring jar mars the delicious harmony. Excuse, however, should be made for his ill-health, and his position, which was never exactly what he rightly thought his merits deserved. His gifts were above the common, and although he could not be said to be a poet of a high order, yet every line he wrote was instinct with a pure and noble spirit. "He was inspired," says one of his warmest admirers, "by something nobler than love of fame, by a sincere and constant desire to promote the best and highest interests of humanity."

A month later, January 1804, the Duchess Amalia writes to Frau Knebel:

"I thank you, dear Rudel, for your good wishes on my birthday, which in truth I need sorely, for my heart is oppressed by the loss we have sustained in Herder's death. In consequence we have had a sad New Year. For my part, his loss is so great that I cannot speak much of it; he is mourned by everybody in all stations in life. I can well believe that your husband's first thought would be to honour the memory of the friend he has lost, by writing a tribute to the nobility of his character and the high aim he had in life. No one could fulfil such a task better than Knebel, and I trust he will lose no time in putting his purpose into effect. To add to my present distress of mind, the Landgräfin of Homburg has arrived, on her way to Berlin, whither she is taking her daughter. This obliges me to show a smiling face. Madame de Staël, who has been here for the last fortnight, wins universal approbation. She unites pleasant manners with an extraordinary understanding and brilliant wit. She is much with me. Your husband would like her.

"AMALIA."

The duchess all through her life showed a wonderful power of throwing off sadness. This was not due to any lack of feeling, but rather to the singular activity of her mind. In a few days we find her quite cheerful. She writes to Knebel:

"Why don't you come to us? We have a veritable phenomenon in the form of Madame de Staël. You *should* know her, you would be charmed with her. She is so agreeable, without egotism or any ridiculous pretension. She knows what to admire and whom to esteem. One must know her to have a proper appreciation of her." Evidently Herder was forgotten!

Madame de Staël came to Weimar as a result of her banishment from France by Napoleon, the banishment being the consequence of one of her witty *bon mots* anent the dictator. She was then planning her great work *L'Allemagne*, and by the advice of Benjamin Constant, who accompanied her, came to gather knowledge of her subject in the German Athens. Some writers tell us she made enemies in Weimar by her sarcasms and her loud manner of talking down every one, man or woman, Heine said she was a whirlwind in petticoats, and someone else that she was the Sultana of the mind.

Goethe and Schiller, whom she stormed with "cannonades of talk," were full of admiration for her extraordinary intellect. Schiller describes her as "the most talkative, the most combative, the most gesticulative of women," but she was also "the most cultivated and the most gifted." The account of her interview with Goethe is most diverting but too long to give here. She frankly told him she meant to print his conversation which naturally had the effect of shutting him up. Nevertheless, she said he was "*un homme d' un esprit prodigieux en conversation.*"

It was an immense relief to Schiller and Goethe when she left Weimar, where her tongue had made her many enemies, but certainly a friend in Anna Amalia, who admired her vivacity, and cleverness, and saw no harm in her. Their friendship was continued in a correspondence. Nevertheless, in spite of her friendship, Amalia must have distrusted her distinguished correspondent, since her letters were always drafted by Wieland, so that no slips might be made for Madame de Staël to lay hold of.

Anna Amalia's correspondence continued to be the business of her life; she answered all letters punctually, and very rarely devolved the task on others. Amongst her correspondents were men and women of all shades of politics — infidels, excellent Christians, together with men and women distinguished in every branch of literature and art. Merck, with whom she had a constant interchange of letters, suffered in later years from mental affliction. The young sculptor, Alexander Trippel, the creator of the fine busts of Goethe and Herder, was amongst her later correspondents. The young artist understood the use of the chisel better than that of the pen, his letters being an extraordinary jumble.

On one occasion he writes to tell the duchess that the busts of Herr Baron von Goeden (Goethe) and Consistorial Rath Herder have been packed and delivered to Herr Reiffenstein. He winds up with remembrances to the Kammerherr Einsiedel and Kammerfrau Göchhausen. Such a breach of etiquette was enough to make the hair stand erect on the heads of the personages named, who had spent their lives in the shadow of the court, and were as thoroughly well trained as two *chevaux de parade.*

Another correspondence of interest was that which passed between Anna Amalia with the Empress of Russia. It owed its origin to the marriage of her grandson, the Crown Prince Carl Friedrich, with the Grand Duchess Maria Paulovna,[105] sister to Alexander, Czar of Russia, which took place at St. Petersburg on 3 August 1804. The sweet disposition of the young princess and her devotion to Anna Amalia were the consolation of the duchess's old age. Her letters to the empress are full of her love for the young Maria Paulovna.

"I find it difficult to express in words," she writes to the empress, "the happiness I feel at the marriage of my grandson with the Grand Duchess Maria. I should be very wanting in proper feeling, if I did not recognise the boon which your Majesty has conferred on us, in giving us a princess who has added so much happiness to our family life. Her fine character, her amiable qualities have won my heart, and my attachment to her will last my life."

Anna Amalia then thanks the empress for conferring on her the Order of St. Catherine. All her letters to the empress are in the same tone of loving affection for the young duchess, who seems to have had on her side the most tender affection for her husband's grandmother.

Fräulein Göchhausen, writing to Professor Böttiger, tells him: "Our dear duchess lives only for and in her grandchildren, who both love her most tenderly and as much as they do their own parents. They are on the most unconstrained and confidential footing with our duchess, to whose life the young duchess especially has given a new happiness. Generally twice in the week she sends her grandmother a little note: "Dear grandmamma, If you will allow us, my husband and I are coming this evening to sup with you." Then, like an old pair who have been comfortably married for years, they come in arm-in-arm and make themselves quite at home: Occasionally they bring two attendants. By a thousand pretty ways they make the evening pass delightfully."

Anna Amalia was indeed charmed with Maria Paulovna, of whom she tells Knebel she cannot say enough, only that she is a treasure and that she loves her with all her heart. These praises were not exaggerated, the young bride justifying in her later years all that was said of her. She was like the woman in the Canticle, a pearl beyond price, who in the days of trouble that were to come was the stay and comfort of all about her.

The spring was now at hand. On 27 April 1805 Anna Amalia writes to Goethe, thanking him for a poem or book he had sent her, with apparently a dedication in her praise, for she says he is too flattering; also she is grateful for his kind hope that she may live long enough to see the results of the creative genius of the newly born century, and these good wishes she returns with the prayer that the Parcae may not interfere with the duration of his or her life, as she does not want an interference from "mythological phantoms."

The arrival of her favourite brother, Frederick Augustus, who all through his life had been devoted to her, gave a pleasant turn to her thoughts, especially as the prince had elected to make Weimar his home. Alas! this reunion of the brother and sister lasted only a few weeks. He had not completed the purchase of his future dwelling when, after a short illness, he died, on 8 October 1805.

"The stern finger of fate," writes Anna Amalia to Hofrath Böttiger, "took him from us. I had only enjoyed the presence of my beloved brother, from whom I had been separated for fourteen years, for a few days, when that Higher Power, to Which we must submit, saw fit to take him from me. The many similar trials I have experienced made me feel this hard stroke of fate so deeply, that I cannot on this occasion say any more. I know that you, like all the good men who knew and appreciated my dear brother, will feel grieved at this sad loss, and this thought lightens my sorrow somewhat, and I trust will give me strength to bear it with patience and submission."

There is a sad yet resigned tone in this letter, which is touching. And now the duchess, looking round her and seeing, as all do who advance in life, the many blanks where once there were loving faces, began to think that her own time was near at hand. Still she was not selfishly taken up either with grief for her own sorrows, or dread of the "king on the white horse," who was now approaching. She still took interest in all those about her. Her letters show the keenest sympathy with the advance in science and modern discoveries, and she listened for hours to the reading of works on such subjects.

Kapellmeister Hummel, from Stuttgart, was invited to Tiefurt, and there was much music; but it was only a semblance of mirth, without any foundation in fact. Goethe remarked: "It is in these moments that it is brought home to one clearly that all amusements and studies, as well as eating, drinking, sleeping, are mere matters of routine, which follow one another in gloomy succession."

But now it would seem that deeper shadows were to darken the closing years of Anna Amalia. Once more France was causing alarm throughout Europe. The masterful genius of Napoleon recognised the necessity of employing the immense army at his command in destroying other countries, while his own greed of power saw therein a means of exalting himself still higher. The war that had broken out between Prussia and France involved the little duchy of Weimar. Karl August's ally at once requisitioned a certain contingent of men to be supplied by the duchy, while Karl August himself was placed in command of the Prussian advance guard, and had to repair instantly to the seat of war.

"Negotiations for peace are going on," writes Anna Amalia to Knebel, on 20 October 1806. "As a matter of fact the French have got all they want, and it is only Bonaparte, who cannot restrain his arrogance or bridle his foolish pride, who insists upon letting matters take their course and see what the issue will be."

Nevertheless, Anna Amalia saw clearly that the prospect was a gloomy one for Weimar. The poor little duchy must serve as a shuttlecock to those belligerent powers. "She has so little strength in herself to resist the powerful demons, who threaten all Europe with fire and sword. There is no longer peace and goodwill amongst the nations of the earth. This blessed condition only exists in small circles or between friend and friend."

From this time the duchess appears to have lost all heart and to have shared the general feeling of hopelessness as to the future of Germany. Still she keeps up her correspondence with her friends. In November 1806 she tells Frau von Knebel that "the Emperor of Austria is hourly expected, and we do not know how long he will stay. Prussians, Russians, English, and Swedish troops are pouring into Hanover; the French are retiring before them. Perhaps Mahometans will likewise come to the assistance of Germany."

And again in December she writes:

"Rüdelchen, you are quite wrong in supposing that, because I have not acknowledged your last two letters, I am vexed with you. Truly I am sometimes not able to write, and at this moment my mind is not in the vein. My soul is troubled by the present unhappy condition of the land in which we are living, which cannot be changed, and must be borne with resignation and courage. These we must seek where alone they can be found, and this is the only hope left to us."

But even in this sad condition the duchess did not lose her interest in the progress of science. In the beginning of 1806 Gall came to Jena to propagate his system of phrenology. Goethe, who attended all his lectures, embraced the new doctrines with enthusiasm, although he was so ill that Gall visited him in his sick room, and there performed divers brain dissections, which made Goethe a convert to the new theories. Anna Amalia followed these new developments with interest, and accepted the office of joint president with Goethe of the Society of Natural Science. But this brief lull was speedily disturbed by the approach of Napoleon's army.

"We are tossed here and there," writes Anna Amalia to Knebel, "like a ship upon the ocean. The Crown Princess is all ready to start for Dresden at the first approach of the French."

A few days later Maria Paulovna left Weimar, and travelled to the north by the wish of her brother, the Czar. Karl August was far away serving with his regiment, and unconscious of the danger threatening his duchy by the approach of the French army, which was opposed by some Prussians, who had been hurriedly sent to the help of Weimar. Their resplendent uniforms cheered the frightened inhabitants, but they were a mere handful as compared with Napoleon's army.

On 14 October 1806, at seven o'clock in the morning, the thunder of distant artillery alarmed the inhabitants of Weimar. The battle of Jena had begun. Goethe heard the cannon with terrible distinctness, but as it slackened towards noon he sat down to dinner as usual. Scarcely had he begun the meal when the cannon burst out in close proximity to the town. Immediately the table was cleared. Riemer found Goethe walking up and down the garden, the balls whirled over the house, the bayonets of the Prussians in flight gleamed over the garden wall... . It was a fine bright day, the birds were singing sweetly on the esplanade, and the deep repose of Nature formed an awful contrast to the violence of war."

What strikes one in this realistic description is the indifference shown by Goethe for the safety of the royal family in the Residenz, and Anna Amalia close by in the *Witthhumshaus*. There can be little doubt from all contemporary evidence that Goethe was not a man of war, but, conceding this point, one has to go farther, and with regret conclude that his fears for his personal safety kept him from flying to the assistance of "angel Louise."

Fortunately the duchess Louise had a brave spirit, and in this emergency displayed extraordinary courage and presence of mind. She at once took her place as director of the movements of the royal party. The grey-haired Duchess Amalia and Princess Caroline were her first thought. She had some difficulty in persuading Amalia to fly, however; but at last she consented to do so.

"We left Weimar in the midst of the thunder, which followed us on our road to Erfurt," writes Fräulein von Göchhausen, "the sky was lit up with the glare of the cannonade. The streets were full of the baggage-wagons of the retreating garrison. The sound of the cannons grew more distant as we drew closer to Erfurt, the road was less crowded by the fugitives. We had been scarcely two hours in Erfurt when the news came, that the enemy was only a few miles distant. Our flight, accompanied by the cavalry, the wounded, and nearly all the inhabitants, was something beyond description. Amidst horrors too terrible to relate we made our way by Langensalz and Mülhausen to Heiligenstadt, where General von Pfül had nothing cheering to tell us. On the 16th we arrived in Göttingen. Here we found letters which instructed us to proceed on the third day to Kassel, where we enjoyed perfect tranquillity, and saw neither friend nor foe. The longing for news of Weimar was indescribable, and on the next day, when we arrived in Eisenach, the good people there would not let the duchess go. She appeared to them as a guardian angel; she helped them in so many ways. At last on the 30th we got back to Weimar. We found a miserable state of things, but we have to thank our good duchess that it was not infinitely worse."

This allusion refers to the Duchess Louise, whose courage in withstanding Napoleon is one of the most romantic episodes of this terrible war. At the risk of repeating what probably is known to most readers of history, I give the incident.

Weimar had been entered by Napoleon's army; a young officer came to Goethe to assure him his house would be secure from pillage, as it had been selected for the headquarters of Marshal Augereau. In spite of this, several troopers made themselves at home in the Goethehaus, broke open the cellars and got royally drunk. In the night there was a tumult outside, and Goethe had to admit a troop of drunken soldiers. Meantime the marshal had not arrived and the pillage went on; houses were in flames, even the Residenz was threatened. At this juncture Napoleon entered the town, and took up his quarters at the Residenz Schloss, where the Duchess Louise had remained with only two or three faithful attendants. Not even the arrival of Napoleon daunted her; her place, she said, was amongst the people whom she had always loved; it was her duty to stand by them at whatever cost to herself.

And so far she judged rightly. When the people learnt that the grand duchess was still in the castle, their joy knew no bounds. When they met they threw themselves into one another's arms exclaiming: "The duchess is here!"

Nor were they wrong in feeling that her presence as a protection to them, for so it proved. When, on the evening of 15 October 1806, Napoleon arrived at the castle, where rooms had been prepared for him and his attendants, the Duchess Louise descended the grand staircase to meet him. Pale, but with calm air of resignation and dignity, she awaited the approach of the "Emperor," on whom everything — the fate of the people and her own — depended. Napoleon regarded her with hostility and in a loud angry voice enquired:

"Who are you, madam?"

"The Duchess of Weimar!" was the quiet reply. "I am sorry for you, madam," said Napoleon, but I must crush your husband." Then, turning abruptly away, he called out rudely: "Let dinner got ready for me in my own apartments." Louise was not daunted; she retired at once, but it was a case of *reculer pour mieux sauter*. Next morning she sent to demand an interview. The request was granted.

Night had brought counsel, and Napoleon, refreshed by sleep and an excellent breakfast, was in better humour. He paid courteous attention to the appeal of this dignified and still beautiful woman, who pleaded her husband's and her country's cause with a boldness and tact which extorted the admiration of her listener. At first, indeed, his face darkened and his heavy brows contracted. Still, the duchess, unmoved by these ominous signs, continued. She defended, with the eloquence of a noble nature, the conduct of the duke, her husband, in his adherence to the Prussian King, whose personal friend he was, and from whom he had received many testimonies of esteem. With a lofty air she enquired how, in the hour of peril and misfortune, he could desert his friend and ally. She then turned her beautiful eyes upon her listener, and with a tinge of colour in her pale face asked him would not his fame be for ever tarnished, if he gave over (as he threatened to do) Weimar and its inhabitants to his lawless troops? And, wonderful to say, Napoleon relented, and not only gave orders that the town should be respected, but rescinded his repeated declarations that Karl August should never set foot again in his own duchy. The conditions which he made were, however, rigorous. Karl August was to quit the Prussian camp in twenty-four hours. Louise, uncertain whether she could prevail on the duke to submit, begged and pleaded for a little more time. Napoleon was inflexible; he had yielded more to this high-minded princess than he had ever intended, but there was to be no further concession; so the duchess hastened away to despatch messengers in all directions to seek the duke, for she did not know the exact place where he was.

Next morning Napoleon waited on the duchess, accompanied by his principal generals and aides-de-camp. His manner was more than courteous, he seemed full of anxiety that the duchess should acquit him of any complicity in the excesses which had been committed by his soldiers on their first entrance into the town. He also assured her that the war was none of his making, and "that it had been forced upon him." "Believe me, madam," he said, "all things are ordained by Providence, and I am now only an instrument to carry out its decrees." As he descended the staircase after this interview, he said, in a tone of enthusiasm: "There is a woman whom even our two hundred cannon could not frighten!"

It is not expressly stated, but no doubt it was in consequence of this visit that Napoleon extended the time he had originally fixed for Karl August's return to Weimar, and made other modifications in the severe conditions he had at first imposed. No entreaties or remonstrances, however, would induce him to abate the fine or contribution he demanded of 200,000,000 francs, a terrible tax on the already over-burdened duchy. All the Duchess Louise could do she did to alleviate the sufferings of the people. Her private purse was drained for them, her jewels were sold for their relief. One is rejoiced to hear that she had her reward in the adoration of her people, in the increasing affection of her husband, and the admiration of all Europe. "She is the true model of a woman," writes Madame de Staël, "formed by nature to adorn the very highest position. She is equally devoid of pretension and weakness."

The meeting between the two duchesses on Anna Amalia's return was very affectionate. Both had passed through a crisis, sufficient to make them bury all remembrance of former differences. The condition of the town was pitiable, and the distress of the people heartrending. Wonderful to relate, the Witthumshaus had escaped the general pillage. "Whether I owe this blessing to the honesty of some French hussars, to the protection of a French adjutant, or to the intervention of some higher Power, I am indeed grateful for being spared the grief of having my house plundered."

A few days later Anna Amalia received by courier the news of a calamity, which was another result of this disastrous war. Her brother, the reigning Duke of Brunswick, had in the battle of 14 October received a severe wound in the head; his life was saved, but the ball had struck his right eye, and he altogether lost the sight of it. The other eye was also threatened, and the surgeons did not give any certain hope of saving it.

Also Karl Ferdinand of Brunswick, who had fought in the Seven Years' War, was driven out of Hamburg by Davoust, and died of his wounds on 10 November. Misery and grief reigned all over Germany.

"Fate seems to pursue us mortals with grief," writes Knebel to his beloved duchess. "Life and death seem to be playing a game and the outcome lies in One All-powerful Hand. It is quite true that two hundred French soldiers have died of their wounds. Bonaparte should bring back their bones with his other relics." And then he asks the question which must have occurred to many minds: "How is it that Frederick the Great has been so soon forgotten, and that not even a trace of his glorious existence remains? Perhaps he neglected to form the nation upon his own pattern; or was it that he tried and failed?"

In Goethe, Anna Amalia met with a bitter disappointment. In place of being a support in these days of trouble he retired into himself,[106] and acted as if the great drama of this cruel war was being played before him, without his having any personal interest in the matter. The duchess complained of this attitude of his, this effort to free himself personally from any participation in the events that were passing before the eyes of all the world. It is well known, however, that it was Goethe's practice to avoid every painful consideration. He could not bear the thought of death, "the eternal fairy tale," and in his later years never mentioned the word or allowed it to be named in his presence.

The alliance with Prussia had brought Weimar much suffering, especially in 1807. Karl August was now in Berlin, where he in vain tried to win some advantage for his duchy out of the web of political entanglements.

"I do believe it would be easier for a camel to pass through the eye of a needle than for us to get anything for Weimar; but there is this comfort, that in the far-off future the evil, with care, time, and self-sacrifice, will amend. Brighter days will come and a rich harvest will be our reward," writes Karl August to Anna Amalia, who, with the Duchess Louise and her granddaughter, was still in Weimar. Her favourite, the Crown Princess, was with her husband at Warschau, where Karl August presently joined them. There were great hopes that the Emperor

Alexander's influence might prove advantageous to Weimar, but the hatred Napoleon entertained for Karl August would not permit him to relax a tittle of the load of taxes he had imposed upon the little duchy. There was even a fear lest this dislike might lead the conqueror to say: "Let Weimar cease to exist," as he had said in the case of Brunswick.

"One must try and live through these bad times, and exercise patience and firmness, else we may get trampled in the dust," writes Anna Amalia, on 4 February 1807, to Knebel. "Honesty counts for nothing and eloquence is not listened to. God grant that all hope of keeping Jena is not lost. Hope is all that we have to sustain us. Burn this letter. The Muses here are asleep, I think; they are not inclined to be friendly, and we are surrounded with so much that is disagreeable that I cannot blame them for not showing us their kindly countenance. Farewell, dear Knebel. Kiss your wife and child for me. "AMALIE."

This is one of the last letters written by the duchess. Neither is her correspondence of this period written with the care formerly bestowed upon every line she wrote. The handwriting is greatly altered; there are signs of haste and anxiety, which was only natural, considering all the anxiety, fatigue, and grief the aged duchess had gone through. The course of the war troubled her tender soul, and, although her means were limited, she strained them to the utmost to relieve the wants of the sick and dying soldiers. At last, peace was concluded with Weimar, in January 1807. Great was the joy that the duchy was not to be severed from the ducal family that had governed it for so many years. But the good news had come too late to revive Anna Amalia; the sufferings both mental and bodily which she had undergone, the hurried flight from Erfurt to Kassel and thence to Weimar, the horror of the situation, and the separation from her son and the grandchildren she loved so dearly, were too much for her aged frame. She summoned up all her energy to receive Chancellor von Müller, who had returned from his mission to the French camp, and for many hours she conversed with him as to the hopes there were for the future. No one who saw her suspected the end was so near. In the evening she asked for Herder's sermons and read them attentively. When she closed the book she said: "All is well with me. I know I shall soon see Herder and also my brother." A few days later, on 10 April 1807, she passed away quietly, her attendant thinking she was asleep. Both body and mind were worn out, and her one sorrow was that her dearly loved son was not with her. By a cruel irony of fate Karl August arrived that same day. He burst into the death chamber. In his wild, passionate way he seized her hand, and finding there was no pulse he rushed out of the room.

A week later the people of Weimar saw their dearly loved duchess for the last time. On 18 April 1807 the doors of the Witthums Palace stood open, and through the garden with its sweet scent of early spring, flowers came a crowd of weeping women and sorrowful men. Many children, too, were there, for the duchess had always loved the little ones. On they came through the large hall into the room where, on a catafalque, lay Anna Amalia in her coffin, which was draped in violet velvet. Over her shoulders was a violet velvet mantle, and she was clothed in white from head to foot. The coverlet which "good old Oefer" had painted for her was thrown over her feet. The large room was draped with black and behind the deceased were the arms of the two great houses of Brunswick and Weimar, together with the Krautenschild for Saxony and white rose on a red ground for Burgundy. Anna Amalia's shield was blue, with the letters A.A. The last resting place of Anna Amalia was in the Metropolitan Church, where Herder is also buried. At the side of the altar, not far from the grave of her brother Frederick Augustus, a small brass tablet has the inscription, "Anna Amalia H.V.S." Some years later a medallion of the duchess was placed on the wall.

Anna Amalia needed no public monument. Her name was enshrined in the hearts of the people who had known her, and amongst whom she had lived, and they handed down their recollections of the good duchess to their children. Further than this no one can expect to be remembered. Nevertheless, I can bear testimony to the fact that although ninety-four years have elapsed since Anna Amalia passed away, her memory is still fresh in the little capital which she loved so well. To the devotion of her grandchildren and the tenderness for her memory which they planted in the mind of Karl Alexander, the late Grand-Duke of Saxe-Weimar, is due the preservation of the Witthüms Palace and all other mementoes connected with the Duchess Anna Amalia of Saxe-Weimar-Eisenach.

THE GRAND DUCAL LIBRARY AT WEIMAR

The grand ducal library dates from the close of the seventeenth century. After the termination of the Thirty Years' War the Dukes of Gotha and Weimar devoted their attention to bind up the wounds, which art and literature had received from the endless wars, that had destroyed all advance in mental culture. It is well known how Ernst, the pious Duke of Gotha, strove to rebuild the schools and restore the colleges, in order that the work of education in the duchy might be resumed.

His grand-nephew was Wilhelm Ernst of Saxe-Weimar, who reigned from 1683 to 1728. A scholar and collector of antiquities, books, and rare weapons was Duke Wilhelm, and to his love for such things, as also to his wish to improve the condition of the people, harassed and decimated as they had been by the Thirty Years' War, Weimar owes the foundation of its fine grand ducal library.

A legacy which came to Wilhelm from the last Duke of Saxe Jena in 1690 gave the first promise of this great undertaking. A few years later, in 1701, the library of Chancellor von Lilienheim was purchased, and in 1704 that of Balthazar Friedrich von Logan, the son of a Silesian poet, who had acquired it during his travels round Europe. This fine collection, which was rich in historical works, was put up to auction in Breslau; Duke Ernst bought it for five thousand thalers. He sent Erbach, a violin player, to receive the books and bring them to Weimar, the books being conveyed in thirty-seven cases to Halle.

The duke's adviser in such matters was his Privy Councillor von Reinbaden, a learned man, distinguished as a linguist, and an accomplished translator of French and Italian verse. It appears that, through his offices, Konrad Samuel Schurzfleisch was offered the post of librarian in 1706. Schurzfleisch had a high reputation for learning; he was a theologian, jurist, historian, and patriot, the last named being his ruling passion. In his correspondence, which he kept up with the most noted men of his time, this political tendency is exhibited in a marked manner. When, in 1681, Strasbourg was taken, he felt more deeply than most of his contemporaries the loss of this bulwark.

"I cannot restrain my tears," he writes to his friend von Gersdorf, "when I think that, not only the whole of Alsace, but also all north Germany is likewise lost to us." Schurzfleisch was not only a singular personality, but was worthy of taking place as an eminent bibliophile. Both he and his brother, a professor of history in Wittenberg, spent time and money in cultivating the love of books. He died in 1708, and his contemporaries, who lamented their colleague, had two medals struck in the honour of this "living library and walking museum."

He was succeeded in the office of librarian by his brother Heinrich Leonard, who came to Weimar in 1708, with a salary of one hundred thalers, and the title of Director of the Library, also a seat in the Consistorium with a vote as Rath or counsellor. Fourteen wagons, each drawn by four horses, conveyed his modest furniture and his large library of books, which were the property of the deceased Schurzfleisch, and which it was understood he had bequeathed to the Weimar Library. Unfortunately, as it sometimes happens, the legacy, if such it was, was not legally secured, and by-and-by Leonard Schurzfleisch, being pressed for money; wished to sell a portion of the books. The duke's lawyers issued a caveat, declaring that when Schurzfleisch was appointed librarian it was understood that after his death the books were to belong to the library of Weimar. Leonard, dying before the law proceedings were finally concluded, his heir acknowledged the justice of the claim (although he had received an offer from a bookseller of ten thousand thalers for the collection), and so the victory was with Weimar. Meantime the books remained where Leonard had placed them, not in the library, but in a large room in one of the wings of the castle, which was then called Wilhelmsburg.

Leonard Schurzfleisch was succeeded in his office of librarian by Johann Mathias Gesner, a man of experience and studious habits, in every way suited for the post of director of a library, which now ranked as the third in order of merit amongst German libraries. Unfortunately, Gesner was involved in the downfall of his patron Von Marschal, and left Weimar, being finally called to the University of Güttingen where he was highly esteemed.

Duke Wilhelm Ernst died in 1728, leaving the library he had founded well filled with rare and valuable books and manuscripts. Great additions were made by the purchase in 1779, of the Schöberschen collection of the writings of the Minnesängers in the fourteenth and fifteenth centuries, and of the Meistersingers in the sixteenth and seventeenth; also curious manuscripts from the time of the Reformation, which were much increased by the purchase in 1782 of the Symbolischen library.

Some remarkable works were secured later, when, by Goethe's advice, the Büttner collection was bought, this being later divided between Jena and Weimar. In consequence of the suppression of the convents, large collections of missals, Bibles and breviaries, with rare illuminations by the monks, came into the market, also chronicles of great antiquity. In 1803 Karl August purchased in Ulm two hundred and seventy heraldic books, to add to the already large number of similar works in the Schurzfleisch collection, and through the munificence of his descendant, the late Grand Duke of Weimar, further additions have been made.

There is, moreover, a full collection of books on costumes, weapons, etc.; of Bibles and catechisms, and of German Singespile from 1450 to 1760. Also the collection of books belonging to the Gore family, who had so long resided in Weimar, which numbered nine hundred volumes; the library of Prince Constantine added in 1804, that of Anna Amalia in 1807, and of her brother Duke August of Brunswick, together with legacies from private individuals, have enriched the already full Library. Mention must be made of the curious collection of playing cards, beginning from the fifteenth century, which attracts much attention.

The charm which is so potent in the library cannot be conveyed by description. It must be seen to be fully appreciated. Its situation, its air of repose and silence, are not so remarkable; these attractions are to be found in many libraries, but not so the associations. These are unique and belong to Weimar. All round the beautifully proportioned hall, with its spiral staircases leading to the gallery overhead, works of art are collected, which even those who are not bookishly inclined cannot (unless they are destitute of all appreciation) fail to enjoy. These include the marble bust, by Trippel, of Goethe in 1788, when he was the young giant of literature; it is faced by that of Schiller, by Dannecker.

Trippel was a daring genius, and while he astonished by his audacity, yet forced even his critics to admiration. He is in strong contrast to the French sculptor, Houden, whose bronze bust of Glück is a masterpiece. In 1774, Karl August, then a young man, saw the bust in the artist's studio, and bought it for four Louis d'or. It is now the only original of Glück by Houden, for the marble bust of him, which was executed by the same sculptor for the Paris Opera House, was destroyed in the fire which consumed the theatre.

The monumental bust of Goethe is by the French sculptor, David d'Angers, who came to Weimar in 1829, to take a cast of Goethe's head. Two years later, in 1831, the colossal bust arrived with a letter from David expressing his satisfaction that he had been able to transmit to posterity the features of the greatest of living writers. The bust was placed in the library and unveiled on Goethe's last birthday, 31 August 1831. A much more agreeable presentment of the great poet is to be found in another room. It is only a pencil drawing, by Schwerdtgeburth, of Goethe in his old age, sitting in his armchair; but it is instinct with life, and must have been a faithful likeness. Dannecker's bust of Schiller, to which allusion has been made, is a fine work, superior to the bust of Goethe by the same sculptor.[107]

The library is also rich in reminiscences of a later circle of literary men, whose intellectual qualities, although perhaps they did not reach so high a standard as the first, have nevertheless claims on the respect of future generations. This second circle included Johannes Schulze, Abeken, Riemer, Franz Passow, Heinrich Boss, and Eckermann; they were led, so to speak, by Meyer, and their general reunion took place at Frau Johannes Schopenhauer's, where all the *littérateurs* of Weimar met twice a week. We are given to understand these meetings were not always serene. Moreover, the autocratic sway exercised by Goethe, especially in his later years, roused opposition in the minds of the golden youth. Neither was the great poet's admiration for Napoleon to the liking of his *confrères*.

Of great interest is the account of Napoleon's presence in Weimar on the occasion of the congress of Erfurt. This was in 1808, when Talleyrand paid a visit to the library. The statesman, who was shown all that was of interest by Johannes Schulze, was greatly interested in the curios of this rare collection, especially the woodcuts of Lucas Cranach, in the translation of the Bible by Luther, which is one of the treasures of the ducal library; also Flaxman's illustrations of Homer. On this peaceful occasion Napoleon received Goethe and Wieland. A few months before the emperor's visit Madame de Staël came to Weimar, accompanied by Benjamin Constant. The bust of this remarkable woman, which is in the library, is by Tieck. Opposite to it is one of Zacharias Werner.

NOTES

1. The Wartburg was the residence of the Counts of Eisenach, It has a commanding situation, standing as it does on the summit of the mountain and commanding a splendid view of the surrounding country. From the highest point an unrivalled panorama stretches before the eye. No sublime thoughts, however, rise to the mind, for the far-stretching landscape is in its character idyllic, while the wooded hills (for they cannot be dignified with the name of mountains) which are called the Thuringian forest, make a background for the highly romantic Wartburg which teems with all manner of old-world traditions. All the world knows it was the Wartburg which afforded Luther "a protecting prison." Luther's room is shown with all its relics, but the mark on the wall, where he threw the inkstand at the persevering devil who was tempting him, has disappeared, having been taken away bit by bit by curious visitors. The late Grand Duke Karl Alexander was very fond of the Wartburg, and constantly stayed there. In the restoration of the ancient Burg great judgment and good taste have been shown.

   The Venusberg, where the amiable goddess Holda (the inventress of Free Love) had her abode, is said to be in the immediate neighbourhood of Eisenach. The knight was a Thuringian, but the love story of Elizabeth is one of Wagner's inventions, and has no foundation in fact.

2. This holy legend makes no mention of Elizabeth's giving her life to save the soul of the Knight Tannhäuser.

3. This was in his early, days; later he made his home at the Court of the great Landgravine of Hesse Darmstadt.

4. The duke had married in 1738 Charlotte, third daughter of Frederick, first King of Prussia, and Caroline Dorothea, daughter of George II Elector of Hanover and King of England. Her mother was the unfortunate Sophia Dorothea of Celle, thus forming a "link" between the present royal family of England and the ducal house of Weimar.

5. The same authority states that the Duke of Brunswick's sister, married to Frederick the Great, was wonderfully handsome, but "as vulgar as a basket woman."

6. There was a connection between the House of Weimar and that of Brunswick, the Margravine of Bayreuth, aunt to Amalia on her mother's side, being likewise aunt to the young Duke of Weimar, In all probability it was the Margravine (who had displayed her match-making powers in marrying Constantine's eccentric father to her mad sister-in-law, Charlotte of Bayreuth), who now suggested this alliance between the young pair.

7. Count Bünau did not leave Saxony. He lived for some years on one of his estates not far from Weimar, and from a letter preserved in the state archives it is evident Anna

Amalia availed herself of his counsels, although apparently he took no part in the government. The letter in question is addressed to her uncle, Frederick the Great, who at this date, 1761, had entered on the Seven Years' War. It is an urgent appeal in favour of the count, who, she says, "is advanced in years, suffering from terrible illness and unable to fulfil the contracts he had made to supply the advancing army with forage and other necessaries." She adds, "I have the more willingly undertaken to intercede with you for the count, as, although he is no longer attached to our service, still he continues to receive a considerable pension, for which he undertakes to give us his valuable advice and the benefit of his experience upon many different points. I greatly desire that he should remain in this neighbourhood in perfect security; and I therefore beg Your majesty to render me this personal service by giving the necessary orders to protect him while he resides in Saxony from being subjected to any bad treatment, such as being made prisoner or otherwise. I need not say that by so doing Your Majesty will confer on me an obligation for which I shall be everlastingly grateful, and with the assurance of my respect and affection."

This letter is addressed to the care of M. Keller, Commandant at Leipzig.

8. Geheimerath in the German Cabinet holds the same position as Privy Councillor. A Geheimerath had a seat at the Privy Council but not an assistant Geheimerath,

9. The "Pro Memoria" is a very long document, which I have spared my readers. It can, however, be found in the archives at Weimar.

10. These books were placed in the Residenz of Wilhelmsburg by Leonard Schurzfleisch. See Introduction.

11. For an account of the grand ducal library see Appendix, vol. ii.

12. The now lovely park was a wilderness situated to the left of the Welsche Garten.

13. Amalia was a very fond mother, and at that time had a decided leaning to her youngest boy. Here is a pretty little letter written to baby Constantine, aged two. The duchess's spelling is not very correct: —

"WEIMAR, 1760.

"Bonjour, mon cher petit Constantin. Comment avez vous réposé. Penses-vous à votre chère Maman? Oui; sûrement, mon petit Constantin me l'a promis. Je me trouve nullement à mon aise ici; je n'ai pas autour de moi ce que j'aime le plus dans le monde, devines ce que cela pourrait être, si vous devines que c'est vous même. Vous avez attrapé juste. Aimes-moi toujours, mon petit Contine cherissez-moi avec un attachement le plus tendre et le plus sincère.

"Votre fidele Mère,

"Amélie."

14. Christoph Martin Wieland, was the son of a parson living at Uberholzheim, a village forming part of the free town of Biberach. Although the parson was probably not possessed of more than the proverbial "forty pounds a year," he was able, living being cheap in Biberach, to give his son an excellent education, and to send him to the university of Erfurt, where he took honours. Law, which was to be his profession, did not attract him, and being drawn to the study of poetic literature, he took when he was twenty-one his own line, and as a first step went to Zurich, where Professor Bodmer was the leading light. He remained with Bodmer two years, during which time he wrote several poems. Later he entered the family of some friends of Bodmer as tutor, and afterwards went in the same capacity to Berne, where he met Rousseau and his friend Julie Bondeli, the latter exercising considerable influence over the young poet. This, however, was not his first love affair. It would appear, indeed, from his own confession. that Wieland was somewhat of a Don Juan, so many were his flirtations. They all, however, being carried on with clever women, contributed to a certain extent to the development of his great mental powers. One of his flames was Sophie

Gutermann, afterwards De La Roche, whose name was well known as one of the most prominent of the "Sentimentalists." As is generally the case, the woman to whose fascinations Wieland finally yielded was of quite a different order from the *femmes savantes* with whom he had dallied. Anna Dorothea von Hillebrand, the daughter of a merchant in Strasbourg, was neither an *illuminée* nor a sentimentalist. "She has little or nothing," he writes to a friend, "of the qualities with which I have been saturated and which I am now convinced would be unsatisfactory food for real happiness, I do not care to find such in my wife. As Haller says, I have chosen her to satisfy my desires and to gratify my heart. She is innocent as a child, unspotted, by the world, a sweet, joyous, delightful creature; not beautiful, but quite pretty enough for an honourable man, who wishes to have his wife for himself and not for the admiration of the world at large." The marriage was a happy one, albeit a year after his marriage we find Wieland writing to the same friend that his wife does not know what the word *verse* means, and has never read a line of his writings. Such was the wife of the man who, in his early days, had raved about Sophie Gutermann and Julie Bondeli.

15. "Danischwende" was tutor to the young prince in Wieland's *Goldene Spiegel* which had first attracted Anna Amalia's attention.

16. A continuation to the "Golden Looking Glass" appeared in *Deutsche Merkur* of 1775, entitled "Danischwende," The *Merkur* was a review of great importance edited for many years by Wieland, to which nearly every man of mark and talent throughout Germany contributed. Wieland's letters to Merck and others contain repeated allusions to the *Merkur*.

17. In one of these long-winded epistles, dated 29 March 1772, she writes:

"You have tranquillised my mind as to the moral character of my eldest son. Many of his inclinations, which gave me much uneasiness since your letter, appear now to my mind in a different light. You assure me that he has a good heart. This I have never for a moment doubted, Nevertheless, I thought there was a certain hardness in his character which in my opinion is a great fault in any one, but worst of all in a ruler. I am, however, convinced by your observations that I was in error on this point; very probably what I considered hardness is merely strength of mind. As we always hope that what we wish may be true, I am satisfied as to the goodness of his heart, and that is the great point for any one who is destined later on to govern; and as far as his understanding and his genius are in question, I may flatter myself that he is the first of the House who has possessed the one or the other. The mean vices of hypocrisy or lying are, I trust, far removed from my son's character; nevertheless, he does not possess the frankness which is generally noticeable in boys of his age. He understands only too well how to be reserved. It I do not mistake, these faults arise from a defect in his education or from his own self-love, which does not allow him to be as frank and open as a high-hearted gentleman should be. I do not doubt that, when you know him more fully, you will find that I am right; and I greatly fear that to cure this defect will be very hard, it not impossible — it has already taken such a deep hold. I confess to you in all sincerity that, if I could begin again, I should bring up my children in a totally different manner. The deep knowledge which you have shown as to the proper treatment for these tender plants has much impressed me, and shall be my guide; the happiness of my children lies so near my heart that I am ready to sacrifice everything which might interfere with the fulfilment of my wishes. You can gauge by this the great obligations which I owe to you. Friendship founded on esteem and gratitude should be the expression of innermost feelings, and such a friendship have I vowed for my life to you and shall always remain

"Your very true friend,

"AMALIA."

18. The ancient Castle of Weimar, which up to the seventeenth century was called Hornstein, was partially destroyed by a fire which broke out in 1424, and which consumed the greater portion of the town. Both the town and castle were rebuilt by Landgraf Frederick IV, called the "Peacemaker." The Bastille and the principal tower, which still remain bear the date 1439 and an inscription. In the floods which rose in 1613 to a great height in parts of Thuringia, the lower rooms of the castle were very much injured. In 1619 a fire destroyed a great portion of the castle, including the church and lower tower. In 1619 Duke John Ernest commenced the new building, but its completion was delayed by the Thirty Years' War. Duke William IV completed it. On 11 April 1654, a banquet was given for the first time in the new hall. On March 28th, the birthday of the duke, the church was consecrated. In 1696 an Opera House was added to the castle by Duke William Ernest. In 1774 the castle was destroyed by fire.

19. It is left uncertain whether Fritsch made the duchess a gift of the house or whether it was a business transaction. That it still remains in the possession of the ducal family would suggest that it was the latter.

20. Stein received a salary of 200 thalers.

21. Jean Paul, in his gently satirical fashion, remarks that there was a universal love for all men and beasts except reviewers, and it is amusing to note how the world repeats its follies, from one generation to another, for in 1774 we find there was a society, or order, of trembling "souls" who drew together in brotherly and sisterly love, helping one another not in any sensible or serviceable manner, but merely holding "spiritual communion" together; and the first commandment of this brotherhood and sisterhood of souls was to love your neighbour and your neighbour's wife! "The cause of these diseased imaginations," says an English writer, "was want of faith in religion, in morality, in philosophy, as well as in politics; and in morals the eighteenth century was ostentatious in its disquiet and disbelief. The old Faith which so long had made European life an organic unity was no longer universal, active, living, dominant; its place of universal directing power was vacant. A new faith had not arisen, and as men's minds should feed upon some form of devotion, we find these makeshifts of universal love, these unholy pacts between men and women, this foolish and sickly romanticism spreading like the upas-tree over the fair pastures of intellectuality." Goethe, although by no means a sickly sentimentalist, was suffering from imaginary passions, first for Lotte, who was engaged to his friend Kestner, and then for Lili, who was one of the "souls," but who nevertheless preferred a rich husband to the adorable youth of Goethe.

22. The name by which Goethe's mother was generally known among her intimate friends.

23. He was eighteen on 5 September 1774, but he did not attain his majority till the following January, when the Court of Vienna gave the necessary release, or *venia aetatis*.

24. From the archives in Weimar.

25. *Life of Anna Amalia*, by Bornhak.

26. Some writers give a terrible picture of the low condition of morality in Weimar. Schiller, whose virtuous, gentle nature was in direct contrast to his friend Goethe, was astounded at the *laisser aller* of Weimar. "All the women," he says, "are coquettes."

27. So far back as May 1775, Fritsch had talked of resigning, being inclined to take this step in consequence of many difficulties and annoyances. In consequence of his father's advice he did not act on this first intention. The older politician writes to his son that it was his duty to remain in office and to act the part of a faithful servant, who is always on the watch with a water-bottle with which he qualifies the wine when it is too strong. But, although Fritz followed his father's advice, circumstances became too strong for him to occupy office much longer.

28. With whom she was connected by the marriage of her daughter Frederica with Prince Friedrich Wilhelm of Prussia, who succeeded Frederick the Great as king.

29. The Landgraf was not so insensible to his wife's merits as he appeared. He kept all the letters his wife had ever written him in a pocket-book, which he carried always in his breast. Such are the curious eccentricities of the human mind.

30. The original correspondence (a voluminous one) of the Landgräfin is written in French, which at this period was the polite language, especially at courts.

31. Goethe's *Werther* was the outcome of sentimentalism, so were Frau de la Roche's novels, and many others of the same stamp, inculcating a maudlin sensibility.

32. Frau de la Roche's novel was called *The Romance of Sternheim.* "Sophie de la Roche," writes Merck, "is a woman of good family with court manners. She speaks French better than German, and her mind travels with extraordinary rapidity from the deepest subject to the gayest trifle. She puts on her mask of sensibility at will." He also makes the discovery which occasionally happens to many of us, who find that our literary idol speaks and acts in an opposite manner to what he writes. Fortunately for Merck, in this instance, Frau de la Roche spoke infinitely better than she wrote.

33. *Anna Amalia u. Karl August*, Beaulieu Marconnau.

34. Wedel, the handsome master of the horse.

35. Lewes, *Life of Goethe.*

36. The signification of the word *misel* or *miseln* is much disputed by German writers. By some *misel* is said to mean demoiselle or young girl, and is related to the Dutch word *meesje.* Miseln signifies to take up with a girl — in other words it means *liebeln*, to make love, or flirt. Therefore the derivation from *demoiselle* may be put on one side. Goethe often makes use of the words *mizeln* and *liebeln* or *geliebelt.*

37. Allowance, however, must also be made for the disappointment experienced by the young duchess, who had looked for something quite different in her "mother's friend" and who, with all the intolerance of her eighteen summers, thought Anna Amalia at thirty-six an old woman, who, it she had not done with the pleasures of life, should at all events have confined herself to amusements suitable to her *advanced* years!

    In their judgment of their elders we notice that the young are always inclined to sternness: nevertheless, there may have been *a shadow* of justice in this reasoning.

38. Goethe's biography.

39. Writing to his friend Kestner, the young poet says (May 1774:) "My rough joke against Wieland makes more noise than I thought. He behaves very well in the matter, so that I am placed in the wrong." The origin of the farce was a strong feeling in the circle of Goethe's friends that Wieland had misrepresented the Grecian gods and dressed them up to please a modern public. One Sunday afternoon the rage for dramatising seized upon the young Goethe, and, with a bottle of Burgundy by his side, he wrote the farce just as it stands. He sent it to one of his admiring friends at Strasbourg, who said it ought to he published; and at Strasbourg it was printed and given to the world. Very few would care to read it now, except as a homage to the composer; the jokes are not easy to understand, and the malice is over the heads of most twentieth century readers. Probably not many of the composer's own nationality have gone through it. But in 1774 it was otherwise. Wieland was a big man to attack, and the audacity of a young writer in so doing was condoned, in view of the spirit and sarcasm, which some readers considered was carried too far. Still, it was talked about and read, and, although some few were scandalised, no one considered it malicious. Wieland took no offence and reviewed it in the paper he edited (*Die Deutsche Merkur*), recommending it to all lovers of pasquinade and persiflage.

40. Dalberg.

41. A variation of blindman's buff.

42. On one occasion the duke and his friend rode from Weimar to Leipzig in eight hours, which, considering the then condition of the roads, was an extraordinary feat of horsemanship.

43. Prince Constantine at this time resided at Tiefurt with his tutor Von Knebel.

44. Bertuch was comptroller of the duke's household.

45. There is very little concerning Goethe to he found in any contemporary literature or newspapers during these first years (1776-78) in Weimar. Not much dependence can be placed on newspaper reports of this period.

46. Stein united the two offices of Master of the Horse, and Gentleman-in-Waiting. He afterwards resigned the latter office.

47. Lewes in his biography does not seem aware of this; he says it was a formal gift to Goethe in 1780.

48. For some time he was in the habit of sending Philip back to Weimar, and staying alone in the Garden House.

49. The *Witthumshaus* was originally built in 1767 by Minister von Fritsch, on the occasion of his marriage, for his own occupation. By the order of the late Grand Duke, everything has been left exactly as it was on the day of Amalia's decease: a volume of music remains open at the place where she had last made use of it: so too with the book she was reading and the piece of embroidery she was engaged upon.

50. Sophie Gutermann, afterwards Sophie de la Roche, born in 1731, was daughter to an eminent physician who was ennobled, under the name of von Gutenhofen. She had been carefully educated, spoke several languages fluently, and had gone through regular training in different branches of science and philosophy. So far as one can judge, she was in advance of our first class Girton girls. But her cleverness did not make her less submissive to parental authority. Fathers and mothers in the eighteenth century were tyrants, disposing at will of the affections of their children. Sophie's case was more than usually hard. She had married a clever and altogether charming Italian physician, Bianconi by name, attached to the household of the Prince Bishop of Augsburg. This marriage was ruthlessly set aside by her bigoted father, who was a stern, uncompromising Lutheran, and who having the law on his side, separated the young and loving couple. Sophie was sent away, a disgrace to her family, to her grandfather, Senator Gutermann, at Biberach. After his death she was placed under the care of Pfarrer Wieland. As a natural consequence, Christopher, who was then about seventeen, fell over head and ears in love with the bodily and mental charms of this fascinating woman, who was, moreover, connected with him by intermarriage. He wanted to make her his wife, but the unkindness of his stepmother to Sophie, together with the intrigues of her (Sophie's) stepmother, separated the young people, after a three years' engagement. In 1754, Sophie became the wife of Hofrath Frank de la Roche. Wieland to the end of his life considered his Sophie a pearl amongst women. It is curious to note that her granddaughter was Bettina Brentano (Goethe's "Bettina").

51. Compare this letter with Wieland's adulation of the duchess in his correspondence with her.

52. Marks must have been a travesty on the name Merck.

53. Once, when Einsiedel was to act the part of a Moor at the theatre, he had his face blacked and dressed for the part early. Presently, forgetting all about the play and his singular attire, he went out to take a walk, and, being in a more than usually forgetful state of mind, wandered a long way, and, being taken for the Moor he was personating, attracted a large crowd, who became by degrees unpleasant, he was rescued with some difficulty from their hands.

54. It will be remembered that one of the first acts of Amalia's regency was the conversion of the Französische Schloss from being an arsenal (for which purpose it has been used by Duke Ernest) to its original purpose, a library. She had all the books brought from the different ducal residences and filled the shelves with them. They did not make a goodly show, but it was sufficient for the duchess's purpose; and later the ever-delightful

library was added, which is now a fitting home for the fine *éditions de luxe* placed there by the duchess and the celebrated circle of Weimar.

55. A sort of mystery surrounds the Gore family. Every effort has been made by the curious enquirer for many years to find out who they were, but in vain. They were, apparently, not connected with the noble family of Arran, from whom nearly all of the name Gore seek parentage. My enquiries into the subject, although I called in the assistance of the invaluable *Notes and Queries*, have produced no solution beyond the already well-known fact that, in 1788-9, an English family of the name of Gore were making the grand tour, and visited Weimar. Father and daughters were so pleased with the geniality and refined tone of the little capital that they returned, and finally made it their home. Mr. Gore, who is described as a wealthy merchant, seems to have been an insignificant sort of lay figure — indeed, the only one of the trio who made a mark was Emily Gore. She was at first honoured by Duchess Louise's friendship, which friendship met with the cordial approval of Karl August, who writes to Knebel of the fine qualities of Emily Gore. No doubt it was her mental qualities that attracted Karl August; it could not have been her beauty, her appearance being in the last degree what was then called *Anglaise pour rire*. Neither personal nor mental qualities made any difference in the ripples of scandal that were circulated anent the duke's attentions. Knebel's sister Henrietta writes to him, 1781: "The English family of Gore are to return here this winter. Weimar is full of gossip; this is very unpleasant for all parties." The Gores fade out of the Weimar chronicles. Emily Gore is, however, buried in the old churchyard. Some money was left either by Mr. Gore or Emily to the town. It has never been realised, in consequence of all trace of the Gores being lost. *See the new introduction: Editor.*

56. It was well known that Frederick the Great shared this opinion of the German tongue, and seldom used it, generally speaking, and always writing, to his intimates in French.

57. This love of the theatre and everything appertaining to it often extends to the playbills, which for ardent playgoers possess a sort of sacredness, as reminiscent of hours of enjoyment never to be forgotten.

58. For his co-operation Eckhoff received, as a present, a gold snuff-box worth £31. His very modest score at the inn — about fifteen shillings for eight days, was also paid.

59. In this piece a device occasionally made use of nowadays was employed. The stage was divided in two by a screen, the action being carried on simultaneously on both sides of the partition.

60. Sometimes written Schroeter but more often Schröter.

61. Professor Musäus had originally been in the Church, but the strict Lutherans of Farnroda in Eisenach refused his ministrations because he had on one occasion been seen to dance. Anna Amalia, who was, as we know, free from such strait-laced prejudices, befriended Musäus, and obtained for him the post of Professor in the Gymnasium.

62. This piece appears in Goethe's works under the name of *Die Geflickte Braut*.

63. An archaeologist of some merit, but whose reputation suffered in consequence of his journalistic indiscretions. He wrote diffusely about Schiller and Goethe; he was on friendly terms with Herder and Wieland; also with the strangers who visited Weimar.

64. *Polissonnerie* — a ludicrous or grotesque act done for fun and amusement.

65. Fritz Jacobi (whose *Waldemar* was pilloried), writing to Knebel, says: "I heard Goethe tell a lady that Herder was the vainest of all the men he ever knew. What Goethe said of Herder all Germany says now of Goethe. His self-importance and pride are making him foolish. Every one knows of Wieland's and Klopstock's vanity, and Lessing sold himself to the devil out of pure vanity."

66. Thusnelda writes to Frau Aja:

"I will only say that Goethe played Orestes in the most masterly manner. His costume was Grecian, so was that worn by Pylades, and in my life I never saw him look so splendid. For the rest, the whole piece was played to admiration. Today it will be repeated, and much as I look forward to seeing it, I would gladly give up my place if I knew Frau Aja would take it."

67. Prince Constantine played the part only once. We are not told the reason, but can imagine it.

68. Sophie De la Roche, the Sentimentalist, was forcing her young daughter Louise to marry a man described by Frau Aja as a monster. She told the duchess that Goethe would grind his teeth and curse under his breath. The eldest daughter of Madame De La Roche had been one of Goethe's many loves, but the mother had interfered, and had forced the girl into a marriage with a wealthy merchant, with whom she was miserable. Hence Frau Aja's indignation.

69. The silhouette of Anna Amalia was cut by Goethe, who had a peculiar talent for this art, which was most fashionable towards the end of the eighteenth century, and continued till the thirties, when the first appearance of the daguerreotype put it in the shade. The art of silhouettes was not to cut an ordinary likeness, but to give to it a *soupçon* of a caricature, by exaggerating some trifling feature, etc. Goethe succeeded in this to perfection.

Whole length silhouettes of the Goethe period, 1775-80, are to be found in the Goethe Museum at Weimar, also in the Witthums palace there is a silhouette of Goethe leaning on a pedestal.

70. Philip Seidel, Goethe's confidential servant. He was a native of Frankfurt, and had been in the service of Goethe's father as a secretary and servant. When Goethe went to Weimar he took Seidel with him. Goethe reposed the greatest trust in him and when he went to Italy Philip was the only one who was in his confidence. He was also entrusted with the charge of his correspondence.

71. Widow of the statesman, and *née* von Stolberg.

72. Bode was known as the translator of Stern and Montesquieu's works.

73. Dr. Wolf, an abbreviation for Dr. Wolfgang (Goethe).

74. The annual fair of Plundersweilern.

75. Frau Aja's letters are published by the Goethe Society.

76. A translation of the original published for the first time in 1892 in the *Tiefurt Journal* collected by the Goethe Society with an introduction by Herr Bernard Suphan.

77. The name Frau Aja has its origin in the *Hermonkindern*, a child's story. It was given to Goethe's mother by the Stolbergs, who were staying at her house in Frankfurt. Wieland, in one of his letters, alludes to the origin of the name. "Our best greetings to Frau Mutter Aja." The *first* great Frau Aja could neither read or write, and yet she was Rheinhold's mother. Rheinhold was one of the Hermons children. Frau Rathin liked the name so much that she always used it.

78. Katherine Elizabeth Goethe, daughter of Rath Johann Wolfgang Textor, Imperial judge or magistrate, was born February 1731, in Frankfurt on Main, married 17 March 1748, Johann Caspar Goethe, became a widow 1782, and died September 1798. She was a woman remarkable for many gifts, and, although she could not spell correctly, her mental powers were recognised by the most remarkable men of a remarkable period. Wieland called her the "Queen of women, and the crown of her sex." Einsiedel says that her whole appearance made a wonderful impression. Merck, the satirical scoffer, declares he is proud because she calls him her son. Prince George of Würtemburg pronounced her to be the only woman worthy of being Goethe's mother. The power exercised by this extraordinary woman over others was remarkable. Writing to Frau von Stein, she says: "I thank God that by His grace no human being has gone away from me discontented —

of whatever position or sex they may have been." An eternal spring and bright sunshine surrounded this joyous nature. She could bear every trial well. "Joyfulness," she cried, like Götz von Berlichingen, "is the mother of all virtues" — and another saying was "He who laughs much can have no deadly sins on his conscience." And yet this fine-hearted woman had met trials enough to sadden her. A weary life it must have been attending upon her invalid husband, whose fretful temper made him at all times "ill to live with."

79. Wieland's kindly sympathetic nature stands out in pleasant contrast to the bitterness which filled the minds of many of the gifted circle. Writing to Merck, Wieland tells him that, "The public sees in this simple and natural excursion a secret intrigue of some kind, and throws all manner of odium on our friend, who has given no ground for their dislike, for he has never injured any one. But since he has been openly declared Privy Councillor (which in truth he has been all along) the fury against him has risen to a height which borders on madness. *Sed vana sine viribus ira.*

80. Karl August's letter to Merck, sending a present of money to Frau Aja, is very characteristic: "I send herewith what I wish Frau Aja to have. She must accept it on the following terms; — first it is not a present; she did much for me in saving me from having to pay dear for bad accommodation at the "Red House" (the hotel in the Zeil); secondly, the old man is to know nothing of our little arrangement; thirdly, Goethe is on no account to hear of it.

81. Bertuch's Magazine was only a magazine of fashion-plates. Bertuch, who was *Legationsrath*, was a pupil of Wieland's and very active in literary matters, with which he combined different official posts, one being the directorship of the theatre. His prudent administration of the funds in these departments gained him the friendship of Anna Amalia and Karl August.

82. A name for Goethe, used by his parents.

83. The house was situated in the Frauen-platz. Goethe bequeathed it to his son and grandson, and the latter left it a legacy to the town.

84. Nothing more is said about this sepulchral groan and the apparition that followed it.

85. Reiffenstein.

86. "She makes great fun of old Reiffenstein (Thusnelda had a mocking spirit, which made her enemies), an antiquarian friend of Goethe's, who devoted his time to showing the antiquities of Rome to the duchess. "He generally comes in the morning;" writes Thusnelda, "and if the *minestra* smells particularly good, remains to dinner. Then we go round through all the corners of Rome. In the evening we sit round a large table and work or draw. We have a new visitor, Abbé Ceruti, who has translated Homer. Herder brought him to the duchess. It appears that such a figure is absolutely indispensable at every house that respects itself."

87. A lovable woman.

88. For Boydell's *Shakespeare*.

89. No translation can be found of Hiuzint metal.

90. From the *Correspondence of Angelica Kaufmann Zucchi with Goethe*; published by the Goethe Society, volume v., 1870.

91. Piper, the duchess's maid, who came with her from Brunswick in 1756. Piper outlived the duchess many years.

92. "The Statue of Apollo."

93. "Old Zucchi is avaricious."

94. There was very little reverence in Caroline Herder's character.

95. Frau von Stein had told Madame Herder that in her youth Angelica had married a villain, who thought she was rich, and had run away with her money and jewels. This was Horn, the valet, who had already a wife. It was the dark shadow underlying Angelica's life.

96. Her letters to Goethe are full of mistakes in spelling.
97. Naples.
98. This seems to indicate Emma Hart, afterwards Lady Hamilton.
99. Vesuvius.
100. These remarks of Anna Amalia recall Talleyrand's acute observation, that "Not even one's best friend speaks *of us* as he speaks *to us.*"
101. "The account of the expenses of this expedition kept by his servant, Paul Götze, shows how cheaply one could live and travel in Germany in 1790." — *Goethe's Life*, by Dr. S. M. Prem, Leipzig.
102. Carl August Herzog.
103. The word "details," as well as the previous expression, "accident," tends to confirm the report as to the duel.
104. Wieland presents a much more amiable, although perhaps not quite so lofty and high-minded, a personality as Herder. Under other circumstances he might have developed into a greater writer. He wrote much, and his teaching is not edifying; but if his works did harm in the time he lived, they are now altogether forgotten, *Oberon* being the only one which has kept its place.
105. Maria Paulovna was niece to the Duchess Louise.
106. From this time Goethe's character seems to have undergone a complete transformation. All contemporary writers and visitors to Weimar mention his haughty demeanour, amounting to insolence. Crabbe Robinson gives an amusing account of his interview with the great writer.
107. Schiller's body was laid on 11 May 1805, in Jacob's Churchyard, in which many noble families, both formerly and later, were interred. In March 1826 the Burgomeister of Weimar, Hofrath Schwabe, undertook to disinter the remains, and remove them to a vault. With much difficulty Schillers skull was identified, and on 17 September 1826 of the same year it was with much pomp and ceremony placed in the library, near to the marble bust by Dannecker, which Karl August had bought from the Schiller family for 200 ducats. The pedestal upon which it stands was intended for the skull to rest upon. Goethe, who was ill, was represented by his son, August von Goethe, who with Ernest Schiller made speeches, while Riemers Cantata, set to music by Hummel, was performed, and then with every mark of honour Schiller's skull was laid on the pedestal. Schiller's remains were afterwards at Goethe's suggestion, disinterred and were brought to the library and placed in a sarcophagus. It was then that Goethe wrote his lines on Schiller's skull, a beautiful composition. There was soon another change. Karl August wrote in 1827 to Goethe, expressing his wish that Schiller's body as well as the skull of which a cast was to be taken should be removed to the "new churchyard;" and laid in the vault which he had built for himself and his race; and in accordance with this wish, so honourable to the deceased, Schiller's remains were once more removed.

It was on Sunday 16 December 1827 that the removal took place. August von Goethe again represented his father, who was ill; the Director of the Library, with six of the head mechanics of Weimar, assembled in the great hall at the sarcophagus, round which six large silver candelabra burned. Upon the coffin there lay a fresh laurel wreath. After a short prayer the coffin was raised and carried by the master mechanics on their shoulders, away from the library and along the road to the park, to the new churchyard and into the duke's vault. In the vault the coffin was received by the Court Marshal von Spiegel, Chancellor von Müller, and Burgomeister Schwabe, and once more the coffin was opened. On raising a beautifully embroidered coverlet the skeleton of Schiller was seen.